Amazed
By Grace

For Kathi - May God bless you as you read this Carole Plemmons

Carole Plemmons

Outskirts Press, Inc.
Denver, Colorado

INTRODUCTION

Many years ago, as a baby Christian, God blessed me with a hunger for His Word, and I began putting on paper what He was teaching me from my daily study of Scripture. That evolved into talking to Him about what I was learning and eventually, I began to journal our conversations.

Out of those journals come these meditations. I share them here so that others will see how He has dealt with an insignificant person like me - the faithfulness, the patience, and the incredible grace and love which He has unfailingly shown to me. And to assure you, dear reader, that He desires to do the same for you.

In order for you to understand my perspective, I must tell you a few things about my life. In the tenth year of our marriage, my husband was diagnosed with rheumatoid arthritis. We had just finalized the adoption of our one year old son. Over the next 32 years, our son and I watched as a painful, crippling disease claimed more and more of the life of this precious man we loved. Although he spent most of his remaining 32 years in a wheel-chair, my husband's sweet, uncomplaining spirit did not falter - truly a shining example of the wondrous grace of God!

There have been other battles to fight. I have experienced two kinds of cancer, months of chemotherapy and radiation treatments; a radical mastectomy; numerous biopsy surgeries; a broken back resulting in chronic, restrictive pain; serious heart problems resulting from the chemo, and a brain hemorrhage requiring emergency surgery resulting from the heart medications. I lump all those together because collectively they were not as difficult for me as the long years of watching the love of my life change from a strong, handsome young man into an invalid needing 24-hour care. That is truly a helpless place to be and yet, by God's grace, I am now eight years past my husband's home-going with a grateful heart. I was allowed to love him 42 years.

I tell you these things not to elicit sympathy, but to convince you that I understand deep in my soul the great love, mercy and faithfulness of our eternal God. I *know* that His promises are sure and certain because I have trusted Him, and He has never failed me. I *know* that His grace is sufficient because in all the places of helplessness and weakness in which I've been, He has brought me through to ultimate victory. Over every difficult path, He has been with me, holding me, loving me and strengthening me.

So I encourage you, as you read these prayers, to let my worship flow into your worship of our magnificent God. Identify with the struggles I have brought to Him because, in reality, we are all struggling in some way. Realize that this walk of faith will not always be a straight, smooth way. Absorb grace and light into your spirit as you spend time in His presence so that when the inevitable dark times come, His grace and light will sustain you. May He bless you abundantly every day of this coming year!

January 1
A BRAND NEW YEAR

The Lord is my strength and my shield;
My heart trusts in Him, and I am helped;
Therefore my heart exults,
And with my song I shall praise Him.
Psalm 28:7

Some of my favorite things, Lord...time to be alone with You, a clean new book to write in, an unblemished new year before us. My spirit is full of joy at the prospect of what this year will bring. Allow me to draw near to You and tell You I love You - to sit with You in quietness and warmth before this busy day begins.

You, Lord, are my light and my protector, my high and holy God whom I worship. My spirit bows down in awe and adoration of who You are - majestic, full of power, full of wisdom and justice. Yet You have given to me the incredible gift of Your actual presence living within me. And paired with that full-of-wonder gift is the promise that You will never leave me.

Joy and praise fill my being, Lord, that these things are true. Your ever-flowing grace fills me and covers me and changes me. My will and my spirit I give to You. Work in them Your sweet work. Make of me whatever You choose.

I do have one specific request for this new year, Lord. I pray that my spiritual ears will be, more than ever before, listening for Your voice. Please help me learn how to maintain that core of stillness within so that I can hear Your softest word to me. I know, Lord, that this is not a matter of straining to hear. It is rather a relaxing - a leaning into Your embrace - a yielding to Your touch. This I long to do, not just for a moment now and then, but for all the days of the rest of this earthly life.

What a blessed existence it is to have this foretaste of heaven! There, all communication will be different - easier. Here, we deal with the paradox of doing a difficult thing by actually doing nothing - except being still and attentive to You. Here, our seeing and our understanding are only partial. There, we will know even as we are known - fully. But, yet, Lord, there is so much more I can know about You even here! I'm eager to learn.

May this coming year in our walk together be the best one yet.

January 2
THE NEED FOR LOVE

This is My commandment, that you love one another,
just as I have loved you.
Greater love has no one than this,
that one lay down his life for his friends.
You are My friends, if you do what I command you.
John 15:12-14

Those words, Lord, are from Your own mouth, teaching Your disciples the important truths they would need to remember in the days ahead. Those words make me think about this inherent need for love that You have placed within every one of us, this desire to love and to be loved. You have taught me that it is only satisfied, truly satisfied, by You. St. Augustine said, "You have created us for Yourself, O Lord, and our hearts are restless until they rest in You." If this God-shaped space is not filled with You, there is an aching void, a visceral need within me. I may try to ignore it by keeping my mind busy but in some unguarded moment of quiet, up pops that haunting sense of sadness. So I push it away and try to bury it again, or attempt to fill it by other means. Yet the end result of looking anywhere but to You will be frustration, unhappiness, and failure. I need You so much more than I think I do! Let's think about that.

All people not yet in Your family are unaware of the riches of Your love. They have that inner longing for it, but have no idea how to satisfy that longing. So they are searching in all kinds of places and, in the process, many are ruining their lives. And there are even Christians who are unaware how to access the storehouse of Your incredible love that is available to them. Those of us who know must be teaching both these groups of people! It has been said that Christianity is as simple as one beggar telling another beggar where to find bread. Oh, may we be telling!

I must never be possessive of any gift You give me because Your blessings flow in and out like a river of living water; a never-ending supply that You desire me to pass on to others. My Lord, may I be discerning in seeing Your provision, wise in my telling others, and faithful to persevere when tempted to get discouraged. Please see within me the praise and gratitude that fills my spirit as I think about Your unsurpassed love for me and for all the world. May each of Your present-day disciples see the huge need for telling this Good News! *It is all about love!*

January 3
THE TRUE CIRCUMCISION
Part One

Beware of the dogs, beware of the evil workers, beware of the false circumcision;
for we are the true circumcision who worship in the Spirit of God
and glory in Christ Jesus
and put no confidence in the flesh.
Philippians 3:2-3

There is an abundance of good substance in those words that Paul wrote, Lord. Any child of Yours reading them would immediately desire to be of "the true circumcision" even if they, like me, have an imperfect understanding of all that means. I definitely don't want to be a dog or an evil worker! Although, to be *my* dog might be pleasant since all she does is eat and sleep. But I think, in Paul's time and culture, dogs were not the pampered members of the family that we have made them today.

But on a more serious note, what I want to think about with You are the three things Paul says are necessary to be the "true circumcision":
- Worship in the Spirit of God.
- Glory in Christ Jesus.
- Put no confidence in the flesh.

Worship in the Spirit of God. I'm still learning what it means to worship, and I humbly acknowledge I have much yet to learn. However, when I look back at where I was, I see that You have increased my understanding. So, please help me see truth about this.

Worship is not only attending church services. Many people, some Christians included, think that when they have gone to church, they have worshipped. But I know, because I've been guilty of it, that it is possible to sit through church on a regular basis and *never* worship. What Paul is describing above is an involvement, a surrender, of all that I am to Your Spirit within me.

My spirit is the part of me, Lord, that communes with Your Spirit and, while that sweet communion can be done in church, it can also be done everywhere else. That is the unique thing about worship in the Spirit of God! Everything I do, all day, everyday, is worship *if I am acknowledging You as Lord of all my life*. My work, my play, how I spend my leisure time, how I spend my money - it all either worships You, or it doesn't. Because You either are my Lord, or You aren't.

Those words may sound harsh, Lord, but are they not true? If You are my Lord, my spirit will bow before You in awe, worshipping You as Creator, as Lord, as Most High God of the universe. My spirit will worship You as I go about my day, and every time my mind is not otherwise occupied, it will return to Your Presence. This is a most blessed thing - to be able to experience You in this way!

3

January 4
THE TRUE CIRCUMCISION
Part Two

Beware of the dogs, beware of the evil workers, beware of
the false circumcision; for we are the true circumcision
who worship in the Spirit of God and glory in Christ Jesus
and put no confidence in the flesh.
Philippians 3:2-3

Glory in Christ Jesus. There are any number of things I could glory in other than You, Lord...my salvation, my physical needs met by Your provision, my service to You. All these things are good. But I am to glory in none of them. It is to be *only* in You, the Giver of these gifts. You are the Author and Finisher of my faith. You are the object of my seeking and of my love. You are my Everything.

How confused and off-track our culture is in what it considers worthwhile and desirable! It glories in everything *except* Christ Jesus! How sad that the devil has deceived millions of people by twisting Your truth so that it appears to the unbeliever to be myth and fantasy.

How sad that even many Christians don't realize the blessings they are missing by not living out this Scripture. You did not give us this instruction for the satisfaction of some egotistical need on Your part, Lord. No, it is for *our* blessing, our building up and spiritual growth that You inspired Paul to write down these words. Oh, that Your people could understand the incredible blessings that come from praising You, the joy and peace that we find kneeling in Your Very Presence, the enormous benefits that are ours by loving You and being loved by You, the delight that is ours when we glory in You.

Put no confidence in the flesh. This is the last condition to be met. It seems that once I understand what it means to "glory in Christ Jesus" leading me to an understanding of who You are and who I am, the only wise thing to do is never, never put confidence in myself. However, You have had to teach me this lesson over and over - this lesson of turning loose of my self-sufficiency and allowing You to be in control. My natural tendency is toward self-confidence. This is a characteristic much admired by the world but in the spiritual realm it is definitely not an asset!

I think, too, that these words mean that I am not to put confidence in *any* person in such a way as to take Your place of honor in my heart, spirit or mind. All human flesh is fallible. Death and destruction have followed when groups of people have substituted a man for You in their worship and obedience. These are obvious wrongs. I can err also, however, in much more subtle ways by looking to others for encouragement or acceptance, by looking to any human being to fulfill my desire to be loved completely. The bottom line truth here, Lord, is that *You desire that I develop this love relationship with You and You alone.* And You desire that same thing for every person. What great good news we have to share with others!

January 5
THE EYES OF GOD

For the eyes of the Lord move to and fro throughout the earth
that He may strongly support those whose heart is completely His.
2 Chronicles 16:9

The eyes of the Lord are in every place,
watching the evil and the good.
Proverbs 15:3

These words tell of an amazing truth! You are able to see everywhere all the time. And even more amazing, You don't just see the outside of me and what I am doing, You see into the very deepest places within me - places I don't know about with my conscious mind.

And here is what is most amazing to me, Lord - You love me anyway! You looked at me in my sinful state and saw all the dirt, trash, doubt and fear that was in me, but You did not condemn. Rather, You cleaned me up inside, and began to change me by loving me. You renewed my mind by showing me a better way. You taught me through every small thing in my life of Your constant, consistent, unconditional love. You taught me that, more than anything, You want my fellowship and love.

You know, it occurs to me, Lord, that no other people have what Your people have - the blessed privilege of being able to love the One who loves us so much. You love unbelievers, too, *but they are unaware of it*. This is what we need to be telling them and telling them and telling them! Love is hard to resist - Paul says it never fails.

And how do I know these things? Because You have done exactly that in my life! I have no words that express my gratitude and love for Your mercy and grace, my Lord. Please look inside and see how they fill my heart and run over, spilling out of my eyes as warm tears of joy. What a great thing it is to be Your child! How glad I am that You are always watching me!

January 6
CONCERN FOR AMERICA

Grace to you and peace from God our Father, and the Lord Jesus Christ,
who gave Himself for our sins,
that He might deliver us out of this present evil age,
according to the will of our God and Father,
to whom be the glory forevermore.
Amen
Galatians 1:3-5

Therefore be careful how you walk,
not as unwise men,
but as wise, making the most of your time,
because the days are evil.
Ephesians 5:15-16

Those words instruct Your people to turn to You; You will supply what we need in order to live faithfully in evil times. Even though we do not hear a lot about fasting these days, Lord, You have been speaking to me about it. Fasting seems to have gone out of fashion. My own feeling is this - if it was ever a useful discipline in seeking You, it still is. But I understand that You are showing me that to fast without prayer, without seeking You, without yearning for Your hand to move, would be an empty exercise in self-denial and of no spiritual significance. Please, Lord, help me to be very aware of Your presence today, even though we cannot always be alone together. I seek Your heart and Your mind. Only You have the unconditional love, power and wisdom to meet the needs of our time.

This country of ours has so much good and so much rotten all stirred up and mixed together. And, Lord, it seems that rotten has the upper hand right now. But I know that, in the end, You and Your people are victorious. Praise Your name for that knowledge! Enable us to clearly see Your great heart of love every time we pray for America. Give us a vision of what You long to do for us as a nation if we would only look to You for guidance.

Please show us, Lord, Your people whom You called the salt of the earth and the light of the world, the tasks we need to be doing as Your coming draws nearer. Make us open to Your will, submissive and obedient to everything in Your Word and give us a greater love for You and for people. May we see that walking very close to You, day after day, is the only way to replenish our saltiness and our light. Oh, God, if only all of Your people could see the truth of that one fact, how different would be our impact upon this nation!

I want to thank You, Jesus, for delivering me from the domain of darkness and into Your kingdom of light. I'm overwhelmed at Your love for me! I love You, too, Lord, more than I know how to say. Help me live that love this day.

January 7
THOUGHTS ON BEING CHOSEN

And so, as those who have been chosen of God, holy and beloved,
put on a heart of compassion, kindness, humility, gentleness and patience;
bearing with one another, and forgiving each other,
whoever has a complaint against anyone;
just as the Lord forgave you, so also should you.
And beyond all these things put on love,
which is the perfect bond of unity.
And let the peace of Christ rule in your hearts,
to which indeed you were called in one body;
and be thankful.
Colossians 3:12-15

I was chosen by You. I am beloved by You. I have been born of Your Spirit. You are the source of all the characteristics listed in this Scripture, such as "holy." I can never be holy on my own. No one can simply set out to be holy and achieve holiness. It is only as Your Spirit is holy *through* me that I can be holy - or compassionate or kind or humble or gentle or patient.

These lovely traits are those of a Spirit-filled, Spirit-led life. People in the world can have these traits only to the degree that self is not impinged upon. A person who has not died to self and made You Lord of their life will not be able to fully and consistently show forth these characteristics. They probably won't even have the desire to do so.

Love, Your kind of love, is the basis of this holiness; the foundation upon which everything else rests; the most important attitude of our lives. Love is the perfect bond of unity. It is the solution to conflicts, whether inner or outer. It is the answer, when rightly perceived, to understanding Your will for my life. It is the motive behind everything You do.

Our world is searching for peace and obviously failing to find it. There have been wars all of recorded history. It seems today that the nations of this old earth are filled, more than ever, with violence and hatred. We are so far from what You desire for us, Lord! And yet this word about peace causes an enormous amount of thanksgiving to rise up within me!

"And let the peace of Christ rule in your hearts" says to me that, in the midst of war and violence and danger of annihilation, Your peace can rule in my heart. And my heart tells me this is so. I have no fear for myself. But I have much sadness for those who don't have this peace in their hearts, too.

Please, my Lord, give me the wisdom and grace to allow You full control of my life. Only You know how much I desire to become all You want me to be.

January 8
SURRENDER OF THE WILL

Submit therefore to God. Resist the devil and he will flee from you.
Draw near to God and He will draw near to you.
James 4:7-8

I have a couple of things concerning surrender to talk about with You, Lord. You know my tendency to want to take control, my natural bent toward self-sufficiency. It has been one of the largest obstacles in my spiritual growth. And now You have given me a task, an assignment, that *demands* I yield control to You at all times because it certainly is not within my power to accomplish this task. It requires Your perspective and Your eternal, unconditional love to be at work in me all the time, not only for special times. And this requires my focus to be upon You and Your desire-to-bless rather than upon me and my weaknesses.

Help me, Lord, to remember that my motive for doing this task is not to be based on emotions but on the very real transactions You and I have made in my will. My emotions may never fall in line as I want them to, but I can still resolve to keep my will surrendered to You. This I do, my Lord. Give me wisdom to speak only words that build up. Give me discernment to see and take every opportunity to demonstrate unconditional love. Help me remember that my responsibility is to obey You, not produce results. Results are in Your hands; therefore*, I need never get discouraged.*

Now, Lord, I am ashamed to even acknowledge that the other issue on my mind is still an issue. You and I have hashed it out so many times! And yet, I find myself still on the selfish side instead of the surrendered-to-You side. Not all the time, but some of the time. And *any* of the time is too much. I do not want to be double minded. I want to will only what You will. So once again, I place my will concerning this small but important thing in Your hands. I surrender to You all that I am and all that I have.

January 9
FREEDOM

It was for freedom that Christ set us free;
therefore keep standing firm
and do not be subject again to a yoke of slavery.
Galatians 5:1

This Scripture causes me to think back over all the kinds of bondage from which you have delivered me, Lord. And I probably don't understand total freedom even yet. I'm not sure I can, in this mortal body, experience complete freedom.

But here is the thought You have placed in my mind this morning - the freedom You offer is made from an entirely different cloth than the freedom we can experience any other way. Your freedom creates a vast, wide, enormous place to be. Maybe I can express it this way. When I was 17 and leaving home to go to college, I was so looking forward to freedom from my parents' strict rules. That was my idea of freedom - to be able to do what I wanted, when I wanted. And it *was* enjoyable to my immature thinking. But what actually happened is that I began to do things that put me in bondage like I'd never known before, bondage from which You would, years later, have to set me free.

So what I thought was freedom resulted in bondage. And as the years have gone by and You have continued to teach me about Yourself, I've learned that *many things I thought I knew about You* were also a type of bondage. As I began to read Your Word for myself and listen to Your Spirit as You explained it to me, I had to turn loose of some misconceptions about Your character and Your grace. Slowly You set me free from my too-small understanding of who You are and what You desire from me, and I began to see the expansive, beautiful place You want all Your children to occupy.

Here is a mystery. At the moment You saved me, You provided all I needed. Included in that was the *finished work* of setting me free of all bondage. *"It was for freedom that Christ set us free."* Past tense - a thing already done. All I had to do was accept that truth and, as Paul said above, stand firm. Had I been wise enough to see that then, the outworking of my freedom would have come to pass much sooner. How grateful I am for Your patience and mercy as You led me step by step through those first years! And all the years since! Because the truth is that, unless I stay alert and stand firm in Your freedom, I am still apt to fall into some type of bondage.

It's a full time job, Lord, this business of being Your child. But what a glorious, joyful, difficult, impossible-without-You business it is! I love You so very much this morning! Please give me grace to show that to everyone who crosses my path today.

January 10
DRAWING NEAR TO WORSHIP

Blessed be the Lord God, the God of Israel,
Who alone works wonders.
And blessed be His glorious name forever;
And may the whole earth be filled with His glory.
Amen, and Amen.
Psalm 72:18-19

Lord, I so much need to come away from everything and enter into Your warm and beautiful presence; to be still and be cleansed; to be filled and be loved. Those are my needs, and they are real. But deeper down, just as real yet more essential, is the need to set all of those aside for a bit and focus on You. This need is a powerful-within-me drive to love You with words, to try to express the reverence, awe, worship and praise that I feel. That is what I want to do first.

I search my mind for words that express my heart. And even as I think of them, I know that You are so much greater and holier, wiser and more powerful than that. But they are all I have.

You are gloriously splendid, shining, glowing with beauty
that far surpasses any beauty we have on earth.
You are pure and holy above all - high and lifted up!
You have all knowledge and nothing surprises You.
You see tomorrow more clearly than I see this moment.
Your power is limited only by Your wisdom.
This means You are *able* to do anything but choose not to do some things.
You created all that exists.
You are still creating in ways of which I am not even aware.
One day, in heaven, I will understand.
Your love reaches every living creature and thing, wherever it is found.
What You have created, You love and care for.
Words like magnificent, wonderful, exalted, Most High God,
these describe You, my Lord.
You are the Pearl of Great Price and
one who knows You is wealthy beyond understanding.

Such a one am I. You have allowed me to become one with You. This grace in which I stand is more precious to me than anything else could ever be. This privilege of spending time with You, loving You and knowing that You accept my love with joy, and return Your love to me - these are such incredible truths!

I'm so thankful You know my heart because even though I've filled all these lines, I have not conveyed all that I feel. Please look within and see my spirit bowing low in gratitude and adoration. You are my Beloved.

January 11
A DARK DAY

For Thou art my lamp, O Lord;
And the Lord illumines my darkness.
2 Samuel 22:29

Lord, I ask for Your help as I try to verbalize my needs, because I don't fully understand what is going on. It feels like something has come between us and yet, when I search for what that might be, I find no specific thing. So I think perhaps it is just a short time of darkness, of You veiling Your face from me for a time. This has happened before and You have always brought me out of it into the light again. And saints through the centuries have told of this "dark night of the soul" that descended upon them from time to time.

If that is the correct diagnosis, I know what to do - just keep my hand in Yours, draw closer to You and keep walking.

In the meantime.....

Please, Lord, don't allow me to get hard spots in my heart. Keep me soft and pliable.

Help me keep my eyes on You, and only You, so that I see everything in my life as coming directly from You to me.

Cleanse me, Lord, of anything that is not good in Your eyes. Wash me white and pure with Your precious blood.

I confess my selfishness and tendency toward wanting to control. Please keep me on a short leash should I start to wander in that direction. I want to be filled to overflowing with You. For my part, I will believe and accept and rejoice. Thank You, Lord, for loving me even if I can't feel it today.

January 12
THE OPPOSITE OF SIN

...the love of God has been poured out within our hearts
through the Holy Spirit who was given to us.
Romans 5:5

Oswald Chambers' definition of sin is *"...deliberate and determined independence from God."* Oh, how that resonates in my soul! How I grieve for the years I walked in independence from You! But my mind is working this morning on the opposite of that definition.

Using this premise, the opposite of sin would be *deliberate and determined dependence upon God.* This, Lord, involves my will, my heart, my mind and all my strength - which is exactly what You said, "Love the Lord your God with all your heart, soul, mind and strength."

And love is exactly the right word for this dependence upon You. I choose to be dependent not out of fear but rather because I, by Your grace, understand Your love for me, and that causes love for You to spring up within my heart, bringing me closer to You, desiring to stay there always. It is a beautiful circular process that begins with Your love being poured out within my heart.

Deliberate - denotes choice, a thing done on purpose, an intentional action taken after considering alternative actions.

Determined - speaks of strong will, perseverance, resolute commitment to a course of action.

Dependence - I have to smile, Lord, when I realize how truly dependent I am upon You. You could stop my next heartbeat and physical life would leave my body! But in context, I am thinking of a conscious, moment-by-moment reliance upon You. I look to You at all times; I seek Your thoughts; I seek Your face. This is a free-will, renewed-every-moment *choice* to rely upon You and all that You supply to me.

Thank You, my Lord, for being patient with me through all those times I was bratty and self-centered. Please continue to teach me to reckon the old me dead so that I may be fully alive to You. And please, Lord, enable me this day to walk in the fullness of Your amazing grace.

January 13
ABSORBING GRACE

Oh, the depth of the riches both of the wisdom
and knowledge of God!
How unsearchable are His judgments and unfathomable His ways!
Romans 11:33

A few solitary moments
to spend in the quietness of Your presence.

I want to enter into that beautiful
orderly
welcoming
place
You and I have created
and sit at Your feet.
I want to tell You I love You.
I want to absorb all the radiance
and grace I can hold.

This is going to be a good day, Lord!

You are my Sovereign God,
in control of all my moments.
You are wise
powerful
loving
merciful
and faithful.

My heart bows low in worship and love.
Thanksgiving and praise fill my spirit.

Words fail,
but glory
honor
and devotion
flow from me to You in wordless worship.

You have given me so much, Lord!
May I walk worthy of You this day.

January 14
THINKING ABOUT JOY

...and though you have not seen Him, you love Him, and though you do not see Him now, but believe in Him, you greatly rejoice with joy inexpressible and full of glory.
I Peter 1:8

You have taught me, Lord, that the joy You give has nothing to do with outward circumstances. It is not caused by them and, in fact, often exists in spite of them.

The basis of this joy is found in our relationship - Yours and mine. It is all inward, though it will manifest itself outwardly. Because its source is You, it is unconditional just as Your love is unconditional. I'm seeing, Lord, that *all* Your gifts are unconditional - Your peace (how vastly different from the world's peace), Your patience, kindness, faithfulness - all of these are unconditional.

It is like I have two columns of characteristics using identical words in each column but one is headed "GOD'S" and the other "MAN'S." Though the list of words is the same, the reality of them, the way they feel to me, and the impact of them upon my life are as far apart as can be. *Like the difference between substance and shadow.*

For instance, love. Even most unbelievers love their spouses, children, parents and siblings. But I know from experience, Lord, that only if I am filled with *Your* love can I love my enemies and those who persecute me.

The same is true for joy. On my own, I can have joy when life is smooth, the family is healthy and the job is stable and well-paying. But the test comes when one, two or all of those situations change for the worse, and I find myself in trouble. Then it is only *Your* joy that can continue to flow like a wide, powerful river through the depths of my spirit, moving me steadily on toward my destination. This joy is a deep, settled peace, a "knowing" that all is well because of You, an incredible sense of interior light even when outward conditions are very dark.

All that the blessings You give are mine *no matter what.* It is a certainty that, because You are my wise, powerful, loving God, I am safe. Thank You, Lord.

January 15
SELFISHNESS

And He died for all,
that they who live should no longer live for themselves,
but for Him who died and rose again on their behalf.
2 Corinthians 5:15

Lord, I need to talk to you once again about my self-centeredness. A few moments ago I was thinking about what a blessing it is to me to have close fellowship with You. Suddenly, Your thoughts came alive in my mind, **"I desire an intimate relationship with every one of My children. It brings joy to Me for you to draw near."**

What an astounding thought! Not only do You give me the gift of joy, I have the potential to bring joy to You! Somewhere in the back of my mind I have known this, but I don't often think about it because I'm always thinking about *my* side of our relationship. How selfish of me!

"To one who loves completely, the loved one and the good pleasure of the loved one fills the thoughts." Thank You, Lord, for once again stretching me out of my innate selfishness. At church we sing, "It's not about me, Lord, It's all about You." But that truth has not always been lived out in my life very well. **"A truth not lived out is much blessing missed for both of us."** How good You are to keep teaching this slow learner!

January 16
RADICAL FAITH

*If anyone comes to Me, and does not hate his own father and mother
and wife and children and brothers and sisters,
yes, and even his own life,
he cannot be My disciple.*
Luke 14:26

The best times of my life, Lord, are when You and I are in communion in my spirit and all else is shut out. Sitting at Your feet, soaking in the peace, beauty and love that constantly flow out of You - that is when I learn more about You, and that is the ultimate experience.

Occasionally, at these times, I get a clearer picture of who You really are and realize how likely it is that I, living in this dark world, am comprehending but a fraction of Your fantastically glorious nature. And this brings me to my "thoughts of the day."

In reading the first chapters of Acts, I'm made to wonder why there was so much power at work in those believers and so little in believers today.

Have You changed? No. You will never change. Are we less needy today? No. We may even be *more* needy than they were. To my finite logic, there seems to be two options - either You were doing a special work then in the birth and establishment of the Church, or our understanding, and thus our faith, is weak in comparison to those believers. And maybe the root of our small understanding is *the low level of our commitment.*

Maybe the truth is a combination of both of those. You *were* doing a special work. But my mind keeps coming back to this word "radical." Those believers had a radical faith that risked everything for Your sake. They jeopardized their very lives in order to walk with You. We are far too careful, cautious and politically correct. We straddle the fence by loving You, wanting to please You and still be "tolerant" and "open-minded."

This may very well be what You were speaking of when You told certain believers they were lukewarm, and You were going to spit them out. You said, at that time, that *cold* was better than lukewarm! No faith at all is better than wishy-washy faith?

"Well, yes. Atheists at least don't pretend."

I stand guilty before You, Lord. I am at times one of those straddling the fence. I confess and repent. I ask for Your Spirit within me to burn with a fervor that is flaming so that my words and actions reflect a radical faith.

January 17
DEATH TO SELF

I have been crucified with Christ; and it is no longer I who live,
but Christ lives in me; and the life which I now live in the flesh
I live by faith in the Son of God,
who loved me, and delivered Himself up for me.
Galatians 2:20

This topic of death to self is one of the most clearly taught in the New Testament. And yet only You know what a struggle I have had in understanding it, in working it out in my life. Help me, Lord, as I think once again about it. Grant me grace to see truth - Your truth.

I see that it is Your work. I also see that You will not do it except with my surrender - my willingly laying down on Your altar. **"Yes, My child, but understand that this is not the Old Testament altar where the priest killed the sacrificial animals. Those animals had no choice. You must lie down upon a cross. Like My Son, you are to die in obedience. Like My Son, you are to die for the joy set before you. Like My Son, you are to be raised in newness of life."**

"This death is not for atonement, because that was taken care of once and for all by My Anointed One. This death is for the slaying of your fallen human nature that would compete with Me for your loyalty, love and obedience."

My Lord, I'm seeing now! There is a very real transaction that takes place in the spirit-world when I ask You to do this work in me! An exchange takes place - my old nature for Your pure and holy nature. That transaction is quite visible to You but not so easily seen by me. I must, by faith, reckon it done. This reckoning is simply the out-working of what You have accomplished. I *am now* dead to self and alive to You. I *am now* emptied of self and filled with You. This Holy Spirit power which is now within me is constant and transforming!

Another thought - this "reckoning" involves choices to be made all day, every day, and could quickly become legalistic unless I realize that my one choice to die has already made the rest of them. This is a wonderfully liberating thought! It frees me to simply look to You, trust that You are guiding me and are quite capable of showing me anything You need me to know. I can relax and rejoice!

Thank You so much for Your love behind this teaching! Will I now be free of struggle concerning this topic? Probably not. Being the slow learner I am, I will inevitably have further problems with self. But I do have a new understanding of Your side of it, and that is incredible to me - both the truths themselves and the fact that You shared them with me. Please look within and see my enormous love for You!

January 18
TRANSFORMED

I urge you therefore, brethren, by the mercies of God,
to present your bodies a living and holy sacrifice,
acceptable to God, which is your spiritual service of worship.
And do not be conformed to this world
but be transformed by the renewing of your mind,
that you may prove what the will of God is,
that which is good and acceptable and perfect.
Romans 12:1-2

Transformed: changed in appearance, condition, nature, or character.

In the beginning, Lord, You made mankind in Your image. Then we ruined that by disobedience. So when I came to You, I had to be changed from what I was into what You wanted me to be, an obedient-because-of-love follower of my Creator God. And the process of transformation began through the renewing of my mind. I think it is interesting that Paul says "*be* transformed" as if it is something done for me, rather than a thing I, myself, do. It is a process not unlike the potter shaping a vessel upon the wheel. The lump of clay has no ideas of its own. It has no goals in mind, no opinions as to what should be done. It lies inert and moldable in the potter's hands.

This is how I was conformed to the world in the first place. From the time I began to understand language, I was shaped and molded by what I saw and heard and experienced. I did not consciously set out to be worldly minded; it just happened. I took in thoughts and attitudes that were formed by hands that did not acknowledge the Lord Jesus Christ as either Lord or Christ. And all this shaping was done in my mind. That's why the mind must be renewed. I think it is significant, Lord, that this phrase *follows* the instruction concerning giving You all that I am - this living sacrifice which is my body and all of my life. Because only as I give it all to You can You begin Your work of renewal.

It's a lot like redecorating a room, isn't it? Some things must go, some can be kept and used, much cleaning needs to be done, many brand new things will be brought into the finished room. This, in a spiritual sense, is what You do in my mind as quickly and efficiently as I allow You to work. The truths in Your Word become the new furnishings in my mind, replacing the lies and half-truths that the world had placed there. The beautiful, precious promises You have given me become the valued possessions that bring joy and peace as I see them and enjoy them.

My part in all of this ongoing work is to stay yielded to You. I rejoice that You love me enough to want to change me from what I was into what You want me to be. One day, when this life is finished, *I'll* be finished. I'll be transformed into Your likeness. How I love You, Lord!

January 19
BEING TEACHABLE

Make me know Your ways, O Lord;
teach me Your paths.
Lead me in Your truth and teach me,
for You are the God of my salvation.
For You I wait all the day.
Psalm 25:4-5

I'm thinking this morning, Lord, about the small incident yesterday with my little son. I was trying to teach him to tie his shoes. But he was certain he knew how and did not want my help. So he kept trying and failing, growing more and more frustrated with how difficult it was. I could have shown him quickly and *wanted* to show him, was in fact *waiting* to show him, but he was determined to do it his way. So I got frustrated, too.

Then, suddenly the whole situation was cast into a new light - *this is exactly how I am with You sometimes!* Oh, I'm so sorry, Lord! That IS exactly how I am. I am so sure I know how to do something, and I barrel ahead without even consulting You. Things don't go as they should; I become upset and frustrated with myself (and others) and only when it is all over do I realize that I was working under my own steam - me, one who has asked to be controlled by Your Spirit at all times.

I see that I must be teachable if I am to learn from You. I must be open to You, listening and obediently trying to do as You say. This is so basic. I don't know why I haven't seen it before!

I see too, Lord, that just as my wisdom is greater than my small son's, how much greater is Your wisdom than mine! Like Job, I lay my hand upon my mouth. You speak and I will listen. Thank You for this lesson.

January 20
PRAISE AND WORSHIP

Praise the Lord in song, for He has done excellent things;
Let this be known throughout the earth.
Cry aloud and shout for joy, O inhabitant of Zion,
for great in your midst is the Holy One of Israel.
Isaiah 12:5-6

Allow me this morning to draw near, Lord, to worship and to praise and to express thanksgiving. You have blessed me all the days of my life. How grateful I am for all the ways of trial-turned-blessing!

My spirit is alight with Your beautiful shining presence, Lord. My heart rejoices; it sings its own song of praise to You. I marvel at Your greatness, Your majesty and holiness. And at the same time, I understand that You are my Best Friend, my Beloved, my Close Companion! You are all of those and more. My feeble comprehension sees only a part of the truth about You and, even at that, is so amazed.

To meditate on Your love
is to get lost in its greatness.
I cannot understand.
I can only try to grasp the nature of it.

To think about Your presence within me,
how incredible is that!
The Creator of all,
able to dwell within this insignificant person
and fill this room
and this house
and this *world.*

And then my limited mind fails, and I come back, full of wonder, to thank You for loving *me*, for living in *my* spirit. Please let me walk very near to You today, my Lord, and may I glorify You.

January 21
BELIEVING IN GOD OR BELIEVING GOD?

And without faith it is impossible to please Him,
for he who comes to God must believe that He is,
and that He is a rewarder of those who seek Him.
Hebrews 11:6

Believing that You exist is not difficult. It doesn't even take a lot of faith. In fact, I think it takes more faith to deny Your existence. And most people, if stopped on the street and asked, "Do you believe there is a God?" would answer in the affirmative. But that belief is a preliminary action. It is like turning the doorknob to a door which opens into an unknown universe but then failing to pull that door open - making no life change, no change in thinking.

But believing You - now, that is a different thing altogether! Believing You is radical because it changes everything! It takes me down roads I could never imagine and demands of me things I cannot do. It teaches me truths that are not even understandable by those who do not believe. Believing You is pulling open that door, placing my hand in Yours and stepping into an experience of such full-of-wonder dimensions that it can only be comprehended by those who possess Your Holy Spirit.

Believing You changes me from the inside out - a change so deep, so fundamental that I can never be like I once was. It is an experience of moment-by-moment fellowship with You, a Holy Friendship. It causes a permeating spirit of love, reverence and submission to flow from me to You. It is a living ever-active relationship, never static, never boring.

Believing You, Lord, stretches my mind, makes my heart beat faster, enlarges my faith and constantly challenges me to grow. It is an experience that takes place on the inside but greatly changes the outside of my life. In fact, there is no piece of my life that is not transformed by this action of constantly believing You. What a great thing it is to be Your child!

January 22
LONGING TO WORSHIP

Oh, give thanks to the Lord, call upon His name;
make known His deeds among the peoples,
Sing to Him, sing praises to Him;
speak of all His wonders.
Psalm 105: 1-2

Praise! That's what I want to do. There are several things I could be anxious about this morning, Lord, but You stopped that quickly with the reminder to "be anxious for nothing." (Philippians 4:6) So I take every one of those things and give them to You, one by one.

It is actually amusing when I think about how useless, how really stupid, it is to waste time and energy on being anxious. Anxiety accomplishes nothing except to make me sick. You are the only one with any power to change the things that need changing.

Thank You, Lord, for taking me to raise. Your love and mercy mean more to me every day that I live. My praise gets all tangled up with gratitude for what You have done, are doing and are going to do for me and for these I love. My needs are great, but Your supply is greater.

I start out to think about and meditate on You - all the wonderful, glorious attributes that are Yours - and soon find myself thinking of how You have blessed *me*. But it's not about me, Lord. Thanksgiving is good, and I'm glad I have a grateful heart. But, at times, I would like to just focus on You - who You are, Your character, Your great wisdom, all the unique and splendid truths about You.

Please take this love and gratitude overflowing my heart and sift out from it the pure praise I long to express. Give me a new vision of Yourself, a new understanding of the majesty and holiness of El Shaddai. Teach me how to worship worthy of You. I do not know how to separate my *need* for You from my love for You. How comforting to know that You accept my efforts and even bless them!

January 23
WHEN GOD TURNS LOOSE OF MY HAND

The Lord is your keeper;
the Lord is your shade on your right hand.
The sun will not smite you by day,
nor the moon by night.
The Lord will protect you from all evil;
He will keep your soul.
The Lord will guard your going out and your coming in
from this time forth and forever.
Psalm 121: 5-8

For a lot of years, Lord, You and I have walked side-by-side, hand-in-hand. This verse teaches me that You are at my right hand. This signifies to me that I am yielding control to You, since my right hand is my "control" hand. During these many years, You have taken me down paths that I would never have chosen, some so difficult that, except for Your strength, I could not have continued. You have at times even carried me because I truly was not able to walk. Through it all, You have been faithful.

Now the thought occurs to me that someday, when this life is ended and the next begun, You will turn loose of my hand and we will stand face to face. Oh, my dear Lord, this causes me to tremble! I will be finished with earthly lessons. My time of living in this dark world will be ended. My opportunities for obedience in this life will be over.

I think about that Day - to stand before You, to look into Your beautiful face, to see the eternal love in Your eyes, this fills me with a "joy unspeakable and full of glory." It makes me long for that day to be today!

Now to Him who is able
to keep you from stumbling,
and to make you stand in the presence of His glory
blameless with great joy,
to the only God our Savior,
through Jesus Christ our Lord,
be glory, majesty, dominion and authority,
before all time and now and forever.
Jude 24-25

January 24
ALWAYS WITH YOU

My sheep hear My voice,
and I know them and they follow Me;
and I give eternal life to them,
and they shall never perish;
And no one shall snatch them out of My hand.
John 10:27-28

It has become the most natural thing to me
to live every moment aware of Your presence.
That, my Lord, is an astonishing thing!

You shield me from seeing You
in all Your Splendor
Holiness
and Magnificence
because I would be unable to function
beholding all that You
in reality
are.
Your wisdom and kindness protect me.

So what *do* I experience?
Your love filling me and surrounding me.
And that love brings with it Your peace
joy
gentleness
and compassion
that are like a wonderful fragrance,
invisible, yet certainly observable.

Sometimes I am aware of Your gentle rebuke and correction.
At times I'm aware of Your strong arms of assurance and comfort.
Sometimes there is much conversation.
At times, just silent companionship.
Always there is the satisfying
of my spirit's hunger and thirst for You.
And yet that hunger and thirst remains!
You are my Beloved,
and I never tire of You.

January 25
BEING ONE WITH YOU

And the glory which You have given Me I have given to them that they may be one,
just as We are one; I in them and You in Me that they may be perfected in unity,
that the world may know that You sent Me, and that You love them even as You
love Me.
John 17:22-23

One of the oft repeated teachings in the New Testament, Lord, is that You want me to become one with You. These words above came from Your own lips. This idea of being made one with You is such a startling thought! That such a thing is possible is astounding. That You *desire* that it happen is equally amazing. One thing I know: It can never happen by my own doing. I am unable to "evolve" from a new-born Christian into this lofty place of becoming one with the Majestic Creator of all.

I see why John said that You are the Alpha and the Omega. From the initial convicting work of Your Spirit, through all the processes of spiritual growth, to the final breath that this body of mine will draw, You are Sovereign and You are the Power of Life.

One of the things You teach me is to see sin for what it is - a fact of every life, a strong force I cannot overcome on my own, a darkness within that will fight for its life and will win when fighting against *me*, but will lose to Your mighty power. I learn to hate sin the way You hate sin.

I learn that either sin will reign or You will reign. I choose but You fight. My battle lies in the *choosing* because it feels as if I, myself, am dying when sin is killed. And, in a sense that's true. It is all the "self" I am familiar with. It is the nature with which I was born and grew up and came to look upon as "self." What I learn is that You replace that dark, sinful nature with a brand new one. My spirit becomes the place in which You Yourself dwell and fill with all precious and beautiful things - a place where I can fellowship with You One-on-one as often as I like because You live there.

This is why Your cross was necessary, Lord, to make this possible. How magnificent is Your mighty plan of redemption. To understand a small part of it is to fall at Your feet and worship! To see the vast, eternal Love behind that plan is more than my mind can grasp. I can only humbly accept. With bowed head and open arms, Lord, I embrace all You have provided for me.

January 26
JOY IN TRIBULATION

Consider it all joy, my brothers, when you encounter various trials,
knowing that the testing of your faith produces endurance.
James 1: 2-3

All of life is a combination of sunshine and rain, isn't it, Lord? And in my short-sightedness, I have many times not even thanked You for the sunshine, much less recognized the rain for the blessing that it is. I should be thanking You for both.

I admit that I have most often yearned for escape rather than opening myself up to what You wanted me to learn from any particular rain cloud. That is about as far from thanking You for it as I could get! In retrospect, I can see that. And seeing that about yesterday shows me I'm guilty of the same attitude today. The circumstances are different; the storm is not the same storm, but still my heart is longing for escape rather than saying to You, "I surrender. Show me what You want me to see."

What I've discovered, Lord, is that You seldom grant "escape" anyway. The better description for what You provide is "deliverance." You walk me on through the entire distance, and no matter how badly I behave, You are faithful to hold my hand and keep going. How much more pleasant it would be if I complied and even *rejoiced* along the way! Is that not Your instruction? Your Word does say, "Rejoice evermore!" That means all the time. That means I need to see all things from Your perspective and never be self-centered. Be God-centered. Be full of joy and thanksgiving and prayer and peace and desire to please You *in my everyday life exactly as it is.*

Please, Lord, allow this blessed truth to sink deep down into me. Change me so that I see every situation as You see it and respond to it with Your love, compassion, gentleness and strength. Both the sunshine and the rain are necessary to shape me into the person You want me to be.

January 27
FAITH

For I am confident of this very thing,
that He who began a good work in you
will perfect it until the day of Christ Jesus.
Philippians 1:6

You are taking, my Lord, what seems to me a very long time to prepare me. And since I don't know what Your finished product is supposed to look like or be used for, that long time often seems like wasted time. That is why You provide me with faith - so that I may continue my "long obedience in the same direction" when I don't know anything except who is leading me.

The important truth here is that *You are all I need.* I don't need to know why or where or how or when because I know WHO. And I am safe.

That truth fills me with joy! You are such an awesome, wonderful Teacher! You never belittle or shame, even when reproof is necessary. Correcting is done with gentleness and clarity. You encourage with love and You correct with love. You *are* love. It shines out of You and all around, even to the depths of my spirit, and it makes me desire to be just that way - so full of Your love that it shines out of me and all around to the people in my life. May it be so.

I acknowledge, Lord, Your great wisdom in veiling the future from me. If I knew all that You know about the future, I would undoubtedly try to take over the leadership role in this walk. What a disaster that would be! I'd rather be surrendered, sanctified and secure.

January 28
SURRENDERING THE EVERYDAY-NESS OF LIFE

Whatever you do, do your work heartily,
as for the Lord rather than for men.
Colossians 3:23

The truth for today from Your heart to mine is that, even on a "good" day, I do not have the resources, on my own, to live for You. In times of great crisis, when the situation is obviously overwhelming, I quickly turn to You because I see my inability to deal with the crisis. And I then continue to look to You until the crisis is past.

The crisis may reveal what is already within me, but it is living faithfully day after day, when no one is looking, that the fruit of the Spirit is produced in my life. It is the perseverance of doing well the things that You have put before me, common though they may be, that builds my character. And to do these tasks well requires allowing You to be Lord. How many years I failed to understand this truth, Lord! I somehow thought I should be able to handle the everyday things in my own wisdom and strength. I thought it was up to me to just deal with them.

This is why everyday stuff is more often my place-of-stumbling than is a great crisis. I see that You are telling me (again) that I am to trust You in *every* situation - listen to You every hour of every day whether that hour brings joy, sadness or contentment. Even in my routine tasks my focus is to be on You, because doing unto You glorifies all that I do.

This business of renouncing self-sufficiency is so essential, Lord. At least for me, it has been a struggle. How many times I have wished You would simply take over and do it for me! But I know You don't work that way. Surrender, by its very definition, is always from the will, freely given. This is so You can have a people who love You and surrender *because* they love You. Once again, I see Your wisdom at work! What an awesome God You are!

January 29
GRATITUDE

I will give thanks to the Lord with all my heart;
I will tell of all Your wonders.
I will be glad and exult in You;
I will sing praise to Your name,
O Most High.
Psalm 9:1-2

It is a beautiful morning.
The sunshine fills my room
and I'm made to think about all for which I'm thankful.

Your grace is so wide - so spacious in all directions,
and my heart is amazed
and humbled
and grateful for that grace.
It represents to me all that You are.

You surround me with a brightness
and warmth
that comforts and protects me.
The comfort brings me joy
and the protection brings me peace.
Together they mingle in my spirit and the result
is an uprising of praise and love to You.

It starts out, Lord, as gratitude for what You have done for me
but it turns to praise for who You are.
For You are not just *my* Lord,
You are *the* Lord.

One day every knee will bow
and every tongue confess that powerful truth,
and Your glory will cover the Earth!

How I look forward to that day!
All life's struggles with pain and weakness and sin will be over.
Then *all* will be surrounded with brightness and warmth
as I am
this moment.

January 30
CHILDLIKE TRUST

O Lord, my heart is not proud, nor my eyes haughty;
Nor do I involve myself in great matters,
Or in things too difficult for me.
Surely I have composed and quieted my soul;
Like a weaned child rests against his mother,
My soul is like a weaned child within me.
Psalm 131:1-2

More than once, Lord, I have come to You confused over how to know what *You* are supposed to do and what *I* am supposed to do in this walk of faith. This usually happens when I come to a difficult place and want to get past it quickly. I get all tied up in knots over, *"Maybe I'm trying to do God's part. I can't do God's part! What if I'm failing at what I'm supposed to do?! How can I know for sure exactly what is my part?!"*

And, so many times, You have hugged me and said, **"My child, you worry too much. Relax and rejoice. Trust Me to show you all you need to know."**

Then I once again see that I'm making it much harder than necessary. I do not need to know "for sure exactly" what is my part. It is as simple as a child walking beside her father and letting him be in control. You blessed me with a wonderful earthly father, one who loved his children and did all within his power to provide and protect and nurture us. I trusted him completely because I knew he loved me. I would never have been afraid to put my hand in his and walk a strange path. I felt safe in his presence.

Looking back, I see that it was not my responsibility to know much of anything except to listen to him and obey him. That was easy! And so is this walk of faith if I can do these simple things on a consistent basis:

Be anxious for nothing.

Relax and rejoice.

Trust You in *every* situation.

Do not quench Your Spirit.

Be still and listen for Your voice.

Obey all that I understand.

Know that You are well able to *make* me understand what I *need* to understand.

How beautifully simple! The older I get, the more I appreciate simple. Did You not say that I need to be as a little child to enter Your Kingdom? Thank You, my Lord, for being patient with my slowness to learn - just like a child. Thank You for Your mercies which are new every day. Thank You for Your precious promise that You will not leave me alone. Truly, I am blessed to be Your child!

January 31
STABILITY

I love Thee, O Lord, my strength.
The Lord is my rock and my fortress and my deliverer,
My God, my rock, in whom I take refuge;
My shield and the horn of my salvation, my stronghold.
Psalm 18: 1-2

Lord, to You all things are seen and understood.
You know my heart and all it contains.
Please help me quiet my mind
bringing order and serenity,
taking every thought captive.

I love You, my Lord.
Circumstances of life may change my emotions.
They may color how I view certain people.
But deeper than these emotions and these perspectives,
there abides an unchanging foundation of Love
which You Yourself have placed within me.
This I return to again and again.
It is my Rock,
the anchor of my life that shields me from the winds of life
that would otherwise blow me off course.

Powerful.
Simple.
Gentle.
Eternal.

Those are a few of the words that describe this ever-solid foundation of Love.
As I think about it, Lord, I am humbled.
I am not worthy of Your *attention*,
much less Your love!

But that is what grace is - unmerited favor.
Not earned in any way, yet freely given.
All I can do is bow
in adoration, worship and gratitude
for that amazing grace and the Giver of it.
Thank You for the stability You give my life.

February 1
J
O
Y

...let us run with endurance the race that is set before us,
fixing our eyes on Jesus, the author and perfecter of faith,
who for the joy set before Him endured the cross,
despising the shame,
and has sat down at the right hand of the throne of God.
Hebrews 12: 1-2

Remember, Lord, when I learned this little acronym as a child?
J - Jesus
O - others
Y - yourself

This was an easy-to-remember reminder of what the priorities should be in my life as Your child. And a reminder that living out this priority would bring joy to You, to others and then to me. I wish I could honestly say that I always lived by it, but we both know I didn't. I know, Lord, the reason for my failures is that I often attempted to live in my own strength. It is seemingly taking me a lifetime to learn this simple but important concept: *I am to walk by the Spirit and not by the flesh.* In other words, even setting priorities is not a thing I do. It is rather a work You do in me. Like many other spiritual truths that seem to be instructions, it is actually a *result* of Your Spirit being constantly at work with my surrendered will. My part is to surrender my will and obey. Yours is to change me on the inside so that it works through to the outside.

It is the same idea, Lord, as Your words "blessed are the pure in heart for they shall see God." This is not an instruction to me to make my heart pure. I have no power to make my heart pure! If I did, You would not have had to die on the cross. It is rather a clear snapshot in words of what You desire to do in every one of Your children - make them pure in heart. The efficiency with which You accomplish it in me, however, *is* up to me and to my ability to be constantly surrendered to You.

So, as You and I walk on toward home, my single-minded purpose is to maintain this joy of being with You. If the joy departs, I know that my focus has become faulty, my surrender has been compromised in some way. I am probably putting "me" first. Or I am allowing "others" to have a power in my life that is not pleasing to You. Because if I am walking surrendered to You, You *will* be my number one priority! So be it, Lord.

February 2
WORDS OF WORSHIP
From Psalm 63
(paraphrased)

Yesterday I read Psalm 63 and this morning You led me back to it to do more than just read it. I love this Psalm because I love You, and the words say what my heart feels. David was just better at expressing his heart than I am. Thank You for preserving his words all these centuries. And please, Lord, accept my words of worship from a heart overflowing with love for You.

O God, You are my God;
I seek You with all my heart.
My soul thirsts for You,
my flesh yearns for You in a dry and weary land
where there is no water.

My spirit is Your sanctuary, Your dwelling place.
How amazing!
There, the eternal part of me meets with You
and there I experience Your glory and Your power,
Your love.
Because Your love means more to me than life itself,
I shall praise You
with my lips
and with my life
as long as I have breath.
My soul is satisfied and I am filled with joy.

Even when I am unable to sleep,
my thoughts turn to You.
I remember all the ways You have blessed me
and delivered me over the years,
and my spirit sings a beautiful song to You.
In Your presence, my Lord, I am safe and protected.
I hold tight to You,
and You will not let me go.
You have promised.
So be it.

February 3
CLEANSED

Come now, and let us reason together, says the Lord.
Though your sins are as scarlet, they will be as white as snow;
though they are red like crimson, they will be like wool.
Isaiah 1:18

Cleansed. What a great word! To be clean from head to toe is a delight that only one who has been denied that privilege for a while can appreciate. I remember, Lord, the time following my back injury when I could not even stand up for weeks much less shower and shampoo my hair. I remember how ineffective were the little "baths in a bag" and dry shampoo that bed patients get - just barely better than nothing. And I remember that first day I *could* get into the shower and delight in the wonder of hot water and sweet-smelling soap. What a fantastic feeling. I think the happiness in heaven is going to be something like that!

But as good as that is, I'm thinking this morning about the cleansing that only You can do, the cleansing of the heart, the forgiveness of sins. This cleansing, Lord, is as far above physical cleansing as the heavens are above the earth. And when You called me, I knew inner cleansing was absolutely essential if I wanted to be a member of Your family. You took away the sin nature with which I was born, the one "red as crimson" and You gave me in its place Your very own nature. That is why that verse says "whiter than snow" because Your nature is pure, without sin.

You not only gave me a new nature, You forgave me the sins I had committed; the acts of rebellion, the disobedience, the selfish lifestyle I'd chosen to live, the bad decisions I'd made. I confessed and You forgave. What a relief to have such a burden lifted from my shoulders! Guilt that I had carried for a very long time was suddenly gone! I searched around for it, but it was nowhere to be found. Later I learned from Your Word that when You forgive our sins, You also remove them…

As far as the east is from the west,
so far has He removed our transgressions from us.
Psalms 103:12

I love it, Lord, that David used east and west here rather than north and south. Because we have a definite stopping/starting point for north and south, that is a distance that can actually be measured. But east and west just go on forever. That is why I could not find that burden of sin I'd carried!

This inner cleansing, I have discovered, is an ongoing thing. You and I keep finding bits of stuff here and there that need to go. The dark world in which I live constantly bombards me with its dirt and some of it sticks. How I praise You, my Lord, for Your faithfulness to keep me clean! Please see the gratitude and love brimming up in my heart.

February 4
RELIANCE UPON YOU

Come to Me, all who are weary and heavy-laden, and I will give you rest.
Take My yoke upon you, and learn from Me,
for I am gentle and humble in heart;
and you shall find rest for your souls.
For My yoke is easy and My load is light.
Matthew 11:28-30

Songs of praise to my God who loves me!
Thoughts of thanksgiving for blessings
too many to number.
Desire to draw near,
to rest in Your presence,
to sit at Your feet and worship.

All of this, Lord, is taking place within me
as I sit in my quiet room this morning.
My needs are many;
my requests for others come from my heart of love
which You have created.

The thought occurs to me
that my dependence upon You would be frightening
if it were upon anything or anyone else.
But it is all on You,
my Faithful Counselor
and my Beloved.

So I am safe and loved and blessed
and so very thankful to You!
May my actions today live out that gratitude in ways visible.

February 5
IT IS ALL ABOUT LOVE

And the Lord is the one who goes ahead of you;
He will be with you.
He will not fail you or forsake you.
Do not fear, or be dismayed.
Deuteronomy 31:8

If it pleases You, Lord, help me understand the application of this verse to all: *"I will never leave you or forsake you."*

I see clearly how it applies to an obedient child. But in my reading last week I came upon the statement that even sin and selfishness and waywardness will not cause You to leave. However, I remember learning as a child this statement: "God will not dwell where there is sin." One of those statements has to be untrue.

Your Word teaches that Your presence is everywhere all the time. In fact, Paul's list in Romans 8 of all those "things" that can never separate us from Your love covers every condition that could ever happen to us. And that *is* one of the messages of the prodigal son - he was selfish and wayward but his father never stopped loving him, never ceased being his father. The son eventually came back home and repented.

But what about one who continues in his sin? What about Hebrews 6? What about "he who puts his hand to the plow and then looks back is not fit for the kingdom of God"? How are these reconciled with You never "leaving or forsaking"?

I think I'm seeing, Lord, it is all about love. And I must understand that You love at all times, but I am not able to *receive* that love if I'm sinning or selfish or wayward. *Love offered and love received are two very different things.* Only "love received" brings my heart-response of loving You in return. Only "love received" causes me to rejoice and praise and be grateful - all conditions which You desire I experience.

I see, Lord, that Your heart is grieved by a child who wanders away from You. Your presence *will* be continually with that one but he will miss the blessed experience of a loving, growing relationship with You. And as for judgment day decisions - You are sovereign, all-wise, just and holy and thus will do what is right. It is all about love.

February 6
OBEDIENCE

Although He was a Son, He learned obedience from the things which He suffered.
Hebrews 5:8

This verse stopped my reading this morning, Lord, as I came to this chapter about You being my High Priest. I do not have the same understanding of the role of High Priest as the people to whom this book was written. They were as familiar with that as I am of the role of pastor. But I understand the concept of obedience. What is amazing to me is that You had to *learn* it - that obedience was not something You knew by virtue of being the Son of God.

One thing this tells me is that obedience is a skill to be learned. I was not born knowing how to be obedient. My parents had to teach me to obey, and when I came into Your family, You continued this training in obedience. I, like You, have learned obedience from the things I suffered. In my case, as a child, it was a razor strap hanging behind the kitchen door. It took very few applications of that to teach me that obedience was the right way to go. The very fact of its presence there, along with the knowledge that my mother was to be relied upon to use it when necessary, was a strong incentive to be obedient. This sounds very old-fashioned today, but it certainly worked for me and my seven siblings.

We are told so little about Your childhood. But it may be that Mary and Joseph had to discipline You as well. Maybe You were not the "perfect" child I envision You to be. But my spirit, Lord, tells me that this type of discipline/obedience is not what was being spoken of here. This has, rather, to do with Your choosing to proceed with the plan of redemption, a plan laid before the foundation of the world. You could have chosen, at any point along the way, to *not* proceed. What an awesome thought! What a frightening thought!

You knew the consequences both of choosing to proceed and of choosing not to proceed. I cannot imagine the mental anguish, the heart pain, the dread with which You had to wrestle, knowing the ramifications of both Your obedience and Your disobedience. That is at least part of the suffering through which You learned obedience.

Being an ordinary mortal, I have little concept of *all* You went through, Lord. But that which I know is cause enough for eternal praise! To be saved from being eternally separated from You fills me with a joy and gratitude that overflows in praise. Thank You for learning obedience.

And having been made perfect,
He became to all those who obey Him
The source of eternal salvation.
Hebrews 5:9

February 7
ENCOURAGEMENT

So then let us pursue the things which make for peace
and the building up of one another.
Romans 14:19

You and I, Lord, have been thinking about how important encouragement is to all people. I am needy of every good thing which flows from someone encouraging me. Please help me as I put down a few of Your thoughts on the subject:

"Encouragement is an expression of love." Yes, and I see that it is Your kind of love - love which is unconditional.

You, my Lord, are the One to whom I should look for encouragement. But You often use Your people to speak it. So I must be sensitive to Your Spirit directing me to encourage someone else and sensitive to others' words as You speak through them to me. I have made the mistake of looking *only* to people for encouragement and it always resulted, eventually, in disappointment.

"Encouragement is a selfless act, an out-working of desire for the other person to be blessed." The longer I walk with You, Lord, the stronger my desire for everyone to experience knowing You as I do. That verse above from Romans speaks of the need for peace and for building up one another. Those are only two of the blessings which follow encouragement.

"It costs nothing to the giver but means much to the recipient." How many times I have been given strength by a word of encouragement! Just as newborn babies fail to thrive if they are not cuddled and held and loved, so we all need the verbal love expressed in encouragement.

"Encouragement rightly received brings humility." Yes, Lord, I see. I don't know why it brings humility, but I see that it does.

Encouragement from You feels like…

…peace filling my mind and heart

…love rising light and bright in my spirit

…joy overflowing

…renewed certainty of Your goodness

…renewed strength to continue this walk.

Perhaps the greatest encouragement I can receive is to read Your promises from the Word and know they are mine! Glory!

February 8
EMOTIONS/WILL

Therefore everyone who hears these words of Mine,
and acts upon them, may be compared to a wise man,
who built his house upon the rock.
And the rain descended, and the floods came,
and the winds blew, and burst against that house;
and yet it did not fall,
for it had been founded upon the rock.
Matthew 7:24-25

Thank You for the reminder that emotions are *never* the measure of our relationship. What matters are the decisions of my will. My will has been placed totally in Your care, submitted to You as fully as I know how, left there for You to work what and when You choose. That is the important truth here.

Emotions can be like the storm in Your story above. They come and go. They are affected by so many changing circumstances. But my decisions, made from my will, stand secure like the wise man's house built upon the rock. (I love it, Lord, that it twice says *the* rock, not *a* rock!) Those decisions are enduring, life-changing-forever transactions that took place.

Thank You for Your gentle reminder of that this morning. Thank You for being The Rock.

February 9
PERFECTION

...God sees not as man sees,
for man looks at the outward appearance,
but the Lord looks at the heart.
1 Samuel 16:7

Let's face it, Lord, I will *never* live up to my own high expectations. I will *always* fall short of my idea of perfection. And this failure will, if I let it, beat me down, depress me and rob me of Your joy.

I see that this is not what You want; neither is it what I want. I also see that Your intent is for me to open myself up to Your Spirit and, moment-by-moment, *walk* in the grace You have abundantly supplied to me.

And then I see that, along with my perfectionist tendencies, I am constantly pestered by the enemy of my soul reminding me of my failures and my hopelessness. How good that You have taught me how to deal with him! All I need to do is resist him and he will go away for a time. And I do this by agreeing that I truly am a hopeless failure without You. "**Apart from Me you can do nothing**." He is defeated, and I am filled with joy because I am firmly "attached" to You.

Please help me set aside forever my own ideas of perfection. They are wrong, anyway! Please fill me fuller than I have ever yet been with Your amazing grace. Fill all the tiny little corners of my spirit, Lord, with Your Light so that there are no dark, hidden stashes of anything contaminating Your dwelling place.

"**The spirit is willing but the flesh is weak**." How true! But does it matter that those words were spoken to Your disciples *before* they were filled with Your Spirit? How well I know that my flesh is weak, but I also know Your Spirit is powerful, present and active in my life. May I live this day by the power of that blessed Spirit. I love You, Lord!

February 10
THE SINFUL STATE

For this reason I say to you, her sins, which are many, have been forgiven,
for she loved much; but he who is forgiven little, loves little.
Luke 7:47

These words from Your mouth came after telling the parable of the two debtors - the one who owed a lot of money and the other who owed only a little. They were both forgiven their debts, and You asked the judgmental Pharisee which one would love the lender more. And, of course, he said the one who was forgiven the larger debt.

His reason for being judgmental was the woman who had come in and begun to wash Your feet with her tears and dry them with her hair. Since she was a "sinful woman," the Pharisee was upset that You allowed such a thing. Which just proves again that You see things not at all like the world sees them. You saw her love for You which motivated this unusual public display of caring. You saw her heart which was repentant for the lifestyle she had lived. You saw the potential for compassion and grace to make a fundamental difference in her life. How that makes me love You, my Lord! How thankful I am that this is how You see me, too.

Because the truth is that, although I had not been a "sinful woman" in the same sense that this woman had, *I was just as lost as she was.* It does not take a huge sin or a multitude of small sins to be lost. It actually takes no action at all to be lost. I was born that way. It is my faulty human thinking that tries to rank sins on a chart from tiny to gigantic when, in Your eyes, it is all sin. And all sin flows from a heart needing Your cleansing.

Of course, I had to repent and forsake a sinful lifestyle. But any attempt to do so without allowing You to completely change my nature would have been futile. It was that inner change that made it possible to live a life that pleases You. Except for the miracle of inner change, I would be lost for all eternity. That is the sobering thought that causes love to rise in songs of praise from my spirit! That is what makes me value Your grace so highly. For without it, I would have no salvation, no fellowship with You, no joy and peace in these days of my life, no reunion to look forward to with people I love very much - in other words, what is most precious to me I would not have *except by Your grace.*

My love for You, Lord, is based in part upon the wonderful truth of what You have done in my life. I was headed toward eternal darkness, and You stopped me, put Your arm around my shoulders and said, "Come, walk with Me." You turned me toward the light and took my hand and, in a moment of time, changed what I was and where I was headed. There are no words in my vocabulary to express my gratitude and love for You! Wordless praise will have to do. All glory to You, my Lord and my King.

February 11
STRENGTH IN PERSECUTION

Listen to Me, you who know righteousness,
a people in whose heart is My law;
do not fear the reproach of man,
neither be dismayed at their reviling.
Isaiah 51:7

It is not a popular thing today to be a Christian. Fewer and fewer people respect You, Lord, and thus fewer respect our faith. This was no doubt true 100 years ago, too, but the disrespect has progressed exponentially since then. Remember 80 years ago when children were taught from readers full of Biblical principles? Remember 40 years ago when our school days were started with Bible reading and prayer? Remember 20 years ago when a traditional prayer over the loudspeaker was spoken before a football game? All that has become forbidden in the public schools of this "Christian nation."

The day may come, and soon, when we will be truly persecuted for our faith. I wonder, Lord, what will happen then. This verse above spoke to me this morning as I read it. It speaks to me of what is important, of what is *eternally* important, and puts this whole subject of persecution in proper perspective. There is only so much that mankind can do to us. They can torture and they can kill the body. But You, Yourself said,

And do not fear those who kill the body, but are unable to kill the soul;
but rather fear Him who is able to destroy both soul and body in hell.
Matthew 10:28

I'm seeing, Lord, that the radical, evil element of our world is growing more powerful. By that, I mean those in other nations and in our own nation who *hate righteousness*. They seem empowered to speak out and garner an audience among what mankind deems to be "the influential." I don't think I'm being paranoid. I do think I'm seeing what is happening before our eyes. I think I'm seeing what Your Word says will happen in the latter days - that men's love will grow cold and evil will wax worse and worse. But, having read the whole Book, I am full of hope! Here is what You say will happen to those who persecute Your people...

For the moth will eat them like a garment, and the grub will eat them like wool.
Isaiah 51:8(a)

Eaten by bugs! Not a very glorious end for these fighters of the God of Heaven! And what happens to those of us who are faithful to the end?

But My righteousness shall be forever, and My salvation to all generations.
Isaiah 51:8(b)

I'll stick with You, Lord!

February 12
PRAISE

Worthy art Thou, our Lord and our God,
to receive glory and honor and power;
for Thou didst create all things,
and because of Thy will they existed and were created.
Revelation 4:11

I'm glad I read that verse this morning, Lord, because it brings to my mind the whole subject of praising You and how often I need to be revitalized in this area of my life. I'm not talking here about a general attitude of love and admiration toward You. I always have that. I'm thinking about on-purpose, focused praise with energy and thought behind it. I'm thinking about a portion of my prayer time being consistently set apart for thinking about who and what You are - not about what You have done for me, not about what I need You to do for me today, not about others' needs, but about *You.*

And even as I write those words, Lord, my mind floods with the blessed results of praising You! Like the fact that praise takes my eyes off me and puts them on You. Thinking about Your greatness, Your power, Your eternal love puts my life and its problems in perspective with no effort on my part. I come away reassured and full of peace that all is well because You are in control of my life.

Reminding myself of all the wonderful attributes that are Yours increases my love for You. The more I magnify Your name in my mind and heart, the more that ever-flowing fountain of love within me fills up to running over. The greater my attempt to glorify You, the more I sense Your great love returning to me. At the end of the day, Lord, this whole business of walking by faith is about love, isn't it?

It seems that praising You opens up invisible, spirit-world channels through which You pour good things into my life. So on days when I neglect praise, I forfeit blessings. You taught me long ago that all Your actions and instructions are motivated by love, and I see how this is true in this area of praise. Praising You *seems* like a gift from me to You but, in Your awesome grace, You turn it into a gift from You to me. I begin with the idea of putting into words the honor and esteem in which I hold You, the exalted place which You occupy in my thinking, and I end up being blessed myself.

So, is this my motive for praising You - to get all these good things? No, Lord. My motive is and always will be to attempt to express a heart and mind full of love and gratitude. Often my praise turns into thanksgiving, but I can't help that. I'm thankful. And thanksgiving is good, too. I can always bring my mind back to praise.

But the real reason is this - *only You are worthy*. You alone are Lord of all. You alone are my Lord.

February 13
CHOSEN
Part One

And so, as those who have been chosen of God,
holy and beloved,
put on a heart of compassion, kindness,
humility, gentleness and patience.
Colossians 3:12

Lord, as I sit in Your presence and think about these words that Paul wrote and what it means to be chosen by You, my mind is filled with thoughts and emotions - all good - but all jumbled up. Please help me sort them out and meditate upon them in some orderly fashion.

When I shop for produce at the grocery store, I look over what is on display and choose what looks best and freshest. How thankful I am that You do not do that! Outward appearance has nothing to do with Your process of choosing because You look at the heart. And when You look at the heart You see it, not in its present sinful state but as it will be when made holy by Your grace. You see the potential for godliness because You are able to see the future as clearly as I see yesterday. You know from the beginning what Your plans are for each person. Plans to bless!

As I think about this, gratitude is the overriding emotion in my heart. I am overwhelmed with thankfulness that You cared enough to choose me. Through all of this time, You continue to be patient with me while I learn and grow. I am filled with a strong sense of gratitude mixed with humility. How incredible that You would choose ME! Such wonder makes me fall on my knees before You and pledge myself to You for all time, forever and ever!

Lord, in thinking about the immense *significance* of being chosen by You, what comes to mind is the excitement of holding the winning ticket to a multi-million dollar lottery. An instant millionaire! Major good news! Immediately, that winner's attitudes change and a brand new outlook on life takes form. So many things are radically different!

But I'm convinced that being chosen to belong to You, to be made holy and beloved, so far surpasses the significance of winning millions of dollars! That money may (and often does) bring more misery than happiness. And even if it brought only joy, it is still temporary; it is only for this life. *Your choosing is for all eternity*! Blessings and grace for this life and then all eternity to live with You and worship You! How blind our culture is to the true worth of spiritual blessings. And how sad that this is so.

February 14
CHOSEN
Part Two

And, so, as those who have been chosen of God, holy and beloved, put on a heart
of compassion, kindness, humility, gentleness and patience.
Colossians 3:12

Understanding the concept that "I am who You say I am" has done much toward helping my faith grow. This Scripture above is a perfect example of who You say I am. You say I am chosen, holy and beloved. On practically any day, at any given time I may feel very far from chosen, holy and beloved. *But my feelings do not change the facts.* My feelings are affected by so many variables and, therefore, may change from day to day. Your facts are rock solid and eternal. And the fact is that, "I am who You say I am." This is an incredible, life-changing truth. A life-long study could be made of Your Word on this subject alone. The abundance of Your grace is amazing. Truly, You are an awesome God!

This Scripture grabbed my attention yesterday because of the list of words following the truth that "I am chosen." (Well, the *real* reason is that Your Spirit *made* it grab my attention and for that, I thank You.) That list contains characteristics I strongly desire to manifest in my own life, and yet, more often than I like, fail to do so....compassion, kindness, humility, gentleness and patience. As You know, Lord, I so often struggle to "put on" these traits; they do not come naturally to me. They are a challenge, and therefore, I must *choose* to override self and turn in all openness to You. I have set out to think on these truths, because I believe that it will further my emotional/behavioral progress. I ask You to bless both the process and the results.

My motive? Simply this: I know that impatience, crossness and grumpiness do not bring glory to You. It hurts my heart that I *say* I love You with all that I am, and yet *behave* at times as though I love no one but myself. I can find no justification for this lack of integrity. Not the fatigue, not the pain, not anything. Because I know, Lord, that You have power to overcome and it is *that* power upon which I need to be drawing. Please help me to do that very thing this very day.

February 15
YOUR WORK IN ME

So then, my beloved, ...work out your salvation with fear and trembling;
for it is God who is at work in you,
both to will and to work for His good pleasure.
Philippians 2:12-13

Lord, the whole book of Philippians is about joy. And these verses bring me great joy because they speak of Your work in me. I used to wonder about the "fear and trembling" part, because those words did not seem to fit with the concept of joy. But You have taught me, my Lord, that what is meant is a holy reverence toward You, an awe, a profound respect for who You are. As I ponder that, the trembling naturally occurs because I begin to comprehend the vast distance between who You are and who I am, the holiness that is You and the utter lost-ness that is me. I'm made to see how strong You are and how weak I am. I realize that, if I was ever to know You at all, You had to take the initiative and make it happen. And You did! What an incredibly glorious thing is redemption!

But the phrase "to will and to work" catches my thoughts this morning. I'm seeing, Lord, that if You want me to do something, You also make *me* want to do that something. Your will becomes my will and thus, obedience follows. That sounds simple and easy. And it is simple. But my experience has been that it is not always easy. I have often wrestled with the inner conflict of knowing what You want, wanting very much to obey but yet postponing obedience because it was difficult, or it was painful to the flesh, or it seemed risky.

You have shown me, more than once, that delayed obedience is disobedience. You have also shown me the wonderful joy that follows obedience. You keep leading me deeper and deeper into myself and bringing me to these crossroads. Will I choose Your way or my way - life or death - misery or joy? These are no-brainer choices, Lord, but still, in my humanness, sometimes hard to make.

Here is my request for today. Please make me wise enough to be quick to obey and to trust absolutely in Your power to keep me from every evil. And please accept my gratitude for Your work in me.

February 16
DEALING WITH REGRET

For the sorrow that is according to the will of God
produces a repentance without regret, leading to salvation;
but the sorrow of the world produces death.
2 Corinthians 7:10

I am working this morning, Lord, on thoughts of forgiveness and regret. Tozer says that if I believe You have forgiven me of the sins and failures of the past, I will not feel the sting of regret. I may have a memory of the sin, but the sting will be gone.

The fact that I so deeply feel my regret tells me we have some work to do. What comes to my mind is "if I will confess my sin, You are faithful and just to forgive my sin and cleanse me from *all* unrighteousness." These are Your thoughts, Lord, not mine. And I have confessed. But I'm seeing that completed forgiveness is a two-part process. Your part is to forgive; my part is to accept that forgiveness and travel on, believing - *knowing* - I'm forgiven. I'm to live with wondrous relief and unceasing gratitude because I've been delivered from the penalty of that sin.

I see now that to continue to feel such sorrow and regret is not pleasing to You. That says I don't really believe You are big enough or powerful enough or love me enough to *truly* forgive. In plain English, *it is doubting You.*

Faith is what pleases You, and You have given me a deep desire to please You in everything. So I accept Your forgiveness, and I rejoice in the relief it brings. May the sting of regret over past actions be covered over by Your grace and mercy. I'm so thankful, Lord, for Your Word. All the promises in it become shining truths for me to live by when I accept them as my very own. What a privilege it is to be Your child!

February 17
FORGIVING MYSELF

How blessed is he whose transgression is forgiven,
whose sin is covered!
How blessed is the man to whom the Lord does not impute iniquity,
and in whose spirit there is no deceit!
Psalm 32:1-2

A disturbing dream last night about two people I love very much. You, Lord, have used this dream to show me some truths about forgiveness. In this case, about forgiving myself of past failures, sins, mistakes and poor judgments. What I now understand…

I work at forgiving myself
by refusing to continually bring to mind
hurtful failings from the past.

Instead, I acknowledge I have given them all to You
and now must leave them with You.

If they come to mind,
I remind myself that You have taken care of them,
once and for all.

I accept Your love and Your forgiveness
as a healing balm to my bruised and painful emotions,
allowing them heal.

I now let the space they have occupied in my mind and heart
be filled with Your peace
and love
and joy
and creativity.

How desperately this world needs to know and practice these truths. How I want this blessing upon every person I know!

February 18
A LAPFUL OF JEWELS

Forever, O Lord, Your word is settled in heaven.
Your faithfulness continues throughout all generations;
You established the earth, and it stands.
They stand this day according to Your ordinances,
for all things are Your servants.
Psalm 119:89-91

Lord, Your truths seem to me a mound of jewels, each one reflecting light and color and affecting the appearance of all around them. All together they are magnificent to behold. Each has a brilliant loveliness of its own, yet when I look at the totality of them, I am astounded at the radiance which is multiplied and reflected.

Some of these precious gems, my Lord, are Your promises I have tested and found to be absolutely true. Upon Your faithful words I can stake my very life. I can remember a time when it was a little scary to step out upon a promise. Like a baby learning to walk, I felt uncertain and uneasy, trying to master the intricacies of muscle movement, balance and forward progress. But You are faithful. By trusting a little, I learned to trust more. By exercising my faith, it grew within me so that each promise I tested became a shining treasure. How I value these gems!

Some of these jewels are instructions on how to live a pure and light-filled life in this dark world. Your Word is full of them! I could fill up pages if I tried to write them all down. But You have already written them down for me! Your instructions are readily available. They are easily understood. They are valuable guideposts along the road to keep me from straying down some dangerous path. They do not change - what was needed for first-century Christians to walk successfully is what is needed today. Conditions, cultures and problems come and go, but Your Word and our inner needs do not change. Thank You for these precious truths and safeguards for my spirit!

Even more precious to me are Your promises that are yet to be fulfilled. I joyfully wait, expectant and eager. I know these promises are sure because all the others have been. So, though I do not know when or how You will fulfill them, I have no doubt that You *will*. Thank You, Lord, for these divine blessings to which I look forward.

But the most prized gems to me, Lord, are the ones You have spoken softly into my listening spirit. Words directly from Your heart to mine. Words that reached deep down into my being, fundamentally changing me so that I will never be the same. These priceless jewels shine with a holy light; they finally made me understand that You truly love me. How I thank You for Your patience with my slow learning. How I thank You for these endearing words of love that melted my heart and made it completely Yours. How I long for everyone to experience Your love!

February 19
FAITH THAT GIVES THANKS

In everything give thanks;
for this is God's will for you in Christ Jesus.
1 Thessalonians 5:18

Every problem, every fault I see in myself, every failure I have experienced, should be the basis for thankfulness to You, Lord. I'm seeing that truth this morning so clearly. I know Your Word already told me that, but I'm just now seeing it as true for ME.

Everything that You allow into my life, whether I see it as good or bad, is the potential avenue to bring me closer to You and to know You better. And isn't this what I desire most?! Of course it is! Nothing sends me running to You faster than trouble. Nothing keeps me right by Your warm side more than on-going problems. Problems for which I can find no solution. Problems that last and last and keep on lasting. These are what keep me on my knees before You.

So instead of being cast down and discouraged when trouble comes, I should be grateful to You for yet another chance to love You more and receive more of Your love. I should be thankful for a golden opportunity to claim Your promises and then watch You work in my life. Please, Lord, make me wise enough to take this truth and live it out consistently.

Besides, the devil is always happy to see one of Your children unhappy and discouraged. That alone is, to me, reason enough to have faith that gives thanks in everything.

February 20
DEALING WITH A PROBLEM

Trust in the Lord with all your heart,
and do not lean on your own understanding.
In all your ways acknowledge Him,
and He will make your paths straight.
Proverbs 3:5-6

I'm learning, Lord, that trusting and acknowledging You is not always simple. I've leaned on my own understanding for so long that its difficult to *stop* leaning on it. When problems arise,. I usually try first to solve them myself. When that fails, then I turn to You. Someday I'll learn to turn to You first. How thankful I am for Your patience!

To see that You *do* want to change something in my life is usually not complicated. I can see that You do, and I can even want You to do it. My difficulty comes in knowing the "how" - what I am to do and what to depend on You to do. But I think I'm seeing a process which answers those questions for me. Please help me clarify it.

Your part. You show me the problem. You are, after all, the Spirit of Light.

My part. I must have a willing heart. I must be open to what You are showing me and agree with what You want to do.

Our part together. Just agreeing is not enough. I must, by an act of my will, make the necessary effort in the direction You are pointing.

There always seems to be a first "something" I must do, and when I take that step, You bless it. Then as I continue to move in that direction, You continue to bless. You will not bless without my obedience. And my obedience without Your blessing would never solve the problem. This truly is a cooperative venture.

Now I know we can never condense Your ways of dealing with every situation down to three simple steps, Lord. But I do think patterns can be recognized that make our spiritual growth smoother. And that is what I believe You have shown me here - a simple-to-understand pattern that gives guidance in problem-solving, whether that problem is a destructive habit to quit, a resentment that seems to hang around even when we want it to go away, forgiving someone or…well, You get the picture. What I know is that it works. And it works because You work. You are working within to perfect me and make me like You! There can be no better life than living with You, my Lord. Thank You for being my Teacher!

February 21
CONTROLLED BY YOUR SPIRIT

And let the peace of Christ rule in your hearts,
to which indeed you were called in one body;
and be thankful.
Let the word of Christ richly dwell within you
with all wisdom, teaching and admonishing one another
with psalms and hymns and spiritual songs,
singing with thankfulness in your hearts to God.
And whatever you do in word or deed,
do all in the name of the Lord Jesus,
giving thanks through Him to God the Father.
Colossians 3:15-17

Words of love spoken in worship are good. They please You, Lord, and they elevate my own spirit to more love for You and for my fellow humans. But they are not all You desire. You want those words put into action and lived out in my life everyday. That is where I am convicted this morning.

All people deal with days of being irritated with things and with people who seem bent on being, well, irritating. I'm sure I'm not the only one with this problem. Nothing seems to go right; things are out of control; I go from this to that and accomplish little. Frustration builds sometimes to the point of explosion. This kind of day, this kind of situation needs "Spirit control."

This is exactly the time that I have an important choice to make - to continue fuming and grow more miserable (making all around me miserable, too) or simply say, "Lord, I give You complete control of my mind and emotions in this mess. Please enable me to have peace within, a smile without and a mouth filled with praise. Thank You, Jesus."

The choice is mine. Those words above that Paul wrote say, "*let* the peace of Christ rule in your heart." You will not rule over my responses without my permission and my cooperation. Submission to Your Spirit must be a constant attitude. Actually, I see that I'm being foolish to wait until things are totally out of control to do this. The smart thing to do is make a lifelong decision to submit to Your Spirit *before* encountering situations that demand patience and gentleness - think through what I need to do and make that all-important decision to do it.

This is much easier to talk about than it is to do. But I know You never give us something to do that is not do-able. So by discipline and practice, it is not only possible but becomes more and more desirable. That is one of the most beautiful things about our relationship, Lord. The more I love You, the more I want to love You. The longer I know You, the closer I want to walk with You. It is a lovely, growing, living friendship, holy yet concerned with everyday problems.

What a great God You are! How fine it is to belong to You!

52

February 22
YOUR WISDOM

But the wisdom from above is first pure, peaceable,
gentle, reasonable, full of mercy and good fruits,
unwavering, without hypocrisy.
James 3:17

Since one of Your goals for me is to make me like You, this verse describes what my mind and actions should be. Or at least becoming.

Pure - only You, Lord, are truly pure. And only You can make me pure. I give You full permission to remove anything within me that would hinder Your purity from becoming the basis of all my thoughts and actions.

Peaceable - that suggests to me calmness, serenity, loveliness, order, the sweetness of Your love flowing through my life. May it be so.

Gentle - tenderness is, to me, one of the most appealing things about you, Lord. You show Your strength through Your gentleness, Your tenderness with fallen men and women and with small children. Oh, Lord, make me gentle like You!

Reasonable - a danger exists in applying this word from the world's point of view rather than Yours. It is *Your* wisdom we are talking about, so reasonableness will always agree with Your Word. A fanatic, in the true sense of the word, is one who goes beyond what You have said or who misinterprets what You have said. You have given us good minds and reasoning powers. Under Your control, my thoughts *will* be Yours.

Full of mercy - I cannot pick and choose who I will bestow mercy upon. My job is to be full of Your mercy to all - not judging, not critical, not harsh and opinionated, but merciful, loving, and reasonable. Jesus, help me be a channel of Your mercy.

Good fruits - my life under Your control *will* bear good fruit. The fruit my life bears may be different than the fruit that my brother and sister bear in their lives. That should not concern me because You know exactly what You are doing with each one of us. If we are submitted to You, we will bear exactly the fruit You desire that we bear.

Unwavering - steadfast, founded on the Rock, unmovable, bold, assured, strong against all foes. This is truly a great characteristic to have, Lord. Give me an unwavering witness to Your glory!

Without hypocrisy - how I desire this! I have asked many times for You to make me transparent so that there would never be a need for covering up anything. Satan's way is to cover up and deceive. Your way is to confess, wash clean, purify and *shine*! So be it, Lord.

February 23
TOTAL HONESTY ABOUT MOTIVES

Now we have received, not the spirit of the world,
but the Spirit who is from God,
that we might know the things freely given to us by God.
I Corinthians 2: 12

Lord, please see my troubled thoughts this morning and help me discern their source. If they are convicting, correcting thoughts from You, I want to surrender to them and allow them to do their work in my heart. You know, my Lord, that my deepest desires are to be transparent before You and to please You.

If these thoughts are from my own over-zealous conscience, may I have the wisdom to turn *from* them and *to* You. It is hard for me to get a strong hold upon this business of motives. About the time I think I've nailed it down, it slips away from me. Maybe this is because my motives come from an unfamiliar-to-me place very deep within. Maybe it is because I do not understand my own heart. I can think my motives are positive and pure; then, as I go forward in that direction, what is initially a tiny doubt comes to mind - "what is my *real* reason for doing this?" That one doubt opens the floodgate for a hundred more to rush in and overwhelm me - which is where You find me this morning.

Then, too, the enemy of my soul is always on the prowl looking to devour, destroy and disturb. He can so subtly plant a doubt in my mind; I can then take it up in a flash and act upon it - which is exactly what he wants! If *that* is the source of these troubling thoughts, I know to stand fast and resist his attack in the power of Your indwelling Spirit. You have taught me that lesson well, Lord!

So I am standing fast. I am turning to You. Do You see how much I need Your wisdom and discernment? You have promised that if I need wisdom, I need only ask for it. And tied to that promise is the concept of my not doubting that You will give it. (James 1:5-8). How do I know that this promise is sure and certain? Because You have proven to me countless times, Lord, that You are faithful to Your Word, faithful to bless, to protect, to pour out Your grace upon Your children. You are true to Your Word even when I fail to be. So I know that I shall have my answer. Thank You for the peace that floods my spirit because my problem is now *Your problem.* So be it.

February 24
FACING TEMPTATION

Read Matthew 4:1-11

Reading these verses, Lord, describing Your temptation by Satan is very enlightening. I don't think You included these verses in Scripture only to illustrate how devilish the devil is, or how steadfast You are. Those facts are both true but what I'm seeing this morning is the direct application to my life: *I am tempted just as You were.*

Satan first tempted You to satisfy the desire of the flesh by suggesting You turn stones into bread. And he did this at the precise time that You would most likely be hungry - after fasting for 40 days. That's one of his best schemes - to attack where and when we are at our weakest. But, Lord, I realize that if I'm not careful, most of my time, energy and money can be spent satisfying the flesh and its desires. If I give in to this temptation of self-satisfaction, he will continue to use it *because it works*. Only through spiritual growth, only by consistently dying to self and allowing You to rule my heart will this temptation be overcome. Then Satan will move it up a notch and try me with his next test - proving You.

Proving You comes about when Satan subtly whispers, "See how godly your living has become? Now that you are in the midst of a need, let's see how quickly all that pays off." If the payoff does not come quickly, doubt and discouragement can begin and Satan wins that round. I see, Lord, that every time Satan speaks, I must listen for the lie. There is always either a lie or a misuse of the truth. In this case, *I do not live for You in order to be "paid off."* I live for You from a willing and loving heart that is eager to please You. You don't have to "prove" Yourself to me - You did that already at Calvary! Once I realize what the devil is doing and tell him that, he will go away - for a season.

He will be back, however, and another of his best schemes is to offer honor and power and glory. How alert and prayed-up I need to be in order to not be deceived! His goal is to steal my faith. Knowing that the worship of anything or anyone other than You will eventually destroy my faith, he might even appear as an angel of light. He desires that I worship him directly, but will settle for my worship to simply be turned from You, the One True God. This could include putting my trust in myself, my mate, a friend, a pastor, a teacher, *anyone* other than You. Sooner or later that person will fail, because we all fail, and my faith will be shaken because it was not built upon the Rock. This could also include doing the right thing for the wrong reason. I must search my motives, and keep them surrendered to You for approval. Bottom line, what is required to withstand this temptation is on-going surrender of all that I am, all of the time.

The adversary is doing everything he can to ruin my relationship with You, Lord. By myself I cannot win. With You, I cannot lose. You have defeated him already! Thank You for taking me to raise!

February 25
MY SPIRIT
YOUR DWELLING PLACE

By wisdom a house is built,
and by understanding it is established;
and by knowledge the rooms are filled
with all precious and pleasant riches.
Proverbs 24:3-4

There is a cozy room - not large, not small. The walls glow a soft yellow, the carpet thick and plush underfoot is a few shades more golden. There are only two chairs, each of them plumply upholstered in a creamy white fabric, inviting and comfortable - the kind to sink into for a time of rest and conversation.

There are beautiful paintings on the walls. There are bookshelves filled with books written by men and women under the inspiration of Your Holy Spirit - books to encourage, to meditate upon, to inspire strong faith. There is soft lamp-light illuminating the whites, beiges, and soft yellows of the room, all blending to create an air of peace and loveliness. There are large windows which look out upon a lawn of ancient trees.

This room belongs to just You, Jesus, and me. We meet there. Sometimes I go to absorb the serenity and quiet that is the room's atmosphere, knowing that You will join me. Sometimes when I go, I find You waiting there for me. What a blessed thing! To one who loves, nothing is more desirable than the presence of the loved one.

Sometimes we talk, and You teach me. Sometimes we sit and rest and say little. Sometimes I have many problems to tell You about. Sometimes I just want to express to You my love and praise, and I try to do that. Every time is sweet beyond telling, and I'm reluctant to have it end, yet strengthened and renewed to return to the physical world.

While this room is the product of my sanctified imagination, the blessings that flow from it are *so very real!* You fill me with joy unspeakable and peace that only You can give. How blessed I am to be Your child!

February 26
AVOIDING ISRAEL'S MISTAKES
Part One

Read I Corinthians 10: 1-11

What a lesson for today! These verses describe a stubborn, stiff-necked people not unlike we are today. You had shown them miracle after miracle in getting Pharaoh to let them go. You had delivered them through the Red Sea when it looked like the Egyptians were going to slaughter them. You had provided manna for them to eat and water for them to drink. You had led them by a pillar of fire at night and a cloud by day that not only led them, but shaded them from the burning sun.

You had even given them the vision, the promise of bringing them into a new land of their very own! This people who had known nothing but bondage now had a future to look forward to and a freedom they had never experienced.

And yet....

They were idolatrous. Their hearts were set upon themselves and what they wanted. When Moses left them for but a few days, they built a golden calf to worship. Oh, Lord, I can be like that, too! Anything or anybody, including myself, I place before You in my mind, heart or love is an idol. "Eating, drinking, playing" - that describes our world today!

They craved evil things. Meat, cucumbers, melons, onions, leeks and garlic - in themselves, these things are not evil. But the people were evil in their greedy desire for them. In their view, the satisfaction of the flesh was *the* goal to be achieved. The words "crave" and "covet" are strong words but fitting, as their desire was intense. All they could think about was "how good it was back then." Please, Lord, do not let me forget the harmful aspects of my "back then." I know that Satan, father of lies, will try to cloud my memory to do just that. May I never forget the bondage of "back then" from which You have delivered me - the bondage of sin, bad habits, fear of death, fears of all kinds.

They acted immorally. Despite Your instruction to the contrary, they allowed the daughters of Moab to join them, and, just as You had warned, this disobedience led to their worship of other gods. They were again focusing upon what *they* wanted rather than what You wanted. Disobedience in this fashion had to hurt You deeply, Lord. And it had to have consequences. In order to teach them the importance of listening to You and obeying, You caused 23,000 of them to fall in one day! What a lesson! May I never hurt You - this way or any other way. Make me moldable and obedient, Lord, I pray. Left to myself, I'll be just as stubborn and stiff-necked as they were.

February 27
AVOIDING ISRAEL'S MISTAKES
Part Two

Read 1 Corinthians 10:1-11

We must finish this, Lord. The lessons are too convicting to ignore. Israel tried You. They spoke against You and against Moses. They lamented their difficult circumstances. Still the sin of self-centeredness - just like today. Instead of "blooming where I'm planted," I have at times complained, prayed, and tried to get out from under whatever You have laid upon me. I have failed to see that You know precisely how, when and where to teach me, and that You do not need my wisdom at all. I'm sorry, Lord.

They grumbled. They complained constantly about everything, but in this case they were protesting against their leaders - laying blame upon them for things not their doing. My lesson? Accept whom You have placed over me as authority, be it parent, husband, boss or pastor, and give them their due respect according to the Word. Do not worry about their faults and failures or try to correct them. Leave the correcting to You. Be, in all things, as I should be and trust You to make the relationship work. And don't whine about anything!

These warnings are convicting to me, Lord! These people failed to keep the vision of God in front of them. Instead of looking at Your goal for them - the promised land - they were looking only at today and its problems, its lacks, its discomforts. Your Word plainly states that I should set my mind on things above, not on things of the earth. When I obey, the petty trials of today fade into insignificance. When I don't obey, they can quickly become overwhelming.

I could sit in judgment upon these people, Lord, but knowing me as I do, I doubt that I would have been any better at seeing what they should have seen. Thank You for teaching me from these examples so that I might avoid making the same mistakes. Thank You for forgiving the times I have made them. Enable me today to look past the troublesome things in my life and stay focused upon things above.

Therefore let him who thinks he stands take heed lest he fall.
1 Corinthians 10:12

February 28
OBEDIENCE AND JUDGMENT

And the Lord said, "Who then is the faithful and sensible steward
whom his master will put in charge of his servants,
to give them their rations at the proper time?"
Luke 12:42

These verses from Luke 12:42 - 48 contain both promises and solemn words of warning. To teach Your disciples the importance of being ready for Your return, You tell a parable about a master and four types of slaves. I'm thinking, Lord, that all four types are believers, and therefore every believer fits into one of these four categories.

The faithful slave. The faithful slave does exactly what his master instructed and when his master returns, is blessed and given much more responsibility. What an incentive to be obedient!

The disobedient slave. The disobedient slave does the opposite of what he was told. He thinks his master will be gone a long while, so he has plenty of time to do as he pleases. Your words about him, Lord, are scary! "…will cut him in pieces, and assign him a place with the unbelievers."

But the person who does anything defiantly, whether he is native or an alien,
that one is blaspheming the Lord;
and that person shall be cut off from among his people.
Because he has despised the word of the Lord and has broken His commandment,
that person shall be completely cut off; his guilt shall be on him.
Numbers 15:30-31

The lazy slave. The lazy slave was neglectful of doing his job. He knew what to do, he simply did not do it. You say that this slave will "receive many lashes." At least he won't be assigned a place with the unbelievers!

The ignorant slave. This one must not have been there when the master gave instructions. Or maybe he just wasn't paying attention. He did not know what he was supposed to do. In real life, Lord, I can think of people this type would fit - people who were born and raised in a godless culture, then hear the gospel and are saved. They are saved, but they are clueless about what to do next. First to come to mind might be those in a dark African jungle. But I also think we have clueless people right here in America. It is our job to be teaching them! I love seeing Your mercy here - You saying this slave will receive but few lashes.

This little story gives me much to ponder. Oh, my Lord, fill me with Your grace!

February 29
A RADICAL THOUGHT

But the Lord answered and said to her, "Martha, Martha, you are worried and bothered about so many things; but only a few things are necessary, really only one, for Mary has chosen the good part, which shall not be taken away from her."
Luke 10:41-42

Some random thoughts about these sisters, Lord. Now I admit, by my human nature, I'm more like Martha and by my born-again nature, I'm more like Mary. So I tend to see this situation from both sides. My contention is that Martha did not love you any less than Mary did. She was simply showing that love by feeding You. I agree, she did have an attitude problem, for which You corrected her, but she would never have been slaving away in the kitchen if she did not care about You. And, on the other hand, I don't think that Mary was lazy and trying to avoid work. She knew the work would get done (she knew her sister!) so she chose "the good part" - to sit and listen to You.

But, Lord, I'm thinking that this lesson is not so much for comparison of these sisters as it is to teach me how vital is the balance between physical and spiritual - that my life should be a balance between the efficiency of Martha (without the bad attitude) and the devotion of Mary.

Martha represents the meeting of physical needs. They *must* be met. Families must be fed, clothed and looked after. I feel sure You expect us to do that. Mary represents the inner person and its needs - the need to spend time with You, to sit and learn and worship and adore. This is so essential! *Both* should be done consistently. *Both* should be done whole-heartedly. *Both* should be done as acts of worship.

So, Lord, here's my radical thought - what if I tithed my time like I tithe my income? What if *all* Your children gave 1/10th of their time to You on a regular basis!

That works out to be 2.25 hours *every day* that we would spend in meeting the needs of our inner person...reading the Word, studying, praying, meditating, sharing with others, experiencing Your presence. What a fantastic people we would be if we each followed that model for daily life!

That truly would be a balanced life, although it may sound unbalanced to our worldly minds. For so long we have lived on half rations, trying to be spiritually strong on 10 minutes a day of reading and praying, that we don't recognize how far out of balance our lives have become.

Two things would certainly result in my life from this radical plan: (1) I would grow more quickly into the person You want me to be; and (2) the remaining 9/10 of my time would be blessed beyond all I can imagine and would prove to be more than enough to meet all my needs. Exactly like tithing my money!

March 1
A TIME FOR PRAISE

O come, let us sing for joy to the Lord;
Let us shout joyfully to the rock of our salvation.
Let us come before His presence with thanksgiving;
Let us shout joyfully to Him with psalms.
Psalm 95:1-2

Help me, Lord, to put aside the details of my life that are clamoring for attention and focus only on You in thankfulness and praise. Truly, You are worthy of all praise, and I can never praise You enough. Even *knowing* that praise expands my heart, I do not exercise it enough.

I praise You for being the high and lifted up God that You are, Creator and Sustainer of all. I thank You for even knowing I exist, much less caring about me and my problems. I praise You for Your infinite wisdom and love that put together such a plan by which I could come to know You - a plan beyond my human reasoning and conception, a plan not entirely comprehensible even with desire and effort. If my effort to understand continues strong for all the rest of my days, I will have touched only the surface of knowing and understanding You. It is all too wonderful!

Even in all the extreme heights and depths of unfathomable love and wisdom, You are merciful toward Your creatures - we who are finite in our ability to understand and uncertain in our day-to-day doing. All of Your powerful attributes must be tempered significantly in order to deal with us. Tempered by love.

How astounding! Love is really what matters - Yours for me, mine for You and ours to one another. If I fail in any aspect of my life, I will have failed because of wrongly directed love.

My goal? To keep You at the center of my life; to have everything revolve around my love and commitment to You; to see You at work in me and through me to others; to simply be Your hands, feet and mouth to someone who may never pick up a Bible and read it.

Well, I started out to praise and I ended up with renewed commitment. Maybe that's okay, Lord. It all speaks of the love, that ever-flowing fountain of love for You, that is within my spirit. Praise God from whom all blessings flow!

March 2
STRUGGLES OF LIVING

He brought me up out of the pit of destruction, out of the miry clay;
And He set my feet upon a rock making my footsteps firm.
Psalm 40: 2

Oh, Lord, You and I know that my goal is to be pleasing to You. But I so easily slide back down into that dark hole of self-pity, self-centeredness, self-concern - self, self, self! This is *not* pleasing to You. When I find myself there (again), I struggle to climb out one more time, back up to the Rock where I should be.

Show me, Lord, am I doing the wrong thing to climb back out? Should I wait for You to lift me out? Or is this on-going battle just part of living this life? This brings up the old questions of what is Your part and what is my part in accomplishing Your will. The hymn I learned as a child says, "*You* pulled me out of the miry clay, *You* set my feet on the Rock to *stay.*" This sounds so *finished.* Is the job truly finished? Am I just wrestling with feelings?

I think I see, Lord, that the hymn and the scripture upon which it is based are speaking of salvation. And truly, salvation is finished. And the work of salvation is *all* of You from beginning to end. My part was/is only to allow Your grace and mercy to enter and live in my heart - to accept what You have done for me - to know I could not save myself, ever.

But my question today is not about salvation. It is about living a life full of joy, peace and victory under any and all circumstances. How much of the burden for that is on *me*? It seems to me, Lord, that *I* have choices to make. I must choose - maybe daily, maybe hourly - to think Your thoughts, to recall to mind Your Word and its promises to me, to choose to believe they really are for me, and to then act on that belief. How can I experience, right here and now, in these days of my life, the Spirit-filled, Spirit-led life pictured in Your Word as Your will for *all* Your children?

"My child, this life *will* be one of struggle. To think otherwise is to be deceived. That is why I gave you instructions on spiritual warfare along with promises of My presence and many, many reminders to not be afraid. Simply believe Me. Just trust Me, trust My love for you. Look to Me for your strength and will to live day by day, even moment by moment. Truly, nothing can separate you from My love. It surrounds you and fills you. I am working in ways you do not now see but you are safe - so safe - within My arms. Rejoice in this and in My plan for you."

Once again I have made things harder than necessary. Thank You so much for Your patience and Your clear answer. Resist the devil, relax in Your care, and rejoice in Your love. I can DO that, Lord!

March 3
SINGING YOUR PRAISE

Let all who seek Thee rejoice and be glad in Thee;
Let those who love Thy salvation say continually,
"The Lord be magnified!"
Psalm 40:16

This Psalm needs more thought, Lord. I'm so grateful for Your words of assurance and encouragement to me yesterday! Today I want to praise and rejoice and sing.

The next verse after the miry clay and the Rock says: "*And He put a new song in my mouth, a song of praise to our God.*" (verse 3) This says to me that You not only redeem me from eternal damnation (although that is stupendous!), but You want me to be full of joy and praise as I live out my life on Earth. Not only do You *want* that for me, You have *provided* for me every good thing I need to walk in Your amazing grace, even in adverse circumstances.

Specifically…

…eternal salvation

…faith to trust You for that eternal salvation

…knowledge and understanding of Your Word with all its promises

…confidence that this day and all my tomorrows are in Your control

…a heart that overflows with gratitude and adoration.

It all comes down to this simple fact: *In any and every circumstance of life, You are worthy of my trust.* Paul talks in 2 Corinthians 11 about "the simplicity and purity of devotion to Christ." We both know I often make things harder than they need to be, and yet You always straighten my path and turn me in the right direction.

How could I not love You, Lord?

March 4
ACCEPTABLE WORSHIP

I urge you therefore, brethren, by the mercies of God,
to present your bodies a living and holy sacrifice, acceptable to God,
which is your spiritual service of worship.
Romans 12:1

Pastor's lesson Sunday on acceptable worship, bringing to You the first and the best, stays in my mind, Lord. The lesson causes me to meditate on the vast distance between You and me - a space so impossible for me to ever, in a thousand lifetimes, travel and reach You. You are holy, high and lifted up, the exalted King over all! How could a weak creature like me ever dream of coming near to You? How could I ever even think about You receiving me with acceptance and love and yes, even a smile? Such an incredible thing You have done in making it possible for Your created beings to know You, love You and worship You!

The realization of it fills me with the desire to bring *only* the first and the best and to bring it, not because You said I should, but because I love You. I see, Lord, that it is only because You first loved me and in that love provided a way - the path to You - that I can sit here in this quiet room, read Your words to me and write my words to You. I am enabled to worship with all that I am and know *You are here!* Your love flows into me, fills me and produces an over-flowing response within of thanksgiving and praise at the wonder of it all. It gives me a renewed determination to live out that love this day - to worship You with my very life.

I'm seeing, Lord, that worship is simply understanding who You are and who I am. So the better I know You, the deeper and more meaningful my worship. And the more clearly I see myself, the more humility covers me over, which in turn, generates even more worship. What an awesome God You are! Your unending supply of full-of-wonder gifts transform me into a holy creature, full of worship acceptable in Your sight. How simple. How beautiful.

March 5
HEARING YOU SPEAK

And your ears will hear a word behind you,
"This is the way, walk in it,"
whenever you turn to the right or to the left.
Isaiah 30: 21

We have a few moments of quiet this morning. My heart is thankful, Lord, for Your presence that fills and surrounds me now, for the good night of sleep just passed, for this home filled with love and care, for the precious people within my circle of influence, and most of all, that You truly are Lord of all my life.

I can simply relax and rejoice because You are my Sovereign God, and all is well. I can walk through this day knowing that Your grace is extended even to me. Allow me to keep my heart still this day so that I can hear Your voice. I very much want to hear You speak, Lord.

Remember the little song that says, "Turn your eyes upon Jesus, look full in His wonderful face"? That visualization helps me maintain the inner core of stillness that I want. My physical ears are not working as well as they used to. I find I hear and interpret the sounds I'm hearing much better when I'm *looking* at the speaker. I'm seeing, Lord, that there is a spiritual parallel here - focusing on You will increase my ability to hear and understand You.

Brother Lawrence said he came to the place where his time of working in the noisy kitchen was no different than his time of quiet prayer. He learned to have inner stillness all the time. He was always looking to You, focusing on You, talking with You and listening to You. That is what I want!

In truth, Your children live life on two levels in this world. The real world is the spiritual level - my relationship with You, and Your grace surrounding me. While the other level is physical and temporary, it is where I practice what You teach me on the spiritual level. I confess to failures here, Lord. It does take practice, this living life on two levels at once! Thank You for allowing this slow learner to keep on trying to get it right. Although I don't know who wrote it, please accept this little prayer as it speaks my heart…

Drop Your still dews of quietness
Till all my strivings cease.
Take from my soul the strain and stress
And let my ordered life confess
The beauty of Your peace.
Amen

March 6
TIME WITH YOU

Be Thou to me a rock of habitation,
to which I may continually come.
Psalm 71:3

I need to be with You, Lord. I know You are always with me, but I need to stop all activity, get still inside and out, and just be *with* You. I want to acknowledge to You that every bit of the harmony, order and beauty in my life is from You, and is of Your design. You continue to enlarge Your dwelling place within me, and for this I praise You! I would have You stretch me, empty me totally of myself so that only You abide within.

See, Lord, the melting of my heart when I draw near to You. I am in awe of Your presence, and yet I am so aware of the acceptance, warmth and love that flows abundantly out of You, into me and over me! There can be no greater joy in heaven or earth than to know I am loved by You! At the thought of this love, my spirit falls prostrate in worship before You. Your grace is unbelievably, incredibly available for the taking! Wrapped in Your grace are all the characteristics of Your glorious Self - mercy, strength, compassion, forgiveness, patience, faith, joy. I could fill this page with words describing Your grace; the riches so vastly more precious than gold. What a privilege to be Your child! The more I know You, the more I want to know You.

I love You with a love that springs up from some depth of my being that I know nothing about. You are the source of that love. You are its sustainer, and You are its object.

"For from Him and through Him and to Him are all things.
To God be the glory forever.
Amen."

That is my song of praise this morning. You are my strength and my joy, my rock of refuge, my everything. Take this busy day and use it to Your glory.

March 7
INTIMACY

For this cause a man shall leave his father and mother,
and shall cleave to his wife; and the two shall become one flesh.
This mystery is great; but I am speaking with reference to Christ and the church.
Ephesians 5:31-32

I thank You, Lord, this cold morning for my warm room and hot coffee. Most of all, I'm thankful for this blessed time of aloneness with You. In the verse above, Paul likened the Christ-church relationship to marriage because marriage among humankind is the most intimate of relationships.

This "mystery" also applies to the One-on-one relationship that exists between You and each individual believer. And it seems to me, Lord, that this relationship is even more intimate than human marriage because *You see my heart and know my thoughts.* There can be no greater intimacy than that! Human marriage partners can only begin to share their inner selves with one another and, perhaps, eventually reach some low level of this "knowing." But You know me fully and, amazing thought, You are teaching me to know *Your* thoughts and *Your* heart.

"My Beloved is mine and I am His
And His banner over me is love."

How incredible that this is so! Paul's love and trust in You were so complete that the threats of certain trouble, persecution, loss of life and loss of loved ones could not move him away from following You. How amazing that You do this interior work in Your children! Truly, You are an awesome God! I give You full permission to do Your work within me as You see fit.

March 8
BEING YOUR MESSENGER

But sanctify Christ as Lord in your hearts,
always being ready to make a defense
to everyone who asks you
to give an account for the hope that is in you,
yet with gentleness and reverence.
I Peter 3:15

Thank You, Lord, for the lesson concerning the significance of prioritizing my thoughts and actions. I'm guilty too often of being wrapped up in my personal walk with You and not enough in the active responsibilities of my assignment - proclaiming Your plan of redemption to all who will listen. No, You did not call me to preach. But You did call me to live every day in the truth of redemption and the power of Your love, to flesh out and express those truths in all my interactions with others. This requires that my heart be surrendered to You.

In these thoughts, Lord, is further training that this life of faith is all about You and not at all about me. You truly are the Alpha and the Omega and everything in between. I find myself at a fork in the road. The choice before me is to grow in spiritual maturity and be used by You, or to stay in a stage of spiritual childhood where the world revolves around me.

I'm seeing that in every human relationship I have, my task is twofold: Communicate Your truth in love to those around me and not be moved at all by the opinions of others, *whether good or bad.* In my relationship with You, I am to stay close by Your side, trusting You fully and loving You with all that I am. As Oswald Chambers says, I choose to be "recklessly abandoned, totally surrendered and separated for Your use."

I'm not so naïve as to think I'm through with this lesson, Lord. I'm not a quick study, but I do see that I am to look to You, and only You, for encouragement, affirmation, correction, and guidance.

The tasks You have put before me can only be successfully completed by Your power. Thank You for Your grace that fills me this moment.

March 9
MORE ON THE FORK IN THE ROAD

Come to Me, all who are weary and heavy-laden,
and I will give you rest.
Take My yoke upon you, and learn from Me,
for I am gentle and humble in heart;
and You shall find rest for your souls.
Matthew 11:28-29

You have kept me thinking about this fork in the road we talked about yesterday. I see clearly that the wrong road would be to see myself as the center of everything. There, I would constantly live my life attempting to meet others' expectations of a "godly" person. What an overwhelming burden that would be! The obvious impossibility of it is huge because every person has different expectations. I would always be concerned with their reactions (or lack thereof). I would never feel I had measured up.

The right road is to take You as my example. And what is Your example? You always spoke the truth. To *everyone*. Even if it sounded harsh, or politically incorrect, or made people uncomfortable. You spoke truth because that is what Love does.

You were compassionate and gentle with the weak, the sinful and afflicted. Whatever the need, You met it with mercy and kindness. You were *not* gentle and kind with the self-righteous. In fact, Your words to them are a powerful motivation for me to *never* allow myself to become self-righteous.

You were filled with purpose, not stress. It is amazing to me, Lord, how You dealt with the tension within of knowing the Cross was before You, and the pressure without caused by the multitudes of needy people who came to You for help. And yet, You stayed calm and simply did what was before You to do. What a lesson!

So, would I be lost and doomed to hell if I took the wrong road? No, I'd still be Your child. But what a miserable way to live. And what a shame to have missed all the blessings of walking with You! May I live every moment of every day with my focus on You. Thank You for the freedom I have in You, my Lord!

Freedom to be who You have made me to be.

Freedom to know that I can please You.

Freedom to bring You joy with my trust and love.

Freedom from trying to please everyone.

Freedom to leave others in Your capable hands.

Thank You for this rest for my soul! May I learn to hear Your Spirit as clearly as You heard the Father while You were on Earth and then fully obey as You did.

March 10
CONTROLLED BY LOVE

For the love of Christ controls us, having concluded this,
that one died for all, therefore all died.
II Corinthians 5:14

This verse has been on my mind for days now, Lord, and this morning I looked it up in the KJV to see how it read…*"For the love of Christ constraineth us, because we thus judge that, if one died for all, then were all dead."* I understand the fact that You died for all, that all believers are seen by You as having also died unto sin, now and forever. You know I have struggled from time to time with the concept of being dead to sin as I worked it out in my everyday life. But please, Lord, help me set that aside for now because my thoughts are on the first phrase, "the love of Christ controlling (constraining) me."

How many times I have wished that You *would* take control away from me and absolutely run my life so that all I do and think, all I am would be pleasing to You! But my wishing did not make it happen. Over the years, I learned that the only way You would ever have control of me is if I voluntarily give it to You. In other words, You would not violate my free will.

Have all of Your children wrestled with this as much as I have? It is almost like a power struggle except that You do not struggle. No, it is all one-sided; I am the only one fighting. You are patiently wooing and working in my heart, waiting for me to once again "see the light." How I marvel at Your longsuffering!

Now, I do not think for one minute that this battle is over because, as You well know, I like to control. But, Lord, here is the thought rising large in my mind this morning - more than I want to control, I want to please You. I say those words from the deepest part of me. I want, above everything, to be found pleasing to You. And I see that the reason for this desire of my heart is "the love of Christ."

I'm uncertain if Paul was saying that what controls me is Your love for me or my love for You. It could be either one, but it's probably both, because the more I understand and experience Your love for me, the more I love You. It is a simple, beautiful, splendid process, this learning about You. The better I know You, the more I desire to spend time with You. The more time I spend with You, the greater grows my love for You. And the cycle continues on, and will until the day I stand before You in glory.

Please forgive my glitches of selfishness when I want to take back the management of my life. Thank You for Your mercy. Keep a tight grip on me, Lord, for I do love You and want You to be in charge! May I keep my focus on You this day, all day.

March 11
HINDERING YOUR SPIRIT

Do not quench the Spirit.
I Thessalonians 5:19

Still pondering on Your control in my life, Lord; I want to think in Your presence about giving Your Spirit absolute freedom in me. Some questions come to mind....

What is there right now, today, this moment, in me that hinders You? How different would my life look on the outside if You had total freedom in me?

Immediately You bring something specific to my mind. Only You know the frustration and guilt I've been dealing with because of my short temper, my frustration at my inability to control it and my guilt for that lack of control.

"My child, you are focusing on the wrong thing. That behavior truly does not glorify Me, but it is not the real problem. What we need to address is the underlying cause of the behavior. The reason behind your too frequent spells of impatience and anger is *pride*. When your authority is challenged, your patience goes out the window and what comes in is definitely not the quiet and gentle spirit that I desire for you."

I'm sorry, Lord. I see clearly that You are right. Pride is such an ugly thing! And the truth here is that I *have* no authority. I gave all my rights over to You, and they now belong to You. Please, Lord, help me keep this truth before me at all times and especially when the situation is a set-up for impatience and anger.

"Remember this, you need to accept all that happens to you as if it were happening to Me. Then your reaction to it will be under My control." Yes, Lord. Oh, how much I want that!

If You were completely unhindered in my life, all the stress, impatience and harshness would just vanish. My words would be softer. They would be spoken from the heart and thus would have positive power in them. Love would always be my motive just as it is Yours. Even when You spoke words that angered people (like the Pharisees), Your motive was love - love for the Father and for lost mankind whom the Pharisees were driving *from* You rather than bringing *to* You. When You drove out the money-changers from the temple, Your motive was love - love and respect for the holiness of the Father and for His house.

Love balanced by discernment can only come from You, Lord. I do not have the wisdom or the power to do this for myself. I can only trust You to do it in me and through me. Thank You for these insights into myself, my Lord.

March 12
NEW VS. OLD

No one sews a patch of unshrunk cloth on an old garment;
otherwise the patch pulls away from it,
the new from the old, and a worse tear results.
And no one puts new wine into old wineskins;
otherwise the wine will burst the skins,
and the wine is lost, and the skins as well;
but one puts new wine into fresh wineskins.
Mark 2:21-22

Lord Jesus, You spoke these words to people of a different culture than ours. In their everyday living, they understood things like patching old clothes and storing wine properly. But Your message was not really about these everyday things. Your message was to show them that God was doing a new thing - a wonderful new thing - and that they needed to open their minds and hearts to what He was doing, that they were to embrace the new and not mix it with the old.

And, Lord, while I don't know much about patching garments or storing wine, I do understand that, inside, I am exactly the same as these people; trying to live my life in my strength; thinking my good, moral life counts for something; thinking that it is all about keeping the rules.

Dying to self is one of the basics of being Your child, and yet I continue to struggle with it. Even though You plainly said that true life is only found by dying to self, I still cling to the tattered rags of my righteousness as though they were worth something.

I am desperately lost without You, Lord. If I am not living by the power of Your Spirit, I have made Your suffering and death of no account. If I am not worshipping in the Spirit, my worship is noise in Your ears. If I am not ruled by Your Spirit, I am in great danger. It is black and white clear.

I ask that You take every bit of self-centeredness, self-sufficiency and every other self sin that exists within me, along with the legalism that seems to be my default setting, and by the power of Your shed blood, wash me clean of their presence and even their smell. Like the new wine of Your Spirit poured into the new wineskin of Your grace, fill me with Yourself.

Here is the bottom line truth: Legalism keeps me focused on me. Grace keeps me focused on You.

March 13
MARVELOUS LOVE

For I am convinced that neither death, nor life, nor angels, nor principalities,
nor things present, nor things to come,
nor powers, nor height, nor depth, nor any other created thing,
shall be able to separate us from the love of God,
which is in Christ Jesus our Lord.
Romans 8: 38-39

In spite of Monday, in spite of having two sick children home from school, in spite of my own fever and achy body, I sit here in my sun-drenched room with such peace and joy. Your presence fills me with warmth just as the sunlight fills my room.

The freedom of living in Your grace is such a precious thing, Lord. I am bound to You by the shining cords of Your eternal love that Paul speaks of in those verses. I never tire of thinking about the fact that You love me. Maybe that's because I had such a hard time believing that fact. Now that You have convinced me, however, Your love is the foundation of every portion of my life. That is why those verses always light a fire in my soul. Your children truly are eternally secure in Your care!

Your love and acceptance of me causes me to love You in return - causes me to desire to dwell very near to You, to hear You and to obey in all things simply to please You. What profound wisdom that designed a marvelous thing like love! By my response of love and obedience, I both please You and am, myself, blessed.

How *blessed* I am to be Yours. When this life is over, I will clearly understand things which I now understand only in part. Then I will wish I had poured much more energy and thought into praise and thanksgiving for the immensity of Your grace. In Your goodness, You provide for *all* my needs. Give me the wisdom, Lord, to live these days of my life out of an unceasing mind-set of deep gratitude that overflows into all my relationships.

March 14
FORGIVENESS

If we confess our sins,
He is faithful and just to forgive us our sins
and to cleanse us from all unrighteousness.
I John 1: 9

I must gather up, sort through and talk to You about all these things bothering me, Lord. Hurtful things - failures to live up to Your high standard of love, my very expectation of myself to be *able* to live up to that lofty standard, the selfishness within me that these things bring to light, my so-very-wrong judgment of another.

I am convicted. I am humbled. I am troubled. I am disappointed in myself, and then I'm ashamed to admit that I believed in myself to begin with. I'm so sorry, Lord.

I guess it just proves again how impossible it is to live this life of faith without You being in charge. I truly *am* desperate for You. The "wanting" is in me but the power for "doing" comes from You. Here is another lesson in relying upon You in *all* things- even the thoughts I have (maybe *especially* the thoughts I have).

The good news in all this is that when You died that awful death on the cross, it was for all sin, for all time, for all who would accept it. So my forgiveness is assured, my relationship to You restored, my heart both wiser and more-than-ever filled with love for You.

Here is what I learned in this lesson: self-righteousness, which is precisely where that judging came from, blocks the channel through which Your love flows to me. Confession removes that block, allowing me to understand a bit more of that vast supply of God-love You want to pour into my heart.

I hate acknowledging these sins, Lord, but how thankful I am that You love me enough to keep pointing them out to me!

By Your grace, I'll try to not fall in that ditch again.

March 15
THOUGHTS ABOUT SURRENDER

Submit therefore to God.
James 4:7

I've been turning over some thoughts in my mind concerning living the surrendered life. I want to think about them in Your presence this morning, Lord.

Surrender, I'm discovering, was a decision of my will that I made at a specific point in my past. But it was not finished by that one decision. No, I find myself often coming to the point of decision concerning surrender, sometimes daily. And this will continue, seemingly, until my life in this dark world is finished. It is as if You lead me deeper into myself, finding new areas that need to be surrendered, and You also allow me to enter new situations requiring new choices to be made.

We speak of "total surrender." That, at first glance, seems redundant to me because if surrender is not total, it is not surrender. However, because surrender is a *process*, what is total today may tomorrow be partial. I believe, Lord, that You hold us responsible only for what we know - not for what we don't yet know. So total today is enough.

I want to think about the "why" of surrender. I'm thinking that the only motive that is pleasing to You is my love for You surrendering to Your love for me. My reason for yielding is not what You will do for me, how useful I will be in Your work, or anything other than from-the-heart love making me desire to give You all that I am.

This is a beautiful picture, Lord, because it says so much. Here is what is wrapped up in that giving myself to You...

...absolute trust in Your love,

...total confidence in Your goodness,

...freedom from any fear of what You may ask of me,

...peace and joy deep in my spirit like a bubbling stream from a never-ending source of living water.

It is true that there are great benefits derived from my surrender to You. But my reason for surrender is not to gain those benefits. It is simply my heart saying "Yes" to Your heart saying, "Come to Me."

The reality of that invitation fills me with the strength and determination to live every day of my assignment with grace and thanksgiving. My moment-by-moment surrender makes You my Lord. And that is exactly what I want.

March 16
HOW ARE YOU?

Let your speech always be with grace,
seasoned, as it were, with salt,
so that you may know how you should respond to each person.
Colossians 4:6

Reading these words of Paul, Your searchlight is showing me an area of my life that needs to change. It involves a simple response to a simple question we often ask one another out of habit rather than out of real concern. And that question is, "How are you?"

In my case, Lord, I really am full of your joy and peace. And yet, when asked that question, the first response that pops into my mind is the amount of pain and fatigue I'm dealing with - which is also true. But that is not how I really *am*. Those negative things are just some of the temporary circumstances of my life. What is important, the eternal truth here, is that I *am* filled with Your powerful presence and all the wondrous things You bring - light, love, singing, joy, peace, perseverance and countless other great things.

Since the question is usually a polite conversation starter rather than concern about my physical well-being, it is a perfect chance to witness to the beautiful inner work You do in the spirit of one who loves You. It is an open door of opportunity to talk about important things, to perhaps get the asker's mind started down a new path that will result in blessing for them.

This old dog needs to learn a new trick - to stop and check in with my spirit, rather than my body, before answering that question. Thank You for teaching me this little lesson. You are *the* Master Teacher.

March 17
WALKING WITH YOU

Walk worthy of your calling
with all humility and gentleness,
with patience showing forbearance
to one another in love.
Ephesians 4:1-2

Humility. Gentleness. Patience. Forbearance. Love. These words speak to my heart, Lord. They are exactly what I want my life to look like because I know they are also Your desire for me. However, we both already know that I cannot accomplish them in my strength. I have no power to make myself any one of those wonderful things, much less all of them.

But You have promised that when I am weak, You are strong. That is what I'm counting on. That is how it will be accomplished. One day at a time, I will be surrendering control to You in every situation as it arises, listening to Your quiet voice giving me encouragement, giving me instruction, giving me the ability to walk worthy of my calling with gentleness and patience.

My heart is full of gratitude for Your mercy and love.
My spirit bows down with praise and exaltation for who You are,
the high and holy God of all the universe.
I worship You with all that I am.
I look forward to whatever good thing You will do next
and anticipate it with joy!

March 18
LOOKING BACK

May the beloved of the Lord
dwell in security by Him,
Who shields him all the day,
And he dwells between His shoulders.
Deuteronomy 33:12

When I look back over the years You and I have walked together, Lord, I see that the paths You chose were not ones I would ever have chosen. Difficult paths, steep climbs, long times of walking without rest, rugged ways of illness and pain and heartache. Had I foreknown those paths, I would have lacked the courage to even begin. How thankful I am that You did not ask my opinion!

Because now I see that You taught me the most valuable truths about Yourself during those hard times. It was then that I learned Your faithfulness, Your gentleness, Your abundant grace. And now I can see that without the demanding conditions of my life I would not have been teachable. I would not have learned the joy of Your presence, the strength of Your love, and the warmth of Your acceptance. These are now more precious to me than gold. You, Yourself, are what I seek, what I hunger and thirst for and what my heart rejoices over.

So every rocky road, every dark night, every pain or sorrow has been the means of incredible blessing now and in the life to come. How amazing is Your wisdom and the sufficiency of Your grace. You shield me all the day, and I dwell between Your shoulders.

March 19
HEAVEN

The Lord is in His holy temple;
The Lord's throne is in heaven;
His eyes behold, His eyelids test the sons of men.
For the Lord is righteous;
He loves righteousness;
The upright will behold His face.
Psalm 11: 4, 7

Thinking about this life and the life to come - here in this life, we are constantly learning and being tested on what we learned. We sometimes pass and sometimes fail, but we learn even from the failures. Maybe especially from the failures. But here is what amazes me - You, Lord, do not really need us for Your kingdom's work here. In fact, we are in the way more often than we are helpful. Like a child learning to make his bed or wash the dishes, Mom could do it much faster and better by herself. But then the child would not learn.

So we are inept, prone to make mistakes, often making things worse rather than better. Yet You continue to assign tasks so that we will learn. You are the ultimate, patient teacher because You see the whole purpose - the *real* purpose. Because of my limited understanding, I can only speculate upon the real purpose.

Are You preparing us for participation in a plan more grand and glorious than anything we could ever imagine? My spirit somehow believes that is true, although my mind is mystified at the thought. I look at Your incredible plan of redemption executed on Earth and see that perhaps it is only the first step of a far more extensive design. You may have vast numbers of souls in unknown-to-us universes, and You are training workers here to become messengers there of Your glory, honor and love for them. Speculation only - but You must have *some* wonderful, over-reaching purpose in order to tolerate our pathetic performance while in training.

Like a child learning to play scales and exercises on a musical instrument, the purpose is not to be able to play scales and exercises. The purpose is to master the skills *necessary* to play them in order to play the "real music" to come later. I think that You are so patiently teaching us now the skills we will need for the "real music" You have for us in the future.

All this, Lord, is not crucial to my daily walk with You, but it is exciting to think that maybe my failures and bumbling around are actually doing some good thing toward some good end. Thank You for Your patience, Your persistence, Your mercy and unfailing love which allow me do-overs when I fail. Look into my heart, my Lord, and see there the deep love for You and the desire to succeed rather than fail.

March 20
SPIRITUAL CAPACITY

But to each one of us grace was given
according to the measure of Christ's gift.
Ephesians 4:7

For through the grace given to me I say to every man among you
not to think more highly of himself than he ought to think;
but to think so as to have sound judgment,
as God has allotted to each a measure of faith.
Romans 12:3

Each of Your children is born with various natural abilities and propensities, and You deal with each of us just as we need, according to those differences. This is what a good parent does, and You are the ultimate Good Parent. There is an area, however, in this walk of faith where my abilities and propensities are not a factor. And that is the area of spiritual capacity, my potential for spiritual growth, my God-space within. That has nothing whatever to do with my in-born natural ability or lack thereof. Rather, it is determined by Your gift of faith to me.

You reminded me early this morning of Dolores - a lady from my childhood who had a child's mind in an adult's body. But what a faith she had. And how she loved You! Even when I was a child, I could see that faith and love, and I admired and respected it. There have even been times when I envied her simple-mindedness. Her life seemed so blessed and so much less stressful than mine. Thinking about her, Lord, makes me realize that this gift of grace is all of You - You living within, filling me, speaking words of love and instruction to me, giving guidance and allowing me to get to know You more and more.

"It's not by might, it's not by power, but by My Spirit says the Lord." It's not intellect or education or natural abilities. Otherwise, Dolores could never have been the shining example of faith that she was. No, my spiritual capacity is mine by faith in Your promises. You have given Your children so many astounding promises in Your Word! And then You have given each of us faith to understand and believe those promises. But in order to grow and strengthen, faith must be exercised. Dormant faith will eventually fade away. Healthy faith, on the other hand, is active all the time. Healthy faith is authentic faith. And authentic faith is simply believing You are who You say You are, and You will do what You say You will do.

Dolores understood this. If You should see her today there in heaven, tell her what a blessing she was to me. May my faith be as whole and healthy as hers!

March 21
MY LIGHT AND MY STRENGTH

The Lord is my light and my salvation;
whom shall I fear?
The Lord is the defense of my life;
whom shall I dread?
One thing I have asked from the Lord, that I shall seek:
that I may dwell in the house of the Lord all the days of my life,
to behold the beauty of the Lord,
and to meditate in His temple.
Psalm 27: 1, 4

You are my light that never fails. Electrical power can fail. Batteries run down, bulbs burn out and must be replaced. But Your light is constant and shall last for all eternity. In Your light I find warmth for my spirit, enlightenment for my mind, and security from the enemy. All of that, together, gives me great peace. Walking constantly in Your light, I'm promised cleansing from all sin by Your shed blood. You *are* my salvation.

You are also my defense, my protector, my strength. I value that truth so much more now than in my younger years. Advancing age has taught me the beauty of Paul's statement, "*but the Lord stood with me and strengthened me.*" *(2 Tim.4:17)* Your Word says that the joy of the Lord is my strength. (Nehemiah 8:10) I have found that to be true, Lord, on two levels: one, my spiritual strength is much greater when my heart is full of joy and praise; and two, even my physical strength is affected positively by a thankful, joyful heart.

The light, the joy and the strength, they are all mysterious God-gifts that, themselves, produce *more* light, joy and strength. Do I understand this process? No. Am I glad it works? Oh, so very glad!

To look in Your face, my Lord, is to worship.
To look in Your face
causes within me a trembling of awe and reverence,
a melting of my heart in gratitude,
and I am strengthened simply by looking.

I am made strong,
enabled to do what You have set before me.
I am filled with Your light.
There may be a fierce, thunderstorm raging outside,
but we are safe, warm, dry and *together*.
That is all that matters - being together.

March 22
QUIET REST

There is none like the God of Israel,
who rides the heavens to your help,
and through the skies in His majesty.
The eternal God is a dwelling place,
and underneath are the everlasting arms.
Deuteronomy 33:26-27

Now, a few quiet moments to rest in Your presence, to experience the stability of Your everlasting arms. I know You are always with me, Lord, even when I'm surrounded by noisy, messy children, but this is the best - when all is quiet within and without.

I want to be still, relaxed and so near You I can feel Your heartbeat. I desire to see with my spiritual eyes all You want to teach me. Or, if You choose, to simply enjoy the warmth of Your presence and soak up Your fragrance, sweetness and love. You, my Lord, are all I need.

Search my mind and my spirit, please, and do for me what You will. I marvel at Your patience with me! Thank You for not giving up! Because of Your presence, my spirit is bright and beautiful. All of my life is blessed because of You, Lord. I do not understand the reason for some of my circumstances, but someday I will. And that is enough for me, because I know You are in control and can change any circumstance in an instant. I also know that every day I live, I am one day nearer home. That fills me with abounding joy!

Your grace is abundant. I wish I were wise enough to appropriate every available morsel of it, using it in such a way as to make others desire You in their lives. It's all about love isn't it, Lord? I open up my mind to understand, and my spirit to experience, all that I can of that ever-flowing fountain of God-love.

You are my Beloved. My spirit bows in adoration and worship before the immensity of Who You are to me. Words fail and praise takes over.

March 23
YOUR PURPOSE

The Son of God appeared for this purpose,
that He might destroy the works of the devil.
1 John 3:8b

Help me, please Lord, think on this statement I read a couple of days ago about a part of Your purpose in coming to live among us as Son of Man and Son of God. At the time I read it, You quickened it to my heart. And again this morning, You reminded me of it. It says, *"You came to destroy every power which resists You and opposes the divine will."*

Your fellow Jews were looking for a political destruction to take place, for a leader of a revolution which would set them free from Rome's rule; therefore, many of them missed Your message. Today we have the advantage of the completed Word to study, as well as 20 centuries of men and women who loved You, were taught by You and were faithful to write down what they were learning. So we understand that this destruction is one that takes place *within* every believer. The sin nature with which we are born must be destroyed because it always resists and opposes You. This we know from Your Word. This we know from others' experiences. This we know from personal experience.

In addition to the sinful nature with which we were born, we are subject to attacks from the enemy of our faith, the devil. This power which resists and opposes You works diligently upon Your children; if not always to make us behave badly, at least to make us so busy as to distract us from Your daily assignment.

That is why, Lord, when I feel within me a resistance to Your will, the red flags start waving in my mind, and I know You and I have some business to transact. I must, with You alongside, search for what is resisting and opposing You. I must listen closely and then obey quickly. I make David's prayer *my* prayer this morning...

Search me, O God, and know my heart
Try me and know my anxious thoughts,
And see if there be any hurtful way in me
And lead me in the way everlasting.
Psalm 139: 23-24

March 24
CHOSEN OF GOD
Part One

And so, as those who have been chosen of God,
holy and beloved,
put on a heart of compassion, kindness,
humility, gentleness and patience.
Colossians 3: 12

You have brought this Scripture back to mind for further thought, Lord. My relationship with You is the one indispensable thing in my life. I can't even imagine (and don't want to imagine) being without it.

There are a few things that I *know*. I know that long ago when I was a child, You touched my heart and let me know You wanted me to be Your child. What an incredibly precious thing that knowledge is to me. Of course, I didn't understand it in just this way then - I only knew, deep down *knew*, that I was a sinner, that salvation was to be found only in Your blood shed for me and I very much wanted to be saved. It started out as fear of being lost but over time, through Your grace, has become profound love and gratitude for that saving grace. And it all started with Your touch upon my mind/heart/spirit.

I know that You are not at all restricted in *how* You choose. You spoke to me through the preaching of the Word. But many people never go to church, and yet I know that, being both just and creative, You have an unlimited number of ways to speak to people about their need of You....

....through the awesome sight of starry skies at night
....through the vast ocean and earth full of living creatures
....through other peoples' love and witness
....through Your Word
....through the circumstances of life
....and on and on and on.

I know that the important fact about being chosen is that it is all of You and not at all my doing. I did nothing to earn it. I've done nothing since to merit it. And, somehow, in some way I cannot understand, I think You choose everybody. Your Word says You are not willing that *any* should perish. That pretty much covers everyone. And yet it is obvious that many are on that broad way to destruction. I can only believe that this is not because You have not chosen them, too, but because they have made the sad choice to not respond to Your touch.

March 25
CHOSEN OF GOD
Part Two

And so, as those who have been chosen of God,
holy and beloved,
put on a heart of compassion, kindness,
humility, gentleness and patience.
Colossians 3: 12

Thinking further about yesterday's topic of being "chosen," Lord, I ask You to allow me access to Your great heart and mind as we think about this. What difference does it make in people's lives to be chosen and to accept Your invitation to come to You?

- They now have a loving and growing relationship with You, the Living God.
- They have the constant companionship of Your Holy Spirit.
- They are the recipient of every wonderful attribute of Your character (such as love, peace, joy, patience, goodness, kindness, self-control) because You actually dwell within them.
- You are their constant Teacher, Guide, Counselor, Encourager, Friend.
- They possess eternal life - today!
- They are forgiven of their past sins, washed clean, made holy.
- They have assurance of continued forgiveness as they confess.
- They have no worries about tomorrow.
- Best of all, they are loved by You.

These are just some of the incredible truths concerning one who accepts Your grace. A whole volume could be written about all the benefits of being Your child. I'm convinced, Lord, that it would be a blessing for every child of God to meditate often upon this subject of being "chosen, holy and beloved." I can see that it would produce greater humility, greater appreciation of Your grace, overflowing love for You, burning desire to see others know this truth, greater dependence upon You to provide all that is needed...so many positive benefits to spiritual understanding just by thinking, understanding and meditating upon this one huge truth!

All of us, Lord, will face hard times in this life - the redeemed as well as the lost. But what a difference You make in *how* we face them! I see all this through the eyes of one who loves You completely. and so my thoughts are from that perspective. But Lord, I know that You want to love everyone just as You love me and that is exactly what I want, too.

How can I express my own heart? What words can explain the deep thankfulness I feel at belonging to You? How glad I am that You know my every thought because my vocabulary is totally inadequate for this high praise! Your Spirit provides even for that need, and my spirit sings for joy!

March 26
CHOSEN BUT LOST

And so, as those who have been chosen of God, holy and beloved,
put on a heart of compassion, kindness, humility, gentleness and patience.
Colossians 3: 12

Evidently we are not through with this subject, Lord. To appreciate the wonderful benefits of fully belonging to You, I must think about the opposite condition - not having those benefits. Those who are touched by You but refuse to come to You are in this "have-not" condition. How sad that is. It is hard for me to think about this, Lord, because I realize how many, many blessings the have-nots are missing.

- They have no relationship with You.

- They may have a sense of fear at the thought of You or simply an unexplained emptiness within that they try to fill with all the wrong things.

- They have no companionship of Your Spirit all day, every day.

- The demands that life makes upon them to exercise characteristics such as love, patience and forgiveness must be met from their own meager, insufficient resources.

- They have no internal teacher, encourager or friend other than their conscience, which may have been warped by their upbringing.

- They have no heaven waiting for them when this short life is over, only eternal separation from You - an unimaginably painful punishment!

- They carry all the guilt and condemnation of their sins.

- They feel all the weight of worry about their future.

- They do not know that they are loved by You - the God who created them!

Deliver those who are being taken away to death,
And those who are staggering to slaughter, O hold them back.
Proverbs 24:11

Those words from Proverbs are so descriptive of these who refuse to come to You! How much they need to be held back and delivered. How convicting to me is this verse and the next one in that passage...

If you say, "See, we did not know this,"
Does He not consider it who weighs the hearts?
And does He not know it who keeps your soul?
And will He not render to man according to his work?
Proverbs 24:12

Oh, God, please help me keep foremost in my thinking what is crucial to You - delivering those being taken away to death. Eternal death.

March 27
A COMPETITIVE SPIRIT

But not so with you, but let him who is the greatest among you
become as the youngest, and the leader as the servant.
Luke 22:26

I'm thinking this morning, Lord, about how filled our world is with competition. We see it in ads for products: which pain reliever acts faster, which laundry detergent washes whiter, which new car is safer. We see it in children's school activities: spelling bees, contests to see who can read the most books, or who can sell the most during a fund-raiser. Athletics - how we see it in athletics! All the way from Little League with its end-of-season tournaments to professional sports. Football has its Super Bowl, baseball has its World Series, and the Olympics - that ever-growing athletic competition on a world-wide basis. We see it in reality shows on television. We see it in music competitions. We see it so much that, oddly enough, it is almost invisible to us.

But it is not invisible to You, Lord. And I'm interested only in Your viewpoint. I cannot think of a single teaching from You or any of Your followers that would support a competitive spirit in Your children. In fact, it is just the opposite. You teach that he who would be greatest must be least. Paul teaches that we are not to be conformed to the world's thinking but rather, transformed by the renewing of our minds by Your Holy Spirit. The disciples, early on, were bitten by the competition bug and found themselves arguing over who would have the place of greatest honor in Your kingdom. You set them straight very quickly on their wrong thinking.

I'm seeing, Lord, that part of our mind-renewal process is doing away with this competitive spirit and replacing the "me first" mentality with "Jesus first." You become first in my love; first in my use of time, talent, money, energy; first in my loyalty. The death of my competitive spirit moves *me* out of the center of my life and puts You there.

Forevermore, all of my life is lived in reference to You. My life is made valuable only because I am Yours. I see, Lord, that this is just a different perspective on the process of being made like You, the Perfect Example of the Perfect Servant. So be it.

March 28
THE AWESOME POWER OF CHOICE

Oh, the depth of the riches both of the wisdom and knowledge of God!
How unsearchable are His judgments and unfathomable His ways!
Romans 11:33

You keep impressing upon me, Lord, the very real power I have to *choose*. Every waking moment of every day I must choose....how to think, how to act, what to do, what to believe, what to say, what to not say. And at the end of this life, I will *be* the result of all those choices. The environment I grew up in, how much education I had, what was done to me - none of those will determine what I *am* when this life is over. How I chose to handle all the circumstances of my life will make that determination. This power to choose is truly an awesome power You put into our hands. How much we need Your wisdom and power to make right choices.

Backing away to study the "big picture," I see, Lord, that You gave Adam and Eve a choice about being obedient. You could easily have designed them to do exactly what You wanted. But Your heart's desire was that they obey because they *wanted* to, not because You programmed absolute obedience into them. You wanted obedience that grew out of their love for You. You wanted them to love You just as You loved them. Who knows how different mankind's history upon the Earth would have been had they obeyed You?

As a consequence of their failure, ever after, all mankind was born with a sinful nature without the power to choose. Your Word teaches that we are in bondage to Satan until set free by You. In 2 Timothy 2:26 Paul says, *"and they may come to their senses and escape from the snare of the devil, having been held captive by him to do his will."* Paul also wrote these words to the Romans: *"knowing this, that our old self was crucified with Him, that our body of sin might be done away with, that we should no longer be slaves to sin."* (Romans 6:6) Slaves and captives have no choice - they do what they are told to do.

So when we accept Your offer of salvation, You restore within us the Garden of Eden with its beauty and its bounty, its fellowship with You, and its awesome power of choice. My belief, Lord, is that when You speak to people's heart about needing You, at that very moment You restore that power to choose or reject Your offer of salvation. In Your mercy, You allow that choosing-power to remain available for a time because some hearts do not decide immediately to follow You. Eventually, however, there comes a time when the power to choose will be taken away from one who continually rejects Your offer. What a terrifying thought!

Oh, my Sovereign God, keep before me, and all of Your children, the importance of making consistently good choices - ones which lead us ever deeper into Your love and grace. And help us see the crucial role we play in influencing the lost to choose LIFE.

March 29
INTERCESSORY PRAYER

And this is the confidence which we have before Him,
that if we ask anything according to His will, He hears us.
And if we know that He hears us in whatever we ask,
we know that we have the requests which we have asked from Him.
I John 5:14-15

I'm guilty at times, Lord, of pushing to the back burner my praying for others, relegating it to "later." Yet I know that praying for others somehow opens ways for You to work in their lives; ways that would not exist if I didn't pray for them. Please help me to have Your perspective on this.

You clearly teach that Your Spirit prays in, through and for all of Your children. This wonderful truth enormously affects intercessory prayer. It tells me that, even with my limited knowledge of others' situations, I can still pray effectively since it is actually *You* doing the praying. My task is twofold:

- to be faithful to lift to You this person or this situation, and
- to keep our relationship, Yours and mine, open and loving, free of barriers.

If I do those two things, You are certain to do Your part. And I see, Lord, that our relationship must be open and free so that I can hear Your Spirit prompting me to pray and even, at times, what to pray. This is very liberating to me, Lord! Those two things are what I want anyway. And this means that the real work is Yours and thus, the results are Yours, too. Yours to receive the praise and glory, or Yours to accept the responsibility. From studying Your Word, I have learned the basics of praying with faith and of praying in Your will. But what I'm thinking about here is deeper than consciousness. It is You being faithful to pray in and through me, whether I'm aware of it or not. It is You knowing what to pray while I often do not. It is Your prayers being certain of an answer, while mine may be off-track.

I realize anew what a privilege it is to be an intercessor. I'm actually just Your helper in blessing peoples' lives. A co-worker with the God of the universe! How awesome is that! May I be so identified with You, my Lord, that time spent in praying for others is valuable to Your work within them.

March 30
PREACHING TO MYSELF

Do you not know that you are a sanctuary of God,
and that the Spirit of God dwells in You?
1 Corinthians 3:16

Dear Lord, please help me to understand how You want to work in these changed circumstances of my life. I was literally "on call" 24/7, facing difficult responsibilities during the terminal illness of my loved one. I now have *all* my hours free from being needed. From the time I get up in the morning until I go to bed at night, I have only myself to see after. *Never* has my life been like this. I look around my neat, orderly house and don't know what to do next. I find that this causes a fear, Lord, a feeling of panic.

But even as I write those words, the thought comes that they are foolish words. I must speak strong words to myself. Is God unable to make me hear and understand? Is anything too hard for Him? Has He taken back His promise to lead me and deliver me safely to His eternal Kingdom? Can I fail because of my lack of knowing how to deal with this new life situation?

The clear answer on all counts is NO! I can totally trust that You will provide for me anything and everything I need. I can walk forward knowing that You are in control of my life because I have asked You to be. I can know that my spirit, heart and mind are renewed day by day. I can know that a part of Your divine design is that I will, with my mind, enter into my spirit where You live, as often as I need. I can know that You will restore the sense of peace, strength and rest that I can find nowhere else. And I so much need that rest. That is probably the most important thing I can do for a while - simply rest.

By Your mercy and in Your love, You have provided for me a place within that is forever available to me - a place where You always have time for me, a quiet, restful, beautiful place. My job is to simply go there, tell You what is on my heart, give You all my anxious thoughts, and tell You again that, though I am very weak and needy, my love for You and my confidence in You are strong. By Your grace, they are strong.

Thank You, Lord, for creating within me this sanctuary, this refuge from the world. Thank You for such love and wisdom that provides, ahead of the need, all that I need. Thank You that all my tomorrows, whatever they bring, will be good because You will be there. Thank You for my sermon to me today.

March 31
HARD QUESTIONS

And let us not lose heart in doing good,
for in due time we shall reap if we do not grow weary.
Galatians 6:9

Thinking about prayer in general and intercessory prayer in particular, I have some challenging questions:

Do I believe Your promises concerning prayer with the same deep, knowing faith that I have for Your other promises?

If not, why not? If I do, why is it often so difficult to pray? What is it in me that must be overcome to get busy and *do* this business of praying?

When this life is over, and I understand things which now I only know by faith, how will I view my prayer life?

- with regret for not seeing the powerful tool You placed in my hand which I too often let lie there unused?

- with sorrow for doubting that You meant what You said when You taught about praying?

- with joy in seeing the things accomplished because I prayed?

- with thanksgiving for being allowed to be useful to You in doing Your work?

Lord, help me search my heart for honest answers - painful maybe, but honest.

Possibly much of my doubt and reluctance hinge on my lack of worthiness rather than on Your promises or Your ability to answer. Thinking that through, however, it's quickly obvious that of course I'm not worthy to ask anything of You! It is only by Your grace I'm even Your child, much less have the privilege of coming to You for my own or another's needs! So *grace* is my answer to that.

How much of my struggle is due to spiritual warfare? Why do I think praying should always be easy? Is other work always easy? Wouldn't it be more realistic to admit up front that I have committed to a demanding task, and that it will require genuine effort and fighting some battles to get it done?

How important are my feelings anyway? Isn't love what You seek? And, while love is a matter of the heart, it is first a decision of the will. If I find love when I look within, is it due to *my* goodness? Absolutely not. Grace again. From beginning to end, what I am, what I have and what I will be are all because of Your goodness and Your grace. The answers to this page full of questions are all to be found in that all-sufficient grace.

April 1

A SACRIFICE OF THANKSGIVING

He who offers a sacrifice of thanksgiving honors Me;
and to him who orders his way aright
I shall show the salvation of God.
Psalm 50:23

As I read this Psalm this morning, Lord, the two verses that talk about a sacrifice of thanksgiving speak to me. Somehow, I know that this is different from just ordinary thankfulness. To the people of Israel, a sacrifice was usually an animal killed and offered to You. But in this Psalm, You say that what You truly value is not the slaying of animals, but a sacrifice of thanksgiving. You could have said "a heart of thanksgiving" or "an attitude of thanksgiving." By using the word "sacrifice," You are saying something different. Help me, Lord, to see what that is.

- A sacrifice always costs something. (2 Sam. 24:24)
- A sacrifice was given totally to You - no part of it withheld.
- Our idea of 'sacrifice' is often *a thing that is hard to give.*
- Being thankful is easy in good times but often difficult in the midst of troubles.

So if I take only those four thoughts and apply them to my life this day, it looks like this:

With all that is within me,
nothing held back or reserved,
I give You thanks for my life
just as it is.

You know, Lord, that there are some things in my life that make it difficult for me to give thanks. I'm sure that is true for most people most of the time. But Your Word is clear. Like I Thessalonians 5:18 where Paul says, *"In everything give thanks; for this is God's will for you in Christ Jesus."* So in obedience, Lord, I give thanks. In all the good things, my gratitude is effortless and flows freely. In what seem to me the "bad" things, I can still be truly thankful because I completely trust Your love. I have such confidence in Your character, Lord, that I know You are not going to allow anything in my life that will not ultimately be for good.

Thank You for accepting my sacrifice of thanksgiving. May a spirit of gratitude continue to rule over my thinking at all times.

April 2
BUILDING YOUR TEMPLE

And the house which I am about to build will be great;
for greater is our God than all the gods.
But who is able to build a house for Him,
for the heavens and the highest heavens cannot contain Him?
So who am I, that I should build a house for Him?
2 Chronicles 2:5-6

Reading those words this morning, Lord, those questions from the heart of Solomon, I'm prompted, also, to ask, "Indeed, Lord, who am I that You, my Lord, my King, should dwell in my spirit?" I cannot build You a place of splendor, gold, silver, bronze and jewels as Solomon did.

No, my spirit is more like a humble cottage. But it can still be beautiful and warm, filled with love, light and joy. Because, just as You provided all the materials for Solomon to build that temple - all the special wood, precious metals and the skilled craftsmen to work with them - so You are the provider of all that has gone into the building and furnishing of my spirit.

Every good and lovely thing within me has come from Your hand. I am filled with Your righteousness. I am renewed daily by Your faithfulness and mercy. I am humbled and amazed at the fact of Your eternal, unconditional love. How can I express the extent of my gratitude that You should dwell within me and love me? What an incredible privilege to be a child of the Living God! And Your promise is that You will never leave me - that nothing can separate me from Your love. Truly, *"greater is our God than all the gods."*

As we walk from room to room this day in my spirit, may You find only what is pleasing to you. Abundant grace and mercy, order, love shining all around for You and for others - may it all be good in Your eyes. I love You, Lord.

April 3
MAYBE

For I am confident of this very thing,
that He who began a good work in you
will perfect it until the day of Christ Jesus.
Philippians 1:6

Thinking about the process of spiritual growth, Lord, I'm made to marvel at Your patience in changing me from my image into Your image. Slow work! We have been working on this project for years, and I'm very aware of how much more there is to learn. Sometime back, You gave me a short reminder to say to myself often; it is my personal statement of faith concerning what I know to be Your will...

I am willing,
You are able,
It shall be done.

No matter what part of my life we are working on, I can count on that affirmation of faith being true. Maybe this work carries over into the next life. Maybe we only get a good start at it here. Maybe we are so hampered and slowed down, dying to our inborn sinful nature, that mostly we just learn to persevere. We struggle against all the self-sins, against the world, against the enemy, against our tendency to unbelief, against our bent toward evil. Maybe, in the next life, when all those difficulties are removed, we go on learning in a brand new atmosphere and are then able to see real progress toward goals we never even envisioned in this life.

What I know for sure, Lord, is that You will be there - visibly present with us. That alone will make it heaven. In the meantime, I will keep my hand in Yours and continue walking with You, trusting You to continue making me into Your image. This day I desire to make You "the source, the center, and the circumference of my soul's delight." (Spurgeon)

April 4
WAITING

Lord, You and I were thinking yesterday about what I call my 'Five Anchors'…

Be anxious for nothing.
In everything give thanks.
Rejoice evermore.
Pray without ceasing.
Quench not the Spirit.

How many times You have used these anchors to bring me back to the path! They have never failed to clear away the fog and enable me to see truth again. But this morning, I'm thinking about the not-so-fun task of waiting, and how we seem to do so *much* of it in our lives. When we are twelve, we can't wait to be eighteen. When we are childless, we can't wait until we have children. When we have toddlers underfoot, we can't wait for them to go to school. When we are forty-five, we can't wait to retire. And on and on and on.

Then there are the times of shorter waits. Some waiting is pleasant anticipation, some done in dread of potential negative outcome. But, once again, Lord, these Five Anchors come to mind as the best, healthiest, most blessed way to occupy our minds for every situation of waiting.

One of the reasons these instructions are so powerful is that to meditate on them makes me *be in the present moment*. Not in the past - not in the future - but in this moment. The past cannot be changed, and the future is completely unknown to me. Only in the present moment can I exercise my God-given privilege of choosing what to think about.

Obeying these instructions also perfectly positions my heart and mind squarely under the spout of Your blessings, ready to receive whatever You desire to give for that particular moment. I must remove all anxieties by giving them to You, one by one, until none remain. Only then can I go on to be thankful, joyful, prayerful, and listening to You.

Best of all, these Five Anchors make me realize the reality of Your nearness. Psalm 73 says, *"the nearness of God is my good."* In James we are instructed to *"Draw near to God and He will draw near to you."* There is no greater blessing, Lord, than to be near to You!

Of course, You knew that already. You designed it all. How wise and loving and full-of-wonder You are!

April 5
THOUGHTS ON ACTS

To these He also presented Himself alive,
after His suffering, by many convincing proofs,
appearing to them over a period of forty days,
and speaking of the things concerning the Kingdom of God.
Acts 1:3

The book of Acts begins where the gospels end. Your followers had seen You *alive from the grave*. They had heard You speak. They had touched You and eaten with You. They had seen You ascend into heaven and then they somewhat settled down to wait for the promised giving of Your Spirit. They probably had questions and maybe even doubts about what would happen next. As I read that first chapter of Acts, Lord, I too have some thoughts and questions.

You said to the apostles (and thus to me), *"It is not for you to know times the Father has fixed by His own authority."* In context, You were answering a question concerning the restoration of Israel. To my spirit, You are saying to not bother myself with things that are not my concern; rather, use the power You have given me to witness Your love and grace for as long as You so deem. And I say, "Yes, Lord, Your will be done."

The apostles may not have learned every lesson well, but they learned one important one: *"These all with one mind were continually devoting themselves to prayer."* What a lesson for Your people today. How foolish we are if we neglect to be of one mind or fail to devote ourselves to prayer! Give us fire in our souls for faithfulness to pray, Lord.

The choosing of Matthias - why do we never hear of him again? Was this Your guidance for them to replace Judas? Or was it their own idea, and You merely allowed it? Maybe it was Your plan for Paul to be considered the twelfth apostle. But there must be some reason for the choosing of Matthias to be included in the Scriptures. I think it is interesting, Lord, that this method of making a decision (casting lots after praying) was never mentioned again after Your Spirit was fully given on the day of Pentecost. Actually, casting lots would be much easier for us than keeping our spiritual ears tuned to hear Your voice. But I've noticed that "easier" is not high on Your list of priorities. Learning to know You and trust You is.

Are the answers to these questions essential to salvation? No, Lord. If they were, You would have put the answers in Your Word. They are just interesting things to think about. We are going to have so much new stuff to learn when we get to heaven. I can hardly wait!

April 6
ONENESS WITH YOU

And I am no more in the world; and yet they themselves are in the world,
and I come to Thee.
Holy Father, keep them in Thy name, the name which Thou hast given Me,
that they may be one, even as We are.
John 17:11

I have been reading about it, thinking about it and praying about it, Lord, what it means to be "one with You." And I'm seeing, strangely enough, a little of the power Your children have to hurt You. By this I mean, if I do not return love to You, that is hurtful to You. How do I know this? Because I know how it hurts me to love someone and have them not love me in return, have them not trust in my love, have them not understand the depths of my love for them. So if this is true of human love, how much more is it true of God-love?

And how do I fail to love You? By being stubborn and self-willed about anything. By failing to see Your provision and depending upon my own scant supply. By neglect, by thoughtlessness, by selfish decisions made without even consulting You. In a myriad of ways, Lord, I can fail to trust the unconditional God-love that is offered to me. How it hurts my heart to think of hurting Yours! Thank You so much for showing this to me! Please make this truth sink deep down into my spirit, work that inner change and enable me to always turn to You with a heart of love, gratitude and praise.

Now, Lord, help me think about how this will change how I do things. I will see all that happens every day as something You have either caused or allowed, and thus accept it from Your loving hand. I will speak often to You words of love and thanks and praise. When the pain is great, I will simply ask for Your help rather than tell You how badly I'm hurting, since You already know. I will think less often of me and what I want, and more often of You and what You want. I will more consistently live out my 'Five Anchors.' Peace and joy will reign in my heart.

Please understand me, Lord. I'm not saying *I'm* going to do these things. I'm saying that when You have completed the inner change I'm requesting, this is how it will look. I think I have finally learned that making to-do lists of better behavior and then trying to live by them is a perfect set-up for failure. No, I'm simply thinking ahead to how my life will be when You have completed this work within my heart. And how do I know You are going to do it? Because I know it is Your will.

April 7
BE JOYFUL

Finally , my brethren, rejoice in the Lord.
To write the same things again is no trouble to me,
and it is a safeguard for you.
Philippians 3:1

Your Word, Lord, from beginning to end tells us to rejoice, to be full of joy. Please help me think about that this morning. Paul, in this verse, says "rejoice *in the Lord.*"

...not in circumstances, even if they are wonderful, and I should rightfully thank You for them.

...not in accomplishments, even if You have allowed me to be successful at what You have given me to do.

...not in the people in my life, even though I love them and they love me.

...not in prosperity, even if You have blessed me with an abundance of material blessings.

...not in my good health, even if I feel whole, strong and pain free.

All of these may be true at times, but in every believer's life there *will* be times when one or more of them will not be true. And I notice that Paul put no conditions on this instruction - like "rejoice in the Lord when your life is really good." No, I am to rejoice in You at all times, no matter what.

That is because You, my Lord, are the one constant in my life. Everything else may change drastically, even today. Look at Job! In a very short time he lost his family, his wealth, even his health. You alone are the unchangeable, faithful God. You alone are worthy of being the object of my love, rejoicing and gratitude.

I see, Lord, that to rejoice in who You are is praise. To rejoice in my standing with You is thanksgiving. And both are essential to my spiritual health. How wise we would be to just obey You without needing to know why! To simply do what You said do because You said do it. How patient and merciful You are to put up with me while I limp along, shuffling and stumbling when You have provided me everything needed to run! Help me, Lord, this day to keep all this in mind and to at least walk briskly. With You.

April 8
THE NEW SELF

...and have put on the new self
who is being renewed to a true knowledge
according to the image of the One who created him.
Colossians 3:10

Lord, Paul is talking here to people who have been born of the Spirit and have received instruction in dying to self and living to You. Only You know how I have struggled with this concept of being dead to self. Please help me think through what You are saying to me this morning.

In the verses preceding this one and some which follow, Paul gives what seems to be the "process" for putting on this new self:

I am to keep seeking things above, not things on earth - eternal versus temporal.

I must consider my body dead to all sin, all immorality, greed, idolatry. Likewise, my mind and heart must be free of sin - things such as wrath, malice, anger, abusive speech.

I must not lie.

I am to be compassionate, kind, humble, gentle, patient, forgiving.

I am to allow Your peace to rule in my heart.

I must be thankful at all times.

Your Word is to dwell richly in me - so I must read it, study it, memorize it and think about it.

I am to do *all* in Your name and for Your glory.

The idea is that all these things listed above should be done on a consistent basis, progressing toward a specific goal: Christ-likeness.

You made mankind in Your image. Paul talks about that in the verse above. So the renewing process that is going on within me is to re-create my inner person to the original plans and specifications - like Adam and Eve before they were disobedient - renewed to a true knowledge according to Your image.

Help me this day, my Lord, to rejoice in the fact that I belong to You, that You and I are walking side by side and that my heart's desire is to become like You. Help me not dwell on my failures or my slowness to learn, but rather keep the eternal as my focus and trust You for what comes next.

By Your grace, I shall not quit learning. I shall continue to read, study, pray and trust. I shall go on reckoning the old self dead and the new self alive to You. I shall love You more tomorrow than I do today. All by Your grace. All by Your amazing grace.

April 9
YOUR WELL-LOVED CHILD

The Lord is compassionate and gracious,
slow to anger and abounding in loving kindness.
Just as a father has compassion on his children,
so the Lord has compassion on those who fear Him.
Psalm 103:8 & 13

How good You are, Lord to welcome back this child even though I am less than I ought to be; less faithful, less truthful, less free of the world, less filled up with You.

Still, You welcome me back, allow me to spend time with You and receive strength and all else I need to go out for another day. Of course, You go with me, but it's not the same "with" as a time of conscious "with-ness" like now, in the early morning.

I see myself this morning, Lord, as a small child at Your back door, grubby and dirty with who-knows-what stuck in my hair. My clothes are a mess. I am a mess. But I want to come in.

So You open the door and without scolding or shaming, You show me how much better it is to be clean. You fill the tub with warm water and scrub me up with sweet smelling soap and shampoo, put me into clean clothes and feed me something warm and good.

You hold me in Your arms and reassure me of Your continuing presence. You talk about important things like how to keep from getting so dirty next time. And where I could go to play that would be better than where I went. And how You will always and forever love me.

Time after time, Lord, You do this for me. Maybe someday I will grow enough to not show up in such a needy state. I love You so much for loving me!

April 10
PARTNERSHIP

Therefore you are to be perfect, as your heavenly Father is perfect.
Matthew 5:48

Those words above, Lord, spoken from Your mouth, are in the middle of an extended teaching session that lasts three entire chapters in Your Word. The things You were telling Your disciples were astonishing! The standard You set is so impossibly high; the expectation so out of reach of any mortal man. If I thought I had to achieve it in my own strength, I would have never had the courage to continue this life of faith. But then, that would not be a life of faith, would it, Lord? It would be a life of works. Which is the equivalent of what the Jews had done all their lives - tried to live by thousands of rules.

But You were not dictating more rules to follow. You were explaining a whole new way of life that was available after the Day of Pentecost and is available yet today - *the 'Holy Partnership' of You in me and me in You...*

I *cannot* do Your part.
You *will not* do my part.
It takes both of us working *together* to accomplish Your will in me.

Most of our projects are matters of the inner person, such as heart purity, attitudes and motives. Once these are submitted to You, the "outer person" problems begin to resolve themselves. Such things as personal relationships, anxiety about material goods, loving my enemy, fasting and praying, judging others, all these and more must be settled first in the mind and the will, and then worked out in life.

I'm so thankful, Lord, for this new and living way! I'm far too weak to consistently follow any path as arduous as this on my own. How awful it would be if I thought You gave me this long list of things that needed to be changed within me and then stood there with Your arms folded, Your foot tapping, waiting for me to shape up. How wonderful to realize that You are in this thing *with* me, and that You will not leave me.

Here's an uplifting thought - a true partnership involves two people who put everything they have at the other's disposal. That's exactly how it is!

April 11
PRAISING YOU

Yet Thou are holy,
O Thou who dost inhabit the praises of Israel.
Psalm 22:3

In learning more about living a life filled with praise, I come to this verse which says that when I praise, You dwell in those praises. This is very mysterious! It does not say You inhabit those who praise You (although, by Your Word I know You do). It says You inhabit the praises.

I may not understand that, Lord, but here is what I do understand. You do not have with an inflated ego that demands praise. No, this word, like all others from You, is given to Your children *for our good.*

"It is only when you are in an attitude of praise that I can bless you. That is when you are able to receive from Me what I long to give, when your attitude is loving and trusting and thankful toward Me. A grumpy, griping child is very hard to bless. One joyful and eager to do as bidden is easy to bless.

Heart-obedience is necessary, even in matters which you do not fully understand. Just trust that my reason for telling you something is to demonstrate My great love for you in a new way. I am always ready to bless, but am hindered by your failure to receive what I have already given you."

Looking back at my own journey, Lord, I see stretches where, even though I was going through most of the right motions and saying most of the right words, my heart wasn't in it. I was an outwardly obedient child. Not a happy child, mind You, but one who was obedient on the outside. Inside, I was entertaining doubts of "how could God love *me?*" I was actually believing a lie of the devil. His goal was to keep me *attempting* to earn Your favor. I was deeply desiring love and at the same time, doubting it. Lord, this is sin. This is unbelief. You can never bless that!

How thankful I am that You saw exactly what was going on in my faulty thinking and patiently taught me Your truth. My song of praise fills my spirit and rises to the heavens as I ponder the honor and glory due Your Holy Name. I surrender my mind and my heart to Your love, my Lord.

April 12
ATTITUDE ADJUSTMENT

The king's heart is like channels of water in the hand of the Lord;
He turns it wherever He wishes.
Every man's way is right in his own eyes
but the Lord weighs the hearts.
Proverbs 21:1-2

In reading these verses this morning, I see once more the power You, my God, have over my heart. You do with it as You wish. And I acknowledge that You are working to show me an unpleasant, problem-causing attitude in me.

I am aware that this is an attitude of long standing. I am aware that simply suppressing it fails - it only pops to the surface later. I am aware that it is probably a lot more complex than I realize.

I am also aware of what Your Word says my attitude should be. That, Lord, is where I set my will. I am determined to not only *do* but to *be* what Your Word says. As nearly as I know how, I open my mind, heart and spirit to You for Your renewing and cleansing touch.

Obviously, I cannot accomplish this in my own strength. So I put my will on Your side, my problem in Your hands and stay submissive to You as You work it out. I will do my best to listen well and to obey quickly. I give You permission to break through the thick wall of protection I have built around this attitude. Soften my mind and heart and, when we have totally destroyed this thing, we will have room within for more of You. That is well worth working toward!

April 13
SOWING AND REAPING

Do not be deceived, God is not mocked;
for whatever a man sows this he will also reap.
For the one who sows to his own flesh shall from the flesh reap corruption,
but the one who sows to the Spirit shall from the Spirit reap eternal life.
Galatians 6:7-8

This is one of the laws of living that You put into place, Lord. It is so obvious in the physical world that to talk about it seems silly. Everybody knows that if you sow corn you shall reap corn. But sometimes we fail to carry that "knowing" over into spiritual matters. That's where my thinking is this morning.

I'm seeing that I am sowing everyday, either subconsciously or intentionally. If subconsciously, I will probably be surprised at harvest time; unpleasantly surprised. If I am sowing intentionally, I have seen Your law for what it is - an instrument to be used for good.

The present is both a time of reaping of the past and a time of sowing for the future. One is fixed and cannot be changed. The other is in my control. I can decide what seeds to plant today. As Your child, I receive Your light, direction and instruction but I make the choice.

I can look at the not-so-happy harvest that I'm dealing with in my present and look back to see what I planted that caused this particular crop to grow. This is a principle You have taught me, Lord, to *learn* from my miserable failures so that something good can come from them.

But here is the important thought. I can, with Your Spirit as Guide, look ahead five years, or ten years, or to the end of my life, and ask, "What is the harvest I want to come from my life? And what do *You* want?" As I read and study Your Word, I can stay alert for Your thoughts of future yields. Then, together, we can plant the seeds that will result in those particular returns.

One more thought: some seeds are so tiny! It would probably take thousands of mustard seeds to fill a teaspoon. And some of the convictions You bring to my heart are also, seemingly, very tiny and not of much consequence. Some small behavior or habit or way of thinking that seems too insignificant to be concerned about. But, Lord, if it is important enough for You to have brought it to my mind, it is important enough for me to do with it whatever You are saying to do! Let me not push aside a gently whispered corrective instruction from You because I think it is not worthwhile.

I ask You, Lord, to keep the soil of my heart rich, and give me Your wisdom in my daily sowing!

April 14
INSTRUCTIONS FOR VICTORY

1 Peter 5:6-11

These verses, Lord, give me some clear instructions to follow in this business of successfully living by faith. As I ponder them and paraphrase them, I ask You to plant Your truth deep in the soil of my heart and let's grow some *good* things in my life.

I am to humble myself under Your hand. You are to be my Lord in deed as well as word, in all areas of my life. If just one area is outside Your Lordship, then You are not Lord.

I must cast all my anxieties upon You because You care for me. What great good news that is! How incredible that You care about the things that make me anxious.

I am to be of sober spirit, taking seriously Your Word and my relationship to You. Please, Lord, enable me to keep my spiritual senses tuned up and in good shape so that I do not miss anything You desire me to understand.

I must be on the alert. The devil is constantly prowling, looking for someone to devour. And I know from experience, Lord, that he is not above kicking me when I'm down. Give me both discernment and wisdom.

I must resist the devil. Don't listen to him. Don't debate with him. Don't let myself get into situations where I know my weaknesses will make me vulnerable.

I am to stand firm in the faith and be strong in the power of Your presence - be strong in my confidence in Your faithfulness.

It is through this process that You can perfect, confirm, strengthen and establish me. Which is exactly what I want!

April 15
FIGHTING SPIRITUAL BATTLES

Submit therefore to God.
Resist the devil and he will flee from you.
James 4:7

The longer I live and the more of You I understand, the more clearly I see the huge disparity between what You want me to be and what the devil tries to make me be. Just in recent months, Lord, the enemy has tried to destroy our faith, tear down our marriage, demolish family relationships, and put an end to our witness. It seems as though we have had no time for anything except fighting him. But You are faithful! You are our protector and shield, our wall about us, our refuge.

As I look back at these most recent battles, I realize anew how *nothing* I am without Your power at work in me. Left to my own strength and resources, I'd be putty in his hands. And I have also seen so clearly Your great love and patience. Please look within, Lord, and see the gratitude for that love and patience! Gratitude is too weak a word! Eternal thanksgiving...? I just don't know any other way to say it.

Another thing I have learned through these battles is to not be so quick to judge other people who are struggling, but instead, to pray for their strength and perseverance. We cannot know what other people are going through in their attempt to resist the devil.

I already knew, Lord, that we constantly have choices to make - that one way is Your way and one way the devil's. One way blessing and life, one way sorrow and death. But I did not know that, often, at the outset, the wrong way could *look* so right. The wrong way can seem pleasant and inviting. But I found that, here again, You are faithful. You will not let me stray off in ignorance. I may *choose* to take the wrong path, but You will not allow me to take it by accident. How thankful I am for that!

I have found that the turning point of the battle is when I make my choice and am able to put my will in line with Yours. Yielding myself to Your will, to Your love, trusting completely that You know what You are doing - that is the major portion of "my part." Then Your power takes over and finishes the victory. Praise God.

Not by might nor by power,
but by My Spirit says the Lord of hosts.
Zechariah 4:6

April 16
FIRST ADAM - LAST ADAM

For since by a man came death,
by a man also came the resurrection of the dead.
For as in Adam all die,
so also in Christ all shall be made alive.
1 Corinthians 15:21-22

So also it is written,
"The first man, Adam, became a living soul."
The last Adam became a life-giving spirit.
1 Corinthians 15:45

I know, Lord, that Paul was teaching here about the truth of Your resurrection from the dead and thus the certainty of our own, but these verses bring my mind back to the marvelous, dangerous power of our free-will that You built into us.

One of the reasons, as I understand it, Lord, for You to create mankind was to have someone with whom to fellowship. Someone who would come to know You and respond to You in trust and love and respect - the respect of a creature for its Creator. In other words, obedience because the creature understands it is loved and wishes to reciprocate that love.

Since this creature had to be a free-will being - not a holy robot - there had to be the possibility for disobedience; otherwise, the obedience would have no meaning.

These verses (and others) make it clear that Your plan called for Adam's decision to have earth-wide ramifications; i.e., what he decided affected every person born after him - all mankind. Meaning, because of his sin, we are born sinners. Do I understand why You did this? No, I don't. This is just one of the issues that I accept as true because Your Word says so. I have faith in Your character; therefore, I have faith in Your Word.

This Scripture above calls You the last Adam. It's like a brand new start, isn't it? *Your decision to be obedient also affected all,* in that it restored to us the situation that existed with Adam. We now have the power to choose; and because of that, we can have the same loving, trusting fellowship with You that Adam had before he and Eve disobeyed.

I'm sure there are deeper theological issues here than I'm aware of, Lord, but my heart sings praises at the realization of what You did on that cross! You, too, had a choice. You could have chosen to avoid the cross. But You didn't. My spirit bows before You in worship and thanksgiving for all that means!

April 17
THE IMPORTANCE OF MIND-SET

Finally, brethren, whatever is true, whatever is honorable,
whatever is right, whatever is pure, whatever is lovely,
whatever is of good repute, if there is any excellence
and if anything worthy of praise,
let your mind dwell on these things.
Philippians 4:8

We clearly have control over what we think, Lord, or You would not have inspired Paul to write this instruction. And we clearly *need* this instruction or, again, You would not have had Paul write it down and then preserved it all these centuries. So those two truths are evident - we do have control over what we think, and we need to be taught about it.

I'm thinking, Lord, that we Christians have not learned this skill very well. We have never taken authority over our mental processes and may not even be aware that we can. But, in truth, we are simply *not* at the mercy of the enemy once we become Your child. Nor are we at the mercy of our past, or of our emotions, or of any other force or power, *even You*. You renew as we give permission and cooperation, and You give us ability and power to do as You say, but *we* still have control.

Here is what You do, Lord - As Master Teacher, You teach us what to do and how to do it. These are the two essentials in any good lesson. This verse is a part of that teaching. It gives me eight excellent things to think about (an alternate translation is *ponder*). Since my mind can only ponder one thing at a time, it is obvious that when I'm obedient to this instruction, I will not be dwelling on negative things like the opposites of these things - false, dishonorable, wrong, impure, ugly, ill repute, base, worthy of condemnation.

It's interesting to me that the two verses just preceding this are the ones that teach us how to gain peace of heart and mind by bringing all our anxieties to You. I'm seeing that this verse is the "how to" to maintain that peace. So in every real-life situation, I can choose how to think, what to think about it, and thus how to react to the other people involved.

I long ago memorized verses 6 and 7 because I very much want Your peace. If I'm to be obedient to verse 8 and "ponder these things," I see I must memorize it also. I also see I very much *need* this discipline in my life.

My choice. How awesome!

April 18
THOUGHTS ON GOOD FRIDAY

And after weaving a crown of thorns, they put it on His head,
and a reed in His right hand;
and they kneeled down before Him and mocked Him saying,
"Hail, King of the Jews!"
And they spat on Him and took the reed and began to beat Him on the head.
And after they had mocked Him, they took His robe off
and put His garments on Him,
and led Him away to crucify Him.
Matthew 27: 29-31

This day, out of all the year, my heart is torn, Lord.
It is divided between sorrow at all You suffered
and gratitude that You chose to do it.

My heart feels somehow rebellious that we call it "Good Friday"
yet must also acknowledge that what happened on this day was,
for us,
unsurpassed good.

I feel emotionally oppressed to think of all you went through, Lord.
I love You, and it hurts to think of You being hurt.
And then I think,
but what if You hadn't?
and my joy returns.

There is a sense of guilt in me that I'm joyful.
You were beaten, mocked and subjected to such shame and suffering.
and yet,
that is how it is.

In other words, Lord, I'm not exactly at peace within.
I *am* looking forward to Sunday
when we can celebrate Your victory over death and the grave!

No mixed emotions there.
Just pure praise and rejoicing.
What an awesome thing,
Your plan of redemption!

April 19
WILLPOWER

But prove yourselves doers of the word,
and not merely hearers who delude themselves.

But one who looks intently at the perfect law,
the law of liberty,
and abides by it, not having become a forgetful hearer
but an effectual doer,
this man shall be blessed in what he does.
James 1:22 & 25

Lord, I am not - *must* not be - at the mercy of my feelings. When my feelings are clamoring for my attention concerning an area of my life and I know the feelings are not pleasing to You, my job is to ignore them and reaffirm where my *will* is.

Is my will still on the side of obedience to the Word? If not, get it there. I am the only one in control of my will. If it is still on the side of obedience, praise You and get busy practicing a little thought control. Deliberately choose what to think about and reject every suggestion from every source that contradicts Your will for the situation.

This is easy, and this is hard. The hard part is the deciding and committing. The easy part is *doing* because You bless every small effort I make in the right direction.

You just made me smile all over!

Remember when You made me quit smoking? How difficult it was for me to be obedient! I wrestled with You for a long, miserable time over that issue. But I finally got to the place where I told You I'd do it if it killed me (which I seriously thought it might).You walked me on through that process. You brought me out the other side of it free of the addiction, healthier, happier, and best of all, full of joy at proving You trustworthy!

One of the ways You helped me through that hard time was teaching me thought control. You instructed me to turn to You with praise every time the craving for nicotine was intense. So I did, and it worked! I overcame the addiction, my ability to praise was increased, and I didn't gain a lot of weight like some do who substitute food for smoking. How wise you are!

Thank You, Lord, for bringing this to mind. It puts my current situation in a whole new perspective; I can simply put my hand in Yours and continue walking on this journey we began so long ago. Please look within and see my spirit bowing in worship and love for Your excellent care.

April 20
LIVING BY FAITH

For I am not ashamed of the gospel,
for it is the power of God for salvation to everyone who believes,
to the Jew first and also to the Greek.
For in it the righteousness of God is revealed from faith to faith;
as it is written,
"But the righteous man shall live by faith."
Romans 1:16-17

You are at the center of my life and You totally surround my life. You are at the center because You chose me, and I responded to Your choosing. You surround me because You are everywhere-present. Both those facts I believe through faith in Your Word.

Faith is hanging on to what I know to be true when all feeling is absent.

Faith is determining to continue reading, praying and striving to know You better in spite of roadblocks, discouraging situations and long-standing problems that go on standing even after much prayer.

Faith is knowing, deep in my spirit, that You are always with me and are completely aware of what is going on. It is knowing that You *will* intervene if/when intervention is needed.

Faith is knowing that, even when I have failed, You love me and are waiting to help me get back on track again.

Faith is a gift from You and all the faith I have, You have given me. And all I have received from You has been *by* faith. So You gave me faith and then, by that very faith, have given me many other wonderful gifts.

Faith is knowing that my response to You, to be pleasing, is to be open-hearted love, reverence and trust.

Faith is believing that as I love and trust, You are able to work in me - not just with the conditions of my life - but *in* me. How incredibly awesome!

For I am confident of this very thing,
that He who began a good work in you
will perfect it until the day of Christ Jesus.
Philippians 1:6

April 21
KNOWING YOU BETTER

More than that, I count all things to be loss in view of the surpassing value of
knowing Christ Jesus my Lord, for whom I have suffered the loss of all things
and count them but rubbish in order that I may gain Christ,
and may be found in Him, not having a righteousness of my own derived from the
law, but that which is through faith in Christ,
the righteousness which comes from God on the basis of faith,
that I may know Him, and the power of His resurrection
and the fellowship of His sufferings, being conformed to His death;
in order that I may attain to the resurrection from the dead.
Philippians 3:8-11

I don't know for sure, Lord, but I think that sentence above must be the longest in all of the Bible! Paul is rather famous for his sometimes complex but always edifying thoughts. In my reading this morning, this particular one grabbed my attention because I've been thinking about this subject of knowing You better.

What does it take, Lord, to grow in knowledge of You? What, in simple terms, should I be doing every day to make progress toward this much desired goal?

"Be willing to be taught by My Spirit. All day. Spend sufficient time with Me in solitude, but be *always* aware of My presence in you and around you. Be quickly obedient to My wishes as you understand them. See the conditions of your life as being directly from My hand. Do this with full trust. Keep your eyes on Me and My provisions. Bring everything, small or great, happy or sad, to me to share."

Thank You, Lord. Those *are* simple enough to understand that a child could do so. But that does not mean they are all easy to do. You know that seeing all the conditions of my life as being directly from Your hand has caused me a struggle or two. "I believe, Lord, help Thou my unbelief."

"Remember that My wisdom is far above your understanding."

April 22
BEING DECEIVED

And the great dragon was thrown down,
the serpent of old who is called the devil and Satan,
who deceives the whole world;
he was thrown down to the earth,
and his angels were thrown down with him.
Revelation 12:9

This war in heaven happened a very long time ago, and Satan and his helpers are still busy with their work of deception. But, Lord, how am I, as Your child, deceived? Do You not protect me from the enemy and the world?

"Well, yes I do. I tell you what to do and how to do it. Your part is to listen and obey."

Okay, Lord, please help me think clearly about this…

All deception takes place through my mind. The enemy chooses a weak spot where it will be easy to tempt me or deceive me. He continually suggests thoughts into my mind to logically convince me in the direction he is leading. *(Think of Eve and the serpent, Genesis 3:1-6)*

If I take them up and accept them, everything I see is interpreted with that slant to it. In this way, I am soon convinced that my way of thinking on this particular subject is right - even if it is directly *against* plain teaching of the Word.

That's pretty scary! Help me, Lord, be so filled up with You and with Your truth that he can never get a foothold in my mind. I see that to do that…

I must identify my weaknesses so I can be aware of his schemes.

I must know Your mind (Your written-down Word) on *that* subject as well as all other subjects. Because, only if I thoroughly know the truth, will I be able to reject the lie.

I must refuse the enemy's suggestions and consciously practice what You say to do.

I must talk to You and listen to You all the time. In other words, "pray without ceasing."

You know what is great about all this, Lord? You do not want me to be deceived! So I know that You will be right alongside me at all times. I'm so glad You are a faithful, loving, powerful God! I truly am safe in Your care, and I love You for that and about a million other reasons, too!

April 23
THE LAW OF LOVE

For you were called to freedom, brethren;
only do not turn your freedom into an opportunity for the flesh,
but through love serve one another.
For the whole Law is fulfilled in one word, in the statement,
"You shall love your neighbor as yourself."
Galatians 5:13-14

The older I get, Lord, the more I am impressed with the importance, the *power* of love. And as I read this whole 5th chapter of Galatians, I'm caused to marvel again at Your grace. Paul was teaching these people about walking in the Spirit, about freedom from keeping multitudinous rules and from measuring themselves by how well they succeeded at that.

We all, at times, substitute some kind of law-keeping for walking by the Spirit, don't we Lord? And it seems to be worse in those of us who grew up in church. We try to substitute dressing right, acting right, speaking right words, doing right things for *being* right. It is *being* that matters.

Now, Lord, let's quit talking about Christians in general and talk about this one in particular. I fall into this legalism trap far more than I should. And I confess it's because legalistic living is *easier* than walking by the Spirit.

Legalism is just going through the motions. Walking by the Spirit forces me to listen to You and then *obey*. Legalistic living can be nothing more than habit. Walking by the Spirit brings the unexpected into my life because You are in charge. Law keeping takes little thought because it is mostly outward. It takes real effort, Lord, to walk by Your Spirit. I have to *think* and *focus* and *persevere*.

If I'm living legalistically, I'm on my own. But here is the good news - walking in the freedom of Your Spirit, I'm constantly aided, encouraged, supported, taught and loved by You! That, to me Lord, is the difference between the bondage of the law and freedom of grace. Law keepers have no interior help. We who have been born of Your Spirit are indwelt by Your Spirit and set free from rule-keeping. This continually amazes me even though it is a truth I've known for quite awhile. Your grace is just so unbelievably full-of-wonder!

One thing I know for certain - Your grace is a demonstration of Your love. I am now privileged to live out that law of love every moment of every day. Your love for me, Lord, is what melts my heart and causes love for You to fill my spirit. Your love for me is what enables me to love my fellow-believers and to love all those people who are not yet believers. Your love is what always draws me back to the law of love when I have gone off down the path of legalism again. How I thank You for loving me!

April 24
THOUGHTS ON INTERCESSION

And for this purpose also I labor,
striving according to His power,
which mightily works within me.
Colossians 1:29

Paul had such a heart of love. That is what shows through to me in this verse above, Lord. The "labor" and "striving" and in the next verse, "struggle" all have to do with prayer. He always mentioned that he had prayed and was praying and did not cease to pray for those who had come to know You. That is love! To pray for another's needs with as much fervency as I pray for my own. There is a vast difference between this and what we sometimes call "praying for others." We say words. Paul interceded. God, teach me to pray like Paul!

Your Word teaches that the real battle for the souls of people is fought in the spirit world. You have given me Your Spirit. You have given me instructions on fighting spiritual battles. You have given me information about my enemy. You will be with me in battle at every moment. You have given me love for those who are lost and on their way to eternal separation from You. Considering this, I'm ashamed at the smallness of my praying.

Paul prayed, then wrote. His instructions for living were the overflow of a heart of love that had been struggling with the enemy for these people. Why do I think his example does not apply to me? Please see, Lord, that I am confessing to a huge gap between what I know to do and what I am actually doing. I'm confessing a grievous sin of omission. I'm confessing giving in to spiritual laziness because intercession is *hard work!* It requires time spent alone with You, apart from all others, working diligently to see Your will done in other's lives. It requires listening to You so I know how to pray for each individual. It requires an open heart and a willing spirit. It requires a sacrifice of time and comfort. It is a demanding task, Lord!

I'm so sorry for my failure to do what I know to do. Please forgive me and fill me with Your love and compassion for people. May my life be so open to the leading of Your Spirit that You can use me in any way You desire. Teach me to see every person as *You* see them. Teach me to intercede as Paul did.

April 25
THE LIGHT

Again therefore Jesus spoke to them, saying,
"I am the light of the world;
he who follows Me shall not walk in the darkness,
but shall have the light of life."
John 8:12

Some people respond to the Light by turning toward You and walking into Your warmth and radiance. Their darkness is behind them. Even their shadow is behind them. As long as they continue walking toward the Light, they will be walking in the Light and the Light is in them. This group is love responding to Love.

Others have to see the blackness of the dark ahead of them before they turn toward the Light. You allow them to see the awful state they will be in if they continue in the direction they are headed. You enable them to experience some sense of what eternal separation from You will mean. How kind and loving You are to instill this holy fear of the high and holy God in them! What a merciful Savior You are! This group can only love after You have taken them under Your wing and removed the fear.

These two groups of people eventually become one - one with You and with each other. The rest of their earthly days are spent walking with Light and learning to be effective reflectors of Light.

The mystery to me, Lord, is this: what about those who continue to ignore the Light and walk on into ever-increasing darkness? Are they blind? Are they totally without knowledge of what You have provided for them? Are they so stubborn and determined to do things their way that they will risk eternal damnation? Is it pride that holds them back from bowing before You? Can they not see that our life span on earth is but a moment in the vastness of eternity?

This group - Oh, Lord, I know Your heart breaks at the stubbornness of humans! It is not Your will that *any* should perish. And yet some will. Some will.

April 26
A FEW CHOICES

For the wages of sin is death,
but the free gift of God is eternal life
in Christ Jesus our Lord.
Romans 6:23

For the mind set on the flesh is death,
but the mind set on the Spirit is life and peace.
Romans 8:6

You are constantly putting before me (and, I'm sure all Your other children, too) some forks in the road, testing me to see if I've been learning what You've been teaching. I want to think about some of them with You, Lord.

For instance...

I can do my praying and giving in secret and thereby add to my heavenly account. Or I can do it to receive praise from others and *that* will be my reward.

I can forgive others so that I may be forgiven. Or I can bear grudges and resentments and become ill both spiritually and physically.

I can love You or I can love money. One way leads to life, the other to death.

I can be merciful and thus receive mercy. Or I can judge harshly and be judged harshly.

I can ask and seek and knock and receive. Or I can not ask, not seek, not knock and do without.

I can trust You for the future and have peace of mind. Or I can be anxious about everything and develop ulcers.

I can surrender to You now as Lord of my life and enjoy our relationship all the rest of my days. Or I can do my own thing all of my life and bow before You as Lord just before I am condemned to be separated from You for all eternity. Your Word says, "*Every* knee shall bow and *every* tongue confess that Jesus Christ is Lord."

Lord, these are no-brainers!

Why would anyone ever choose to live their life without You?!

April 27
WARNINGS AGAINST HYPOCRISY

But the greatest among you shall be your servant.
And whoever exalts himself shall be humbled;
and whoever humbles himself shall be exalted.
Matthew 23:11-12

You pronounced seven woes upon the Pharisees in the verses following those above. And You had already spent several minutes describing them in decidedly unflattering terms. I can only understand, Lord, that hypocrisy is high on Your list of despicable behaviors because You spoke Your harshest words to and about the Pharisees. So as I read this chapter, I must use it as a measuring stick for myself lest I become as they were. Let's think about that.

"You shut off the kingdom of God from men. You are not just a neutral force but an actual obstacle to men finding God. You are a hindrance rather than the help you are supposed to be." Because I belong to You, I have such a responsibility to *live* as though I belong to You! Am I acting in any way that dishonors You?

"Greed controls your life even though you pray long prayers as a cover-up. For this you shall receive greater condemnation." Lord, may I never pray for show and may I keep a wise view of material possessions.

"You work and work to make one convert and end up making him twice as evil as you are. Evil leaders result in evil followers." History proves this over and over. My job, simply stated, is to point people to *You.*

"You are blind to truth concerning things of God. Your eyes are upon material things as being of supreme value when the spiritual is the true priority." Help me keep my focus on eternal truth, not things of earth.

"You tithe to the last cent and think you have won My approval for it. Tithing is good but you are neglecting justice and mercy and faithfulness, which also matter to Me." It's more about how I treat *people* than how I treat *things*, isn't it, Lord?

"On the outside you look alright but inside, you are full of evil. If the inside were clean, the outside would take care of itself." Oh, Lord, please make me transparent!

"You honor the lives of the prophets who have gone before saying, 'If we had been there, we would not have mistreated them.' You are no different from the killers of the prophets for you are their sons." I do tend to judge myself by a different standard than I judge others. Help me see myself exactly as You do, Lord.

There is a lot of instruction in those words on how *not* to be. Please keep my conscience tender and my heart listening to Your reproof. May I be wise enough to take their bad example and use it for good.

April 28
THE PRODIGAL'S BROTHER

And he said to him, 'My child you have always been with me,
and all that is mine is yours.'
Luke 15:31

In Your story about the Prodigal Son, Lord, those words were spoken by the father to the older son. The older son was feeling quite sorry for himself because he had been the "good" son, stayed home, worked hard and never asked for much. And now his younger brother had returned home from wild spending, wilder living and was received like royalty! Unfair!

I must confess, Lord, that I have been both these brothers at different times in my life. For a number of years, I was the prodigal. And just like the prodigal, when I came to my senses (through Your grace) and realized (through Your grace) I needed to return home, You received me back with love and warm acceptance, even joy, when I didn't deserve any of that.

But this morning, as I read this beloved story, these words to the older brother were spoken from Your heart to mine *because I so often fail to see all You wish me to have.* Your voice was tender, not scolding, and that hurts more than scolding. Your tenderness melts my heart, Lord.

I *know* that Your provision is abundant! And yet I sometimes live as though the opposite were true. I live like You give me a small blessing and say, "Now make that last because you won't get another for a *long* time."

A couple of thoughts: One, Your provision is exceedingly greater than I know. I can never come to the end of it. And two, You say that I have not because I ask not. So if I am living out on the edge of Your blessings, it is my fault. You will not force me to be blessed. But You do remind me.

Thank You for Your gentle reproof. Do You see all this love in my heart for You?

Now to Him who is able to do exceeding abundantly
beyond all that we ask or think,
according to the power that works within us,
to Him be the glory in the church
and in Christ Jesus to all generations forever and ever.
Amen
Ephesians 3:20-21

April 29
CONDITIONS FOR BEING BLESSED

Bring the whole tithe into the storehouse,
so that there may be food in My house,
and test Me now in this, says the Lord of hosts,
"if I will not open for you the windows of heaven,
and pour out for you a blessing until it overflows.
Malachi 3:10

Watching the children play in the lawn sprinkler yesterday, Lord, made me think of how You provide such an ever-flowing fountain of blessings to Your children. The blessings are always flowing, but it is up to me to get under the spout.

All I need to live this life of faith successfully, You have abundantly provided. But You will not follow me around and dump these blessings upon me when I decide to be still for a moment. No, You prepare them but I must withdraw from my busy, noisy life and get away with You, get under the spout in order to receive them into myself.

Draw near to God and He will draw near to you.
James 4:8 (a)

I've relied on that promise countless times over the years, Lord, and not once have You failed to keep Your part of it. That's because *You are always near*! I am the one who wanders off. So, of course, when I sense a distance between us and draw near to You - there You are, waiting to welcome me back. How good You are, Lord, to this unworthy child! How I love You for first loving me!

Thank You for showing me that, just as that lawn sprinkler doesn't hop around the yard following the children, neither do You bless me until I fulfill the condition of drawing near to You, with my heart ready to receive that overflowing blessing You want me to have.

April 30
DYING TO LIVE

Truly, truly, I say to you, unless a grain of wheat
falls into the earth and dies,
it remains by itself alone;
but if it dies, it bears much fruit.
John 12:24

In Your words here, Lord, I see the necessity for a grain of wheat to die to be of use. This is a productive death because through dying, it springs into new life. It is changed from one small grain with a big potential into that big potential. It now has many, many small grains each full of the identical potential.

You were speaking here, however, of Yourself, Your impending death and resurrection and the redemptive potential that would be made available to all mankind. You knew that unless You died, Your life would not bear fruit. And that is true. Many men have been excellent teachers of fine doctrines and have come and gone with little remembrance. It is Your death and resurrection that set You apart as the Son of God. The cross and the empty tomb are what have meaning.

But this concept of dying to bear fruit also applies to me, Lord. Not my physical death, but my dying to myself. At the very moment I relinquished my hold on the sinful nature with which I was born, You began to fulfill the potential that was and is Your plan for me. There was quite a bit of cleaning that had to be done in me. I learned that I must turn loose of all my rights, my opinions, my prejudices, all that even suggests evil; then You could continue this mysterious, wonderful work in me that changes me from what I was to what You are.

One small grain of wheat is pretty useless left to itself. It isn't enough to feed anyone. But in the farmer's care, it gets planted, sends up that little shoot of life and, when combined with all the other planted grains, produces an abundance, which *is* enough to do good. We, Your children, are that way. Only under Your direction and care will our lives count for anything. Only as we die to self and live to You will there be fruit borne for Your Kingdom. So be it, Lord.

May 1
SOME TRUTHS ABOUT PRUNING

I am the true vine, and My Father is the vinedresser.
Every branch in Me that does not bear fruit, He takes away;
And every branch that bears fruit,
He prunes it, that it may bear more fruit.
John 15:1-2

I'm so thankful, Lord, that You provided spiritual lessons by using everyday things like gardening. Even those like me who are not gardeners can understand these truths and apply them to the healthy growth of our spirit. For a child of Yours, there is nothing more important than to "see" the inner workings of their spirit interacting with Your Spirit. So, please Lord, help me as I think about these truths this morning.

Pruning is a blessing because it happens only to those branches which are bearing fruit. Unproductive branches are simply cut off and thrown away. So, though pruning may be unpleasant to the flesh, my heart rejoices in this evidence of Your loving care.

Pruning in nature is cutting away any portion of the branch which will, in the opinion of the gardener, cause it to be less fruitful. The spiritual parallel here is clear, Lord. Anything You see in my life that is hindering my bearing fruit *must* be cut away. And Your "seeing" is far more than just opinion - it is absolute and certain knowledge. I'm thinking that this thing to be cut from my life could even be something I consider worthwhile. But if it is sapping strength and life from me without producing fruit, it must be removed so that something better may grow.

Pruning often hurts because it is a separation from something that has been a part of me. So I must learn and practice submission with a total trust that *You* are good, and that all You *do* is good.

Plants left un-pruned eventually cease to bear fruit at all. How awful would *that* be?!

I see, Lord, that being only a branch, I do not have any in-put as to how You are pruning my neighboring branches. Since I don't even understand everything about myself, how could I judge and instruct You on how to prune them? *Even if it is someone I deeply love.* I must learn to turn loose of them, allowing You to do as You know best, because You know exactly what You are doing.

Pruning will be a life-long experience.

How grateful I am, Lord, that You are in charge of all this gardening work. You do not make mistakes.

May 2
THE DIFFERENCE YOU MAKE

Come unto Me, all who are weary and heavy-laden,
and I will give you rest.
Take My yoke upon you and learn from Me,
for I am gentle and humble in heart;
and you shall find rest for your soul.
For My yoke is easy and My burden is light.
Matthew 11: 28-30

These words, my Lord, are some of my very favorites. How many times I have turned to them, allowing their warmth and healing to flow into and through my spirit, refreshing my exhausted soul. Truly Your Word is living and active. But the sad and disturbing thought in my mind this morning is how many of Your people don't even know that this rest is available to them.

I don't know anyone who is not often weary and heavy-laden with some kind of burden. But I do know many who are not coming to You for rest. Day after day, they are just plodding along under a dark cloud, trying to make things work on their own. They have worries on the job, problems in the home and uneasiness in their spirit. There is never enough money, enough time or enough love to cover the needs.

This invitation is for them, too! You are the answer. It isn't just that You have the answer. You *are* the answer. Your living, abiding presence in a life is the answer. The two conditions to be met are explained clearly:

"Take My yoke upon you" - a yoke is a working tool, a device to make it possible for two animals to pull together and do a job which is too much for one animal alone to do. How clear! Alone I cannot - yoked with You, I can. The yoke You provide always fits perfectly because You made me and know exactly what I need. Putting on the yoke means agreeing to work with You, pulling with You, letting You guide and control. I must allow Your yoke to be put upon me.

"...learn from me" - These people, Lord, who so much need Your rest, have spent years and years learning from the world. They are filled with the world's knowledge. How crucial that they learn from You! And the only way they will do this learning from You is by learning from Your Word, from good teachers of Your Word, and from walking daily yoked with You. It will take effort but, see the reward! Peace of mind, a spirit full of joy, a growing love relationship with You; blessings without number will reward this one who learns from You!

A joyful spirit makes the ultimate difference in a life filled with care and trials. Oh, how we need to be showing others that the "all" in this invitation includes them!

May 3
CLEANING HOUSE

... wait until the Lord comes
who will both bring to light the things hidden in the darkness
and disclose the motives of men's hearts;
and then each man's praise will come to him from God.
I Corinthians 4:5

Lord, help me right now to clean house in my Spirit where You dwell so that there will be nothing hidden when You come - absolutely nothing! No bad attitude, no resentment saved away, no small, grubby grudge stuck back in a dark corner, nothing that would cause me to stand before You on that day and hang my head.

You are not the honored guest here. You are the Owner. You are *Lord*. At times, I'm slow of understanding, stubborn or just plain lazy. But, deep down, my desire is for You to be Lord of all.

I'm a sorry builder, as You know. In the past, I have jumped ahead and built whole rooms without You - rooms out of square and unusable. They have all been torn down now, and I am content to wait upon You, the Master Builder, to do any more building. You also are the One in charge of this cleaning project - You say what needs to go, and I'll see that it goes.

Let's clean house until every room, every shelf and every closet is sparkling, tidy and fresh with the wind of Your Spirit blowing through. Then on that day, I can look into Your eyes and be filled, truly filled, with the knowledge of Your love. Now I know only in part; then I shall know fully, even as I am known. How I look forward to that day! How I love You, my Lord!

For You and I, Lord, to walk
hand in hand
through the rooms of my spirit,
deciding and discussing
how You want them furnished,
and there be no conflict,
no rebellion,
no stubbornness on my part,
just willingness
and eagerness to please,
that is being filled with the Spirit!

May 4
THE WORLD OF THE SPIRIT

But God, being rich in mercy, because of His great love with which He loved us,
even when we were dead in our transgressions,
made us alive together with Christ (by grace you have been saved),
and raised us up with Him, and seated us with Him in the heavenly places,
in Christ Jesus, in order that in the ages to come
He might show the surpassing riches of His grace
in kindness toward us in Christ Jesus.
Ephesians 2:4-7

How incredible is this truth - that I am already raised up with You and seated with You in the heavenly places! There is a whole world of spirit beings, spirit places and spirit happenings that we are only dimly aware of here on Earth. Many people even deny that such things exist. But to me, Lord, the world of the spirit is more real than the world of the physical because all the things I can see, touch and feel are temporary and will someday be merely a pile of rubble. Only the things of the spirit are enduring and eternal.

There are a host of unseen helpers, waiting to do Your bidding for Your children. These are beings of which I have little knowledge, but which You have created for Your own purposes. That world is already experiencing eternity, free of the limitations of time and space. No past, no future, only an eternal NOW. They experience no limits from the laws of physics that we must live by, like gravity.

Our lives are so bound and restricted, so structured and planned that that kind of living sounds far-out. Yet Your Word says that because I am Your child, I am already a part of it! All the action words in the verses above are past tense - loved, were dead, made, saved, raised, seated - these are all things that have already happened. I have passed through death and been made alive. I already have eternal life. I am now seated in heavenly places with You. So, do I understand how I can be there with You and yet know that I am here on Earth, in this room, on this day, at this hour? No, Lord, I do not understand it. But still I know that there is a dimension in which it is true.

For Your own reasons, You have chosen to veil the world of the spirit from us for the most part. It is faith that pleases You, isn't it, Lord? Believing something because I can *see* it takes no faith. But believing something simply because You said it, requires me to trust You implicitly, to love You though I have never seen You, to believe Your delivering power and love for me simply because You have promised an abundant supply of all that I need - those are the things that please You. And that is the desire of my heart, Lord - to please You.

Someday I will be a full-time citizen of that incredibly fascinating, eternal world of the spirit. I love to think about it!

May 5
PREPARATION FOR ETERNITY

And he showed me a river of the water of life, clear as crystal,
coming from the throne of God and of the Lamb, in the middle of its street.
And on either side of the river was the tree of life,
bearing twelve kinds of fruit, yielding its fruit every month;
and the leaves of the tree were for the healing of the nations.
Revelation 22: 1-2

In any kind of training, we learn how to succeed at what we will do when the training is over. The better the teacher, the better the training. The more willing the pupil, the more ground covered. No training is ever absolutely complete. Some things are only learned through experience in the field. But good training enables us to begin our work, knowing that we have been taught the necessary basic skills.

Those facts above, Lord, are well known. Here is where my thoughts are this morning: I am now in the preparation stage for my *real* work. I am in school for whatever work You have waiting for me, not only in this life, but *also on the other side.* You, my Teacher, are the very best! My indwelling Private Tutor. I don't have to leave home and go to boarding school for this training because You live within me, teaching me as much as I'm able (or willing) to grasp. You lead me into all truth. You prepare me for what You know is ahead.

One thing is certain, Lord. My concept of what heaven will be like is inadequate, to say the least. I do not understand much at all about it. Evidently, with the mind, we are not capable of understanding, or maybe we don't need to understand. Either way, I see that my present task is to trust You as my Master Teacher. I am to trust that Your dealings with me here in this life are not only for this life. Many, perhaps most, of them are preparing me for my work in eternity.

Thank You for patiently teaching me. Thank You for all the instructions You've given, for the guideposts You've placed along the way to keep me on track. I love You so very much, Lord!

May 6
A SLOW PROCESS

In a new-born Christian, You begin
bit by bit
to replace ignorance with knowledge.
But knowledge, without grace, makes arrogance.

So You prompt actions to be taken
upon that new knowledge.
This we call obedience.

Many failures occur - a few successes.
Failures produce dismay and sorrow in me.
But, oh how much I learn from failing!
Failing teaches me the meaning of grace.

Successes are wonderful
but not nearly so instructive.

And slowly,
so very slowly,
knowledge turns into wisdom.

All along this slow path,
there is constant input given
and constant improvement encouraged.

When I fail, You are gentle in correcting me.
Much more gentle and patient than I am with myself.

This process takes so long, Lord!

May 7
VICTORY IN BATTLES

Stand firm therefore, having girded your loins with truth
and having put on the breastplate of righteousness,
and having shod your feet with the preparation of the gospel of peace;
in addition to all taking up the shield of faith
with which you will be able to extinguish all the flaming missiles of the evil one.
And take the helmet of salvation and the sword of the Spirit,
which is the word of God.
With all prayer and petition pray at all times in the Spirit,
and with this in view, be on the alert
with all perseverance and petition for all the saints.
Ephesians 6: 14-18

Lord, everything You have given us to do battle with is protective except the sword and prayer; the Word is our sword and we are instructed to pray always. These two alone constitute our offensive weapons.

Now, here's my question this morning: do we wait for the battle to come to us? Or, like David, do we pursue our enemies and take over their land and possessions? The children of Israel had to conquer the land of promise from the enemy. In modern day wars, often the battle is for the purpose of claiming new territory; progress means taking the offensive. But, in Ephesians 6, Lord, we are instructed over and over to stand fast and resist. So this *sounds* like our battles will come to us. I need Your help.

"Stand fast and resist is your task. You don't have any territory to take from the enemy. It has already been given to you. 'I have overcome the world.' The enemy will attack and try to take it from you, but it is yours. I have already defeated the enemy and given you the victory. Your part is to receive it, stand fast in it and don't let him steal it from you. 'All authority has been given Me in heaven and on earth.'

All the ground you defend successfully will be inner victories that lead to stronger faith and a surer foundation in My truths. Stand fast and resist with all your armor in place and, being armed with the sword and unceasing prayer, victory is assured."

I see, my Lord, once more that You have provided everything. From beginning to end, this walk of faith is one of simple trust and obedience. I try to make it harder than that, don't I? Thank You for keeping me. Thank You for your promise that You will never leave me.

May 8
THOUGHTS ON BEING A SHEEP

The Lord is my shepherd, I shall not want.
He makes me lie down in green pastures, He leads me beside the still waters.
He restores my soul; He guides me in the paths of righteousness for His name's
sake. Psalm 23:1-3

Lord, I have this strange picture of two sheep in my mind. Each is reading this well known and much loved psalm. One is a puffed up sheep with a heart full of pride. Here is how I hear him reading …

"The Lord is MY shepherd, I shall not want…Surely goodness and mercy will follow ME all the days of MY life…." The emphasis all the way through is on "I," "me," "mine." This is one smug, self-righteous sheep! Although he may never say it out loud, he has an underlying attitude that says, "God is really lucky to have me."

Many of the other animals, looking on from outside the fold, may see him as being a leader and a role model. And maybe a few of the sheep new to the fold see him in the same way. But it soon becomes clear that this loud, proud sheep is not learning what the Good Shepherd is teaching.

Then I see the second sheep with a heart full of love and humility. Gratitude overflows his spirit as he meditates on all the blessings You provide him. This sheep has a smile on his face. His emphasis is…

Love - for One who loved him first

Trust - in One who has never failed him

Security - because he is watched over by Someone strong

Praise - to One who cares for him even when he strays away, indeed, *especially* if he strays away.

You and I both know that we are not talking about sheep here, Lord. We are talking about Christians and how we can either be prideful or grateful. We can become expert at comparisons. We compare ourselves to other Christians, to sinners yet unsaved, to anyone and everyone except the One who is supposed to be our sole example. And since we can pick and choose to whom we will compare ourselves, we can come away feeling pretty good about our "righteousness." How that must grieve You!

As sad as that smug sheep is, Lord, it is even sadder to think of all the people who never come into Your fold at all. They will never come to know, never experience the love and care of the Good Shepherd. It is such an incredible privilege to be one of Your sheep! I wish everyone could understand that.

May 9
TRANSPARENCY

Arise, shine; for your light has come,
And the glory of the Lord has risen upon you.
Isaiah 60:1

Again therefore Jesus spoke to them saying, "I am the light of the world;
he who follows Me shall not walk in the darkness, but shall have the light of life."
John 8:12

Lord, I need so much to be able to shut out the world with its demands, and just be with You. I need the renewing that comes only from Your presence and Your touch upon me. I want to think about this ever-shining Light within that is You - this Light that both illuminates and warms, that causes everything within reach of its rays to be changed and to glow in reflection of its glory.

You, my Lord, took me from the path where I was walking in darkness, headed toward an even deeper darkness - an everlasting darkness - and You transported me, in an instant of time, into Your kingdom of light. If You never did another good thing in my life, that one initial blessing would be enough to praise You for all eternity! To have the darkness removed without and within. To be filled and surrounded instead with light - but not just any light - the radiance of Your glory! This is hard for my mind to grasp, but my spirit recognizes this beautiful, warm glow as Your light.

What I'm thinking this morning, Jesus, is that You don't do this marvelous work only for me to enjoy. You say in another place that we, Your followers, are also to be the light of the world. And I know that on my own, I can never be even a dim beacon much less one that will do this old world any good. The only way for me to shine effectively is for You to shine through me constantly. I must be transparent.

Lord, You have placed within me a Light
steady, glowing, shining;
and a desire to stay transparent.

This 'staying' some call walking in the Spirit,
some call holiness, or living the sanctified life,
or abiding in Jesus.

All these are correct.
And yet transparency says it best to me.
because if I am clean outside and clean inside,
Your Light will shine through, steady and glowing.

So be it, Lord.

130

May 10
CONFESSION TIME

He who conceals his transgressions will not prosper,
but he who confesses and forsakes them
will find compassion.
Proverbs 28: 13

Lord, You are showing me some things lingering in my thinking - clinging, actually - that I long to see uprooted, and forever gone. These are what A.W. Tozer calls the "hyphenated sins of self" that just continue to plague me. These self-sins, among other disgusting outcomes, can result in mixed motives and in expectations of others that do not reflect a heart submitted to You. I agree with You, my Lord, that these are present. Please forgive my wrong thinking and my slowness to reach the level of right thinking to which You are trying to elevate me.

You and I have not just now arrived at a brand new place. We have been around this mountain before. I'm tired of the scenery, Lord. I wish I could deep down *learn* this lesson so we can go forward.

"Some basic truths to absorb and remember:
Look only to Me for encouragement.
Look only to Me for correction.
Look only to Me for your sense of accomplishment or failure. What you may think is failure may be exactly My will for you.
Look only to Me for instructions.
"In other words, have My mind - see all as I see it - all people, all circumstances."

And my part is?
Submission
Obedience
Continued trust

I see, Lord, that these are very liberating truths; I am set free of needing others' favorable opinions of me. Relationships on the horizontal plane are important, but not so important that I allow other peoples' opinions and thoughts to shape me and how I see myself. That must come only from You. You want me to understand myself, my circumstances and my value from *Your* viewpoint. Ultimately, I answer only to You.

I sense that this is a very narrow path we are on right here, Lord, and there is just enough room for You and me to walk if we walk really close together. What could be better than that?! You are my Beloved. All I desire is nearness to You. Praise and thanksgiving well up in my heart, my Lord, for the fact that You love me enough to teach me this lesson over and over.

May 11
REASONS FOR PRAISE

Be Thou exalted, O Lord, in Thy strength;
we will sing and praise Thy power.
Psalm 21:13

Psalm 21 was written by King David but, strangely, so many of his reasons for praising You are also my reasons. And praise You is what I want to do this morning. Your blessings to me, Your presence with me, Your amazing grace in which I stand; all this and more make me want to praise You with all my heart, soul, mind and strength. So reading David's psalm this morning inspires me to borrow his thoughts....

In Your strength, I will be glad. You even provide strength for praising when my own meager supply runs out. In Your salvation, I will *greatly* rejoice - not just a little - a lot!

You have given me the desire of my heart. You have listened when I prayed and have not withheld answers. Many prayers You have answered in obvious ways. And I believe, Lord, in a way I don't fully understand, that *every* desire of my heart has been given. I am not able to see them all yet because I can't see further than this moment in time.

You meet me with the blessings of good things. So many good things! And the best is yet to come. I asked You for life, and You gave it to me. Life forever spent where You are. Nothing could be better than that.

You have placed within me Your glory and splendor and majesty. It is not mine. It is Yours. My entire life is lived in the warmth and glow of it. You make me most blessed and full of joy and so very glad *in Your presence*. I don't know any words capable of expressing the high regard I feel about Your presence with me, Lord. If I were to rank all the good things You have given me, it would certainly be number one on the list. And You have promised never to leave me!

I completely trust in You and in Your grace. I will never be shaken. Many circumstances of life have tried to shake me and in every one, You have kept me steadfast. Oh, we have had some battles with the enemy! And I'm sure they are not over. But I know I'm already the victor because You have given me everything I need to be victorious. You will swallow the enemy and devour him; he may plan evil for me, but he will not succeed. In Your strength and Your power, I can always overcome.

I'm very glad David wrote Psalm 21!

May 12
YOUR POWER IN ME
Part One

Now to Him who is able to do exceeding abundantly beyond all that we ask or think, according to the power that works within us, to Him be the glory in the church and in Christ Jesus to all generations forever and ever. Amen.
Ephesians 3:20-21

For the word of the cross is to those who are perishing foolishness, but to us who are being saved it is the power of God.
1 Corinthians 1:18

Paul says that You are able to do exceeding abundantly beyond all that I ask or think, according to the power that works within me. There is dynamite strength and dynamite promise in those words, Lord. Then I read his words in 1 Corinthians, and they tell me that the word of the cross is the power of God.

Now, I may not know exactly what Paul meant by the 'word of the cross' but allow me, please, to think in Your presence about this whole idea. I'm thinking, Lord, that a solid understanding of Your cross is necessary, and it seems right to me to look at it from three viewpoints:

As You, Jesus, experienced it
As You, Father God, witnessed it
As I, Your redeemed child, benefit by it.

Your obedience unto death. Your cross, Lord Jesus, is the center of our faith and understanding it, deep down in our being, is the source of spiritual power. Without Your death and resurrection, there would be no power at all in our faith. No other religion has a God who lived, died for a specific purpose, and lived again. Probably Your death, burial and resurrection are the most well-known facts about Your life by the "un-churched." And yet, though what You did is so well known, it is yet so *unknown*. I have heard preachers preach on this subject all my life. I have numerous times read the Gospel writers' accounts of that last week in Your earthly life. I have seen the "Passion of the Christ." I sat in the theater and cried while my heart ached for the abuse and pain You experienced.

But what You endured was so much more than the horrific physical pain; there was the separation - the darkness of soul that came to You at being separated from the Father - the sense of being forsaken, for the first time ever, by Him. To me, Lord, that is far worse than any physical pain. I cannot imagine a more awful condition than to be forsaken by You! And yet, You chose to do the Father's will, leaving heaven and becoming a man, knowing all that was ahead of You. How incredible! What kind of love is behind such a sacrifice?! My mind cannot grasp it.

May 13
YOUR POWER IN ME
Part Two

The heartache of God. I can only begin to know the grieving of Your heart, Father God, as You watched Your Beloved Son go through all that rejection, abuse and pain. And then to be totally separated from Him for a time. That had to be as heartbreaking for You as it was for Him. Most earthly parents would much rather suffer themselves than see their child suffer. Even unto death. How much more for You who are all-knowing. And yet You chose to stand by and watch, feeling the agony of Your Son as if it were Your own.

I cannot know how much Jesus dreaded what was ahead of Him, but however much He endured in looking ahead, You also endured. I get lost in awe as I think about Your sovereign power, Your limitless intelligence, Your boundless creative power. I'm sure, Father, that the Three of You could have come up with another plan that did not involve such pain and suffering! And yet this is what You chose to do. And behind it all was love. Your everlasting love for this creature You fashioned and called mankind. Love that kept loving in spite of our unworthiness and our wickedness. Maybe the plan had to be something that would touch us to the depths of our being as we meditated on it, something that would convince us of a love past understanding. Redeeming love - our song for all eternity!

The redemption of Your children. I do have some understanding of what it means to be redeemed. I have been Your child for many years now and each year that passes, I grow more thankful for Your saving grace. I'm certain that heaven will be more wonderful than I can imagine and hell much worse than I can know. Yet redemption is more than avoiding hell and getting to heaven. *Today's* benefits of redemption are to be highly valued: the freedom from sin's penalty and power over me, the joy of fellowship with You, the peace of mind that sustains me, the love that we exchange, these and a thousand other gifts are all a result of being redeemed.

And redemption could not have happened except for the cross. These thoughts are very simplistic I know, Lord. There are many mysteries tied up in all of this. The mystery of Your existence outside of time, from before You created all that is; the mystery of a love so great that it created a way for us to become again how You created us in the beginning; the incredible mystery of Your Spirit indwelling and changing us from the inside; the mystery of this plan of redemption that was laid before the foundation of the world. My only response can be to praise You for being the awesome God that You are!

Your *love* for me is the eternal well-spring of power in my life. From that unending source comes everything needed to do Your work and Your will. The more I understand and meditate upon it, the more love for You and for my fellow man is created in my heart. And at the end of the day, that *is* Your will for all of us. It's all about love.

134

May 14
WHEAT AND TARES

The kingdom of heaven may be compared to a man
who sowed good seed in his field.
But while men were sleeping, his enemy came
and sowed tares also among the wheat, and went away.
Matthew 13:24-25

I just read that Scripture, Lord, and am seeing, for the first time, a truth that has always been there but I've missed until now. Somehow I skimmed over Your explanation and thought that the good seed were the truths of Your Kingdom and the tares were the work of Satan in attempting to destroy Your Kingdom.

But in explaining this story, You tell the disciples that the good seed (the wheat) are the sons of the kingdom of God and the bad seed (the tares) are the sons of the evil one. So that means that I'm a good seed! And all my Christian brothers and sisters are good seeds in the midst of the tares! And if we produced enough good seeds, the wheat would outgrow the tares. That is our mission, our reason for being - to die, sprout, grow up and produce *an overflowing quantity* of good seeds.

I think about the abundance You supply in nature -
in a watermelon with its dozens of seed,
a cantaloupe with its hundreds of seed,
an oak tree with its thousands of acorns
and each seed with the potential to produce many times again that much. Such lavish supply! This gives me a vision of what You want my life to be and what You will do with me if I will surrender and obey.

Now that I understand that both the good and bad seeds are people, a note in the margin of my Bible further expands my understanding. It says that tares are weeds that closely resemble wheat. I know some very kind, moral, generous people who are not saved. I also know some who profess salvation yet live like they're lost. So, like the tares and the wheat, they can appear very similar to each other. It would be easy to get confused if we had to decide what to pull up and what to leave. Thankfully, it is not the wheat's job to weed out the tares. The landowner's instruction to his slaves is to let them alone and allow them to grow together until the end of the age. Then the angels will do the reaping and the separating.

The Son of Man will send forth His angels,
and they will gather out of His kingdom all stumbling blocks,
and those who commit lawlessness, and will cast them into the furnace of fire.
Then the righteous will shine forth as the sun in the kingdom of their Father.
He who has ears, let him hear.
Matthew 13:41 and 43

May 15
EARLY MEDITATIONS

Therefore having been justified by faith,
we have peace with God through our Lord Jesus Christ,
through whom also we have obtained our introduction by faith
into the grace in which we stand;
and we exult in hope of the glory of God.
Romans 5:1-2

It is now five a.m. and I have been awake since three a.m. What a blessed thing it is, Lord, to wake into Your presence! My heart sings the old hymns; I read and think and talk to You about it all. You, my Lord, are the joy of my life.

I think about the places of surrender to which You brought me, the struggles I went through before surrendering, and then the immense peace that followed. I think about the strength my spirit gained through conflicts won while learning to endure. I think about the joy that came from sacrifice. I think about the incredible sense of freedom when You liberated me from the tyranny of my own will.

In all these instances, Lord, there were battles and hardships and choices to make, and it was difficult and painful. Yet, looking back from this vantage point, I'm mostly aware of two things:

First, Your Word says these are "light and temporary burdens," and second, they are achieving an eternal and weighty glory in eternity. This is a wonderful promise. I'm looking forward to seeing what is waiting for us in heaven. Only You know how eagerly I anticipate the life to come. It *feels* like being homesick, and I guess that's not too strange because that really *is* my home. The longer I walk with You, the more I feel like a misfit in this dark world. You have given me such a foretaste of glory by allowing me to draw near to You that I long to be there rather than here. You have gathered to Yourself so many of the people I have loved, and I'm eager to see them again. So this is my bright hope. But the second is, to me, just as bright...

Through these troublesome and hurtful times, You taught me to stay on my knees before You, to depend upon You, to realize I did not have strength enough to handle life on my own. You taught me that *You love me* and also how to love You in return. You taught me that You will never leave me. These alone are worth every sorrow, conflict and heartache that came with total surrender to You. I know, Lord, that the only way I would ever have allowed You to make me whole was by showing me how truly broken I was.

So, my Lord, my todays are blessed with Your sweet presence and my future is bright with happy expectation. How good You are to me. I'm so looking forward to seeing You - to stand before You and look into Your beautiful face and tell You in person how much I love You. That will be glory!

May 16
A LITTLE POEM FROM YESTERDAY'S MEDITATION

Sadness and Joy

Age brings within my heart
a strange mixture of
joy and sadness,
sadness and joy.

Sadness that most of my earthly
life is gone;
Joy that my coming home to You
is nearer than ever.

Sadness in recalling missed
opportunities to love;
Joy in ones that were taken,
those that are present and those yet to come.

Sadness that physical pain and fatigue
prevent my doing all I want;
Joy that my spirit is whole
and strong and constantly renewed.

Sadness that I have no mortal
person with whom to share my heart;
Joy that You, my Immortal Beloved,
know my deepest thoughts.

Because of You, Lord,
the joy makes even the sadness
glow with a holy light.
How blessed I am to be Your child!

May 17
FAITHFULNESS

I thank Christ Jesus our Lord,
who has strengthened me,
because He considered me faithful,
putting me into service.
I Timothy 1:12

Today, faithfulness is a very convicting subject to this child! I ask Your forgiveness, Lord, both for my slowness to learn and, what is worse, my sometimes deliberate refusal to yield. I see my present-day struggles as another chance to learn the same lesson that the circumstances of past years were trying to teach me. The situation is far different, but the lesson is the same. Here is what I am hearing You say:

"Acknowledge My sovereignty.
Worship even in the hard circumstances.
Yield fully to Me.
Do not murmur and complain.
Expect no explanation from Me, just trust.
Be thankful and joyful."

It is clear to me now what I must do. Through a lot of my yesterdays, all I knew to do was cling to Your hand and ask for help. And You were faithful! You delivered me *out* of a few things and *through* many things, and I know that my own actions were not always pleasing. *But You were faithful.* How can I not love You?!

"And see, My child, that those things listed above would seem harsh and demanding coming from a tyrant. But given, as they are, from My heart of love with the intention of only good, *eternal* good, look upon them as beautiful and blessed and glorious."

I do see, Lord. You have once again directed my thoughts into a path I had not intended. I started out to confess my unfaithfulness to You and ended up acknowledging Your faithfulness to me! And it occurs to me that maybe that's all I was supposed to learn in years past - *that You are, and always will be, faithful.* It certainly is a vital and wonderful thing to know. My grateful heart is full of praise for Your glorious grace upon this unworthy specimen.

May 18
ATTITUDE TOWARD OTHERS

Do not judge lest you be judged.
For in the way you judge, you will be judged;
and by your standard of measure,
it will be measured to you.
Matthew 7: 1-2

I'm thinking this morning that I may need an attitude adjustment, Lord. I tend to drift toward thinking that everyone should have the same values that I do. And as I was sitting here mentally listing all the ways others were failing to live up to my standards, Your gentle, correcting voice reminded me of some important truths...

"Your values, My child, are yours as the result of many years of experience. You cannot expect others to have the same ones. Your past has shaped you and made you who you are just as others have been shaped by their past experiences. What you are doing, truly, is judging and I think My words above are clear on that subject. You need to simply relax and rejoice (have you heard *that* before?) and leave others to Me. Don't try to do My job."

Thank You, Lord, for that rebuke. That is actually a liberating thought. It is not my responsibility to see that other people meet some goal just because that goal is mine. So I can focus on You. I can focus on taking care of my own business.

I also know from experience that You are well able to make it plain to me if You need my help with someone else. (Smile)

May 19
OBEDIENCE

For whoever does the will of My Father who is in heaven,
he is My brother and sister and mother.
Matthew 12:50

I just read those words of Yours, "whoever does the will of My Father." The key word is *does*. You did not say "whoever *knows*." The Pharisees knew but did not live out what they knew. You called them hypocrites and white-washed tombs. To their face!

Lord, You know I consider it a high and holy privilege to be a part of Your family. And You know I have always hated hypocrisy. Being a person of integrity has always been especially important to me - to be transparent, to have nothing hidden or secret from You. I'm sure the root cause of this is Your Spirit at work in me. And this morning it is making me desire to settle an issue with You.

Please look within my heart, Lord, and see that there is *nothing* more important to me than my close relationship with You. You have already shown me that the underlying cause of the disturbing incident yesterday was a self-sin. So that is what I'm recognizing and confessing. I am learning more and more how truly despicable these self-sins are. The closer I get to You, the more I abhor them! I would love to once-and-for-all renounce them and turn and walk away, never to be bothered with them again. But Your plan seems to be small advances, one victory at a time, like driving out the heathen nations before the children of Israel. So I guess this is one more battle to be fought.

Please, Lord as I am walking in the light, help me to remember that it is *Your* light, not the light of my conscience, to which I need to be paying attention. We both know my conscience is sensitive to the point of hypochondria. I am slowly learning to ignore it and hear only Your voice. Help me do that with this battle.

You are such an amazing God! So full of mercy and grace, and yet so holy and powerful that it terrifies me. Awesome and fearful You are. Yet the deepest yearning of my spirit is to draw ever nearer to You. That is where I can learn more of You. That is where I can bow before You in worship.

May 20
TESTING TIME

And a poor widow came and put in two small copper coins,
which amount to a cent.
And calling His disciples to Him, He said to them,
"Truly I say to you this poor widow put in
more than all the contributors to the treasury;
for they all put in out of their surplus, but she, out of her poverty,
put in all she owned,
all she had to live on."
Mark 12:42-44

I've got to talk to You about this, Lord, because it is weighing heavily on my heart. I see that I'm getting a lesson from You in "Don't Make Vows Unless You Mean Them." This small incident yesterday is very insignificant in the eternal scheme of things, but You are using it to teach some eternally important truths:

I have *said* that I believe You are Most High God, sovereign over everything.

I have *said* that I want to be used up in doing whatever You want me to do.

I have *said* that I want You to be in control of my life and the details of it.

Then along comes yesterday's situation and my first thought is selfish. "Just what I need! Something else to make demands on my already small supply of energy!"

Almost immediately the questions started:

"Do you really believe that I am sovereign over all?

Did you mean what you said about being used up?

Are you still fighting for control or have you actually given it to Me?

Are all of those nice words just nice words, or can you now stand by them in real life?

Do you, in fact, trust Me or is that simply wishful thinking?

Am I unable to provide for you *whatever* is needed?"

Then this morning I opened my Bible to where I have been reading in Mark, and there was the story of the widow who put the last of her money in the church offering. Out of her poverty she gave all she had. Talk about convicting! You know, Lord, that my poverty is not of money but of energy. But the principle is exactly the same. Just as that widow gave all she had, trusting You for future provision, I need to do the same. If this is how You choose for me to use my time and energy, who am I to question or complain? You *are* well able to provide whatever I need. So I apologize, Lord. I confess my self-centered attitude. By Your grace, I will do whatever You want done, and I will depend on You for strength and energy to do it.

May 21
THE PRIDE PROBLEM

Pride goes before destruction,
and a haughty spirit before stumbling.
Proverbs 16:18

Webster's definition of pride is "a high or inordinate opinion of one's own dignity, importance, merit, or superiority; an unduly favorable idea of one's own appearance, advantages, achievements; often an arrogant assumption of superiority in some respect; an exaggerated estimate of one's own attainments."

Not a pretty picture. Your Word, Lord, also has quite a bit to say about pride, and what it will do in a life if left unchecked. But what led me to thinking about pride this morning is its connection with my search for joy. Only You and I are fully aware of my tendency toward depression. For quite a while now, You have been revealing to me what is needed to be joy-full. And what I'm seeing this morning is that pride is the foundation and root for *all* the self-sins to which I am to die. Growing from that root of pride is self-pity which in turn, is closely linked with depression. Pride is ugly, and its fruit of self-pity is foul and disgusting! I know this because there was a time when my life bore much of that fruit. I want never to be there again!

I'm not sure if this is true of all Your children, but the self-sins are the ones I most frequently battle. So this is enlightening to me; if I allow You to kill off every root of pride in my heart, the self-sins will simply die for lack of nourishment.

Oh, Lord, I see a new-to-me truth here! If pride is the root of the self-sins, then humility is the root of the fruit of Your Spirit - love, joy, peace, patience, kindness, goodness, faithfulness, gentleness, self-control. You uproot the pride and in its place, You plant humility. You do the work, I allow Your power to flow unhindered through me.

I need to see myself as I am, simply one of Your created beings.

I need to see You as You are - the all-powerful, sovereign, merciful God.

Then I need to be filled with abundant gratitude and praise for Your amazing love which loves me in spite of myself. Those thoughts fill me with humility and wonder at Your grace.

May 22
SEEING YOUR POWER

For Thou art the Lord Most High over all the earth;
Thou art exalted far above all gods.
Psalm 97: 9

My lessons from You this morning have to do with Your power. I read first in 1 Samuel 19 about Your power over all men. Then I read in Psalm 97 about Your power as God Most High to change the hearts of men, then in Luke 23 about the incredible events of the day You were crucified, Your awesome, terrifying power! My first thought was, why do we not see that display of power today? You have not changed. You will never change. Certainly we are needy.

Here is what I understand:

The men in 1 Samuel 19 who came under Your power gave *outward* signs by prophesying. The things that occurred on the day You were crucified (darkness in the middle of the day, earthquake, veil in the temple tearing from top to bottom, resurrection of some dead) were *visible* things that only You could do. And in both instances, Your purpose was to show to all who would see, the power of God Most High - El Shaddai. Many did see, and perhaps many were changed by what they saw.

But I think the answer to my question about seeing Your power today is in the Psalm.

Light is sown like seed for the righteous,
and gladness for the upright in heart.
Be glad in the Lord, you righteous ones;
and give thanks to His holy name.
Psalm 97:11-12

Your power *is* still at work in the world in a mighty way. But since Your death and resurrection, since the giving of the Holy Spirit, it is working quietly, one person at a time, sowing light and gladness like seed in a heart, changing that person from the inside out. And here is the good part - that is even more miraculous and phenomenal than the outward demonstration of Your power! Only Your power can take a dark and sinful heart, work from within and make it righteous, full of light and gladness.

Oh Lord, I am so apt to take this for granted, yet to think of it staggers the mind. That the Almighty God who created the universe and keeps it running, literally like clockwork, lives within this ordinary weak human and loves, teaches, corrects, and forgives me. But this is the gospel. This is Your new covenant with us! May I never overlook how incredibly wonderful this is and how much it cost You to accomplish it. How *great* is the power of the indwelling Holy Spirit! How amazing is this grace in which I stand. I shall be glad in You, my Lord, and give thanks to Your holy name.

May 23
THE FATHER OF LIES

Be of sober spirit, be on the alert.
Your adversary, the devil, prowls about like a roaring lion,
seeking someone to devour.
But resist him, firm in your faith,
knowing that the same experiences of suffering are being accomplished
by your brethren who are in the world.
I Peter 5:8-9

Here is my latest lesson learned - You have already provided me with everything I need in order to do what You have given me to do, even if the task seems beyond my strength. Satan's best weapon against me is deception, and he is highly skilled at using it. So, my job is to *know* what You have given me and to put it to use on a daily basis. I must be aware that lies, discouraging thoughts and questions designed to make me doubt You are Satan's attempts to derail my faith. Awareness! That is so important! Stay alert for his lies.

Here is a time when the power to choose is truly awesome. My "fork in the road" is either to take the bait Satan drops into my mind and allow it to discourage me, hurt me, distress me in some way, or simply hand it to You and say something like, "Lord, You see the hurt in my heart because of this. Please work to remedy this situation as You choose."

I may not always know Your immediate purpose for allowing hurtful circumstances in my life, but I do always know Your underlying motive. And that is love. Everything You do and everything You allow in the life of a child of Yours is motivated by Your eternal love. It took me many years and many heartaches to learn that lesson. But You taught it well, and I do not intend to ever forget it. I know that Your Word is eternally true. I can stake my very life on it.

May this small battle won be the opening of a larger space within me for Your joy to rule.

May 24
DELIVERANCE FROM THE ENEMY

Blessed be the Lord, who daily bears our burden,
the God who is our salvation.
God is to us a God of deliverances;
and to God the Lord belong escapes from death.
Psalm 68:19-20

Lord, I just read in Psalm 44 some wonderful words I want to paraphrase and make our own - Yours and mine.

You are my King, O God; command victories for me.
Through You I will push back my adversaries;
through Your name I will trample down
those who rise up against me.
For I will not trust in my strength
nor will my power help me.
But You have saved me from my adversary
and You have put to shame those who hate me.
In You I have boasted all day long
and I will give thanks to Your name forever.

I have no physical adversaries like the Psalmist did, Lord, but I do have spiritual enemies who hate me and seek to destroy me. I know of specific times in my life when You have delivered me from harm, and certainly there are times in my past that You protected and delivered me from dangers unknown to me. Truly, You are my King and I do boast of You. I know that Your power is greater than any weapon the enemy can use. I know Your promise of protection is trustworthy. I know Your love envelops me and holds me and warms me. I know I shall be victorious *because of You.*

And then in Psalm 68 again…

O God, Thou art awesome from Thy sanctuary.
The God of Israel Himself
gives strength and power to the people.
Blessed be God!
Psalm 68:35

How thankful I am, Lord, that I may lean upon Your strength and power! Because of that, I have no fear of the future. My heart's desire is to honor, praise and exalt You with my life. So be it.

May 25
LEARNING THROUGH ADVERSITY

They band themselves together against the life of the righteous,
and condemn the innocent to death.
But the Lord has been my stronghold,
and my God the rock of my refuge.
Psalm 94: 21-22

This psalm has some notable words of assurance in it, Lord, which I want to think about in Your presence this morning (paraphrased):

Blessed is the child You correct, O Lord,
and teach out of Your law;
that You may grant them relief from the days of adversity
until a pit is dug for the wicked.
For You will not abandon Your children
nor will You forsake Your inheritance.
Verses 12-14

In the midst of correction and learning a lesson, I don't always feel "blessed," but these verses say I am. They also say *why*. You are faithful to correct and teach me so that You can then either take me out of the situation, or walk me on through it. Your sure promise is that You will never just go away and leave me alone. Though I may feel as if You have, still You are present and working. What a tremendous truth to know!

Truly it is the power of Your love that causes Your children to be melted, poured out and reshaped into what You choose. And it is this love that grows within us to the point that we become full of it and emptied of self. That is our ultimate goal, isn't it, Lord? To be totally empty of self and full to running over with Your love. Then when we get into tight places in the days of adversity, we look inside for help and there it is!

Thank You for these beautiful words to feed my spirit this morning.

May 26
CONTROL ISSUES
(Again)

Come, let us worship and bow down;
let us kneel before the Lord our Maker.
For He is our God,
and we are the people of His pasture,
and the sheep of His hand.
Psalm 95: 6-7

My life seems to be a series of problems to solve, many of which are beyond my ability to control. These drive me to my knees and into Your presence, Lord, just as these verses say, and this is a good thing. I *am* Your child, Your sheep, and You are my God. I so much welcome Your work in my life.

So why do I still become frustrated in every new situation? What is going on in this brain of mine? Please help me as I think through this in Your presence.

In all problem situations, human instinct is either "fight or flight." Instincts are, by definition, built into us as a part of our hardwired control panel. And I can testify to the truth of the fight or flight concept. My first thought in every unpleasant situation is *escape* - get me out of this! And if that is not possible, then my next thought is, "How can I fight this thing?"

Here is the frustration. Even though I have given You control of my present and my future, when a new crisis pops up in my life, the "fight or flight" instinct also kicks in. But because I have submitted *all* decisions to You, neither of those is the clear, immediate answer for me any longer. So I'm frustrated that I can't be in control, and I'm frustrated that You work at Your own pace, rather than on my desired schedule. And then I'm disappointed with myself for feeling those frustrations, because I see that You are simply doing what I have asked You to do! Which is, make me like You.

You continue moving deeper into my will, conquering and claiming for Yourself more and more of me. And, Lord, with all my heart I welcome that and invite You to continue. Help me remember the lessons of the past and apply them to the present. Please allow me to place this whole bundle of 'me and my wants' into Your keeping, knowing that is the safest, most secure place I could ever be. You will work things out far better than I could if You were to give me full decision-making powers.

Now, that's a scary thought, Lord, my having full decision-making powers! I take my hands off and leave it all to You. I ask only for grace to live each day with patience, kindness and Your blessed presence. Thank You for not giving me control. Again.

147

May 27
A BROKEN HEART ON A BAD DAY

In everything give thanks;
for this is God's will for you in Christ Jesus.
1 Thessalonians 5:18

"Do you want My will in your life?"
Yes, Lord.
"Then this simple instruction must be obeyed."
It is too hard!
"Have I said it would be easy?"
No, Lord, but I feel today that it is not even possible.
"Have I ever failed you? In all the many ways you have trusted Me, have I ever let you down?"
No, my Lord. I know You can be depended on to do Your part because You are faithful. But I also know You will not do Your part until or unless I do mine. And I'm seeing that mine is an attitude of the heart that needs "fixing." You must do the fixing, but I must agree to it and even ask You to do it. Oh God, give me the strength to ask! What will it take to fix this hurt in my heart?
"Trust...
- that I am in control of the world and of your life
- that I see the whole picture, from beginning to end
- that I reward those who love me
- that I have supplied for all your needs.
"Obey...
- by coming to Me for rest
- by turning loose of your own ideas on how things *should* be
- by allowing Me to renew your mind in My way
- by permitting Me to apply My salve to your aching heart."
Trust and obey - just like the old hymn...

> "Trust and obey,
> for there's no other way,
> to be happy in Jesus,
> but to trust and obey."

Thank You, Lord! The simplicity of Your grace is beautiful. Relax and rejoice.

May 28
YOUR PROVISION OF PEACE

Be anxious for nothing, but in everything
by prayer and supplication with thanksgiving
let your requests be made known to God.
And the peace of God,
which surpasses all comprehension,
shall guard your hearts and your minds in Christ Jesus.
Philippians 4: 6-7

These words, Lord, are some of the most precious in all the Bible to me. I so often need to be reminded that Your peace is available if I will only come to You and talk to You about what is bothering me. You have taught me that it is impossible to feel anxious and thankful at the same time. This morning, I don't really feel anxious so much as unsettled, but I know that these words of wisdom apply to that, too.

So here is what is making me feel unsettled - I am always wanting something for which I am not yet ready. From the very first day of my walk with You, I have looked far down the road and said, "Lord, *that's* where I want to be." Even in this present day, I'm looking ahead to times/things that are Yours alone to determine, and I'm focusing on them rather than where we are *this* day. Maybe some looking ahead is beneficial because it keeps me going in the right direction. but too much of it robs me of the joy of today.

"Yes, it is good to have your destination in mind. But to constantly look ahead and want *that* is to miss the good in *this* moment. Always looking far ahead takes your eyes off the path and off Me, and makes you more likely to stumble. Wanting what you don't yet have makes you discontented with where you are. You miss the fragrance and beauty of all that is around you. You fail to hear the music surrounding the present moment. You miss opportunities to express My love to others in your life *today*.

"My advice to You is to relax and rejoice. These are familiar words by now, but I use them again because you are still learning how to follow them. Slow down, take a deep breath, enjoy the sacredness of each moment of your life. Feel the joy in every small blessing that comes your way and don't be so anxious to get down the road. All things in good time."

Thank You, Lord, for slowing me down again and reminding me to enjoy life as it is. I'm sorry I'm so driven. Give me wisdom to actually live out the good that I know. You are an awesome Teacher, Guide and Companion on this journey! I give You full control of the speed at which we travel.

May 29
DAILY LIVING

Whatever you do, do your work heartily,
as for the Lord rather than for men;
knowing that from the Lord
you will receive the reward of the inheritance.
It is the Lord Christ whom you serve.
Colossians 3:23-24

After a night of not sleeping very well, I woke up this morning tired and a bit depressed. I searched around within for Your Presence and did not instantly sense it. But I *did* immediately have the thought, "It matters not at all *what* I feel or *how* I feel; God is faithful to His promise to be always with me," and that was the end of the depression. Your love flooded through my spirit with such joy and peace that I just had to write it down.

Then, while reading Your Word, the thought came to mind that living is much harder than dying. Now, I know that's not original, Lord. But it startled me in its truth. So much of life is made up of menial little drudgeries that seem to have little or no significance; certainly there is no obvious eternal importance to them. But You have taught that the faithful doing of them pleases You, and that faithfulness-to-small-things works to develop our character. In those verses above, You taught that we are to do our work, whatever it is, as unto You rather than unto men. So it *is* eternally important to do what You have put before me with a glad and thankful spirit. This, somehow, is not always an easy task for me. Living is just so *daily,* so seemingly without relief from the constant pain and fatigue.

But I see that this, my Lord, is exactly what makes me draw upon Your grace every moment. I must constantly ask You for quietness of mind, for gentleness, for strength and joy. And maybe that is exactly what You are trying to teach me - that I *must* look to You every moment of every day for what I need in order to live pleasing to You.

What I know for certain is that when I depend upon You, You are faithful to provide. When I fail to depend on You, I fail. Period.

I know that my days upon earth are finite, and I look forward to what You have prepared for me there. That will be the easy part. But in the meantime, You have given me work to do here. Help me live this day, Lord, with my eyes on You and my heart wide open to Your grace.

May 30
CONSISTENT PRAYER
Part One

And it was at this time that He went off to the mountain to pray,
and He spent the whole night in prayer to God.
Luke 6:12

As I read those words this morning, Lord, I realize anew how important it is to pray. "Important" really is too weak a word - a better one might be "vital" or "crucial." Please think Your thoughts in me as I confess my failures and as I reaffirm my trust in Your love. How comforting to know, in this evil and violent world, that I am shadowed over by Your almighty power, and that absolutely nothing can reach me without Your knowing and allowing it. How awesome is the width, depth and height of Your love. But how little I avail myself of it.

I see, Lord, that I sometimes exist on crackers and water when there is a feast spread out for me in the next room. And I believe that the door to that room is prayer. Yet I find it so challenging at times to be consistent in praying. What is it that prevents prayer?

Not enough time.

Distractions.

Laziness.

No place to be alone.

These four seem to be the sticking points in my life. Please help me be honest with You and with myself.

Not enough time - Since I must be at work by 8 A.M., I have set my meditation/prayer time for 5 A.M. This allows me an unrushed hour with You. If I stay in bed too long, I am saying that a little extra sleep is more important to me than spending time in Your presence. That may sound harsh, but it honestly is at the heart of it. It is a matter of choosing who will have priority in my life - me or You. If I could only impress upon my mind once and for all that *I* am the loser when I omit prayer time. Praying is not something *You* need, it is something *I* need - in fact, must have to be spiritually healthy.

Distractions - This is a constant. My own mind is difficult to control, and the enemy stands ready to distract me, interjecting thoughts to get me off track, Lord. But You have given me power over the enemy through Your Name. I must exercise it, however. It is not automatic. These distracting thoughts can also be handed over to You one-by-one as they occur so that the spirit and mood of prayer is not broken. I think, too, Lord that the consistent discipline of prayer will develop within me the ability to better control my thoughts. It is a skill which will improve with practice, especially when blessed with Your grace and mercy. To further deal with distraction, You have greatly blessed me in this discipline of journaling. When writing, I think more clearly and maintain my train of thought more easily.

May 31
CONSISTENT PRAYER
Part Two

Laziness - This one is tough because it truly is work to pray, and the flesh does not like to do work. I can get up at 5 A.M. and then spend our whole hour in whatever good book I'm reading at the time.. I confess that I have done this, Lord. It is so much easier to read than to pray. Now, reading is good and good reading is better than sleeping, but my early morning reading should serve only one purpose - to lead me into Your very presence and help begin our conversation. *Talking directly to You and being still in Your presence to listen is the absolute best!* Only by Your grace, Lord, can my mind be convinced that the "sacrifice" of effort and persistence is worth it; that the reward of prayer is a closer relationship with You and a consistent witness of my love for You. Again, it is my choice.

No place to be alone - This simple thing can be a problem, Lord. I remember reading that Susannah Wesley, who had a large number of children, simply put her apron over her face and head, and that was her prayer place. Her children knew not to bother her then. Fortunately, You did not bless me with so many children, but solitude is still hard to come by. That's another reason I've been so thankful that You taught me to journal. Because even if another person is in the room with me, when I'm immersed in writing to You and listening to You, *I have solitude.* The imaginary walls around me shut out the world, and only You and I exist within them.

That awesome power of choice! It places a lot of responsibility on me, Lord. You have provided all that I need, but I must choose to take it. I probably could find a myriad of excuses to try to justify not spending time with You. But the deep down truth is that they would be nothing but dust in my mouth on that day when I stand before You. Oh, Lord, on that day, may I be able to look into Your beautiful face and with spoken words and silent tears, thank You for loving me throughout all my days on earth. This is my heartfelt desire. My heart beats faster just thinking about it! This is my goal! To not have to hang my head in shame on that day. To simply confess this truth - "I can stand before You, my Jesus, only because of Your saving grace." Glory!

June 1
MY HOPE

This hope we have as an anchor of the soul,
a hope both sure and steadfast
and one which enters within the veil.
Hebrews 6:19

You, Lord, are my Anchor.
You are my Hope.
You are both sure and steadfast.
You are the Eternal God
who has entered within the veil on my behalf.

Thinking on these truths brings
a peaceful heart
and a calm mind.
Even my body relaxes.

In the rush of everyday life
I can begin to think I am called upon
to be everything to everyone,
knowing I shall fail miserably
at this impossible task.

It was never Your intent that I live this life
in my strength.
Your plan from the beginning
was that I would rely upon You.

This hope is not wishful thinking, Lord.
Nor is it only for the future.
It is an earnest *expectation* of Your blessing
every moment of every day.

You, Yourself have instilled this expectation in me.

"My hope is built on nothing less than Jesus' blood and righteousness."

June 2
RUNNING THE RACE

Therefore, since we have so great a cloud of witnesses surrounding us,
let us also lay aside every encumbrance, and the sin which so easily entangles us,
and let us run with endurance the race that is set before us.
Hebrews 12:1

Oh Lord, that verse speaks volumes to me! Please help me sort out the thoughts colliding in my mind and put them in some kind of order.

First, the fact that the departed may be witnesses to our journey. What a stupendous thought that is! What an encouragement to put into practice all that You have taught me!

"Encumbrance" - per Webster*: something useless or superfluous; a burden; a hindrance.* I see, Lord, that a determined-to-win runner would never carry anything that was unnecessary, would weigh him down and could cause him to lose the race. Am I not a determined-to-win runner? Yes, I am. There are undoubtedly things in my life that use my time without giving any lasting benefit, or activities that squander my energy without accomplishing anything of value. May I be honest in my evaluation of them.

Then we talk about "sin" - All sin is an encumbrance but not all encumbrances are necessarily sin. To me, Lord, sin is *anything* that comes between You and me. The good news is You will not allow me to continue sinning in ignorance. You are faithful to show my sin to me, bring me under conviction and make me victorious over it.

"Endurance" - continuing to run until I reach my destination. No sitting down and camping at some pleasant spot along the way; no whining that it is too hot, or I am too tired or this is too hard; remembering that endurance is coupled with patience - not just gritting my teeth and plodding my way on through life. No, endurance involves following Your running rules. And that means I'm to be bearing the fruit of the Spirit all along the way. Grumpiness is not one of them.

Now comes "the race that is set before us." I'm thinking, Lord, that the race You have set before me is specifically mine, just as the race you have set before each of my brothers and sisters is specifically theirs. We all have the same destination, but You have laid out our individual courses through many different terrains, climates and distances. That's why I am so safe allowing You to make decisions on this journey. You *know* what is up ahead, and I don't, so looking to You is the wisest thing I can do. Thank You for the grace which supplies my stamina and determination to finish this race with You. My grateful heart runs over with joy at the thought of the rest of our journey.

June 3
SOME THOUGHTS ON PRIDE

Submit therefore to God.
Resist the devil and he will flee from you.
Draw near to God and He will draw near to you.
Cleanse your hands, you sinners;
and purify your hearts, you double-minded.
Be miserable and mourn and weep;
let your laughter be turned into mourning, and your joy to gloom.
Humble yourselves in the presence of the Lord, and He will exalt you.
James 4: 7-10

The first five verses of this chapter in James concern things we are to avoid. Things like quarrels, lust, envy, wrong motives and friendship with the world. Then in verse 6 he says, *"But He gives a greater grace. Therefore it says, 'God is opposed to the proud, but gives grace to the humble.'"*

Now, there are two things of which I'm certain, Lord: (1) I do NOT want You to be opposed to me, and (2) I am very needy of Your grace. Thinking about the problem of pride - how sneaky it is, how deadly, how the enemy is always attempting to lure me into it, how my own nature is already bent that way, and how often I've failed in attempts to control it myself. Finally, I know that truly it is only Your "greater grace" that will free me from pride. Please help me think through these instructions You gave through James to fully understand living in this greater grace.

Submit to God - presupposes belief in Your Word and Your goodness

Resist the devil - I must *recognize* his tactics

Draw near to God - truly the only safe place to be

Cleanse your hands - my outward behavior

Purify your heart - my mind/will/heart given to You (where behavior originates)

Be sad and sorrowful - about my sin (see sin as You see it)

Humble yourself in the presence of God - and I am full circle back to the top.

In a few words, Lord, James outlines the simplicity of walking humbly with You. I tend to always make things harder than necessary. Help me keep these beautiful, clear words in my thinking today so that my focus will be on You rather than me. That will take care of pride, and You will be glorified - which is exactly what I want.

June 4
WRONG THINKING

...for I have learned to be content in whatever circumstances I am.
Philippians 4:11

Lord, You are showing me that discontent is, at the heart of it, sin. If I am discontent with even one thing, I am saying to You that You are not doing a very good job, and I could do much better if I were in charge. What arrogance against a wise and loving God! I see that being discontented is actually a form of rebellion, and rebellion grieves Your heart. Your desire is for me to accept things - all things - as coming directly from Your hand and to be thankful. How wrong my thinking can get.

For instance, I can dwell upon what I consider an unfair or uncomfortable situation, play the role of victim and soon have myself full of self-pity - the most disgusting frame of mind possible. I can play and replay the mental tapes that tell me how difficult it all is. This may gratify self; it surely makes the devil happy, but it is *not* pleasing to You, Lord. Seeing it in the cold light of day makes me realize how truly abhorrent these attitudes are. Please help me see Your wisdom in preventing this.

"The time to cease wrong thinking is at the introduction of the thought to your mind. It matters not at all whether it is from your own thinking or a suggestion of the enemy. Do not entertain it for a moment once you recognize it for what it is - a way of thinking that leads to heartache, sorrow and eventually depression. Simply make the choice to turn full face to Me with words of thanksgiving for everything in your life. This is truly a sacrifice of thanksgiving at first, but you will find that with a consistently thankful attitude, your whole mind set changes and you begin to see all of your life in a different light.

"You must understand, My child, that My instructions are all given to you for *your* good. The life I want for you is one filled with peace and joy and contentment, no matter what your circumstances are at any given moment. I can do this for you but only if you obey my Word."

Finally, brethren, whatever is true, whatever is honorable, whatever is right,
whatever is pure, whatever is lovely, whatever is of good repute, if there is any
excellence and if anything worthy of praise, let your mind dwell on these things.
The things you have learned and received and heard and seen in me,
practice these things;
and the God of peace shall be with you.
Philippians 4:8-9

June 5
UNDERSTANDING YOUR LOVE

For I am convinced that neither death, nor life,
nor angels, nor principalities, nor things present, nor things to come,
nor powers, nor height, nor depth nor any other created thing,
shall be able to separate us from the love of God,
which is in Christ Jesus our Lord.
Romans 8:38-39

This morning while reading those verses, Lord, I thought about how, as a baby Christian, it was so difficult for me to believe You actually loved me. I believed You loved other people. I believed Your death on the cross was for me. But I just could not feel that *You loved me.*

Then You showed me some truths that planted deep within my heart a "knowing" that has never left me. And You did it by comparing Your love for me to my love for my small son.

"How much do you love your son? How strong is your desire to see good come to him rather than ill? How much do you enjoy the person he is while yet seeing the potential for growth? How much do you enjoy hearing from him some evidence that he loves you, too? How much would you sacrifice to help him become the person I want him to be?"

The answers, Lord, to those questions are: a *lot;* very strong; oh, *so* much; with all my heart; my very life.

I see! If I can, in my humanness, love my son so much, how much more can You, perfect in every way, love Your children? I realize we are not comparing apples to apples here, Lord, but it makes such a clear picture for me. Thank You for allowing me to see it! Thank You for expanding my heart to receive all You want to give. Thank You for being the wise and loving Father that You are, for the unconditional acceptance I sense flowing from Your heart to mine.

I also realize now, Lord, that to doubt Your love would grieve Your heart. May I never do that! May I learn to trust Your love in every circumstance of life.

June 6
BEING SINGLE MINDED

Make your ear attentive to wisdom,
incline your heart to understanding;
for if you cry for discernment,
lift your voice for understanding;
if you seek her as silver,
and search for her as for hidden treasures;
then you will discern the fear of the Lord,
and discover the knowledge of God.
Proverbs 2: 2-5

Thank You, Lord, for a peaceful night of rest and a lovely quiet time with You before I go to work. Thank You for those words of promise from Proverbs. This proverb on wisdom led my thoughts to the book of James. In James 1:5-6, You promise to give wisdom if we but ask and believe.

Some of what I see: Many "small" inner conflicts simply disappear if I am single minded in my devotion to You. Your Word says that double minded people are unstable, unpredictable, unsteady, not dependable (James 1:7-8). This is *not* the kind of person I want to be. Nor is it one that can be useful to You.

How do I get to be single-minded? The foundation upon which single-mindedness is built is love; I'm to love You with all my heart, soul, strength and mind and to love others as myself. As a result of loving You, my love for others grows, and my thoughts and intentions become pleasing to You. That, Lord, is my constant goal.

So my (our) task is to identify those things in my life which prevent my loving You with all that I am. That brings us back to familiar territory because it is the old sins of "self" that immediately come to mind…the desire to be self-sufficient, the selfishness, self-love, self-centeredness, self-anything/everything. These must go.

So this single-mindedness leading to wisdom is an act of the will first, followed with many choices as situations arise where I must decide "my way or God's way." It is not an easy, one-step act. It is a slow process that is worked out in an array of challenging, daily decisions. Being single minded means I consistently choose Your way. It means demonstrating my love for You to through obedience. It means putting aside my innate self-confidence and allowing You to change it to God-confidence. It means recognizing You as my Source of all that I need. So be it.

June 7
PERSEVERANCE

For whatever was written in earlier times
was written for our instruction,
that through perseverance and the encouragement of the Scriptures
we might have hope.
Romans 15:4

Thank You for showing me the application of Your Word to my situation, Lord. I'm seeing that the problems in which I find myself at this particular moment can have two results: I can allow the enemy to have his way and destroy my faith, my marriage, my family, my relationship with fellow believers, everything that is worth anything, or I can place my hand more firmly in Yours and say, "Lord, I don't understand but I trust You and love You, and I intend to continue on with You."

I can be destroyed or built up. What determines which it will be?

My response to the problems,
my attitude,
my behavior,
my mind-set,
the placement of my will.

In other words, it is my choice. Lord, give me grace.

Now may the God who gives perseverance and encouragement
grant you to be of the same mind with one another
according to Christ Jesus;
that with one accord you may with one voice
glorify the God and Father of our Lord Jesus Christ.
Romans 15:5 & 6

June 8
TRUE LOVE

Read I Corinthians 13

Because of pleasant childhood memories, this is one of my favorite Scriptures, Lord. I helped my brother memorize this chapter so he could win a prize. But now I have put away childish things, and these verses are living and active in me for other reasons - because they tell me about unconditional love - the love with which You love me.

"Even if I can speak in every known language, if my words are not spoken in love, they are just irritating noise. I might know all there is to know about everything and have faith to move mountains but if I fail to love, I am nothing. I can give away everything I have, *even my life*, but if I don't do it for love, it profits me not at all."

Those three verses reveal the high priority that You give to love. It is so far above all the other excellent things that we humans value! The next four verses tell what love is...

"Love is patient, kind, not jealous, not boastful, not arrogant, doesn't act unbecomingly. It bears and believes and hopes and endures all things. It does not seek its own, is not easily provoked, does not carry grudges, does not rejoice in evil. It always rejoices in good."

Here is what I'm seeing this morning, Lord, as I ponder this well-loved chapter. This love is not a goal which I should be pursuing. Rather, this love, and all that ensues from it, *will result* in a life that is Spirit cleansed, Spirit filled and Spirit led. That will be the natural outworking of the inner working of Your Spirit. I don't "try" to *be* any of these attributes. To do so takes my eyes off You and Your abiding in me, and puts them on me and my trying.

I simply keep my eyes on You, listen to You, walk with You step by step and hour by hour, respond to each situation that comes as You say to respond. In this way, You are in control. That's exactly what I want. Thank You for this new perspective. Thank You for this beautiful picture of who You are and what You are making me.

June 9
SPIRITUAL ABUNDANCE

But the fruit of the Spirit is love, joy, peace, patience,
kindness, goodness, faithfulness, gentleness, self-control;
against such things there is no law.
Galatians 5:22-23

As I read this chapter in Galatians this morning, Lord, I think of the abundant provision You have made for Your children and of appropriating that provision into my life.

There is no doubt that Your supply is abundant. This Scripture is only one list of the blessings You want me to have. When I was born again by the power of Your Spirit, You moved into the center of my life, into my spirit. With You came all that You are, not just parts and pieces of You but all of You, Yourself, in the Person of the Holy Spirit. All these beautiful things listed above are therefore already within me because they are the fruit of *Your* Spirit.

What this means is that if I lack one or more of these virtues listed above (or those listed elsewhere in Scripture), *it is my fault*. They are there for the taking. It is Your will that I take them. But You will not force them upon me. I must "do something" to appropriate into my life every good thing You provide. Please help me think through this "something" I must do.

I must know what is available. That means I must read Your Word. I must see and understand all that You desire for me to have. I must have my mind open for Your Spirit to teach me. This takes mental discipline, Lord. It takes surrender. It takes desire to know You. It takes responding to You drawing me.

I must *desire* to have every good thing You want me to have. If I don't desire it, I will never ask You to give the manifestation of that particular virtue in my life.

I must then prepare for You to begin working. I'm convinced, Lord, that the situations of my life at this very moment are the answers to prayers. I have asked You to do something wonderful in me, and You have begun to do it. It often, even *usually*, does not seem like an answer to prayer. It often seems like problems and pressures and adversity and difficulty. But I see, my Lord, that if I will trust You, keep my hand in Yours and allow You to do Your work, the good and wonderful will come about in due time. How do I know this? Because You have promised.

And we know that God causes all things to work together for good to those who
love God, to those who are called according to His purpose.
Romans 8:28

June 10
STRAYING FROM YOU

Let Thy compassion come quickly to meet us;
for we are brought very low.
Help us O God of our salvation, for the glory of Thy name;
and deliver us and forgive our sins, for Thy name's sake.
Psalm 79:8(b)-9

Your wisdom, Lord, is complete. There is nothing beyond Your knowledge and understanding. Your power is over all, greater than any other power. And You *are* love. Your love is a wise and almighty love, knowing what is needed and bringing it to pass.

Why, then, is it so difficult for me to continue walking in that knowledge, secure in the fact that You know all and will best handle every situation? Why do I pull in the other direction? Why do I want to rest when You say walk or keep walking when You say rest? Why is it so difficult to keep Your perspective on life and its situations? Why is it so challenging to stay soft and moldable in Your hands?

Hardness creeps in, rebelliousness sneaks in, tiny bits at a time until I find my spirit cold and indifferent. I realize I'm not enjoying Your presence anymore. I do not want to live this way! Please help me see truth here and use that truth to restore my spiritual health. I'm thinking, Lord, that there are at least two reasons this happens:

The enemy is trying for all he is worth to ruin my relationship with You. He knows my weak spots, and he throws darts exactly there. If I am not dressed in the armor You have provided for me, and walking in Your holy presence, his darts find their targets and the damage is done. Which brings me to reason two.

At some point, I made a wrong choice. I chose to think about the wrong thing, or I chose to skip feeding on Your Word for a day or two, or I chose to *not* bring something to You and ask Your opinion. Bottom line, I simply did what I wanted. That wrong choice led to more wrong choices until I find myself in a place far from You. I am lonely for You here, Lord.

I know that all I have to do is acknowledge to You my sin in straying and, turning full face toward You, repent of that sin. In Your mercy, You bring me back. Once more You set me on the right path, going in the right direction. Oh, that I could be wise enough to never do this again! Maybe I've finally learned this lesson, Lord.

June 11
THE SIN OF ACHAN

So Achan answered Joshua and said, "Truly, I have sinned against the Lord, the
God of Israel, and this is what I did: when I saw among the spoil a beautiful
mantle from Shinar and two hundred shekels of silver and a bar of gold fifty
shekels in weight,
then I coveted them and took them; and behold, they are concealed in the earth
inside my tent with the silver underneath it."
Joshua 7:20-21

You had plainly told the sons of Israel that when they overthrew Jericho they were NOT to take any of the silver, gold, bronze or iron for themselves. All such articles were to be considered holy and placed in Your treasury. But one man was overcome by his greed; he took silver and gold back to his tent and hid it, thus disobeying a clear instruction from You. He broke the commandment concerning coveting, and then attempted to conceal his sin. His attempt failed. We cannot hide things from You.

When Joshua next led the sons of Israel into battle at Ai, they suffered a humiliating defeat. And when Joshua fell on his face before You, he found out why: someone had sinned, and You would not bless them with victory until the culprit was identified and punished. You helped in the identification of Achan. Israel took him and all that belonged to him, including his sons and daughters and all his animals, and stoned them to death and burned them with fire. And Your fierce anger was turned away.

Here are a couple of lessons I learn from this story, Lord. First, Achan's sin brought trouble, heartache and death to many. All the men slain in the battle at Ai, all his sons and daughters and animals - dead because of him. I may think that my disobedience (sin) affects no one but myself, but that is not true. It affects people all around me in ways I may not see and may never know. But most grievous of all is the effect it has on our relationship - Yours and mine. You cannot bless sin.

The second lesson I learn is that Joshua was able to take the appalling defeat and use it creatively in his next battle plan. He had to be listening to You, Lord, because that is exactly what You do - You take failure and redeem it into victory. The second attack upon Ai was a rousing success. How good that Joshua listened and was obedient to You. It was good for Joshua, good for all of Israel, and, today, good for me.

So Joshua burned Ai and made it a heap forever,
a desolation until this day.
Then Joshua built an altar to the Lord, the God of Israel.
Joshua 8:28 & 30

June 12
SPIRITUAL BATTLES

For our struggle is not against flesh and blood,
but against the rulers, against the powers,
against the world forces of this darkness,
against the spiritual forces of wickedness
in the heavenly places.
Ephesians 6:12

At times, Lord, I get so tired of fighting spiritual battles! Is it my fault the battle is so long? Surely it is! Please help me understand what I need to do differently.

Let's think about adverse circumstances. Often, circumstances may dictate what I do, but they cannot dictate how I feel about them. That is my choice. My response to any circumstance may be godly or it may be "fleshly." If my response is godly, You are pleased, the enemy is defeated and I am blessed in spite of the adverse circumstance. If I choose the "fleshly" route, the interior battle is on-going. It continues because You are a gracious and merciful God; You do not want me to make wrong choices. Oh, Lord, give me wisdom to choose well!

The enemy's goal is to destroy every good thing You have given me. And his tactics frequently are subtle and effective. But, as Your child, I have conquering power through the work of Your Spirit in me. You teach me how to recognize his attack, to detect his lies quickly, to be always dressed in my protective armor with my sword and shield ready. *Your work and my cooperation will defeat him every time.*

The helmet of salvation is crucial in protecting my mind. By salvation, I mean more than the crisis experience of conversion. That is only the beginning. Salvation is also the power and grace You pour out upon me, *keeping* me through this training period we call life. The final chapter of salvation will happen at my death or Your return, whichever comes first. That helmet protects my mind from doubts, fears and uncertainties that the enemy tries to interject. *I consciously put it on by knowing, believing and reminding myself of Your promises to be with me and protect me.*

Therefore, take up the full armor of God,
that you may be able to resist in the evil day,
and having done everything, to stand firm.
Ephesians 6:13

Help me take the truths stated here and use them, by Your grace, to stand firm, resist and be victorious.

June 13
TRUSTING YOU

Trust in the Lord with all your heart, and do not lean on your own understanding.
In all your ways acknowledge Him, and He will make your paths straight.
Do not be wise in your own eyes; fear the Lord and turn away from evil.
Proverbs 3:5-7

Trust You with all my heart. My first step in learning to trust You was seeing that my parents trusted You. Because they trusted You, I had some level of trust as well. The second step was my personal experience, and that is where "all my heart" comes in. Because until I came to know You personally, my trust was pretty superficial. Only as I got into Your Word for myself and began to see "the real You" did I discover that You truly *are* worthy of a trust without reservation. I'm so thankful for parents that loved You and lived out that love before me and for my own growing relationship of love with You. May I be an example for others as my parents were for me.

In all my ways acknowledge You. There is that "all" word again. That is all-inclusive, leaving out no part of my life. And what does it mean to acknowledge You? I think it means to accept everything You have said about Yourself as being absolutely true. And the only way I can know what You have said is to read and study Your Word.

Fear You. Fear in this context means reverence, respect and even awe. It means seeing Your powerful wrath and justice as clearly as I see Your mercy and love. It means understanding Your hatred of evil and sin wherever it is found. It means seeing Your holiness and unsurpassed majesty, and yes, it means trembling because I also see my unworthiness.

Turn away from evil. That is easy, Lord, when I ponder the subject of fearing You; I want to be as far removed from evil as I can possibly get.

Don't lean on my own understanding. As Your child, I am to lean on You. Period. I am to look to You for my understanding of all things. Oh, the implications here of the necessity of Bible study and of times of solitude spent in Your presence!

Don't be wise in my own eyes. If I understand the instruction above on fearing You, there is not much chance that I will consider myself wise.

The promise is that You will make my paths straight. And best of all, You will be right beside me every step along that straight path. I am both filled and surrounded by Your presence. What could be better?

June 14
KNOWING AND DOING

...we have not ceased to pray for you and to ask that you may be filled with the
knowledge of His will in all spiritual wisdom and understanding, so that you may
walk in a manner worthy of the Lord, to please Him in all respects, bearing fruit in
every good work and increasing in the knowledge of God; strengthened with all
power, according to His glorious might,
for the attaining of all steadfastness and patience;
joyously giving thanks to the Father,
who has qualified us to share in the inheritance of the saints in light.
Colossians 1: 9-12

This prayer by Paul is my prayer this morning, Lord. I so much desire to know Your will in the current conditions of my life, to understand what You want and how I am to walk in a way that will please You. Here are some things I *know* I must do:

I must see clearly that all these requests of Paul for his people are also Your will for me. Because if I know it is Your will, I can pray in confidence. I must determine to open my mind and heart to You for whatever work You see needs to be done. My request for guidance implies my obedience, Lord.

I must remember that I cannot change other people. I am only responsible for me. I must realize through the day, at crisis times, my need to allow control to remain in Your hands, and quietly step aside so that I am responding to You rather than my situation. This is difficult for me. Please help me be aware *at those times* how clear-cut my choice is: Your control versus mine.

I must be joyously thankful. I see, Lord, that the attitude of the inner man should be shaped by eternal facts rather than temporary situations. The fact is that You have already qualified me to share in the inheritance of the saints. The job is done! Knowing that creates within me an attitude of joyous thanksgiving. May it reign over my day.

I realize that I cannot do any of those things in my own power, Lord. Only by Your boundless grace can I be successful in both knowing and doing Your will in this circumstance.

I am willing.
You are able.
It shall be done.

But if any of you lacks wisdom, let him ask of God,
who gives to all men generously and without reproach,
and it will be given to him.
James 1:5

166

June 15
BEING QUALIFIED

...giving thanks to the Father, who has qualified us to share in the inheritance of
the saints in light.
Colossians 1:12

I see we are not through with this passage. I'm thinking about these words this morning, "the Father has qualified me." Please, Lord, guide my thoughts.

The *Father* has qualified me: You are the beginning, the end and all in between. It is Your calling, Your grace, Your work within me that has accomplished this change from what I used to be to what I am now, and that will continue to perfect me until this life is over.

The Father *has* qualified me: Past tense - a thing already completed in Your eyes. This tells me I need to relax and rejoice in this full-of-wonder thing You have done in me. Relax because You are in charge and rejoice because - well, because You are in charge. You are, after all, the One with all wisdom and power.

The Father has *qualified* me: You have done this through Your awesome plan of redemption - paying a price that I could never have paid. I was in the domain of darkness, under the control of the enemy, lost and away from You. You called me to Yourself, cleaned me up by giving me a new nature in place of my sinful nature, and transferred me into Your Kingdom - a Kingdom where You, Yourself are the Light. All of this, Lord, *qualifies* me to share in that Kingdom.

The Father has qualified *me*: Until I came to believe that all the good news contained between the covers of my Bible was written for me, my faith was shaky and my joy non-existent. What an incredible, blissful fact it is that You love me! I somehow never get tired of thinking about it. And because You love me, You have qualified *me* to inherit the same glorious eternity with You as the saints of the past. Like Paul and Abraham and John and Elijah and Peter - hallelujah!

For by Him all things were created, both in the heavens and on earth,
visible and invisible, whether thrones or dominions or rulers or authorities - all
things have been created by Him and for Him.
And He is before all things, and in Him all things hold together.
Colossians 1:16-17

June 16
WALKING ON WATER

And when the disciples saw Him walking on the sea,
they were frightened, saying, "It is a ghost!"
And they cried out for fear. But immediately Jesus spoke to them, saying,
"Take courage, it is I; do not be afraid."
Matthew 14: 26-27

This morning, Lord, let's talk about this event in the disciples' lives. Help me clearly see what it means to me in my life experience. First, some facts about what happened...

The disciples were doing just what You had *told* them to do - it had not been *their* decision to cross the lake. Interesting. And now the boat was being battered by wind and wave, and they were frightened - even before they saw the "ghost."

Only one out of twelve had the courage to step out on faith. Then *his* fear became larger than his faith, too, and You had to save him from drowning. The whole situation was, if not designed by You, certainly used by You to further reveal to the disciples Your power and authority over the laws of nature. You were building their faith.

Only the disciples saw this miracle. The multitudes were not there.

Here are the lessons for me: Troubles and trials will come my way *even when I'm living in Your will.* And, just like the disciples, they are for the purpose of teaching me Your power and authority, for making me realize my need of You and Your desire to bless me. Hannah Smith calls these the "chariots of God" sent to bring me to You. Beautiful thought!

Fear is the natural man's reaction to conditions beyond our control. Only a spiritually renewed mind, fixed upon You, will not fear under fearful conditions. What might be called courage is actually trusting You.

Peter's motives may have been mixed. We cannot know what was in his mind. But the important thing is that, even if there was a little of the "look at me" in his thinking, You honored his request anyway. This makes me believe, Lord, that You honor and build upon every scrap of good within us and, in Your grace, over time, You weed out the not-so-good.

Sometimes You come to me in a "different" way - an unexpected way. I may be startled and even fearful at first, but You calm those fears. I'm amazed, Lord, at how my concept of You has changed over the years. And I still have so much to learn. I need to stay close to You to learn these lessons You want to teach me. Close and teachable - exactly where I want to be. I love You, Lord.

June 17
BEING LIKE YOU

But we all, with unveiled face beholding as in a mirror the glory of the Lord,
are being transformed into the same image from glory to glory,
just as from the Lord, the Spirit.
2 Corinthians 3:18

All Christians should share a goal to become more like You, Lord. This verse tells me that I *am* being changed into the glory of Your image. In Romans 8:29, Paul uses the phrase *"become conformed to the image of His Son."*

What I'm thinking about this morning is how necessary it is for me to have an accurate concept of who You are. It is foundational to my being changed. Because if I do not see You as You truly are, I'm likely to resist changes Your Spirit desires to work in my own transformation. And I learn who You are by looking into the mirror of the Word.

When I started reading the Bible for myself, I was surprised at the many mistaken concepts I had. I had much to unlearn before I was able to learn, and my preconceived ideas slowed me down considerably.

One outstanding revelation to me was Your attitude toward people. You were always tender to the needy, the afflicted, and the children. To me, Your gentleness became a picture of Your strength. It fills my heart with love to see that tenderness toward those who needed You so much. But, at the same time, You were very outspoken, even harsh, with the Pharisees and others who were caught up in hypocritical legalism. For them, You had strong words of condemnation.

You looked at a person's heart, not their outward appearance, and it was to their heart You spoke. You were never deceived. You were in constant touch with Your Father and spoke what He said speak, did what He said do and saw what He showed You. You did all of this without concern as to whether people "liked" You or not. You were definitely not out to win a popularity contest. Your words and actions were always motivated by love, but sometimes love meant honest words and bold actions.

I see, Lord, that my potential for having those same qualities in my life is in direct proportion to the strength of my relationship to You. If I am growing more like You, I will be ministering compassion to those who need it, and acting with tough love when warranted. I will be looking to You for what to say and how to say it. I will be always listening and obeying. I will be seeing clearly that whether people like me or not is of no consequence. The only opinion that matters is Yours. This really is not an extreme concept, is it, Lord? It is simply being led by Your Spirit. So be it.

June 18
THE PARABLE OF THE LAMP

Now no one after lighting a lamp covers it over with a container, or puts it under a
bed; but he puts it on a lamp stand,
in order that those who come in may see the light.
For nothing is hidden that shall not become evident,
nor anything secret that shall not be known and come to light.
Therefore take care how you listen; for whoever has, to him shall more be given;
and whoever does not have, even what he thinks he has
shall be taken away from him.
Luke 8:16-18

A lamp is for giving light. You, my Lord, are Light, illuminating all that is within me. Sometimes You shine upon something which I must do away with; sometimes, a truth about which I need to pray or think. At times the Light is thrown upon a long-ago hurt whose time has come to be healed. My job, as I understand this verse, is to simply let Your Light shine. Don't hide it under the bed or try to cover it over. Just welcome its glow.

What is hidden shall become evident, what is secret shall be made known. At first glance, this may seem like a threat or a warning. But to me, Lord, it is a wonderful promise. It is an assurance of Your faithfulness; You will bring to my attention what is in my heart. *I* may not know the things hidden there that need to come out, but there is nothing hidden from *You.* And the terrific news is that You will work with me through all that is revealed. You don't just point it out and then sit back waiting for me to take care of it. You walk every step of the way with me.

"Therefore take care how you listen." That is a strange statement, Lord. You didn't say, "Take care to *what* you listen;" You said, "take care *how* you listen." Perhaps You are cautioning, "Listen carefully" because there are so many barriers to overcome and pitfalls to avoid in order to truly listen. I cannot truly listen if I have an attitude of having already made up my mind, or I think I know what You are going to say so I don't need to hear it. Or worse, I think I know what You are going to say, and I don't *want* to hear it.

So *how* I listen is indicative of the deepest desire within me, isn't it? To say 'I love You with all my heart' means nothing if I then ignore Your speaking to me. To say 'I want Your guidance in all areas of my life' is a lie if I then don't listen carefully when You are giving that guidance. I see, Lord, that it is imperative to listen with an open heart, an eagerness to learn, and a teachable spirit.

The rest of verse 18 must be a significant spiritual principle because it is written down five time in the four gospels, *"...whoever has shall receive more; whoever only thinks he has, even that will be taken away."* It evidently applies to all areas of faith. What I know, Lord, is that whatever area we are talking about, I want more, not less.

June 19
LIFELESS LIVING

Now to Him who is able to do exceeding abundantly beyond all that we ask or think, according to the power that works within us, to Him be the glory in the church and in Christ Jesus to all generations forever and ever. Amen.
Ephesians 3:20-21

It is possible, Lord, for Your people to become dull.

Dull of hearing,
unable to hear Your soft words,
missing tender blessings.

Dull in thinking.
Slow in understanding new eternal truths,
forgetting what is known.

Dull in vision,
not wanting to see the sickness of the world around them
or the healing You have for it.

Just a gloomy plodding day after day,
"Oh, just get me through this day!"
An existence far short of abundant life.

Oh, God, may we wake up to the excitement of living with You!

The joy of Your constant presence and
the power of Your love shall be to us an
invigorating,
compelling,
fragrant way of life
that is contagious.

June 20
MAGNETIC LOVE

And it happened that as He was reclining at the table in the house,
behold many tax-gatherers and sinners came
and were dining with Jesus and His disciples.
Matthew 9:10

Lord, the tax-gatherers and sinners were drawn to You. They came and joined with You at meals or just to hear You speak. They had become accustomed to equating "godly" with "judgmental," but suddenly here was One who was definitely "godly" and yet was compassionate! They knew, without words, that You loved them and love always draws the unloved to itself. Your condemnation was heavy upon those who were self-righteous and hypocritical. But upon the ignorant, the sick and sinful, You showered a quiet, healing, radiating Love that drew them in.

Here is what bothers me, Lord. I look today at myself and my fellow Christians, and I don't see an abundance of this compassionate magnetism going on. Christians and non-Christians are pretty much living in two separate worlds. We Christians travel in our own circles, spending most of our time with fellow-believers, praying for our family and friends and teaching spiritual principles to the already-saved. This is all worthy, Lord. You did some of this, too. But it is not all You did.

You spent a *lot* of Your time out in public places where the lost could get close to You, feel the compassion flowing out of You and into their thirsty souls, where they could see You and hear You speak words of life. You were never too busy to stop and minister to anyone who needed You. You obviously saw the importance of every person and every need that crossed Your path. You had no agenda other than that. That *was* Your agenda...*to seek and to save that which was lost* (Luke 19:10).

I fear, Lord, that the world today looks at us Christians with the same attitude that it looked at the Pharisees - as being self-righteous and judgmental. I also fear it is somewhat justified in that view. Some of the most outspoken representatives of Christianity *are* self-righteous and judgmental. But the really sad and convicting-to-me thing is that the rest of us are doing so little to refute that perception. We continue on with our decent, safe, little lives rather than putting dedicated thought and effort into ways to minister to those who need it most - those who are lost, hopeless and on that broad road to destruction.

Oh, how we need to be driven by Your agenda! How we need to be filled with Your compassion! The harvest is great, the workers are few and our time is short.

172

June 21
RIGHTEOUSNESS, PEACE AND JOY

For the kingdom of God is not eating and drinking,
but righteousness and peace and joy in the Holy Spirit.
Romans 14:17

In this chapter, Paul was teaching about principles of conscience, how rule-keeping is *not* what You are interested in, and about having compassion for my "weaker" brother. Paul says that Your kingdom is not about what we eat and drink (or any other of the multitude of daily-life things). Your kingdom is about Your power to change me from the inside through the indwelling of Your Spirit.

These words fascinate me this morning, Lord. They are a small, one-sentence description of what happens inwardly when a person becomes a member of Your kingdom. I'm quite sure there are deep theological meanings to this word "righteousness" but, not being a theologian, it simply means to me that, because of Your grace, I have right standing before You. You have accepted me as I am. You love me unconditionally.

These facts never fail to astonish me, Lord! I am amazed anew each time I realize that I am loved and accepted by You. It melts my heart and causes me to once again commit all that I am and all that I have into Your keeping. It opens up my spirit to be filled once again with every bit of You for which I have room. And as I meditate, I realize that this very state of being is the *source* of peace and joy.

Peace and joy are tied closely to trust, aren't they, Lord? If I have doubts and fears, they crowd out both peace and joy. And trust is tied closely to *knowing You as You are*. And the only way to do that is spending time in Your Word, talking to You and listening to You. Christians may get tired of hearing "read your Bible and pray," but there is no better advice if they desire to know You fully.

So, as I come to know You, my trust level rises. And as my trust grows, so does my capacity for peace and joy. And as that capacity enlarges, You continue to pour in more and more blessings. It is a divinely-designed process that repeats itself and unceasingly brings me "heaven on earth." How generous You are to Your children to give us these precious, priceless gifts of righteousness, peace and joy in Your indwelling Holy Spirit!

June 22
MORE ON JOY

Blessed be the God and Father of our Lord Jesus Christ,
who according to His great mercy has caused us to be born again to a living hope
through the resurrection of Jesus Christ from the dead.
And though you have not seen Him, you love Him, and though you do not see Him
now, but believe in Him, you greatly rejoice with joy inexpressible and full of
glory.
1 Peter 1:3, 8

Lord, I'm still working mentally on this subject of being filled with joy. Only You know the off and on battles with depression I have had for long years. I have never understood the "why" of it, but the fact is that I've struggled with it since childhood. So the subject of joy is especially appealing to me.

What I'm understanding is that Your joy in me comes from knowing a few facts: that You love me and won't stop loving me; that Your promises are for *me,* too; that Your power to deliver on those promises is unlimited; that You have already given me the greatest gifts possible - eternal life and the privilege of fellowship with You.

These, Lord, are eternal, unshakable truths. Conditions cannot change them. They will be as true next week or next year as they are today. Because You do not change, Your truths do not change.

How do I know these facts? By faith - faith that You are who You say You are, faith in Your character, faith in Your Word. Hebrews 11:6 says:

And without faith it is impossible to please Him,
for he who comes to God must believe that He is,
and that He is a rewarder of those who seek Him.

So, if I want to please You, I am to believe not only that You exist, but also that You are good to those of us who want to know You. I'm seeing, Lord, that You don't urge me to believe You just because it pleases You. No, You desire my trust because *only when I come to You in faith will my life be open to You to bless and make joyful.* Once again, I see Your motive of love behind a truth. It always comes back to love, doesn't it, Lord? From beginning to end, it is all about love.

So, knowing all this, will my tendency toward depression disappear forever? Maybe not. I don't know what causes it. What I do know, my Lord, is that even on days when all seems dark and lonely, You are still with me, still holding my hand, still loving me. So I will just stay steady until the darkness passes once again. Joy always returns. You are indeed an awesome God!

June 23
BY YOUR GRACE

And He has said to me,
"My grace is sufficient for you,
for power is perfected in weakness."
Most gladly, therefore,
I will rather boast about my weaknesses,
that the power of Christ may dwell in me.
2 Corinthians 12:9

An overwhelming sense
of my inadequacy
walks beside
an equally intense desire for
serving You.

Where are these two going?

Toward the radiating
all-encompassing
sufficiency found only in You.

I can do all things
because of Your strength in me.

Thanks be to God for His indescribable gift!
2 Corinthians 9:15

June 24
CONFIDENCE IN YOUR CARE

But we have this treasure in earthen vessels,
that the surpassing greatness of the power may be of God
and not from ourselves;
we are afflicted in every way, but not crushed;
perplexed, but not despairing.
2 Corinthians 4:7-8

Even though conditions and problems may box me in on all sides, nothing can interfere with my relationship to You, my Lord. Nothing can stop my fellowship with You except my own attitude and choice. I need to remember this because I'm tempted sometimes to allow my feelings, rather than facts, to dictate my actions.

The fact is…

For I am convinced that neither death, nor life, nor angels,
nor principalities, nor things present, nor things to come,
nor powers, nor height, nor depth, nor any other created thing,
shall be able to separate us from the love of God,
which is in Christ Jesus our Lord.
Romans 8:38-39

Thank You, Lord, for inspiring Paul to write both those truths. It does me much good to be reminded that I am only an earthen vessel. You know I have this bent toward trying to be everything to everybody and then severely castigating myself when I fail, which I always do.

Once again, I confess this weakness and look to Your surpassing greatness. Take this earthen vessel with all its problems and stresses and give me grace to be strong in *Your* strength. I affirm the treasure within. That treasure is You, Yourself in the Person of the Holy Spirit. I know You will let nothing separate us. My heart overflows with gratitude for that, and the overflow becomes warm tears running from my eyes. What a great thing it is to be loved by You, my Treasure!

June 25
TRUSTING IN DIFFICULTY

Though the fig tree should not blossom,
and there be no fruit on the vines,
though the yield of the olive should fail,
and the fields produce no food,
though the flock should be cut off from the fold,
and there be no cattle in the stalls,
yet I will exult in the Lord
I will rejoice in the God of my salvation.
Habakkuk 3: 17-18

Lord, I praise You for this moment, for this situation in which we find ourselves, for these exact conditions. I did not want to ever find us in such again, but here we are and I'm claiming Your promises that You are here with us.

Being human, the first thing I think of, Lord, is ESCAPE. How to get out, or at least how to change this situation from what it is to what we wanted it to be. But Your word and intention here may be TEACH. Your purpose may be a further lesson in faith.

What I *know*, Lord, is that deep down, we want above all to be pleasing to You. No matter what happens, all will be well if we are pleasing to You.

"True security comes not from people, not from things, but from a vital relationship with Me. People change and can pass out of your life; things can be taken from you or wear out. Only your relationship with Me is eternal.

"Be secure in My love, trusting Me and accepting your days as ordered by Me and as coming from Me. For, truly, I am in control of your life. But only as you are pliable in My hands am I able to do for you all I wish. I am waiting to bless - simply trust, be at peace and full of joy."

The Lord God is my strength,
And He has made my feet like hinds' feet,
And makes me walk on my high places.
Habakkuk 3: 19

June 26
WHO HAS STRONG FAITH?

For we who live are constantly being delivered over to death for Jesus' sake,
that the life of Jesus also may be manifested in our mortal flesh.
2 Corinthians 4:11

As I picked up my journal this morning, Lord, this thought was in my mind: "Untested faith is weak faith." Now, I know this is not an original thought. Saints through the ages have known this truth. But it is a truth well worth thinking about. Please help me as I do that.

In this country, where we are able to worship as we choose, freely and without fear, You must test our faith some way other than persecution. Our tests usually come in the form of illness, death, financial troubles or relationship problems. Here is what I'm seeing this morning, Lord. Perhaps my brothers and sisters in China and those under other repressive governments, risking death for their faith in You, are the *blessed* ones, while we in America are not.

They make their original commitment to You knowing that it might cost them all they own, including their lives. So they *begin* their journey far down the road, where most of us are only after a lifetime of lesser demands. The trials and tribulations we go through, when held up beside theirs, seem almost petty, Lord.

They learn early and thoroughly to trust You with all their heart while it takes us years to get to that point. It is through much hardship that they practice their faith. Many do not even have a complete copy of Your Word! Meetings must be held in secret and so are infrequent. There are no Christian bookstores in every town stocked with helpful teaching resources.

But they have *You*, Lord! And I believe You minister to them, in Your unlimited mercy and love, in ways we cannot know in our sheltered and, yes, pampered lives. You do not need Bibles and books to teach. All You need is a listening, loving heart.

They possess a spiritual strength we only talk about. Many of them have so little in the way of material possessions that their minds truly are set on things above, not on things on the earth. Oh, how much we think about material possessions! At the end of the day, Lord, all this stuff we have spent our time and effort and money on will be just rubbish in a landfill. Our priorities are so backwards.

We are often urged to "thank God you were born in America with freedom to worship." But I wonder, Lord. I wonder.

Remember the beggar Lazarus and the rich man?

June 27
KEEPING GOD'S PERSPECTIVE

And working together with Him,
we also urge you not to receive the grace of God in vain.
2 Corinthians 6:1

Well, I guess we are not through with this subject, Lord. In reading this chapter, I see again how the persecution of the early Christians strengthened them and gave them a powerful faith that is rare today in America. As I read the things Paul writes in the first ten verses of this chapter, they seem to fall into two categories:

Things we don't want	Things we want
Afflictions	Endurance
Hardships	Purity
Distresses	Knowledge
Beatings	Patience
Imprisonments	Kindness
Tumults	Holy Spirit
Labors	Love
Sleeplessness	Power of God
Hunger	Weapons of righteousness
Dishonor	Glory
Evil report	Good report

Now here's a thought - what if we get the things we want only through experiencing some things we don't want? I think that shouldn't even be a question, Lord. I think it is a truth. We *do not* gain the things in the second list without experiencing some of the things in the first.

Even a cursory reading of the New Testament shows that first century Christians were far different from those of us living twenty centuries later. Their faith was strong *because* they had to face all that in the first list. Is ours weak because we don't?

The day may come, Lord, even in my lifetime, that we in America might have to endure some of those things that require a strong faith. We need to give it some serious thought. We need to use our sanctified imaginations to strengthen our commitment and play out in our minds how we would respond to those experiences. We need to seek You with all our heart. We need to open ourselves up to all that You desire to do within us. We need to be willing to do whatever it takes to be strong in the Lord.

The end of all things is at hand;
therefore, be of sound judgment and sober spirit
for the purpose of prayer.
1 Peter 4:7

179

June 28
CLOTHED FROM ON HIGH

I will rejoice greatly in the Lord,
My soul will exult in my God.
For He has clothed me with garments of salvation,
He has wrapped me with a robe of righteousness.
Isaiah 61:10

This morning, Lord, I do not feel that I am clothed in garments of salvation or a robe of righteousness. But I must remind myself that this life with You is, at present, lived by faith - not by feeling. So, by faith, I affirm that this is true of me.

As I meditate on this verse, my spiritual eyes begin to see the garments of salvation. They are soft and white and fragrant with purity. The first garment of salvation goes on next to my clean self - clean because You have washed me clean. The next garment goes over that, flowing, glowing and beautiful.

Then comes the robe of righteousness. It completely covers me, head to toe. It is what You see when You look at me. It is made to fit *me* and therefore is both comfortable and comforting. To be wrapped in it is to know the ultimate in security and peace. This righteousness is not mine, Lord, because I had no righteousness when You saved me, and still have none of my own. The salvation and ensuing righteousness are all of You. How good You are to give such gifts to this unworthy child.

Thinking about this, Lord, makes me long for the time when I will know these experiences fully. A time when faith becomes sight. Fill my heart and mind with Your Spirit today, and all the rest of my "todays," so that You may be glorified by my thoughts, actions and words. May my spirit be strengthened more and more by Your work in me.

Go then, eat your bread in happiness,
and drink your wine with a cheerful heart;
for God has already approved your works.
Let your clothes be white all the time,
and let not oil be lacking on your head.
Ecclesiastes 9: 7-8

June 29
SECOND CHANCES

And Peter remembered the word which Jesus had said,
"Before a cock crows, you will deny Me three times."
And he went out and wept bitterly.
Matthew 26: 75

Peter *thought* he was brave and strong. After he denied You three times, and realized what he had done, "he went out and wept bitterly." How he must have grieved those next days! The guilt and remorse he felt were, no doubt, overwhelming.

Obviously it took something this drastic in his life to make him understand that, in himself, he was *not* brave and strong, that he needed to trust in You rather than himself. Thankfully, he did learn that because he went on to be a bold and powerful minister of Your good news.

Peter's experience, and my own, tell me it is only when something knocks the props out from under my self-sufficiency that I experience the wonderful security of Your everlasting arms. As long as I think I am able to handle life and its problems, I will not depend on You. But then life hands me something far beyond my ability to control and, like Peter, I discover my limitations the hard way - by failure.

When I think I have totally blown every chance I had of ever being what You want, You are merciful. You extend Your hand of love and grace to me yet again, restoring me to acceptance and fellowship with You.

That is what You did for Peter, and that is what You have done for me more than once. Wise people learn to depend on You at all times. The rest of us seem to realize our weakness and turn to Your strength only when we're knocked flat on our backs, facing BIG problems.

The account of Peter's lesson encourages me greatly, Lord, because it tells me You are the God of second chances - and third and fourth, if necessary. You are on my side. You don't give up on me. Thank You.

The eternal God is a dwelling place,
And underneath are the everlasting arms.
Deuteronomy 33: 27

181

LOOKING BACK

Indeed we had the sentence of death within ourselves in order that we should not trust in ourselves, but in God who raises the dead; who delivered us from so great a peril of death, and will deliver us, He on whom we have set our hope.
2 Corinthians 1: 9-10

Lord, I just finished reading through my journal that was written during a hard time in my life. In a span of 18 months, I received a diagnosis of advanced cancer (with no effective treatment available), experienced a car wreck which broke my back in five places, got a second opinion on the cancer and went through six months of radiation and chemo-therapy, became addicted to pain medicine and went through withdrawal and was diagnosed with breast cancer resulting in a radical mastectomy.

As I read through those pages, I was surprised to find page after page, entry after entry, of just Scripture - promises that You were with me, promises that You would not leave me, reminders that You wanted me to be full of hope and joy, urgings to praise You, instructions to bring You all my anxieties because You love me. I must have gone page by page through my Bible and pulled out every positive Scripture I could find!

Looking at that now, my Lord, I realize how much You taught me during that time about Your love for me. What I felt at the time was sick and weak and in so much pain and totally dependent upon You. Now, I see it as a holy time, a time of deep change within me, a time of learning much about You.

I remember reading and re-reading those Scriptures I had written in my journal. Several times a day, I would read them all again. I didn't realize it at the time, but they were pouring healing into me each time I read them. They were literally a life line for me. The words were living and active. They did their healing work deep in my spirit and in my body.

So here I am, nine years later, both cancers in remission and no addictions to battle. The chronic pain from the back injury is constant and restrictive but bearable. The heart problems resulting from the chemo slow me down a bit but cause me no anxiety. The brain surgery, resulting from medication given for the heart problems, fixed the brain hemorrhage with no lasting impairment. In other words, Lord, I am so very blessed!

It has been a revelation to me today to think through all this. A revelation of Your goodness, Your faithfulness, Your grace which is abundantly sufficient, Your power to work in the life of this child. I love You so very much, Lord. I can hardly wait to hug Your neck!

July 1
WORDS OF WISDOM

With what shall I come to the Lord
and bow myself before the God on high?
Micah 6: 6

I come to You this morning, Lord, the same needy child as yesterday. Do You get tired of hearing my needs? I do. Let's do something different. Instead of telling You what I need and want, allow me to ask You, "What would *You* like for our time together today?"

"I want to give you some truths about loving Me:

"A child who loves Me very much will, because of that love, consider Me in all things. There will be no struggle to 'put God first.' Love will make it so.

"That child who loves Me very much will, because of that love, trust Me completely. There will be no anxiety, no fretfulness, no irritation at petty inconveniences. Rather, a total trust that this day is in My control and rejoicing that this is so.

"A loving trusting child will be listening to Me, open to My leading in all situations, will have a sensitivity to My Spirit all day long. Obedience will follow listening.

"A child loving Me will be compassionate with people, ready to help any and all with My help.

"A child with My compassion will, because of that compassion, have a deep hatred of sin and what it does to people."

Love
Trust
Joy
Listening
Obedience
Compassion
Hatred of sin

By Your grace, Lord, may all of these become true of me.

July 2
MORE THOUGHTS ON LOVING

Now the God of peace...equip you in every good thing to do His will,
working in us that which is pleasing in His sight...
Hebrews 13: 20-21

This morning, Lord, I'm still thinking about yesterday's subject. Since those are characteristics that please You, then obviously their opposites would displease You. So it looks like this:

Pleasing to You	Displeasing to You
Love	Indifference
Trust	Doubt/Fear
Joy	Murmuring/Discontent
Listening	Heedless
Compassion	Hard Hearted
Hatred of Sin	Tolerance of Sin

Listing the opposites makes it very clear to me. I'm convicted, Lord, because many of my days as Your child have been characterized by the wrong list. I'm convicted because I see what a powerful witness of Your grace I could be if I took this to heart and began to live it.

What if every one of Your children would do this?

Is it actually do-able?

Yes, but only by Your grace. Can I count on Your grace to provide?

Absolutely,

For as many as may be the promises of God, in Him they are yes;
wherefore also by Him is our Amen to the glory of God through us.
2 Corinthians 1:20

This is Your Word, Lord. And those beautiful words from Hebrews at the top of this page assure me that You are more than ready to work in me to accomplish these things. How good You are to Your children! Help me this day to be pleasing in Your sight.

184

July 3
LEARNING TO PRAISE

Let them praise the name of the Lord
for His name alone is exalted;
His glory is above earth and heaven.
Psalm 148: 13

This psalm is a 14-verse-long encouragement to praise You. The whole creation is invoked to praise You, not only as Creator but also as Sustainer of all that exists. You alone are exalted and holy and worthy of our praise. I'm learning, Lord, that a requisite part of praising is *reverence*. And reverence carries with it a sense of respect and awe and wonder, even mystery. Mystery because You are so much more than my mind can understand. But I cannot let the limitations of my mind keep me from digging deeper for a clearer, more comprehensive concept of You, with the motive being *learning to praise*. The end result is worth far more than any effort expended.

You know, Lord, that through the years I've had to shed old "pictures" of You and appropriate new ones. Perhaps this continues as long as this life lasts. But what I'm seeing today is that my perception of our relationship, Yours and mine, is based on what I *know* about You. Thus, it is key that I have accurate knowledge of You.

Seeing who You really are brings spontaneous praise. And I am only able to see that by faith - faith in what Your Word says about You. I must have the simple, childlike trust of a much-loved, well-cared-for child in a loving, powerful, filled-with-goodness Father. Praise is simply a heartfelt response of love to Love. It is words of love spoken that tell You how I feel - not how I *ought* to feel or how I *want* to feel - but how I do feel toward You. It is communication on an intimate, honest level; You know all about me so there is no need for pretense.

Worship and praise are recognizing who You are and who I am. Here we have only talked about Creator, Sustainer and Father. The picture of Father/child is precious to me, Lord, because I understand it through my earthly life experience. But there are so many more pictures. Like.....

- You are Savior, I am saved
- You are Lord, I am servant
- You are King, I am subject
- You are Redeemer, I am redeemed

Any one of these is abundant reason to praise, but put together they are an awesome reminder of Your majesty and holiness!

185

July 4
DISCIPLINE

Keep watching and praying that you may not enter into temptation;
the spirit is willing, but the flesh is weak.
Matthew 26: 41

Total honesty with You is what I want, Lord, as I think about these words of wisdom from Your mouth. They so much describe me! Within me is this driving desire to get into Your Word, to praise and worship, to pray, to meditate. But all those things take effort, and my flesh truly is weak. I'm so easily persuaded by tiredness or distractions and I readily give in to the idea that I cannot put forth the necessary exertion.

And, Lord, when I give in, I know that I'm the loser. You have not given me this driving desire for *Your* sake but for mine. It is only when I allow Your Spirit to rule, that I am able to live my life as You want. Because that is when I learn; that is when I experience change.

But I say, walk by the Spirit, and you will not carry out the desire of the flesh.
Galatians 5: 16

If I would always see this situation as the spiritual battle that it is, I believe I'd be more ready to stand firm, determined to win through Your grace and strength. I'd learn to ignore the flesh and just obey Your Spirit. Temptation to sleep would not be a factor. Temptation to allow distractions to divert my mind would melt away. Temptation to just read whatever good book I'm reading at the time would no longer be strong.

Please, Lord, give me grace to fight this battle for as long as necessary in order to establish this discipline in my life. These things are too important to allow failure. Besides, I absolutely do *not* want the enemy to win.

No temptation has overtaken you but such as is common to man;
and God is faithful, who will not allow you to be tempted
beyond what you are able,
but with the temptation will provide the way of escape also,
that you may be able to endure it.
I Corinthians 10:13

Thank You for that encouragement. Thank You for Your faithfulness!

July 5
GOD'S PRESENCE

If therefore there is any encouragement in Christ,
if there is any consolation of love,
if there is any fellowship of the Spirit,
if any affection and compassion,
make my joy complete by being of the same mind,
maintaining the same love,
united in spirit, intent on one purpose.
Philippians 2: 1-2

Those are some of the wonderful things about consciously being in Your presence, Lord. Encouragement is essential, and Your encouragement is supreme above all. You have built us with a great need for love and acceptance, and we find both in Your presence. Fellowship of the Spirit! How incredible is that? The High and Holy God of all the universe takes time to fellowship with me. Affection and compassion - those words, like fellowship, are "friendship" words. And You *are* my Friend.

All of this, my Lord, is for each and every one of Your children. You accept us as we are and begin to change us, bit by bit, into what You desire for us. When we try and fail, You accept us all over again. When we don't even try, You discipline us and bring us back into Your presence for another dose of Your love. Eventually Your love does its blessed work of causing us to love You more deeply and to *want* to try. The depth of Your patience, Your power and wisdom are beyond my comprehension.

The second verse above talks about being same-minded, taking You as my example and living by the leading of Your Holy Spirit. If all Your children are doing this, we *will* be of the same mind, maintaining the same love, united in spirit, intent on one purpose. It is exactly the same principle as the symphony members all tuning to the oboe. If all instruments are in tune with the oboe, all will be in tune with each other and beautiful music will result.

I'm so glad, Lord, You are teaching me beautiful music in my life. My spiritual goal is the ability to focus on You so completely that it becomes my second nature to pray without ceasing. Because the truth is that I'm *always* in Your presence. Then my very life can be a song of praise to You.

July 6
GOD *WILL* SAVE

But I have trusted in Thy loving kindness;
my heart shall rejoice in Thy salvation.
I will sing to the Lord,
because He has dealt bountifully with me.
Psalm 13: 5-6

David is praying for help in a time of trouble. This little psalm is only 6 verses long, and the first 4 are spent telling You his troubles, asking when You are going to come and rescue him. I've been there, Lord. I've wondered how much longer You are going to wait before You provide some particular thing I think I needed yesterday.

I've been through times of wondering, "How long shall I take counsel in my soul?" I've felt an urgent need for Your wisdom but, like David, *seemed* to be left to handle things on my own. I have felt like You were hiding Your face from me and, like David, that the enemy was winning. Not a happy place to be, by any means, but such a lesson in faith! Through those situations, I learned to *not* trust in how I felt, or in what I thought, *but to keep my eyes upon You.* I'm so encouraged by what David does next.

What he does next is speak to You those words of faith and praise above. In between verse 4 and verse 5, he recalled all the past times in his life that he was in trouble, and how You had *never* failed to deliver him. And his recollection settled each of his questions. It did not give him answers, but it gave him peace in the midst of his uncertainties.

Those who know tell us that "the best indicator of future behavior is past behavior." That certainly is true of You. One of the greatest faith builders I have is to simply remember all the ways You have been faithful to deliver me over the years. And how You were faithful to deliver my parents before me. And how You were faithful to every one Your children throughout the Bible. With all those past deliverances, why would I ever do anything but trust in Your loving kindness, rejoice in Your salvation and sing to You? Truly, You have dealt bountifully with me!

In peace I will both lie down and sleep.
For Thou alone, O Lord, dost make me to dwell in safety.
Psalm 4: 8

July 7
GIVERS AND TAKERS

...and hope does not disappoint,
because the love of God has been poured out within our hearts
through the Holy Spirit who was given to us.
Romans 5: 5

I'm seeing, Lord, that I must be both a taker and a giver - inflow and outflow - to be in balance. It is impossible to be just one or the other. Not just hard, but impossible. Before I have any blessing to share with anyone, I must first have received it from You. And You are constantly ready to give, but I must *take*. There is a vast difference between *having something available to me* and *taking it for my own*. Because, it's only when I have *received* that I have something to give.

So I am a taker from You and a giver to others. This inflow/outflow is Your design, Lord. You pour Your love into my heart. I receive it and then must dispense it to others. If I don't pass it along, the inflow stops. The rate of inflow is determined by the rate of outflow. Unless it is flowing out, it cannot flow in. Unless it is flowing out, what is there evaporates, stagnates, trickles away or just sits there collecting dust. Not a pretty thought.

Your supply is unlimited and as long as I'm giving, I can never run short. Only by ceasing to allow it to flow out into the lives of others will the incoming supply dwindle. If that happens, I cease to become either a taker or a giver, and I become something else entirely - an empty shell. An empty shell that gets harder and thicker and uglier, and soon all fellowship with You is gone. And so is all fellowship with my spiritual brothers and sisters.

Now on the last day, the great day of the feast, Jesus stood and cried out saying,
"If any man is thirsty, let him come to Me and drink.
He who believes in Me, as the Scripture said,
from his innermost being shall flow rivers of living water."
John 7: 37-38

I'm seeing that generosity applies to so much more than just money. You want me to be a cheerful giver of everything You have given me - which is everything I have!

Your grace is a flow,
a refreshing, cleansing inflow
which washes away the dustiness and mustiness of my soul.

An outflow can then occur which reaches out to those around me
and gently touches their lives.
Lord, may I be generous!

July 8
YOUR WORK IN ME

For it is God who is at work in you,
both to will and to work for His good pleasure.
Philippians 2: 13

It is a beautiful morning, Lord, and my heart is so full of gratitude and love that I must put some of it down on paper. The enemy of my soul would have me be depressed with the thought of another long day to get through with this pain and fatigue. This was present in my thoughts when I woke up awhile ago. But immediately came the thought:

This is the day which the Lord has made,
let us rejoice and be glad in it.
Psalm 118: 24

And my whole inner being became joyful, peaceful and full of light. I got my coffee, my Bible and my journal and got back into my chair to spend wonderful time with You. What an incredible privilege to be Your child, to know that You love me and that I'm secure in Your care. My spirit rejoices, Lord, and my heart bows low in worship and thanksgiving!

I read this statement yesterday, "Life is not salvage to be saved out of the world, but an investment to be used in the world." This sentence speaks volumes to me because, as You know, I often feel pretty useless and unable to do anything of worth - for You or for anyone. But this tells me that, as Your investment, I *am* useful because You are the one doing the work, not me. All I have to do is stay close, abide in You, and trust that You are at work.

My desire, Lord, which You have placed within me, is to be used by You to make a difference in the lives of the people in my circle of influence. So be it.

I am willing.
You are able.
It shall be done.

July 9
FAILING A TEST

The fear of the Lord is clean, enduring forever,
the judgments of the Lord are true;
they are righteous altogether.
Psalm 19: 9

Thank You, Lord, for allowing me to see a little glimpse of how much work there is yet to do in me. Yesterday's situation, I'm convinced, was a test. The sorrow in having done poorly is outweighed by the joy in realizing two critically important things:

You are at work in me.
If I want the job completed, I must work *with* You.

It is, first of all, an amazing thing that You are at work in me! I'm so thankful for that. And I do want the job done, Lord. Once more I turn full face toward You and admit my weariness, my lack of everything needed.

I also stand upon Your Word that through You, I *can* do it. I'm very aware that there has to be a change deep inside me. Help me to simply do what is before me, listen carefully to You, and cooperate fully as You make the inner-man-changes in me.

Let the words of my mouth and the meditation of my heart
be acceptable in Thy sight,
O Lord, my Rock and my Redeemer.
Psalm 19: 14

July 10
YOUR CONTROL

Do you not know? Have you not heard?
The Everlasting God, the Lord, the Creator of the ends of the earth
does not become weary or tired.
His understanding is inscrutable.
Isaiah 40:28

You, my Lord, are in control of the circumstances of my life. Whatever happens, You can use for good. That inner assurance gives me a completely new perspective on the past, present and future. Many things in the past I don't understand; often in the present I tend to ask questions; and the future is so uncertain - mine, the nation's, the world's. But knowing You are in control is the key to peace and joy and power in daily living.

Having said all that, I, like the Jews, sometimes long for a "sign" that You really are in control. Increase my faith, Lord, and increase the depth of my love for You and for all people.

.....next day.....

That prayer above, Lord, was prayed one ordinary work-day morning and was answered in an extra-ordinary way the same morning. The hilly country road from our home into town was covered with ice, and I got into my car at the bottom of the driveway where I had left it the evening before. I started slowly down the icy road and suddenly felt my car sliding sideways toward the edge of the road - an edge that went down a long way into a deep ravine. I had absolutely no control over my car.

That is when You answered both the prayer above for a "sign" and the one which involuntarily came out of my mouth at that moment, "Oh, God, please make this car stop!" And You did! It absolutely stopped - a few inches from the edge and cross-wise in the road.

Then I continued to pray, both prayers of thanksgiving for not going over the edge and supplication for "now, how do I get backed up and facing the right direction?" Somehow, Lord, You blessed my ignorance of what to do, and enabled me to get turned around and headed in the right direction.

Do I believe You are in control? *With all my heart!* Will I ever, ever again ask for a sign? I don't think so.

Do not fear, for I am with you;
do not anxiously look about you, for I am your God.
I will strengthen you, surely I will help you,
surely I will uphold you with My righteous right hand.
Isaiah 41:10

July 11
CHOICES, CHOICES

For the flesh sets its desire against the Spirit,
and the Spirit against the flesh;
for these are in opposition to one another,
so that you may not do the things that you please.
Galatians 5: 17

We always do those things we really want to do. True or False?

Lord, we are faced with decisions and choices every day, many times a day. As a follower of You, I weigh these and at times find myself in the position of choosing what I know to be the "right" thing even though it is not what I'd really like.

So is the above statement false? I *don't* always do those things I really want to do? No, I think the statement is true. Because in making that choice to do "right," I *am* doing what I really want - I want what is "right" more than I want what I want.

What I've found, Lord, is that once I get past the struggle of choosing, I still face the problem of living out those decisions. This can be treacherous territory because it is a perfect breeding ground for doubt, resentment, and bitterness. I can conveniently forget that I made the choice and begin to blame the situation on another person or on You or on my past - whatever the enemy can dredge up that will cause me to have a negative attitude.

This erosion is deadly, and I can see it takes diligent work to prevent it. What *does* it take to successfully live out my decisions to be 100% obedient to You?

A vital, growing relationship with You.
A "heart commitment" as well as mental assent to Your will for my life.
Absolute trust in You.
Consistent obedience to what I know to do.
Sometimes life is so hard! How thankful I am for Your grace.

And let us not lose heart in doing good,
for in due time we shall reap
if we do not grow weary.
Galatians 6: 9

July 12
STRESS AND STRUGGLES

For though we walk in the flesh, we do not war according to the flesh,
for the weapons of our warfare are not of the flesh,
but divinely powerful for the destruction of fortresses.
We are destroying speculations and every lofty thing
raised up against the knowledge of God,
and we are taking every thought captive to the obedience of Christ.
2 Corinthians 10: 3-5

Dear Lord, I need to sort through the jumble of my mind this morning and take some thoughts captive. I need to destroy some speculations and fortresses. Help me to set aside the opinions of others as well as my own. I want specific help from *You* in my mind as I go out to begin this busy day that is ahead of me.

I confess, Lord, that part of my problem is that I *know* Your Word much better than I *live* it. I so need to live my everyday life with a full-of-trust obedience to all I know of Your Word. Even simple instructions like:

Rejoice evermore.
Pray without ceasing.
In everything give thanks.
1 Thessalonians 5: 16 - 18

I can see that to consistently obey only these three instructions would bring a transformation in my life. Jesus, let me draw on Your strength. I seem to have come totally to the end of mine.

I also see that the battle, the real struggle, is spiritual no matter what form it takes on the surface. I find it interesting that merely *acknowledging* that fact clears away side issues and presents my mind with a simple choice: God's way or Satan's way? Right or wrong?

I'm convinced, Lord, that when I *will* to do what You want, all the forces of heaven are gathered to my side to see that I am victorious. The will is the key thing. I have no wisdom in myself to make right choices, so I ask that You continue to pour out Your amazing grace upon my life. Today I shall, by that grace, obey the three directives above. I really am learning, Lord. Don't give up on me.

July 13
ENCOURAGEMENT

From 1 Corinthians 1: 2-9

My heart overflows with gratitude this morning, Lord, as I think upon the encouragement from these verses. Paul uses the word "saint" to identify the believers to whom he is writing these noble words. I seldom (in fact, never) think of myself as a saint. But, well, here are the truths in Your Word.....

I have been sanctified in You, set apart to belong to You, made holy by Your grace at work within me.

I call upon Your name for everything I need to live this life of faith in a dark and sinful world.

I have received both grace and peace from You. Grace for living and peace which is greater than any the world has to offer - Your peace.

In You, I have been enriched in everything - both speech and knowledge, material and spiritual.

The truth about You, Lord, has been confirmed in me by the work of the Holy Spirit.

I am eagerly awaiting Your coming back again. Today would be a good day!

I have the promise of being confirmed by You to the end, and found blameless on that great day.

I have the assurance (and the experience of long years) that You are faithful.
I am called into fellowship with You. How glorious is that?!

I so much needed these encouraging words this morning. Only You, Lord, know the rough patch I've been going through and the weariness it has caused - both physical and spiritual. I feel strengthened now to make it through this day. These are wonderful thoughts - each of them a jewel and, all together, a beautiful crown for every believer. Even me.

July 14
A SMALL LESSON ON FAITH

For by grace you have been saved through faith;
and that not of yourselves, it is the gift of God;
not as a result of works,
that no one should boast.
Ephesians 2: 8-9

You've given me a new insight today, Lord. Please help me understand it.

When I told You that I desired to belong to You 100%, the first giant step was taken. If I have not, since then, disobeyed or been rebellious, I must consider the work to be progressing *whether I see it or not*. I must also believe that You are well able to make me understand anything You need *me* to do.

To be constantly taking my spiritual temperature is not necessary and maybe not even pleasing to You. My initial salvation was by grace and grace alone. My working out of that salvation day-by-day is also by Your grace. You are in charge and do not need me to help You run things.

"Be anxious for *nothing!*"

Even something as important as this?

"Yes."

I see, Lord. I am to trust in Your care and simply rejoice that I belong to You. *That* is what I need to be doing. Relax and rejoice.

But the Lord is faithful,
and He will strengthen and protect you
from the evil one.
2 Thessalonians 3: 3

July 15
MORE ON FAITH

*...for I know whom I have believed
and am convinced that He is able
to guard that which I have entrusted to Him
until that day.*
2 Timothy 1: 12

What *have* I entrusted to You, Lord? Well, every small and large thing concerning myself and every person within my circle of influence, complete with all of our problems. I have brought it all to You. You are the one with the answers to our needs, so why would I go anywhere else? But do I fully trust that You are working on these situations? I want to give serious thought to those words, "which I have entrusted to Him."

If I have entrusted a problem to You, I have placed it into Your hands; it is no longer mine. If I find myself still working at it and worrying over it, then I have taken it back. I can therefore expect no solution from You.

So I must give the situation to You and *leave* it with You, full of assurance that You will take over from there and will answer my prayer. Perhaps Your answer will not be the answer I'd choose, but it will be the *best* answer.

The challenge for me, Lord, is practicing the patience necessary to wait upon You. My nature is to get busy and get things done. So for me to sit... and wait... and trust... is *very* difficult.

Grant me mercy, please my Lord, until I learn.

July 16
STRENGTH FOR FIGHTING

Finally, be strong in the Lord, and in the strength of His might.
For our struggle is not against flesh and blood,
but against the rulers, against the powers,
against the world forces of this darkness,
against the spiritual forces of wickedness
in the heavenly places.
Ephesians 6: 10 & 12

The struggles of life seem endless, Lord. At work, at home, in our extended families - there seems to be no end to the problems, some of them sizeable. Your Word says these struggles are not against flesh and blood, even though most of our problems are "people" problems, but against the rulers of darkness. In other words, they are, at base, spiritual problems.

The very first piece of spiritual armor we are given with which to protect ourselves is *truth*. We are to gird ourselves with the truth. I know, Lord, that what I think is not necessarily the truth; nor what I feel, nor even what I see. *Your Word is truth*. You, Yourself, are truth; therefore, I can know that a thing *is* the way You say that it is. Help me to keep that in mind as we progress with these thoughts.

A few things I know about my battles:

It is foolish to fret over the past. I cannot change the past. It is far better to spend that energy, and the wisdom gained from my failures, in changing the present.

What I do today directly affects my tomorrows and those of everyone around me. The choices which shaped my life to the present day were *my* choices. So all thoughts of self-pity or blaming must be consistently turned away until they are silenced by exhaustion, and never return. The enemy will try to convince me to blame *anyone* rather than myself - even You - because then I could be the "victim." My task is to resist him.

I am not strong enough for these struggles. I used to think I was emotionally and physically capable of handling most things that came my way. Now I know I am not. Neither am I wise enough to consistently make right choices. And there are many yet to be made. I'm depending upon You for both strength and wisdom. And perseverance. Don't forget perseverance. You, my Lord, are my Rock and my Refuge!

July 17
MY SECURITY IN YOU

He who dwells in the shelter of the Most High
will abide in the shadow of the Almighty
I will say to the Lord,
"My refuge and my fortress, my God in whom I trust!"
Psalm 91: 1-2

What better way to start a day than to affirm Your words to my heart.
Words of promise,
words of love I claim as mine,
not because I'm worthy
but simply because You love me.

Incredible!
The Most High God stoops to love
His undeserving creatures!
And yet that is Your entire message from Genesis to Revelation.

You love me,
desire my fellowship,
want to bless me,
and the best is yet to come.
For ultimately, I will behold Your salvation.
I can hardly wait!

Each new day is like standing on the verge of the unknown,
and yet my spirit is at peace,
I am secure in Your love,
because You know exactly what is ahead.
I have no fear.

Through the hills and valleys, You will be with me.
I will drink water from the rain of heaven to strengthen my spirit.
I will have everything I need supplied to me.
My heart overflows with thanksgiving.

July 18
ETERNAL TRUTHS

And His voice shook the earth then, but now He has promised, saying,
"Yet once more I will shake not only the earth, but also the heaven."
And this expression, "yet once more," denotes the removing of
those things which can be shaken, as of created things,
in order that those things which cannot be shaken may remain.
Therefore since we receive a kingdom which cannot be shaken,
let us show gratitude, by which we may offer to God
an acceptable service with reverence and awe;
for our God is a consuming fire.
Hebrews 12: 26-29

As I read Your Word, as I read the writings of men and women of faith who have lived in the years since You walked this earth, as I sing the old hymns of long ago, I'm made to realize a wonderful thing, Lord. Their words resonate deep in my spirit with truth and my heart says, "Yes, that is how it is with me, too!"

This is astonishing to me! These writers each lived in a culture and environment completely different from mine. The circumstances of their daily life would be quite foreign to me. And yet their words about their love for You, their faith and their struggles are like they have been reading *my* journal.

This is everlasting truth making itself evident, isn't it, Lord? This is You at work showing me that the truths of the spiritual world are *eternal* truths. As the Scripture above says, they are unshakable and thus will remain for eternity. Like You, they are unchangeable...

Jesus Christ is the same yesterday and today, yes and forever.
Hebrews 13: 8

How hopeless it would be to live this life of faith if this were not true. If You changed Your mind about things every few years, we would not know what to do or what to expect. I'm so filled with gratitude right now, Lord, that You are immutable.

How great to know that my faith is founded upon the Rock, that I'm a part of that unshakable kingdom! What an awesome thing is this grace in which I stand. Truly, Lord, it is with reverence and awe that I bow before You in gratitude and worship.

July 19
UNSHAKABLE PEACE

And this expression, "Yet once more," denotes the removing of those things
which can be shaken, as of created things,
in order that those things which cannot be shaken may remain.
Hebrews 12: 27

I'm still thinking about this Scripture this morning, Lord. I think the author was speaking of a cosmic, world-wide shaking that would happen. But I'm thinking of how it applies to my own heart and life.

I have experienced this shaking in my life, Lord. Gradually over time, it seems that everything that can be shaken *has* been, in order that only things which cannot be shaken may remain. I no longer count my life or any of my possessions dear to me. I hold them out to You with open hands. *Therefore, nothing has the power to move me from the peace You have given me.*

I have learned to rest only in You. It is truly a blessed place to be. A separation has occurred between me and everything/everyone else. I'm detached - cut loose - and ready to finish these days here and come home to be with You. I understand what Paul meant when he said:

For to me, to live is Christ, and to die is gain.
Philippians 1: 21

We are of good courage, I say, and prefer rather
to be absent from the body
and to be at home with the Lord.
2 Corinthians 5: 8

So am I elevating myself to the lofty heights of the Apostle Paul? Not at all. I'm just saying that what You did in Paul's heart, You have also done in mine. And when I think of all the hymns and gospel songs written about heaven, I see that You have frequently done this work in Your children. You loosen our grip on the things below and make more and more precious to us the things above. We begin to see the temporal for what it is - quickly passing away - and the eternal as the shining blessed promise before us.

But, like Paul, I acknowledge that the power of life and death is in Your hands, Lord. I want only Your will worked in my life, however much longer that may be. Because I belong to You, I have glorious security and unshakable peace.

July 20
INTERCESSORY PRAYER

Jesus said to him, "I am the way, and the truth, and the life;
no one comes to the Father, but through Me.
John 14: 6

It seems to me, Lord, that these words spoken by You embody one of the most fundamental statements in all of Scripture. There is so much truth packed into those few words. As I come to You this morning with the burden of intercessory prayer on my heart, You show me a facet of truth in this verse to ease that burden.

You know, Jesus, that 100% of what I'm asking is for people to come to You - for salvation, for complete surrender, for spiritual healing or physical healing, for whatever You know they need to successfully live this life of faith.

What I hear You saying through this verse today is that this is *Your* work. Initially and finally, beginning to end, this is Your work. I can't convict anyone of their need for You. I can't cause their heart to long for You. I can't give them the heart-knowledge necessary for them to come to You, confess, repent and accept You as Lord of their life. The whole package is Your job.

So what is my part?

"Love one another.
"Bear much fruit.
"Ask the Father.
"Be full of My joy.
"Abide in Me.
"Keep My commandments."

These are my instructions, Lord. I am to live a life of obedience and transparency. I am to faithfully bring these people and their needs to You in prayer. I am to simply trust that Your prayer promises are absolute truth. Keep me faithful, Lord!

July 21
PURE JOY

Blessed is the man who listens to me,
watching daily at my gates,
waiting at my doorposts.
For he who finds me finds life,
and obtains favor from the Lord.
Proverbs 8: 34-35

Please, Lord, allow me to thank You for the blessing of yesterday that was so real to my spirit and my mind. Help me describe it.

Yesterday, while working in the flower beds in my backyard, I had a revelation of You as a God of joy - *a new-to-me sense of the lightness, happiness, glee and pure joy that are vital ingredients of who You are.* It was not like a vision, for I saw nothing. There was no audible speaking. It was simply a beautiful, complete, shining fact dropped into my mind that made me drop what I was doing, stop in my tracks and turn my full attention to You.

The revelation had an immediate effect upon me, one which lasts still - an easing of my own burden, and a stronger sense of confidence that I can rejoice because *You* are in control. Now, obviously, this is not new knowledge. But, somehow, I know it *better,* with greater certainty, more deeply than I did before.

Then my reading this morning was in Proverbs 8 which is about wisdom and all of her attributes, worth, history and mission. These astonishing words, speaking about creation, stood out for me:

Then I (wisdom) *was beside Him, as a master workman;*
and I was daily His delight,
rejoicing always before Him,
rejoicing in the world, His earth,
and having my delight in the sons of men.
Proverbs 8: 30-31

Both times the word "rejoicing" occurs, the alternate translation of that word is given: "playing." "*Playing always before Him, playing in the world, His earth.*" This is affirmation of what You showed me yesterday and is, to me, a whole new and unique way of seeing You. I absorb it with my whole heart, Lord, because: (1) I sense it is of You and (2) I am very much inclined, if left to myself, to focus on things in the opposite direction.

By Your grace I will this day rejoice evermore with a light and happy heart - one full of love for You, my God of pure joy.

July 22
BORNE ON EAGLES' WINGS

You yourselves have seen what I did to the Egyptians,
and how I bore you on eagles' wings,
and brought you to Myself.
Exodus 19: 4

Lord, I know I've read this many times before, but this morning it was like You had flashing lights around the words to draw my attention. You were speaking these words to Moses for him to pass them on to the sons of Israel. And it is true that they *had* seen what You had done to the Egyptians; incredible things that should have been very convincing. But... "borne on eagles' wings"?

I imagine that if Moses had sent out his administrative staff with their pads and pens to poll the Israelites on whether or not they had been borne on eagles' wings, 10 out of 10 would have said, "No way!"

They were terrified when Pharaoh's army pursued them. Then they ran out of bread. Then they had no meat. Then they had no water fit to drink. And during all this time, they walked and walked and walked. And complained and complained and complained. I'm certain they would not consider that being "borne on eagles' wings."

To me, Lord, and probably to them, this phrase conjures up the scene of an effortless, wonderful life lived far above all the dust and hurts of daily existence. No pain, no weariness, just resting and soaring high. But this I *know*: You said it, so it is true. And then You showed me why it is true.

You were totally in control every minute - every second - of that process of moving Your children out of Egypt and into (or at least toward) the Promised Land. You had a plan, and You were working that plan. You delivered them by Your power from every problem. You supplied their every need - bread, meat, water, a cloud to lead them by day and a pillar of fire to lead them by night. Were they grateful? Not very. Did they totally understand Your plan and fall right in with it? Not exactly. Am I any different? Not much.

But Lord, I do see the lesson You are trying to teach me: every detail of this past eventful, stressful, painful month has been under Your control and part of Your plan. Do I fully understand? No, but I fully trust that You will show me anything I need to know when I need to know it. In the meantime, here is what I do know.

I know that I was very near death, and yet I'm alive. I know You provided what I needed precisely when I needed it. I know that You are good, and all that You do is good. I know that I am safe in Your hands. I know I love You with all my heart, soul, mind and strength. I see clearly, Lord, that You *were* bearing me up on eagles' wings.

July 23
SOVEREIGN GOD

He who is the blessed and only Sovereign,
the King of kings and Lord of lords;
who alone possesses immortality and dwells in unapproachable light;
whom no man has seen or can see.
To Him be honor and eternal dominion!
Amen.
1 Timothy 6: 15-16

I love these words, Lord. I memorized them long ago because they say beautifully what my heart feels but has trouble expressing. So when I come across them again in my study of the Word, it is like re-discovering a sparkling, exquisite gem. I am so grateful for writers like Paul, David and Isaiah and for Your inspiration within them to write such powerful, wonderful words.

Today the words "sovereign," "King," 'Lord," and "dominion" are what grab my attention. Lately I've been thinking about Your control over the affairs of men, Your absolute sovereignty both on earth, where we experience it every day, and in heaven, about which we only speculate.

Sure, there is evil in the world. Seemingly, a lot of it. And yet Your Word teaches that none of it occurs without Your permission, that Satan is on a leash and completely under Your command. I must admit that I don't fully understand why You permit the evil except that it is somehow necessary to Your overall purpose. And for right now, that includes a world that seems to be growing more evil every day.

How incredible that, as You work out Your grand plan for all mankind, you also work out Your plan for every single believer's life! I cannot comprehend *how* You can do this but, because You are God, I know You can.

Thoughts like these make me realize how small is my concept of You, Lord. I get comfortable with my thoughts of You as my Counselor or my Friend or my Father. And You are all of those to me. But this Scripture stretches my mind and reminds me that You are so much more than I know! In all humility, my awed spirit bows down before the eternal sovereign King who dwells in unapproachable light. To You, my soul gives honor.

July 24
A WEARY PILGRIM

Come to Me, all who are weary and heavy-laden, and I will give you rest.
Take My yoke upon you, and learn from me,
for I am gentle and humble in heart;
and you shall find rest for your souls
for My yoke is easy, and My load is light.
Matthew 11: 28-30

These soothing words always speak to me, Lord, maybe because I always seem to be weary and heavy-laden. I think I must have been *born* serious minded and solemn in attitude. But this morning, You are showing me a new-to-me truth from them. It is this. If I find myself struggling and working strenuously at *anything*, I need to back off and take an honest look at the situation. When I do that, I will always find the old problem of self-sufficiency present and at work.

Your promise is that You *will* give me rest. I have proven this specific promise many times in the past, and I know that none of Your promises fail. At times I fail to qualify for them, but Your promises do not fail. So if my daily life seems to be getting harder and harder, and I'm becoming weary and heavy-laden, it is my fault. I have slipped out of Your yoke and am, once again, laboring under my own steam, bent down under the burden. You *have* exactly what I need, but I must come to You and receive it.

You would think - well, *I* would think - that I should have totally killed off self by now. But I too often find myself back at this point of dealing with it again. I see, though, that You are giving me a "positive" to fill the space that death-to-self leaves behind.

For sometime now, You have been working into my mind the concept of *trusting* what You are doing in me. You have been showing me that while rejecting my self-sufficiency, I must also whole-heartedly *accept, honor, value, and trust* the truths You are teaching me. I must share them at every opportunity You give me. I must be bold to speak Your word, with the pure motive of bringing glory and honor to You.

In summary:

My Part	Your Part
Come to You	Give me rest
Take Your yoke	Suit Your yoke to me
Learn from You	Teach me
Share	Provide opportunities

Thank You, Lord, for Your patience with this slow-learner. It takes a lot of practice, doesn't it?

July 25
STILLNESS

Let go, relax and know that I am God;
I will be exalted among the nations,
I will be exalted in the earth.
Psalm 46:10

How strong my need
my desire
to be calm and still in Your presence.
My mind, my will, my heart are subdued.
The quietness of eternity has settled down within me.

You have placed within me such a hunger for more of You, Lord.
This requires there be less of me.
I am willing.

I choose to know Your will.
To know and to do.
There is nothing I cannot give up at Your word.

You have the highest place of honor and authority in my life.
My heart is at peace,
my mind is stilled,
my spirit Yours, my Lord.

Be Thou exalted.

July 26
SIMPLE FAITH

Surely I have composed and quieted my soul;
like a weaned child rests against his mother,
my soul is like a weaned child within me.
Psalm 131: 2

Simple faith is child-like faith. Children who are loved learn to trust and love those in charge of them. This kind of faith is so appealing to me, Lord, and I believe it is because You have planted deep within me the knowledge that this is what pleases You, too.

As You know, George Müller is one of my heroes. He had this uncomplicated faith about which I'm thinking. He took all Your Word as truth, believed it and put it to work every day of his life. And time after time, year after year, You honored Your promises and his faith. His life is an amazing account of what You can accomplish through a person who will consistently believe You.

I ask You, Lord, to teach me this kind of faith. Teach me to take, for my own, every promise that is mine. Teach me to quickly dismiss every thought that would come against Your Word. Teach me to love and trust You as a well-loved child does its father or mother.

In the very act of asking these things, I realize that You have already done so much of this! So I turn my supplication into praise and thanksgiving. Thank You, Lord, for bringing me this far down the path toward a beautiful, simple faith. My spirit is full of praise for the God of compassion and mercy, so wise and full-of-power! I give You freedom to continue Your work.

July 27
YOUR PRESENCE WITH ME

The grace of the Lord Jesus Christ,
and the love of God,
and the fellowship of the Holy Spirit,
be with you all.
2 Corinthians 13: 14

Lord, I read a few minutes ago this benediction Paul wrote - this prayer for the believers in Corinth. These are the things Paul's great heart of love desired for the people who had become believers under his teaching. And he desired these things because *You* desired them as well.

The grace of the Lord Jesus Christ - that phrase slips off the tongue so easily, Lord. But oh, how much it cost You to provide it! May I never forget or take for granted the price paid that enables me to stand in the fullness of that marvelous grace. My entire being worships at the foot of the cross upon which You died - that death that was my eternal salvation.

The love of God - so much has been written and sung and preached about the love of God. And yet, with all I know, I have only a dim understanding of its depth. You have shown me how it is like a good father's love for his children. That is an illustration which is clear to me because I had a good father. You have shown me love through Your compassion and mercy in my own life. You have shown me love, perhaps most of all, through the plan of redemption. You willingly sent Jesus to die! Love for Your creature man was great enough to see Your Son suffer and die a horrible death. That is a love beyond my limited comprehension, Father God, because I, too, have a son.

The fellowship of the Holy Spirit - this is probably one of my favorite subjects in all the world. There are no words in my vocabulary to express the exalted value in which I hold the fellowship of Your Spirit! It is so far above every other thing in my life as to be in a completely different realm. I know that within Your fellowship are both the grace of Jesus and the love God, and every other good thing You pour out upon those who fear You and love You. Although not yet tested, I believe I could do without all my physical blessings if I still had the fullness of Your fellowship. Without that fellowship I would not want to live even five minutes, no matter how many physical blessings I possessed. That may be poorly said, Lord, but You know my heart. I'm saying, I love You with all that I am!

Like Paul, this is my prayer for everyone I know. These words are to me like a warm blanket on a cold day. How I would that *every* believer be covered over and wrapped in Your grace and love and presence.

July 28
EVIDENCES OF YOUR SPIRIT

I, therefore, the prisoner of the Lord,
entreat you to walk in a manner worthy
of the calling with which you have been called,
with all humility and gentleness, with patience,
showing forbearance to one another in love,
being diligent to preserve the unity of the Spirit
in the bond of peace.
Ephesians 4: 1-3

I'm thinking still about the inflow-outflow of this life of faith. You have called each of us, and I'm so amazed, Lord, at the variety of ways we can express Your work within us. The filling of Your Spirit is always the same in that it is the same Spirit, producing the same love, adoration and praise in our hearts. But the responses - oh, how different!

We respond and react differently because *we* are so different. The work You do within us is filtered through our personality when expressed to others. Some write songs, some sing those songs, some dance, some preach, some teach, some write books, some just quietly shed tears. But it is the same Spirit filling each. And here is the focal point: You are pleased with each one who is freely allowing You to flow through their life, however it comes about, as long as it is glorifying to You.

If my goal is simply to please You with my life, which it is, then that statement becomes very liberating. I am set free to be myself as You made me. I don't have to do the things others do; I don't have to reach some standard set by man; I don't have to measure up to *anything* other than Your opinion of me. You, Yourself, are the Creator of all this variety. You fashioned us to be what we are and never, never, did You expect us to be all alike. You love the loud expressive one just as much as You love the reserved and quiet. You love the writer of the song just as much as You love the singer.

How great it would be, Lord, if every believer could know how accepted and loved they are - how much joy they give You by being themselves. How solid and steadfast we could then become because our confidence would not be in ourselves but *in Your work in us.*

How great it would be, also, if knowing this truth, we would never judge a fellow-believer. Please, Lord, make us humble, gentle, patient and loving with each other.

July 29
YOUR GOODNESS TO ME

One of the greatest ways You have blessed me over the years, Lord, is teaching me to take Scripture personally; that is, to allow it to speak directly to *my* mind and heart.

This morning as I read in Titus, I came to these lovely words. I want to paraphrase them as being the affirmation of my heart to Yours....

Your kindness and Your love for me came and saved me,
not because I'm worthy or good, but because You are merciful.
You washed away my filthiness
and made me a new person - all by the power of Your Spirit
whom You poured out upon me abundantly.
By Your grace You made me an heir of Your family
and gave me eternal life.
Titus 3:4-7

Thank You for inspiring Paul to write these words and then for preserving them through the centuries so that I could be blessed by them this morning. Thank You for washing me in regeneration and pouring Your Spirit freely into mine. Thank You for allowing me to be a part of Your big, wonderful family.

Truly You are a great and awesome God,
full of grace and glory.
May this day be one of unceasing prayer and worship.

July 30
THE FATHER OF LIES

You are of your father the devil, and you want to do the desires of your father.
He was a murderer from the beginning, and does not stand in the truth,
because there is no truth in him.
Whenever he speaks a lie, he speaks from his own nature;
for he is a liar, and the father of lies.
John 8:44

Lord, I read the following statements awhile ago and they distressed me. I need to talk to You about them. They said, "The supreme satisfaction is to be able to despise one's neighbor and this fact goes far to account for religious intolerance. It is evidently consoling to reflect that the people next door are headed for hell."

Those words fairly drip with evil and hatred! I wish I could talk face to face with this person. I wish, too, that I could argue that religious intolerance does not exist, but I cannot because I know that it does exist. But it angers me for this writer to plunk that concept down into the middle of despising and being glad your neighbor is headed for hell. It angers me that all faith, all worship, all "religion" is lumped into one homogenized conglomerate and all scorned. It angers me that there could be one who would think that the supreme satisfaction is to despise one's neighbor. Because I *know*, Lord, that the *only* satisfaction in life comes from loving, not despising. And it is actually exactly the opposite of what this writer says when a child of Yours reflects that a neighbor might be headed for hell - *disturbing* - not consoling.

How sad that this person is so bitter toward You and Your children. How unhappy and cynical he must be to express such thoughts. He is, in actuality, in bondage to Satan and is either completely unaware of it or denies it. His words are but a small picture of the lies and hatred he has been fed.

Once I get past my anger, to think about him does two things in my soul. It makes praise and thanksgiving rise up to You with all joy. How great it is to belong to You, my Lord. You are such a good and loving God!

And it makes me want to pray for this person to be touched by Your merciful and powerful grace. Please, Lord, speak to his mind as only You can and enable him to see truth. Give him courage and strength to look at the facts instead of looking at what he *wants to believe* are the facts. Give him a glimpse of Your enveloping grace - grace large enough to cover all his hatred and bitterness, and all the causes of them. I pray that You will touch him, this moment, with Your heart-healing touch and change him for all eternity. For You are not willing that any should perish.

July 31
THE KINGDOM OF HEAVEN

Matthew 13

I just finished reading this chapter, Lord, and I'm wishing I could have been there to hear these stories from Your lips as they were spoken the first time. Sometimes I would like to erase all I know about You and come to Your Word with the mind of a child, ready to be taught truth. Since that is not likely to happen, I'll settle for the next best thing - asking You to enable me to see all that *You* want me to understand from these parables.

The first two stories You told were the "Sower of Good Seed" and the "Tares Among Wheat." These two tales do *not* paint rosy pictures. The sower planted his seed in four different conditions, and 75% of it failed to grow to maturity. Then a man planted good wheat in his field and an enemy came and sowed tares, a weed very similar in appearance to wheat.

No, these are not pleasant illustrations, Lord, but they *are* realistic. They are truth. This life of faith is *not* easy. Much of any ministry's seed is planted in hearts that just do not support sprouting and growing. But what a joy there is to be found in the 25% that do grow and bear fruit. Joy great enough to keep the sower sowing. And I'm sure the wheat farmer would have preferred a crop of pure wheat without any tares. But that doesn't happen in our life of faith either. The enemy is always on hand to derail us in any way he can. You were simply telling the truth to prepare us for real life.

Then comes the story of the "Mustard Seed." *"The kingdom of heaven is like a mustard seed, which a man took and sowed in his field."* This speaks to my heart this way, Lord - I never know when a small something, a kindness, a smile, a word of encouragement spoken to someone will plant a seed of Your Kingdom in their heart. That seed will later take root and grow into a mature and useful plant in Your Kingdom's garden. Your beginnings in every life are small, but, over time, they become shining examples of Your grace and power in a variety of ways. Oh, God, may I be a sower of these small seeds of Your Kingdom.

"The kingdom of heaven is like leaven, which a woman took, and hid in three pecks of meal, until it was all leavened." (Verse 33) This analogy tells me two important facts: First, the leaven, because of its nature, changes all of whatever is around it; and second, the change takes some time to happen. Your presence within me has changed me in so many ways and will, if I allow it, change those around me also, not because of what I do but *because of what I am - filled with Your Spirit.* We humans tend to get very impatient, but Your work does not transpire quickly. It is a slow process.

Thank You for these valuable truths, Lord, for they present a practical picture of walking by faith. They teach me to relax and rejoice in being a part of Your Kingdom's work.

August 1
A DISCONTENTED HEART

Watch over your heart with all diligence,
for from it flow the springs of life.
Proverbs 4: 23

The older I get, the more "simple" appeals to me, Lord. Somewhere, sometime over the years I turned away from "more" and embraced "less." Your Word says that where my treasure is, there my heart will be. (Matt. 6:21) My heart is *not* in material possessions. I appreciate the things You have provided that make my life comfortable, but I'm thinking this morning about excess - having *so much more than is needed.* And I'm thinking about the vast number of people in the world, not just America, who set their sights upon having more, more, always more. It is an epidemic of discontent. We are inundated with incessant ads pushing that very thing. Perhaps the advertising fuels the discontent or maybe just capitalizes upon it, but the situation certainly indicates that our culture is blind to what is truly valuable.

Here are a few random thoughts about the delightful side of "less." The less I own, the less of my time and energy is needed to care for it. The fewer "valuables" I own, the less anxiety I have about theft or damage. And just think how much closet and cabinet space we could reclaim if we tossed all of the surplus - things we don't use, don't need, many times don't even know we possess.

We waste a significant amount of money on all those things, but more importantly, all that clutter negatively impacts our minds and spirits. This is personal opinion, Lord, but I think that living in the midst of excess and discontent produces fractured, cluttered, disorganized minds - minds with an inability to remember well or think clearly - minds that have a hard time ever being at rest or full of peace. I love the sense of peace that comes with having all the hidden places orderly.

And here is perhaps the most important thought: Your Word teaches us to give thanks in everything. (I Thess. 5:18) But a discontented heart *cannot* be thankful. At some point, we must say "this is enough" and stop accumulating more. Only then are we able to experience fulfillment through owning less; only then will we experience the joy of a contented and thankful heart. This is why monks and nuns live in simple surroundings with only life's basic needs provided. Theirs is a lifestyle bare of things but full of beauty.

Somehow, Lord, this is all tied into the concept of "transparency." My inner life is an open book to You, so my desire is to keep it clean and in order. My outer life should reflect that same order. So it works both ways, doesn't it? The inner life directly affects the outer, but the outer life also affects the inner. Is any of this crucial to eternal salvation? Probably not. It's just where my thoughts are this morning. Thank You for listening.

August 2
REMEMBERING

Seek the Lord and His strength;
seek His face continually.
Remember His wonderful deeds which He has done,
His marvels and the judgments from His mouth.
1 Chronicles 16: 11-12

I've been thinking about times of testing and how a mountain-top time is so often followed by a deep valley. While I was driving to an appointment just an hour ago. Lord, You gave me a great thought concerning the valuable resource of *remembering.*

Early this morning, I read in Genesis about Joseph and the seven lean years of famine which followed the seven fat years of abundance in Egypt. Here is the excellent thought You dropped into my mind: *My journaling is like Joseph storing grain during the abundant "fat" years for the famine he knew was coming.*

Many of Your children, I'm sure, can just sit down and *remember* the blessings of the fat days, but I am somehow not able to do that. So it is extremely reassuring for me to open my journal on a down day, go back and <u>read</u> what I wrote on my fat days. What I've found, Lord, is that it is very difficult to generate positive thoughts when depressed. But I *am* able to realize that words of love and worship written to You previously were true at the time and that, therefore, *they are still true.* I'm able to understand that only my feelings have changed - not the facts. So, for me, those written words become comfort, encouragement and strength in the midst of a dark time. Every blessing that flows from Your presence within me is *there* whether I'm able to feel it or not. Peace and love for You flood my spirit because Your Word says that You will continue this work until it is completed. (Philippians 1:6)

Just as Joseph knew the seven lean years were coming, there is no doubt that the dark times will come. The lean times are simply a part of living - they come to all. But, Lord, You are my stability. You not only keep me steady, You keep me moving in the right direction. You allow me to seek Your face continually. You are gracious and merciful to me, even though I am undeserving. Thank You so much for loving me. I love You, too. Even on a lean day, I know that.

August 3
WILLING TO LIVE

But whoever drinks of the water that I shall give him shall never thirst;
but the water that I shall give him
shall become in him a well of water springing up to eternal life.
John 4: 14

Life!
You, Lord, are the fountain of Life
springing up within all who are willing.
And what does it mean to be willing?

It means understanding that this marvelous thing is possible
only because *You* made it possible.

It means seeing what it cost
for You to do so.

It means thirsting
desiring
longing
for You.

It also means,
on the practical side of things,
creating conditions in my life that open me up to You
like solitude
quietness
meditation on Your Word
worship
confession.

These things prepare my spirit
for Your living water
to spring up within me
unhindered
powerful
and
beautiful.

Life-giving!

216

August 4
GOOD AND EVIL

But you said in your heart, "I will ascend to heaven;
I will raise my throne above the stars of God,
and I will sit on the mount of assembly
in the recesses of the north.
I will ascend above the heights of the clouds;
I will make myself like the Most High."
Isaiah 14: 13-14

One of the great mysteries of life is the existence of evil. Evil had to exist long before You created mankind, before Lucifer rebelled and attempted to become like You. Otherwise, there would have been nothing to tempt him to such independent actions. And we know that one of the consequences of his rebellion is that the powerful, beautiful, bearer-of-light Lucifer became Satan, the personification to us of all evil. We tend to think of angels as created beings without free will - as eternal creatures made for Your own purposes and who always do Your will. But, since Lucifer chose to rebel, he obviously had been given, by You, the power to choose.

So evil existed before You created Adam and Eve. Adam and Eve may have successfully withstood many temptations to disobey before this particular one in which they failed. We do not know. What we do know is that for Your overall plan for mankind to work, there had to be a choice given between good and evil. There had to be both a *choice* and *the power to choose.*

In other words, redemption was not an afterthought, was it, Lord? You knew from the very beginning that creature-man would fail and would need to be rescued. You purposely set the standard high so we could quickly realize how impossible it was to reach it on our own, so that we would turn to You and call upon You for divine help.

Through the ages, some did turn to You and some did not. Moses leaned heavily upon You after trying (and failing) on his own. The consequence of his failure was 40 years on the back side of the desert being a herder of sheep. Abraham, too, learned the hard way to believe You for the promised son, after taking matters into his own hands. The world is still reaping the consequences of that independence.

We are no different today. Man, with all his great technology and advances in knowledge, is still unable to truly live without Your constant input. We still try, fail, repent and start over. Sometimes we repeat that cycle many times. Sometimes we more readily see truth and allow You to do *in us* and *for us* what You never intended that we do for ourselves. You always intended that we live this life on Earth by a strong faith in a good God.

So be it.

August 5
MOTIVE

And He came to Nazareth, where He had been brought up, and as was His custom,
He entered the synagogue on the Sabbath and stood up to read.
Luke 4: 16

This was the beginning of Your public ministry in Nazareth, the town in which You grew up, the synagogue in which You had worshipped, with the people who had known You as a child and a young man. You read the Scripture from Isaiah 61 about "the Spirit of the Lord is upon Me" and then stated, *"Today this Scripture has been fulfilled in your hearing."* And all was well. The people were speaking highly of You. They were wondering, knowing You were "Joseph's son," about the words You were speaking, but they were listening.

But You knew what they were thinking. They had heard of miracles You had done in Capernaum and wanted You to perform miracles for them. You knew that this mind-set was *not* the fertile soil needed in which to plant seeds of the Kingdom of God. You were focused on Your mission. Your actions and words always reflected that intense focus which came from being in constant communication with Your Father.

The examples You chose to use, of Elijah and Elisha going to foreigners and blessing *them* rather than blessing someone in Israel, angered the people, as You knew it would. They were so enraged they tried to kill You.

You were telling them that God has an agenda of His own and, just like their forefathers had done in the past, they were completely missing it. *God's purpose in having a people was always to be glorified through them.* And here, in these two examples, He had to send His prophets *outside His own people* to find someone who would fulfill that purpose. You were saying that, like their forefathers, their perspective and their priorities were all wrong. Some of the hearers were able to see the truth and repent. More were not. But Your motive was to present the truth for those who would accept it, who would become willing to be changed by Your love.

I see in this, my Lord, a principle of correction for myself. My purpose, also, is to glorify You. All day, every day, to walk by the Spirit and have my perspective and priorities be aligned with Yours. Food for thought.

218

August 6
FAITH FOR ANOTHER

And behold, they were bringing to Him a paralytic, lying on a bed; and Jesus
seeing their faith said to the paralytic,
"Take courage, My son, your sins are forgiven."
Matthew 9: 2

Often, Lord, by Your divine design, we receive people in our sphere of influence who are not believers and thus do not yet have faith. Yesterday as I prayed, the questions I asked You were, "Is my faith enough? Must this person have his own faith before You can bless him? Or can You, will You, honor my faith and do this thing for him?"

And then this morning I came to Matthew 9 and this story. I'm not sure why I'd never before noticed that particular truth from this passage, but it clearly answers my questions.

These men carried their paralytic friend to You to be healed. It does not say the paralytic asked to be carried. It does not say that he, himself, had any faith for being healed. But Your Word says, *"...and Jesus seeing their faith..."* I have underlined that word "their" in my Bible because it is definitive.

And then I stop and think - "Of course, You honor one person's faith for another person's blessing!" Why else would a mother pray for her wayward children? Why would we ever pray for a baby's healing? Why would we pray for the power and effectiveness of a missionary teaching the heathen? Does the wayward child have faith? Can the baby believe for himself? The heathen certainly don't have faith - that is why the missionary is there - to teach them about faith.

I'm amazed at my denseness sometimes, Lord! But I'm equally amazed at Your gentle patience. You don't scold me for being dense. You just give me the answers to my questions, and we go on. How could I not love You?!

August 7
THE SIGN OF JONAH

And as the crowds were increasing, He began to say,
"This generation is a wicked generation; it seeks for a sign,
and yet no sign shall be given to it but the sign of Jonah."
Luke 11: 29

A quick review of Jonah and his experience can be summarized like this: You chose Jonah to go preach to the wicked people in the city of Nineveh. Jonah chose to disobey and tried to escape Your presence by fleeing to Tarshish. You arranged for him to be thrown overboard from the ship in which he was fleeing and to be swallowed by a big fish. Then Jonah prayed. You heard his cry and saved him from a slow and certain death. *Then* Jonah went to Nineveh and preached. The people repented, and Jonah was angry because You had mercy on them.

Jonah was not a very full-of-grace person was he, Lord? He seems to be a "good example of a bad example." His reason for not going in the first place was that he didn't *want* the Ninevites to repent and receive Your grace! It is startling, the contrast between his narrow-mindedness and Your compassion.

You saw a wicked people who needed to know about Your love and mercy. He saw a wicked people who deserved punishment. You wanted to see them change so You could bless them. He wanted to see them punished. You got what You wanted because You are a powerful God. He failed because he was just a man.

I learn a couple of important things here, Lord. One, You can use *anyone.* Even a Jonah. I find that reassuring. Two, You *will* complete what You begin. That, too, is reassuring. It shows me how unlimited Your resources are for getting the job done. Nothing is impossible with You. I knew that already, but it is good to be reminded.

Oh, the sign of Jonah. Well, I'm not a Bible scholar, as You know, but I think the story of Jonah preceded his arrival in Nineveh. The people had heard what had happened to him and what You had done about it. They saw both Your infinite power and Your compassionate heart in Jonah's experience. And Your power is a frightening thing to behold for anyone not on Your side. They decided the most desirable place to be was on the receiving side of Your compassion. In other words, Jonah was a living example of what You wanted *them* to know - just as You were the living example for the generation that heard You preach.

For just as Jonah became a sign to the Ninevites,
so shall the Son of Man be to this generation.
Luke 11: 30

220

August 8
PRAYING A PSALM

Teach me the way in which I should walk;
for to Thee I lift up my soul.
Teach me to do Thy will,
for Thou art my God;
let Thy good Spirit lead me on level ground.
Psalm 143: 8(b), 10

This prayer of David's for guidance is also mine this morning, Lord. He says, *"Hear my prayer, O Lord, give ear to my supplications! Answer me in Thy faithfulness, in Thy righteousness!" (v. 1)* David needed rescue from his enemy who was incessantly harassing, pursuing and persecuting him. David's method of dealing with this problem was to turn to You for deliverance and guidance, to remember all the good things You had done for him in the past, to stretch out his hands to You in prayer, trust and longing.

That is exactly where I am right now, Lord. I have no physical enemy as David had, but I do have a very real enemy. And I am aware of his schemes. I am also determined by Your grace to not fall into his trap. By the power of Your strong Spirit within me, I stand fast and resist his actions toward me and my home. Your will, and my desire, is that each of us and our dwelling place be filled with Your peace, love and joy this day and all our days.

In verse 6 of this psalm, David says, *"I stretch out my hands to Thee; my soul longs for Thee, as a parched land."* This, also, is my heart's cry this morning. My spirit longs to be in Your visible presence, to bow in worship and adoration. But it also rejoices in the awareness of Your blessed presence in this room at this moment! This is a gift in two ways - Your being here and Your giving me faith to know it. Both gifts are incredibly precious to me. But it is *You* I love.

Thank You, Lord, for the assurance in my heart that Your guidance is a certainty - that You never leave Your children abandoned and searching for their own way. I place my hand in Yours again to continue this journey home. May this day in my life bring glory to You.

August 9
THE IMPORTANCE OF SURRENDER

For the word of God is living and active
and sharper than any two-edged sword,
and piercing as far as the division of soul and spirit,
of both joints and marrow,
and able to judge the thoughts and intentions of the heart.
Hebrews 4: 12

Some attitudes are bothering me, Lord,
and the actions resulting from those attitudes.
They grieve me because I know they grieve You.

I have given You total access to my spirit and mind
to root out everything unlike You,
to establish firmly all that is like You.
Again, I invite You to do that, but this time
with the knowledge that I must then *cooperate* with You,
not try to run the operation.
Surrender is the key word.

I affirm that my will is on Your side.
See into my heart, Lord.
See the very real grieving over my failures.
You must increase, and I must decrease.
Fill up every little space in me until self is no more.
Show me clearly what I must do in this process
in addition to surrender.

A note to myself:
surrender is just another word for *obedience*.

I am willing.
You are able.
It shall be done.

August 10
RULES OF YOUR SCHOOL

To whom would He teach knowledge?
And to whom would He interpret the message?
Those just weaned from milk?
Those just taken from the breast?
For He says,
"Order on order, order on order,
line on line, line on line,
a little here, a little there."
Isaiah 28: 9-10

It is frustrating to me, Lord, that Your concept of time is so vastly different from mine. I am so driven, so attuned to instant answers, immediate results, quick work and the job is done. But You do not work that way. Teach me to slow down my expectations to match Your pace of teaching - to accept without angst the fact that I'm still learning lessons that I think should have been completed 20 years ago.

It is as if You continue to go deeper into my heart, finding more issues to hand up to my will, each item requiring a decision from me. What *I* would like is for You, *today,* to shovel out everything that needs attention so we could be finished with that job. Obviously, You don't operate that way. No, Your way is "order on order, line on line, a little here, a little there."

When I think about Your view of things, I am awed by the fact that You stand outside of time! We creatures know nothing about living in eternity where time is no more because we live *all* our days by clocks and calendars. We need to gain some measure of peace in imagining ourselves in an existence where time is not a factor, don't we, Lord? I believe that level of peace would then carry over into our hurried mind-set of today.

So, I once again place my will, with all its driven-ness, totally in Your control. I shall, for my part, *by Your grace* stay teachable and patient. I will not be anxious. I will be joyful and thankful and prayerful. And I will listen closely to Your Spirit within me. By Your grace.

I love You so much, Lord, and am filled with an immense amount of gratitude and joy that You love me! Your grace truly is amazing!

But do not let this one fact escape your notice, beloved,
that with the Lord one day is as a thousand years,
and a thousand years as one day.
2 Peter 3: 8

August 11
CONSEQUENCES

Do not be deceived. God is not mocked;
for whatever a man sows, this he will also reap.
Galatians 6:7

One way we teach our children to obey is by consistently demonstrating that there are pleasant consequences for obedience and unpleasant consequences for disobedience. Thus, even toddlers soon learn that they have some control over what happens to them. I'm thinking this morning, Lord, about a law that You have built into our existence that, like gravity, functions whether we understand it or not. That is the law of sowing and reaping.

This law has the "consequence" concept as its basis. How empowering is the idea that I can, *on purpose,* sow seeds today that will result in the crop You and I desire. Especially in the area of relationships, this approach seems to be a largely untapped storehouse of potential good. Here is what I mean - I can look at my relationship with anyone, including You, my Lord, and think, "What do I want this relationship to be a year from now, five years from now, at the end of my life?" And then I begin, with Your wisdom at work in my mind, to see actions *I* must take to bring this about.

So, do I have full control over every relationship? No, but I do (or *can*) have significant impact on them. You have taught this very idea through Paul...

If possible, so far as it depends on you, be at peace with all men.
Romans 12: 18

"So far as it depends on you" denotes the importance of my attitude, my behavior, my decisions. I *am* responsible for my side of things.

This exercise is not just for troubled relationships, Lord, even though we do tend to only bring You the problematic ones. This is a pro-active, full-of-hope endeavor that can make *any* relationship better. Your law of sowing and reaping *always* works. We don't have to wait until faced with an unwanted crop to understand it. Instead, we can put this truth to work for our benefit long before harvest time. That, in fact, is the intended way to perceive the law. It would be foolish to plant corn and then be surprised and dismayed at harvest to find a corn patch. Why do we think life is different? This simple, powerful law should be harnessed to mold us into people of integrity and godliness, people that make a positive difference in the lives we touch. Help me to think *before* I sow, Lord.

August 12
MORE ON CONSEQUENCES

Finally, brethren, whatever is true, whatever is honorable, whatever is right,
whatever is pure, whatever is lovely, whatever is of good repute,
if there is any excellence and if anything worthy of praise,
let your mind dwell on these things.
Philippians 4: 8

More thoughts, Lord, on yesterday's subject of my responsibility for consequences and Your laws that make me responsible. Today, I'm thinking on the law of seeking and finding. The bottom line is that I need to be careful what I seek because I *will* find it. It's a law. Your Word promises that those who seek You will find You. That is the law in its positive application. But it is just as true in its negative application. If I seek evil, I will find evil. So the wise thing, in every relationship or in every situation, would be to purposefully seek for the good.

The list above in Philippians is the place to start because that is what my mind should be *dwelling* upon - not only visiting occasionally, but living with day in and day out. And who controls what I think? Can Satan control my mind? No. Do You control my mind? You could, but You don't. You never take away my power of choice. I'm the one who must choose where my mind will dwell. So, since my thoughts will result in words, I must seek for the good, lovely, and excellent in all situations and people. Then the words that I speak will be encouraging and kind.

One more thought on seeking. The other day I read about the idea of seeing You in every person I meet and allowing that to change how I respond to them. This is a profound thought to me, Lord, because it applies to the slow person in front of me at the check-out line, the driver who is rude to me in the parking lot, the somewhat smelly, dirty man asking for money on the sidewalk downtown and well, *everybody.* And have You not already taught me that principle of non-partiality? Yes, but this convicts me of my failure to live it out very well. To see You in each person I meet requires a shift in my perspective; a shift from me and what I want, to You and Your desires.

Truly, Lord, You are a compassionate and generous God! How incredible that I can sow fruitful seed and seek for virtue in everyone, knowing that those actions will result in blessing upon them and me! How precious is the promise that You work for good in every situation in my life, even though that working and that good may not be visible to me. You, my Lord, are worthy of my trust.

August 13
BOLD FAITH

Why are you so timid? How is it that you have no faith?
Mark 4:40

These words of Yours were spoken to your disciples when all of you were caught in the middle of the lake, in a raging storm. Weary from a long day of dealing with needy people, You were asleep in the back of the boat. Your disciples came to You in their fear, and their question, essentially, was, "Don't You care that we are about to die?" And, in response, You asked these two brief questions, "Why are you so timid? How is it that you have no faith?"

This morning, as I came to this chapter in Mark, You asked *me* those questions. I must accept that rebuke, Lord. I am guilty as charged. I, too, have been caught in a storm, not of powerful wind and rain, but of destructive doubt and fear. I've lived long enough to know that attacks from Satan are inevitable, and that attempts to handle them myself are ineffective. Your disciples did exactly the right thing by coming to You immediately. You were not rebuking them for that; the rebuke was for their fear and their lack of faith.

My failure, Lord, has been that I did *not* come to You quickly. Instead, I allowed the storm to grow, the doubts and fears to increase. Rather than coming directly to You, my timid faith began to search within myself for the answers. It tried to find answers in something I had done, or something I had *not* done. I allowed myself to be convinced it was surely my fault that these misgivings and uncertainties were filling me with darkness. And, in a sense, it was!

That's why those questions from You this morning jolted me. They opened my eyes to the truth of what I have been doing. They made me see clearly that, just as You were the solution to the disciples' storm, so You are the solution to mine. The *only* solution.

So, what does bold faith look like? Well, in this instance, it would have looked like me coming to You quickly, opening my heart and mind to You in all honesty, talking to You about the uncertainties, the worries, the shadowy, scary things lurking there. I would have confidently asked for Your everlasting mercy and grace to take control. Then I would have accepted whatever came next. Perhaps You would have immediately dispelled the darkness. Maybe You would have simply taken my hand and led me on through it. The important thing, Lord, is that my heart would have been at peace *because You were in charge.*

Let us therefore draw near with confidence to the throne of grace,
that we may receive mercy and may find grace to help in time of need.
Hebrews 4:16

Is this new knowledge? No, I've known this truth a very long time. I've even taught this truth many times. But now I've learned it in a brand new way. Thank You, Lord, for this lesson in bold faith.

August 14
PRAYING YOUR WORD

I Peter 1: 3-9
(Paraphrased)

Lord, I want to use some words this morning from Your own treasure house of truth and beauty - words which speak my heart's longing to praise You and thank You. The great apostle Peter and I probably have little in common other than our love and high exaltation of You, but his words say so well what my heart wants to say.

Blessed be the God and Father of my Lord Jesus Christ,
who according to Your great mercy
has caused me to be born again to a living hope
through the resurrection of Jesus Christ from the dead,
to obtain an inheritance which is imperishable and undefiled and will not fade
away, reserved in heaven for me
because I am protected by Your power through faith
for a salvation ready to be revealed in the last time.

In this I greatly rejoice even though now for a little while
I have been distressed by various trials,
that the proof of my faith may be found to result
in praise and glory and honor
when You come back.

And though I have not seen You, I love You.
And though I do not see You now,
but believe in You,
I greatly rejoice with joy unspeakable and full of glory!
For the end result of my faith is eternity with You.

What a glorious future awaits Your children!

August 15
BALANCE

The Lord has established His throne in the heavens;
and His sovereignty rules over all.
Psalm 103: 19

I love all of this 103rd Psalm, Lord, because it is filled with so many wonderful words extolling Your character. But my thoughts this morning go to this verse and the facts it brings to mind.

Fact #1. You are Lord and sovereign ruler over *all* of my life.

Fact #2. Therefore, if I murmur or complain, I am doing so against *You*.

Fact #3. So, the good and right thing, at all times, is to love, trust and praise.

The reason, obviously, these facts come to mind is that I'm guilty at times of murmuring and complaining. Putting it down in black and white reveals the spoiled attitude I display when I complain about anything. I'm sorry, Lord. Thank You for showing me so plainly that, even in the difficult times, my spirit can be full of love, and trust and praise. *And peace* - Your glorious peace ruling in my spirit. Those beautiful things are present within me because *You are present within me*. I can, however, choose to override them and behave like an ill-mannered child. That behavior has at least three negative results: You are not pleased, I'm a poor example to those witnessing my selfishness, and I feel terrible about both of those.

What we are talking about here, Lord, is a life lived in balance. You have been teaching me lately about how important endurance is to You. Endurance is essential to learn to walk in balance. To be balanced is to be stable. To be stable is to be single-minded in my devotion to You, to be focused upon You, to live my entire life in reference to You. This way of living must be learned. Learning always encompasses failure as part of its process, followed by endurance to try again.

You are my example of both these characteristics - balance and endurance. Your priorities were always in perfect order because You were always listening to the Father. You did not have times of being selfish or out of His will as I do. I've got so much to learn. May I never, ever take lightly Your sacrifice or Your rightful place as Lord of all my life. Because if I truly understand the price You paid and the love behind Your willingness to do so, then my only response can be love, trust and praise. And this will result in a life of balance.

Thank You for Your mercy that lets me fail and begin again. Thank You for Your grace that gives me the desire to start over. Thank You for Your love that is behind everything You do for Your children. Help me keep my eyes upon You this entire day.

August 16
CLOSER HOME

For I am the Lord your God,
who upholds your right hand,
who says to you,
"Do not fear, I will help you."
Isaiah 41:13

The enemy of my soul
would have me quit;
just give up,
give in
and quit.

Your Spirit, Lord,
bids me see the possibilities.
Or at least the faint outline of them.

There are still many things
I can do
even though there are
many more I cannot.

Help me put away the pain
of the cannot do
and rejoice in the
can do.

You, Yourself will bring to pass
good and blessed things
in my remaining days.

But I must listen to You.
I must look to You for strength
to continue this journey home.

August 17
STAY AWAKE

For He delivered us from the domain of darkness,
and transferred us to the kingdom of His beloved Son,
in whom we have redemption,
the forgiveness of sins.
Colossians 1: 13-14

Pride	Humility
Greed	Contentment
Luxury	Moderation
Wrath	Peace
Gluttony	Simplicity
Envy	Joy
Sloth	Diligence

Listed on the left are seven sins common to the devil's "domain of darkness." And even though I have been delivered out of that domain, I still live in the world, and those sins are ever present around me. In this life, left to my own devices, I will never come to a place of growth where I am free from their influence, both within and without. It's as if the enemy stealthily sneaks in, sets up housekeeping in a small un-used corner and then begins to slowly expand his territory. It happens quietly and without fanfare. One day I stumble over one of these sins and am caught off guard because I was not paying attention. Then I have clean-up work to do.

The good news, Lord, is that this doesn't need to happen. You have told me to stay awake and alert to the deceitful tricks of the adversary. (1 Pet. 5:8) I can be deceived because the devil is able to disguise himself, to appear even as an angel of light. (2 Cor. 11:14) I can be lulled to sleep and be unaware that spiritual warfare is going on within me and around me. But You never sleep and are never deceived. So the *only* safe thing to do is to keep my eyes upon You and my ears tuned to hear You.

And further good news - by Your grace I can experience, in this life, the *complete list* on the right. Those are gifts You *want* me to have. In fact, I have them already because You brought them with You when You came to live within me. One big difference between those of us in Your kingdom and those in the domain of darkness is that we have a choice to make. We can *choose* to allow You free reign in our hearts and when we do, You bring to pass the abundant blessings listed on the right. Oh, God, make me consistently wise enough to choose well. And please help me stay awake, alert and very close to You.

August 18
WORDS OF LOVE

To Thee, O Lord, I lift up my soul.
O my God, in Thee I trust.
Make me know Thy ways, O Lord;
teach me Thy paths.
Lead me in Thy truth and teach me,
for Thou art the God of my salvation;
for Thee I wait all the day.
Psalm 25: 1, 4-5

How good You are, Lord! So faithful and so wise. How foolish I would be to not trust You completely. You are teaching me, seemingly, many fundamentals at once:

How truly weak and helpless I am;
how *present* and strong You are;
the reality of spiritual battles;
how to win them;
the power of Your Word;
that many of my problems go away when I focus on You;
that Your ways are not my ways;
that You are in charge;
that I am so safe *because* You are in charge;
that I must make choices;
that those choices make an enormous difference in my view of everything.

When You are finished with this work, it will be time for me to step out of time and into eternity. In my spirit, I rejoice to think about that! This joy is a sure and steadfast anchor of my soul. It gives me strength for endurance. I love You.

Therefore we do not lose heart,
but though our outer man is decaying,
yet our inner man is being renewed day by day.
2 Corinthians 4:16

August 19
A GREAT EVIL

...But we are committing a great evil against ourselves.
Jeremiah 26:19

This phrase, Lord, speaks much to me as I pray for others, some of whom are failing to be fully devoted to You. It applies to anyone who is Your child but not allowing You to be Lord of his life. It applies to me if I am refusing to be obedient in any area of my life.

In Jeremiah, the nation of Israel was guilty of bad choices, and a few of the elders were wise enough to see the truth. They heard the words You spoke through Jeremiah and said, "Yes, that's right. We are committing a great evil against ourselves."

Israel's sin was no different from our unbelief of today. They had turned from the One True God to serve the world's worthless idols. Are we not still doing that? Even born-again Christians can fail to keep You the #1 priority in this life and consequently make wrong choices. Maybe that is why, Lord, every time I try to pray for the lost, I end up praying for the found. *We* are the needy ones because we are called to be Your hands, feet and mouth to the lost. And, to a great extent, we are spending our days in self-absorption. We are 98% occupied with self and its needs, wants and well-being.

You show me that being Your child is to live a radical, fundamentally different life from the "world" and its ways. To live a life that is so illuminated with Your light inside that the contrast is obvious - a piercing light in a dark world. I cannot read Matthew 5 and 6 and *not* see how truly, *radically* different we are to be! And You know, Lord, that I don't mean becoming an unbalanced fanatic. I mean being so full of love, joy, peace, patience, kindness, gentleness, goodness, faithfulness and self-control that our lives simply radiate those things. And the only way that can happen is if we are *emptied of self and full of You.* These are Your characteristics which You bring into a life given over to You. This is Your will for every child of God.

What this statement from Jeremiah says to me is that *we must push on through every barrier we encounter on the road to becoming emptied of self and full of You; otherwise, we have committed a great evil against ourselves.* To be content with less is to lose much both in this life and in the life to come. Your admonishment is that we forget about earthly treasure and instead, lay up treasure in heaven - treasure that will last for all eternity. If only we could *see* what could be accomplished through lives completely devoted to You! To see opportunities in which we could make a difference. To see hurting people to whom we can bring Your love and peace. So, once again, I ask You to increase the ability of our spiritual eyes to see; increase our hunger to become fully devoted disciples; increase our desire to be completely Yours. We are so needy!

August 20
LIBERATION

For I consider that the sufferings of this present time
are not worthy to be compared with the glory
that is to be revealed to us.
For the anxious longing of the creation
waits eagerly for the revealing of the sons of God.
And not only this, but also we ourselves,
having the first fruits of the Spirit,
even we ourselves groan within ourselves,
waiting eagerly for our adoption as sons,
the redemption of our body.
Romans 8: 18-19, 23

Lord, see into my heart this morning; give me strength and grace to quiet down its eagerness and longing for liberation. Yes, Lord, I well remember another morning when I felt fenced in on all sides, and You reminded me then that the way *up* was open - the way to You. You showed me then that life and its demands upon me could never close off my access to You. What great news!

That access is still open. I can sit here in my chair and enjoy a bit of heaven because You are here, too - filling me, surrounding me. Your blessed presence is my comfort, my strength and my joy. You turn my longing into loving. How good You are, and how very blessed I am to belong to You!

Lord, this longing,
this eagerness to come home to You
is a gift You have given me,
not to bring dismay or discontent in staying,
but to bring delight and joy upon every thought of coming home.

It has become an exquisite, radiant object;
a promise made visible to my spiritual eyes
that I may look at, or hold close to my heart
or, probably best,
allow You to store for me.

Then I enjoy it only when *You* choose.
That is my decision.
Please, Lord, be the Keeper of all my joys.

Truly, You are both the Keeper and the Source.

August 21
MY SONG

The Lord is my strength and my shield;
my heart trusts in Him, and I am helped;
therefore my heart exults,
and with my song I shall thank Him.
Psalm 28: 7

This verse is one of my favorites. Here, David says exactly what I want to say to You. How blessed I am, Lord, to be able to experience Your presence in me and around me! More precious than anything is that gift. You have made my life a song.

Only You really know what music has meant to me all my life, from very early childhood even until now. It is such an integral part of me. I believe that if You took it away, I wouldn't be me anymore.

However, the song that has been with me was not always a song of joy. There were years when I thought I didn't need You in my life; the song then was muted and played in a minor key. But the music never stopped. It haunted me constantly through those years of rebellion and, if I had had the courage to be honest at that time, I *knew* it was You, gently speaking to my wayward heart.

Thank You, Lord, for not leaving me in my rebellion! Thank You for waiting me out until I turned around and began this walk beside You.

Truly You are my strength, my shield, my joy, my song. You have taught me Your song through many hard times and through many good times. Someday we will sing our song together, and it will blend, harmonize and flow into beautiful music.

Victor Hugo wrote about it this way, "Heaven lights me with its unknown worlds. The nearer I approach the end, the plainer I hear around me the immortal symphonies of the worlds which invite me."

That day cannot come too soon to suit me, Lord. Today would be a good day!

August 22
SELF-CONTROL

(my words to You)
You are my hiding place; You preserve me from trouble;
You surround me with songs of deliverance.
(Your words to me)
I will instruct you and teach you in the way which you should go;
I will counsel you with My eye upon you.
Psalm 32: 7-8

Truly, Lord, You are my hiding place - the refuge to whom I run when in trouble. You and I have been working for some time now on this project of my constantly being of a "quiet and gentle" spirit. I know this is Your will for me, and it is certainly *my* will for me. So far, the road getting there has not been smooth. So here I am again.

Self-control *sounds* like something "self" does. But it is actually one of Your gifts made available to all in whom You dwell. Unfortunately, since I'm slow to learn, having it available and *appropriating* it are poles apart. I'm seeing this morning, Lord, that You are equally as present and powerful in any stressful moment as You are at a moment like this one - sitting here without pain and without demands on me. I must remember that truth. I must especially remember it when the stress level is high and the pain is everywhere. Because it is then that I get swallowed up in *them* rather than You. Teach me to pause at *that* moment and look to You.

Verse 8 above declares that You will counsel me with Your eye upon me. This tells me two important things: (1) I must be *looking to You* or I won't even know You are trying to help me; and (2) our relationship must be close, even intimate, for eye contact to have a message.

Thank You, Lord, for this clear instruction. And thank You, too, for the reminder to "relax and rejoice" that You just prompted. If I will simply relax and "be" in the moment, much of the stress will disappear. This is such a fundamental truth - certainly nothing new - but basic to well-being. I need to be present in the moment and allow Your joy to fill me. *That is the message Your eye sends to me - relax and rejoice!*

Together we can do this.
Alone I will fail.

August 23
DISCOURAGEMENT

And it shall be said,
"Build up, build up, prepare the way,
remove every obstacle out of the way of My people."
For thus says the high and exalted One
who lives forever, whose name is Holy,
I dwell on a high and holy place,
and also with the contrite and lowly of spirit
in order to revive the spirit of the lowly
and to revive the heart of the contrite.
Isaiah 57: 14-15

I just finished reading several journal pages covering about a two-week period of time when my loved ones and I were dealing with a very discouraging situation. Please, Lord, help me take those pages and pages of pouring out my heart to You and distill them down to truths I learned.

I learned that You are worthy of my trust. You are faithful to Your Word, and You *are* working in our lives. While I may strain to see what and where and how, my real task is to stay the course and continue to trust You.

I learned that my capacity for grasping the complex plan You are orchestrating is so limited! If I had even a partial understanding, I would undoubtedly try to take the ball and run with it which would *not* accomplish Your purposes. So what I need to seek is *peace* instead of answers. Peace, ultimately, comes from confidence in You.

I learned that it takes courage to stand firm and wait upon You. I remember dark days and nights in the past that You and I walked together, Lord. Sometimes the wait was long and grueling. Many times I asked for answers and got silence. But even in those darkest times, You somehow made me understand that I must stay the course - *simply keep on doing what I knew to do.* I learned that that is good advice for any circumstance!

I learned that there is much activity going on in the spirit world of which I am unaware. That activity is all under Your control. That is good news! So what You are saying is, **"My work *will* be accomplished. Keep your hand in Mine and listen to Me. Keep your eyes on Me so I can guide you. Let Me love you and love others through you. Continue to pray for these and know that I am working in their lives. The work is My responsibility; yours is to love Me fully."**

August 24
GRATITUDE FOR GRACE

Create in me a clean heart, O God,
and renew a steadfast spirit within me.
Do not cast me away from Thy presence,
and do not take Thy Holy Spirit from me.
Psalm 51: 10-11

Those words of David are my prayer this morning. This, Lord, is my constant desire - that my heart will always be clean, my spirit steadfast, and that I will know in ever greater measure the presence of Your Spirit and the joy of Your salvation.

David was praying these words from a place of great brokenness after being confronted with his sins of adultery and murder. I have not committed those sins, Lord, but I have been forgiven for others equally as shameful. I know how it is to be apart from You. I know how it feels to suffer guilt, condemnation and the sickness of soul that they bring. Knowing this, Lord, makes me realize I never want to be there again. It makes me rejoice - absolutely revel - in the grace that floods my spirit when all is well between us.

You are my Rock and my Refuge. Your faithfulness and love are never-ending. Your promises are sure. And how do I know this? Because I am filled with Your grace.

Only one who has been forgiven
can understand the powerful freedom of that forgiveness.
Only one who has experienced lost-ness
can value the immense worth of being found.
Only one who has been blind
can truly appreciate the joy of seeing.

All of this, Lord, is Your love being poured out
upon me and into me
solely because You are good,
loving
and merciful.
All of this is grace!

Emotions flood my mind and heart when I think about these truths! I search for words of praise that express my emotions; there are no adequate words. Wordless praise will have to suffice until I am granted the honor of bowing in Your very presence. Perhaps then I will have a new language with which to convey my love and gratitude to You.

August 25
PRAYING AND BELIEVING

And whatever you ask in My name, that will I do,
that the Father may be glorified in the Son.
If you ask Me anything in My name, I will do it.
John 14: 13-14

These words, Lord, were spoken to Your disciples to help them understand Your oneness with the Father, to help them see that the Holy One of Israel had, indeed, become Man and lived among them. I'm not sure if they could clearly understand this "asking and believing" business. They had not yet been through Your arrest, crucifixion, resurrection and ascension. Your Spirit had not yet been given to them in all fullness. But here is what is astonishing to me, Lord. *We have* Your completed Word; we have centuries of the witness of saints; we (can) have the fullness of Your Spirit within, and yet I must question if *we* believe Your words!

We read them, we quote them to one another, but do we wholly *believe* them? You are God and do not change. Your power today is just as it was the day You parted the Red Sea or walked on the water or stilled the storm or raised Lazarus from the dead. We change; our feelings change; we grow weary. But You do none of these. How guilty we sometimes are of attributing our own weaknesses to You!

"Nothing lies beyond the reach of prayer except that which lies outside the will of God." My heart knows this statement is true. All the prayers I have made for these I love *have been heard and are being answered* for I have asked for nothing outside Your will. It is Your will that the lost be saved, and that the lukewarm be heated up and that all of us learn what it means to be made "one with You." It is Your will that we experience being filled to overflowing with Your Spirit. You desire that every individual, every marriage and every home acknowledge You as Lord. These are all prayers that originated in Your heart, Lord.

So, does this mean that I, personally, will see all the changes in these lives? Not at all. I am not responsible for the changes - that is Your work. I'm only responsible for the asking and believing part. It gives me great peace to realize that seeds planted may lie dormant for a long time before sprouting. We plant and we water but You, my Lord, cause the growth. Glory!

Accept my praise and thanksgiving today for what You are planning for tomorrow. And for the gift of faith to believe it with all my heart.

August 26
YOUR UNCHANGING GRACE

Therefore having been justified by faith, we have peace with God
through our Lord Jesus Christ,
through whom also we have obtained our introduction by faith
into this grace in which we stand;
and we exult in hope of the glory of God.
Romans 5: 1-2

I'm thinking this morning about the strength You give Your children. It is important that I grasp this, Lord, because now, more than ever, I realize my need for that strength. I think I actually *needed* it more in years past but, because I was physically strong then, I made the mistake of depending on my own strength. Now I have very little physical strength. You have had to take drastic measures in my life to make me understand Your ways!

But here is what is amazing to me, Lord. Even though I did a poor job of appropriating Your strength back then, still You gave it to me - strength to go on for a great distance. Now I look back down that long road and see that Your grace is "all of one piece" like Your seamless robe. I tend to divide up Your blessings and talk about Your love, faithfulness, power, holiness, wisdom and strength as separate gifts. But, incredibly, I realize that *all* are present in me in the form of Your Holy Spirit! Your presence within brought me then, and brings me today, *every* good thing You are.

When I'm comfortable in my chair with my Bible and my journal, Your grace is abiding. When I'm trying to accomplish some task and dealing with the stress of increasing pain, Your grace is abiding. And what is true today has been true every day of our walk together. Thank You, Lord, for making me see that truth this morning, for the eye-opening realization that *Your abundant supply does not depend upon my faulty understanding. It depends only upon Your great and glorious grace!*

You are unchanging. How truly blessed I am to belong to You. May my devotion today be total and my behavior show it.

August 27
SPEAKING TRUTH

Her priests have done violence to My law and have profaned My holy things; they
have made no distinction between the holy and the profane, and they have not
taught the difference between the unclean and the clean; and they hide their eyes
from My Sabbaths, and I am profaned among them.
Ezekiel 22: 26

And all in the synagogue were filled with rage as they heard these things; and they
rose up and cast Him out of the city, and led Him to the brow of the hill on which
their city had been built, in order to throw Him down the cliff.
Luke 4: 28-29

My readings in the Old Testament and the New Testament coincided this morning, Lord, into one message - "fulfill the purpose of God." In Ezekiel, Your priests were severely scolded for not acknowledging Your holiness, for not teaching the people the difference between the holy and the profane. In Luke, You boldly spoke the truth in Your hometown synagogue, and Your audience turned against You. At first (verse 22) they were very pleased with Your words, and You could have kept it that way. But Your purpose was not to win friends and influence people No, Your purpose was to preach and teach the Kingdom of God, and that requires *truth*. Obviously, the crowd did not receive it well.

I see this same steadfastness displayed in the apostles' lives as they went out to teach and preach Your Kingdom. They were caught in Your grip, their lives were given over to Your purposes, and they did not water down Your message. Through much persecution, they also spoke truth.

So what does all this mean to me? You have not called me to preach. I have no congregation to teach or flock to tend. I'm not an evangelist speaking to hundreds of lost souls. No, my circle of influence is much smaller. But does its size make it less important? No. For my life, too, has been given over to Your purposes. I pray, Lord, that these thoughts be more than just theory on paper. Instead, make them a real experience lived out before my small audience. Do not loosen Your grip on my life. My only reason for living is to "fulfill the purpose of God."

August 28
COMPLETED FAITH

And a woman who had a hemorrhage for twelve years,
and could not be healed by anyone,
came up behind Him, and touched the fringe of His cloak;
and immediately her hemorrhage stopped.
Luke 8: 43-44

I just finished reading this 8th chapter of Luke this morning, Lord, about this long-diseased woman who touched the hem of Your cloak and was healed. In a crowd of people, there were many touching You. Yet, her touch of faith was different, and You felt power go out of You.

I wonder, Lord, how did this woman come by her faith? Had Your Spirit been at work in her heart to give it to her? Had she simply heard about all the miracles of healing You had done and so believed? Is there more than one way to receive faith? Was she so desperate that she would try anything? Maybe the answer is "yes" to all of those questions. Maybe I don't see the whole truth about receiving faith. Or maybe I don't see the truth about *completed faith.*

However this woman got it, she had what was necessary to bring about the healing of her disease. It is interesting to think about the fact that she knew believing alone was not enough. True, You told her it was her faith that made her well; yet, if she had not made the effort to push through the crowd, get near You and stoop down to touch the hem of Your cloak, that believing alone would not have brought her healing. She somehow *knew* that just believing wasn't enough, that there was some action she had to take. That is what, in my mind, is *completed faith.*

That's an eternal principle, isn't it, Lord? This is what James was talking about when he said, about Abraham, *"You see that faith was working with his works, and as a result of the works, faith was perfected."* (James 2:22) And in verse 26, *"For just as the body without the spirit is dead, so also faith without works is dead."*

When I ask You to do something for me, Lord, an action on my part is always involved in order to make my faith complete. There is Your part, and there is my part. I cannot think of a single time, in Your Word or in my experience, when faith did not result in action. If my "faith" is only mental agreement to a truth, without action from me, then my heart and viewpoint remain unchanged.

This woman had her viewpoint changed! She was willing to risk public humiliation to be healed of this sickness. O God, make me like her!

August 29
THE POWER OF TOUCH

...and touched the fringe of His cloak...
Luke 8: 44

How different, Lord, are the ways in which
we touch and are touched.

The comforting touch
of a mother's hand
on a tired child

the electrifying touch
between lovers

the hug of a friend

the slap of an enemy

the indescribable touch of
Your hand upon a life

all of these are possible
because of this wonderful God-given
sense of touch
we so take for granted.

One of our greatest hungers
we are told
is to be touched with love.

You knew this, didn't You, Lord?

And so You gave us this sense of touch
and one another.

May we be generous
with our touches of Your kindness and love.

August 30
YOUR GOAL FOR US

...that you may be filled with the knowledge of His will
in all spiritual wisdom and understanding,
so that you may walk in a manner worthy of the Lord,
to please Him in all respects...
Colossians 1: 9-10

Once again, Your desires for all believers are spoken and written down for us, here by Paul. To know You, to become one with You, to be completely filled with You - these are all ways of saying the same thing. Your intent, Your goal, is that all believers shall *experience* You in their lives.

Being the good and loving God You are, You invite *every* believer to draw near. Some feel that longing within themselves and obey it. Others feel it and try to ignore it or satisfy it with something else. Neither tactic works. To ignore Your calling creates in us a misery that cannot be tolerated for long. Any attempt to find something (or someone) else to satisfy that longing is futile. There *is* nothing or no one else that is able to appease that yearning.

To accept Your invitation, to draw near and begin to learn the pure pleasure of being with You, *that* is what brings happiness and joy. How I wish I could communicate this truth to everyone I know! It is, without doubt, the most important thing I've learned in my long years of living. Fellowship with You in this life doesn't get the positive press it deserves. As believers, Your goals and desires for us are fulfilled through fellowship with You. How could *anything* be better than that?!

The rest of that prayer says...
...bearing fruit in every good work and increasing in the knowledge of God;
strengthened with all power, according to His glorious might,
for the attaining of all steadfastness and patience;
joyously giving thanks to the Father,
who has qualified us to share in the inheritance of the saints in light.
Colossians 1: 10-12

To fellowship with You, Lord, is a journey through our daily life now, bearing fruit and learning more about You, that continues into heaven, where we will share in the inheritance You have prepared for all the saints. How very grateful I am for Your calling upon my life that You *would not* let me ignore. Give me grace and opportunity to tell everyone I know about this wonderful, life-changing truth of fellowship with You.

August 31
PEACE WITHIN

The Lord bless you, and keep you;
the Lord make His face shine on you,
and be gracious to you;
the Lord lift up His countenance on you,
and give you peace.
Numbers 6: 24-26

A clean page, a new day and a quiet moment before the family wakes up. Thank You, Lord, for these beautiful words I just read from Numbers. Thank You for this most precious time every morning with only You and me. Thank You for the knowledge that when I leave this time of being with You, I'm still with You! And as often through the day as possible, I can return to this peaceful place deep within me where You dwell.

It's like I'm both Mary and Martha. As did Mary, I much prefer to sit at Your feet, and my choice would always be to do that. But my circumstances demand a good bit of Martha's daily attention to duties and tasks. The busy times are the hard ones for me, but You give me strength and common sense to handle them.

How I would love to learn to operate out of that deep peaceful place in me all the time. Is that possible, Lord? *You* were never hurried or harried. That quiet and gentle spirit has been my goal for some time now and what an excellent situation to work on it. How generous You are to give me a "want" and then spread out a banquet table before me with the means of satisfying that very desire. Such is my circumstance.

Praise wells up in me, my Beloved, for Your wisdom, Your goodness in creating these days of growth for me. You are an awesome, ever-faithful Protector and Provider. You have forgiven me much, and I love You much.

September 1
THOUGHTS ON OBEDIENCE

Now then, if you will indeed obey My voice and keep My covenant,
then you shall be My own possession among all the peoples,
for all the earth is Mine;
and you shall be to Me a kingdom of priests and a holy nation.
Exodus 19: 5-6

You never coerce my obedience, do You, Lord? You set up the circumstances, You make known to me what is wanted, and You promise to honor my obedience. Then I have to make a choice.

The most wonderful blessings have come to me through obedience. The joy, *the pure elation in my spirit from doing what You want done, is worth any amount of hardship in the obedience itself.* That is such an understatement! How I would love to make those words glow with a bright light! There are many, many experiences distilled down into that one statement - I could write pages on any one of them. But for now, suffice to say that obedience is surely the high, smooth road, much preferred over the rocky path of disobedience.

And I know that to be true because there have also been times I disobeyed. With that disobedience came a dreadful inner ache in my spirit, harder to bear than physical pain. There is no pill available to ease that kind of pain, Lord. That tells me that, once the human spirit has experienced Your life and joy, to live without it is misery. And Your life and joy come fully to a child who is fully alive, which is to say, walking in all the light that You give. So obedience is life and disobedience is a kind of death.

But, Lord, even in the midst of the hurt was the knowledge that You still loved me; that the way back into fellowship with You was open if I chose to take it. It required contrition and repentance on my part. It required me to be honest about what I did, and why I did it. And then Your grace took over.

You give me chance after chance to learn my lessons, Lord. You build into this growing-of-the-spirit a space for wrong choices and repentance. How glad I am for that.

At this stage in my earthly journey, I have clearly learned that the most blessed choice is to always be obedient - even when the task seems too difficult. My trust in You has matured. I now know that You never ask anything of me that will not result in blessing for me. Your wisdom and knowledge of my needs are from an eternal perspective, while my own are so limited. Now, if I can just be wise enough to *live* by what I know! Thank You for being my Beloved Companion on this journey!

245

September 2
A PEACEFUL DAY

I am the Lord, and there is no other;
besides Me there is no God.
the One forming light and creating darkness,
causing well-being and creating calamity;
I am the Lord who does all these.
Isaiah 45: 5, 7

Another valuable lesson learned this morning as I talked to You about my petty frustrations. You showed me that I'm still trying to maintain control over issues that are not mine to control, actions which need to be understood in light of recent teaching; that is, *doing all things for the right reason - for You.*

If I will consistently put into practice what You have already taught me, so many of my stresses and unwanted critical thoughts will simply disappear. I know the enemy is egging on all these annoyances, Lord, but I am determined that *Your way shall be my way;* he shall have no power in my life.

Your grace within me strengthens both my will to obey and the actual *doing* of Your will. You, my Lord, are the beginning of everything worthwhile in me and in my life. What You have started, You *will* complete. I want very much to work with You - never against You.

This lovely summer afternoon, sitting in the shade watching the boys play mini-golf, I'm so aware of the beauty of Your world - the pleasant breeze blowing and the patterns of sun and shadow that are made on the grass, all the variety of trees I can see from this one spot. And I know that this is but a tiny sample of what heaven will be like. I am fulfilled and at peace as I watch the boys have fun. It is well with my soul to just enjoy the "sacrament of the present moment." It is pure contentment to belong to You!

September 3
A THANKFUL HEART

O come, let us sing for joy to the Lord;
let us shout joyfully to the rock of our salvation.
Let us come before His presence with thanksgiving;
let us shout joyfully to Him with psalms.
Psalm 95: 1-2

The thought I want to think about this morning, Lord, is thanksgiving - having a thankful heart - living and operating out of a place not only of quietness and gentleness, but of thanksgiving, praise and joy.

You remind me again of something I've known for a long time, yet allowed to be crowded out of my mind by lesser concerns - *that You are pleased by a thankful heart, and I am blessed by having one.*

How easy it is to slide away from this place of gratitude! I confess, Lord, that I often fail to maintain a thankful heart. Forgive me, and I will start again today. A thankful heart will increase my ability to "relax and rejoice." It will alter the very atmosphere around me. It will prompt me to count my many blessings. It will change the way I see my everyday life, and it will also change my prayers for others. Which brings me to the second thought swirling in my brain...

It is exciting to think about all the activity occurring right now in the world of the spirit: the prayers I have prayed for these I love that are in process of being answered; their needs I have brought to You that are being met in ways I never envisioned; the ways you are changing me and making me more nearly into Your image; the lessons I am learning about You and about myself; the battles being fought on all sides; seeing that, even if I lose a battle I'm still the winner because, in Your economy, losing is an incentive for spiritual growth. So even failures become victories!

You have made this world of the spirit so very real to me, Lord, and I thank You for that. Thank You for bringing me to the end of my self-sufficiency. Thank You that You have taken me by the hand and are teaching me, one step at a time, how to depend on You for all things, even for having a consistently thankful heart. If I'm ever successful at any part of this life of faith, it will be by Your grace. Only by Your grace.

September 4
WORSHIP

I will extol Thee, my God, O King;
and I will bless Thy name forever and ever.
Every day I will bless Thee,
and I will praise Thy name forever and ever.
Great is the Lord, and highly to be praised;
and His greatness is unsearchable.
One generation shall praise Thy works to another,
and shall declare Thy mighty acts.
On the glorious splendor of Thy majesty,
and on Thy wonderful works, I will meditate.
Psalm 145: 1-5

This quiet morning, Lord, I desire to worship You in a way that satisfies my need to tell You I love You but, surpassing that, honors and pleases You.

The longer I live, the more I realize Your supremacy, Your majesty. The more I know about You, the more exalted You become in my thinking. It scares me a bit to think about all that You are, because then I see the vast difference between You and me. I am reminded of my smallness, my utter poverty and blindness, my wretchedness without You. Only by Your great grace can I be, will I *ever* be, anything of worth.

Your love is so amazing and hard to understand! It took me so long to believe that You loved me. Now, Lord, I hold firmly to that love, I value the incredible privilege of *knowing You*. I so look forward to an eternity with You where I will be able to learn abundantly of Your glorious nature and goodness.

My mind staggers at the fact that the Almighty Creator, God of the universe, knows my name! I search for words to express the wonder and awe my spirit feels, but my search is in vain. Please look within and see the love, the gratitude and praise, the hunger and thirst, the longing for You.

You speak to me through Your Word; thus, all of it becomes a precious possession. Your promises encourage me, sustain me and give me confidence. The honesty of Your Word tells me that those men and women were not perfect either; yet, You loved them and used their lives to Your divine purpose. The poetry of Your Word deeply touches my spirit. The wisdom of Your Word, Lord, I want to *absorb and live out* in my everyday life. All these desires of my heart are ones which You have placed there. Therefore, I can know that they *shall* be accomplished.

You are the Sovereign God of my praise, and my intimate Friend!

September 5
ANOTHER LOOK AT WORSHIP

But godliness actually is a means of great gain
when accompanied by contentment.
1 Timothy 6:6

Paul talks here about contentment being an important characteristic of Timothy's life. And Paul tells the Philippians that he has learned to be content in all circumstances. (Phil. 4:11) So this tells me that contentment is not an inborn gift but rather an attitude to be learned. I read yesterday, Lord, that being contented is a way to worship You; it is a lived-out expression of my faith in Your sovereignty and Your goodness. That statement spoke to me because I want to learn all I can about worshipping You.

You know, my Lord, how difficult it was for me to accept and understand that You are, indeed, in control of every detail of my life. I wrestled with that concept for a long time and tried, times without number, to prove it wrong. But the truth won. *You are sovereign.*

Therefore, discontent becomes, in actuality, rebellion against You. And rebellion is sin. That is a harsh statement, Lord, but truth is truth. It is so easy to think of contentment only in terms of monetary things, material possessions. But the concept of being content applies to all of life - to *every* situation in which we find ourselves. So, does this mean I should just apathetically accept every difficulty in my life without trying to change it? No. It means that I should, in every difficulty, seek You and see what You are wanting to accomplish through it, seek to understand Your perspective.

Andrew Murray, an exceptionally wise and godly man, understood this concept. He wrote: "In time of trouble, say, 'First, He brought me here. It is by His will I am in this strait place; in that I will rest.' Next, 'He will keep me here in His love and give me grace in this trial to behave as His child.' Then say, 'He will make the trial a blessing, teaching me lessons He intends me to learn, and working in me the grace He means to bestow.' And last, say, 'In His good time He can bring me out again. How and when, He knows.' Therefore, say, 'I am here by God's appointment, in His keeping, under His training, for His time.'"

What a contented life this would produce! I think the greatest benefit of applying this truth, Lord, is that *it keeps me constantly looking to You.* To assimilate this simple process would be life changing for any believer who struggles with problems, which is to say *any believer.* Thank You for teaching me.

249

September 6
HOW GOOD YOU ARE

I permitted Myself to be sought by those who did not ask for Me;
I permitted Myself to be found by those who did not seek Me.
I said, 'Here am I, here am I,'
To a nation which did not call on My name.
Isaiah 65:1

Those words, Lord, remind me of the
hopeless, desolate despair
of the place
in which those are who know You not.
They speak to me of Your great grace
which allows us to find You even when not looking.

There was a time in my life when those words described me.
I was not asking for You.
I was not seeking You.
I was not calling on Your name.

Reading them today causes my spirit to bow in utmost humility before Your
mercy.
I am Your child because of Your mercy and grace and love,
not because of any worthiness on my part.
All the good things You have done
and are doing
and have planned for me
are because of who You are
- a great and awesome God of love -
not because I am anything.

What does this knowledge do within me?

It strengthens my faith.
It makes me desire a more focused, single-minded devotion to You.
It increases the desire already present to be a useful vessel in Your hands.
It makes me look forward eagerly to that wonderful day
when I can
in person
bow before You in worship and love and thanksgiving.

You, my Lord, are my heart, my treasure, my home.

250

September 7
CONTROL

The Lord will protect you from all evil;
He will keep your soul.
The Lord will guard your going out and your coming in
from this time forth and forever.
Psalm 121: 7-8

My Psalm this morning, Lord, was 121 - one of my favorites. It is full of information about You and what You do for those You love. But I noticed a truth in verse 5 this morning I had never noticed before:

The Lord is your keeper;
the Lord is your shade on your right hand.

Now, I've known You were my keeper. I've counted on You being my keeper. I've been thankful You were my keeper. It is the next line that jumped off the page at me. All the years You and I have been walking together, I have always pictured myself at Your right hand which would mean my left hand would be in Yours. Since I am right-handed, this would leave my right hand free to maintain control and "do things." So this was a revelation to me to see the truth - *You are at my right hand*!

Isn't this the exact issue with which You and I have been dealing? *Control.* Seeing that verse lit up in my mind the fact that I am at Your *left* side, and You are holding my *right* hand. This is of serious consequence to me, Lord, because I'm not able to do a lot with my left hand. And assuming that my right hand is "immobilized" at all times, *I am actually removing my hand from Yours when I try to take control of situations.*

Yielded-ness or surrender or submission take on new meaning when I consider this picture of spiritual truth - that my right hand is in Yours. *That is exactly where I want it to be, Lord!*

Thank You for showing this to me. By Your grace, I will begin this hour to think of myself walking beside You, my right hand captured in Your left hand, just as my heart is captured by Your love.

September 8
CONFESSION

He who conceals his transgressions will not prosper,
but he who confesses and forsakes them will find compassion.
Proverbs 28:13

I'm claiming that promise right now, Lord, before I read anything further this morning. Yesterday's small incident gave me a glimpse into myself that shocked me. All I know to say is, "I'm so sorry" and, "Without Your grace at work in me, I will never behave differently."

Please forgive me. If I need to do more than confess and receive Your cleansing, please let me know. Nothing in my life is more important than being right with You.

So, what have I learned through this painful experience? That there is work yet to be done in me; I certainly have not "arrived." I see how much it hurts to think I have disappointed You. I see that, though I was surprised by this, You were not. You knew my tendency to err existed and would eventually manifest itself. I see that a portion of my heartache is disappointment in myself - that I depended upon me rather than You; I know better. And so, Lord, I should be *thanking* You for the whole incident. Through it, I see that I must draw even closer to You, listen to You more intently, and then *act upon Your Word.*

"*My grace is sufficient...*" (2 Cor. 12:9). That is present tense - today - for this circumstance - Your grace is large enough. Is it my goodness or righteousness that give me power to live this life? No! So why should I ever think I can depend on such a flimsy, unsubstantial foundation? Of course, the answer is, *I shouldn't.*

You, my El Shaddai, are able to turn what seems to be defeat and failure into unmistakable victory. Your Word say so. "*All things work together for good...*" (Rom. 8: 28). Part of that victory is my learning a very valuable lesson - that my sinful, human nature is still able to affect my behavior.

I've learned, again, that the life committed to living totally for You is a paradox - it is full of blessing, joy and peace but it is also full of heartache, warfare and struggle. The heartache, warfare and struggle are, seemingly, crucial to our spiritual development. The blessing, joy and peace are given as a foretaste of what eternity with You will be like. It is all good.

These "*momentary, light afflictions*" (2 Cor. 4:17) truly are well worth it. Thank You for picking me up again, allowing me to draw near to You, to confess and be cleansed and go forward with new understanding of Your love, grace, faithfulness and goodness. And with a new view of my own weakness. "*For when I am weak, then I am strong.*" (2 Cor. 12:10)

I love You so much, Lord.

September 9
YOUR HEART OF LOVE

By this the love of God was manifested in us,
that God has sent His only begotten Son into the world
so that we might live through Him.
In this is love, not that we loved God,
but that He loved us and sent His Son
to be the propitiation for our sins.
By this we know that we abide in Him
and He in us, because He has given us of His Spirit.
1 John 4: 9-10, 13

On this tranquil morning, Lord, my mind is filled with all the life-giving truths You teach me in Your Word juxtaposed with all of my inadequacies and needs. Yet my spirit overrules my mind. My spirit longs simply to be in Your healing, loving presence and to worship You. To speak to You, spirit to Spirit, of how much I love You and how essential You are to me. Please, O God of my praise, see in me what I desire to express.

"The heart that serves and loves and clings
hears everywhere the rush of angels' wings."

There is, deep within in me, the certain knowledge that You, the magnificent and awesome God of all creation, dwell with me and order the circumstances of my life. You are my loving, sovereign God, my Refuge. You envelop me with a love that does not depend on me, or on what I do or don't do. You *are* love.

It is that love, Lord, that breaks my heart and causes me to want to be and do only what pleases You. To know You is such an incomparable privilege! Even with all my faults and failures, You allow me to draw near to You, to be with You and try to tell You how very precious all that is to me. Praise and thanksgiving fill my spirit! All is light, warmth, joy and peace in my spirit, my Lord, because *You* are there.

"With my hands lifted up
and my mouth filled with praise;
with a heart of thanksgiving
I will bless Thee, O Lord."

September 10
CHILDLIKE TRUST IN YOU

O Lord, my heart is not proud nor my eyes haughty;
nor do I involve myself in great matters,
or in things too difficult for me.
Surely I have composed and quieted my soul;
like a weaned child rests against his mother,
my soul is like a weaned child within me.
O Israel, hope in the Lord
from this time forth and forever.
Psalm 131

This is one of my very favorite psalms. Each time I read it, my heart is reminded that You are a strong, compassionate Father who always has my best interests at heart. The words make me recall that it is You who are wise beyond all understanding, that You see the end from the beginning. How foolish I am, Lord, if I fail to rely upon You with the unquestioning confidence of a well-loved child.

It seems ironic to me that, as parents, we begin teaching our children self-sufficiency and independence at an early age; and then, when we respond to Your calling upon our lives, You must begin teaching us the opposite - to *not* be self-sufficient and to be *totally* dependent upon You.

Maybe I'm thinking about these things because it is taking me all my life to learn them. Maybe that is why this little psalm is so appealing to me. At times, I become so weary of the struggles in the lessons I must learn, the "daily-ness" of life. Then I can come to Psalm 131 and allow its picture of peace to wash over my tired soul and bring rest. I am able to relax in Your loving embrace with no special need except a wish to let go and trust - what a beautiful, full-of-joy picture! I do not need to worry about anything; I am in Your safekeeping.

After a time of rest, I am ready to take up my life with new strength. Truly, You are a good God! See how much I love You?

September 11
THE MYSTERY OF THE WILL

The will is a slippery thing, Lord. When I think I've learned something about it, suddenly it slides into a different shape, and I see that my newly discovered "fact" is not fact at all. For instance, I talk about "giving You my will" and my desire that You be in control of it. But in actuality, that can never happen, can it? My will, in this life, shall *always* be under my control; otherwise, it would not be the free will You created it to be.

But then, Lord, I read Ephesians 1:5, *"He predestined us to adoption as sons through Jesus Christ to Himself, according to the kind intention of His will."* This seems to say that at some point in time, perhaps long ago, You decided who would become children of Your family and so by the "kind intention of Your will," it happened.

And then there is that verse which says You abide within "both to will and to work" in me. (Phil.2:13) Does that mean that You are in there changing my will so that I can then work as *You* choose? How many times I have wished that this were so! But it isn't. The truth in that verse is that You do abide within me to make Your will known to me, and You are at work. You make clear the choices before me, but I must make the choice. That is Your job - the "make clear" part. My job is, has been and always will be to *choose*. That is why the phrase immediately preceding that verse says, *"work out your salvation with fear and trembling."* There would be no working out of my salvation if You were doing all the jobs of the will.

Then there is James 1:18. It says, *"In the exercise of His will, He brought us forth by the word of truth…"* Again, it sounds as if it were completely Your will in action, not the will of man. I think, Lord, that this weak swimmer is in deep water, indeed!

Here is my simple-minded answer to a complex situation (remember Psalm 131!): Paul gives it in Romans 9: 19-21, *"You will say to me then, 'Why does He still find fault? For who resists His will?' On the contrary, who are you, O man, who answers back to God? The thing molded will not say to the molder, 'Why did you make me like this,' will it? Or does not the potter have a right over the clay to make from the same lump one vessel for honorable use, and another for common use?"*

The simple truth is that all of the above is true. You *have* given us free will; we *do* have to constantly make choices and yet, You are Sovereign God. You always and forever will rule over all. You created us, and You can step in and do with us as You choose because You are Sovereign God. All I need to do is read Your words in Job 38-42. That solves the whole dilemma in my mind, Lord.

Two truths to remember - I should never be dogmatic about this subject and truly, You are Lord of all. I'm so glad You are in charge!

September 12
YOUR BLESSINGS TO ME

Ephesians 1: 3-14

These verses, Lord, are a wonderful list of spiritual blessings that You have given to all Your children. I want to think about them in Your presence this morning.

You chose me to be Yours long before I was born. Here is the mystery of Your will working and my will working. Both were involved, weren't they, Lord?

You have made me holy and blameless in Your eyes, even though I'm still learning to walk.

You adopted me to be Your child. This especially resonates in my spirit because our son, too, is adopted and is so greatly loved by us. He has brought so much joy and love into our lives which we would not have known if he were not our son. This is how You look at me!

Your intentions toward me are kind. Hebrews 11:6 says that I must not only believe that You *are*, but also see that You are a *rewarder* of those who trust in You - not a punisher, not a tyrant, but a God full of kindness who desires to bless.

I have been accepted by You into an abundant grace. The longer I walk in it, Lord, the more I see its abundance. It is wider, higher, longer and deeper than I can understand. It supplies everything I need to become like You.

Because You shed your blood, I have been redeemed, bought back, from the kingdom of darkness. Your death provided for my forgiveness, an all-inclusive forgiveness that I receive simply by asking and repenting.

You have given me wisdom and insight as I walk with You, day by day, into the mystery of Your will.

You have laid up for me an inheritance - *eternal life lived with You.* You have sealed me with Your promised Holy Spirit as a pledge of that inheritance.

You have worked all things after the counsel of Your will.

This list, Lord, is awesome! That You would do all this for weak creatures who often are not even *aware* of Your blessings, much less thankful for them, is astounding to my mind. Please accept my gratitude and praise this morning for all that You are and all that You do. I love You, my Lord.

September 13
TEMPTATION

No temptation has overtaken you but such as is common to man;
and God is faithful, who will not allow you to be tempted
beyond what you are able,
but with the temptation will provide the way of escape also,
that you may be able to endure it.
1 Corinthians 10: 13

This verse, so familiar to Christians, is brim full of information that I just must talk to You about it this morning, Lord. First, *"but such as is common to man."* I am often guilty of thinking that I'm the only one who has ever experienced this particular set of trying circumstances. Not so. What I experience is what all people experience in one way or another. Our lives may look very different on the outside, but inside, we are all alike. And the tests (or temptations) we are given are common to all of us.

Next, *"God is faithful, who will not allow you to be tempted beyond what you are able."* Your faithfulness, Lord, has been proven again and again to me. It is a fact, not subject to question. There have been times I thought You might not be paying attention, and allowed my testing to go on a bit too long. There have been situations where I was seemingly hanging on by my fingernails, moment-by-moment, before You intervened. But did I fall? No. Did You fail to intervene? No. So is this a true statement? Absolutely!

Then, *"will provide the way of escape also."* This is another statement You have demonstrated to me to be fact. I must admit I have not always wanted Your way of escape. Sometimes what I wanted was *immediate escape,* and that was not Your provision. Those were the times I learned more perfectly that perseverance and commitment are two qualities high on Your list of importance, Lord. Those were also the times that I realized that Your grace truly *is* sufficient.

Lastly, *"that you may be able to endure it."* And what is endurance but perseverance and commitment? You provide the strength, both physical and spiritual, to endure anything which You allow into the life of Your child. You provide the faith by which I receive that strength. From beginning to end, Lord, it is all of You. Thank You for having Paul write down these words for me to think about today. I love You so very much.

September 14
CONTROL ISSUES
(Again)

My soul, wait in silence for God only, for my hope is from Him.
He only is my rock and my salvation, my stronghold; I shall not be shaken.
On God my salvation and my glory rest;
the rock of my strength, my refuge is in God.
Trust in Him at all times, O people;
pour out your heart before Him;
God is a refuge for us.
Psalm 62: 5-8

Lord, I am such a needy child. As You know, I'm really struggling with this particular control issue. I look back and see the mistakes of my past, where I made wrong choices. Then I look at today and see that I have been given a second chance in this same area to make right choices.. I also look ahead and see what bad things could happen if I *fail* to do it correctly.

I know Your good word to me would be, **"Just relax, let go, let Me be in control."** And I want this, Lord. I really do. And for my own life, it is even easy to do. But in another's life, how does it work? How do I know *they* will allow You to have control?

I don't.

But did You appoint me to be God in their life? Are You not able to orchestrate circumstances for them just as You have for me? Are You not the all-powerful God of the universe? Is anything too hard for You?

My fear seems foolish, Lord, when I see it in light of my power versus Your power. So my faith says, *"Just relax, let go, let God be in control."*

I will both relax and rejoice.
Do as You please in the life of this one I love.
Thank You for being my Rock and my Refuge!

September 15
NO ANXIETY

For this reason I say to you, do not be anxious for your life,
as to what you shall eat, or what you shall drink;
nor for your body, as to what you shall put on.
Is not life more than food, and the body more than clothing?
But seek first His kingdom and His righteousness;
and all these things shall be added to you.
Matthew 6: 25, 33

I do not know what is happening with my body to produce these new and distressing symptoms…the severe dizziness and weakness. But You know, so I'm not worried. I will just hold on to my Five Anchors.

Be anxious for nothing.
In everything give thanks.
Rejoice evermore.
Pray without ceasing.
Quench not Your Spirit.

Knowing that You are in control, I am able to turn loose of anxious thoughts. This causes great thankfulness to well up in my heart, Lord, because You are my all-powerful, majestic, awesome God. But what melts me down and breaks my heart is Your love. It is beyond belief that You love me! What joy fills my spirit when I think about how wide and deep and immense is that love! It has always given me enough space to fail, fall, be picked up, dusted off and to go on again.

How faithful You have been. Through many dark days, You have been there with me; therefore, I have no fear of any dark days ahead. Just confidence in You. One of these glad mornings, the light I see is going to be Your radiant face!

So be it.

September 16
SINGING YOUR LOVE

I love the Lord, because He hears my voice and my supplications,
because He has inclined His ear to me.
Therefore I shall call upon Him as long as I live.
Psalm 116: 1-2

Finally, after six days of feeling lousy, I think I have enough energy to both think and write. I've talked to You a lot these past days, Lord, just not on paper. Thank You for hearing me, no matter how I speak. You are able to hear even the faintest thought directed toward You! I love You and I am filled with praise and thanksgiving for Your goodness to me.

You are faithful; You do not change. Your lovingkindness is everlasting. You continue to love me even when I am not lovable. Your intentions for me are to prosper and not to harm. It is only because of the painful death You suffered that I can someday stand before You, holy and blameless. What an extraordinary, unbelievable, astounding, amazing Person You are to love like that! Never in a million lifetimes could I be worthy of that love. But still, it is mine!

Moments ago, I picked up my journal and read the final statement of the previous entry. The words so speak my heart, Lord. I look forward with joy and great anticipation to that glad, glorious morning!

...My Beloved is mine and I am His ...
His banner over me is love.
Song of Solomon 2: 4, 16

I will sing unto the Lord while I live;
I will sing praise to my God while I have life in me.
My meditations of Him shall be sweet;
I shall be glad in the Lord.
Bless Thou the Lord, O my soul!
Psalm 104: 33-34

September 17
WAITING UPON YOU

Wait for the Lord;
be strong and let your heart take courage;
yes, wait for the Lord.
Psalm 27: 14

Waiting is very hard for some people, Lord, and I am one of them. Waiting takes strength and courage, as David said in that verse. Waiting makes me loosen my grip on my agenda and to trust You. In the first verse of this psalm, David said, *"The Lord is my light and my salvation; whom shall I fear? The Lord is the defense of my life; whom shall I dread?"*

These are helpful and soothing words to this child of Yours who so much likes to *get things done.* This is actually yet another control issue, isn't it, Lord? I see that I need to stop pulling ahead. I need to keep my right hand in Yours, allow myself to relax in Your care, be filled with joy and peace and keep on walking *beside* You.

All the things I am tempted to be and could be anxious about are so *safe* in Your control; if I were in charge, that would not be so. What a relief, Lord! What a wise and loving God You are to disregard my fretting and murmuring. You continue loving and blessing me, urging me to grow up, to see how self-centered I am. Your patience and love are my example. I am to be patient in my waiting for Your promises to be fulfilled, just as You have been so very patient with me.

Thank You, Lord, for carrying the too-heavy-for-me burden. Please look into my heart and see there the love, gratitude and praise that fills me up and runs over the top. You are my El Elyon, my Beloved. My heart's desire is to live out *Your* agenda.

September 18
A "HOW-TO" LESSON

Cease striving and know that I am God.
Psalm 46: 10

Such a short, simple sentence, Lord, but the task within is not easily accomplished. Please help me organize my thoughts on getting still before You so that I can outline this process for my class. As there is infinitely more knowledge than I possess, I open my mind to You; teach me more if You so choose.

I know this: before I can experience inner stillness, I *must* talk to You about any burden I'm carrying and *give* it to You. This might include confession; it could be anxiety I'm feeling about a situation; it is anything in my mind creating distraction. I must hold nothing back from You.

I must then permit Your searchlight to illuminate *to me* any issue I need to bring before You. My knowledge is partial; Yours is complete. This allows You to bring to my mind things of which I may not even be aware. Again, utmost honesty on my part is necessary.

The next step is for me to relax. Rather than "trying hard" to get still, I focus on relaxing both mind and body. Actually, "trying hard" *creates* tension. What I find, Lord, is that my mind can relax only if my body is relaxed. So I simply think about loosening bodily tension starting with my toes and working my way up to my head. Amazingly, in mere seconds, hidden and unsuspected tensions are released. Now to relax my mind, I recall a memorized verse of praise, or just read one from my Bible. For instance:

Enter His gates with thanksgiving,
And His courts with praise.
Give thanks to Him; and bless His name.
Psalm 100: 4-5

Then comes worship. Lord, You know that I never feel my worship is adequate. Still I know that You, being the good and gracious God that You are, accept it with all joy. Thank You for that! During this time, if the enemy attacks with distractions or my thoughts wander, I quickly jot them down on nearby paper. In moments, I am able to refocus and return my thoughts to You. For me, worship includes speaking words of admiration and love to You, writing down the thoughts You bring to my mind and times of just being still in Your presence, simply enjoying being with You.

I'm so thankful that You created us all differently, to worship You in our individual ways. Bless these practical encouragements to my students, Lord. May we see that the important thing is not *how* to worship. The important thing is simply to worship - with all that is within us.

September 19
YOUR ETERNAL WORK IN ME

For the gifts and the calling of God are irrevocable.
Romans 11: 29

I need to capture this elusive thought before it slips away, Lord - the thought about having no doubts about Your power (or Your *anything*) and many about myself. I have said such words to You many times.

What I think I'm seeing is this: if You are dwelling within me in Your fullness, which You are, and if I have given You control, which I have, then to doubt myself is the same as doubting You. I am in effect saying - or, more accurately, thinking - that You are not up to the job of running my life, that You are not going to keep Your promises.

I need to adjust my perspective so that it reflects truth. Here is truth: once I make a commitment to You on any level and on any subject, You consider that a finished transaction. From Your side of things, it is a done deal. You proceed with carrying out Your side of the transaction and expect me to do likewise.

My side always involves trust and obedience, doesn't it, Lord? *Trust* that You are working and know what You are doing, and *obedience* to You in everything I am supposed to do. To be deficient in either of those tasks will throw us off track and slow down our progress. *But my deficiency doesn't negate the contract.* That fact is essential to my absorbing truth, here, Lord. A commitment is, in Your sight, forever.

This forever-ness goes a long way toward explaining Your amazing patience. You plainly see that You have forever - literally - to do Your work in me. You see clearly that You have absolute sovereignty over my life in all its complexity. Consequently, You have no reason to ever be anxious or impatient. You can wait 40 years for me to come to my senses and allow You to do what You need to do.

But I see, Lord, that if I waste those 40 years in unbelief and disobedience, *I am the one who loses.* I am still Your child. I will still get to heaven. But I will be so ashamed when I see Your other children, the trusting, obedient ones who allowed You to work through them, receiving their rewards while I stand there with nothing.

But You know what, Lord? The disappointment of no rewards will be insignificant compared to my anguish of heart at having failed You. Oh, God, may it never be! You who have done so much for me - how could I fail to love You with all that I am, trust You in every situation and obey You as quickly as I understand my assignment?! I pray, Lord, that You will take these thoughts and impress them so deeply upon my heart that I am unable to do other than Your complete will.

You are worthy.

September 20
WALKING BY THE SPIRIT

But I say, walk by the Spirit, and you will not carry out the desires of the flesh.
Galatians 5:16

In Your eternal wisdom, Lord, You use the circumstances of my life to bring about the inner changes that You wish to effect. I began my Christian life with a lot of the "world" in me. This is true of every believer, whether the baby Christian is 7 years old or 47 years old. All the wrong with which we were born and all the wrong which we have learned must be replaced with right.

Instead of using up my entire life to ever-so-slowly, one-by-one *learn* these things, You could, in a moment of time, simply remove every particle of that wrong and fill me with every good thing You want me to have. Well, I could be mistaken, Lord, but my understanding of Your Word is….that is *exactly* what You do! At the moment of my being born of Your Spirit, You did away with all the wrong and gifted me with everything I would ever need to live a holy and pure life from that day forward - Your Very Presence within me. I actually became a new creation.

Therefore if any man is in Christ, he is a new creature; the old things passed
away; behold, new things have come. (2 Cor. 5:17)

So, why is the universal testimony of believers one of struggle, trial, failure/confession and seeking answers? Because the "new creature" applies to my spirit only. It is my spirit that was "dead" and is now alive. It is my spirit in which You dwell during this life. It is my spirit-filled-with-You that is now to be the driving force of my life. Not my mind/will. It is the same mind/will with which I was born. It must learn to yield to Your Spirit living in my spirit. The driving force is not to be my emotions. They are affected by everything from the weather to waking up with a headache. They, too, must be subject to Your Spirit living in my spirit. Not my body. It is the same body the moment after salvation as it was the moment before. I must learn to "bring my body under subjection" to Your Spirit living in my spirit.

It is this process of *changing all the rest of me* that takes so long. It is this process where You use the circumstances of my life to purify me. If You truly are Lord of my life, all the mysterious infrastructure within me becomes, through this process we call walking by faith, exactly what You desire. Man, for all his progress in knowledge and technology, has barely begun to grasp the complexity of human nature. But You created it; You know how to bring about the needed changes.

Thank You, Lord, for Your grace which provides everything I need to live out this life of faith. Without that provision, I would be spiritually dead and on my way to an eternity without You. Do You see the immense gratitude in my heart? My cup runneth over.

September 21
BEING TAUGHT BY YOU

For his God instructs and teaches him properly.
This also comes from the Lord of hosts,
who has made His counsel wonderful and His wisdom great.
Isaiah 28: 26(a), 29

I'm still thinking about yesterday's fascinating subject, Lord - the miracle of how You change us from the inside out. This truly is a miracle as great as healing the blind man or parting the Red Sea. You do it all around us, all the time, and yet Your very own children are apt to say that the day of miracles is past! What is more miraculous than the Almighty God of The Universe living in me, caring about the details of my life, and changing me?! I'm convinced, Lord, that this is as great a miracle as there could ever be.

This inner transformation appears to be a life-long process. I learn spiritual truths just as my child learned to speak words - one at a time. I do believe that I could grow and learn faster if I were wise enough to allow You full control. But since I've never known anyone who did that, it is only a theory.

The words above from Isaiah tell me that Your counsel is wonderful and Your wisdom is great. This means that You have sound reasons for the way You work. And what comes to mind first is the virtue of *perseverance.* How would I have learned perseverance if You and I had done 35 years of work in two weeks? Perseverance, like every other virtue, is perfected only by practicing it in adversity. And, obviously, perseverance is high on Your list of desired attributes.

And *patience.* Patience, too, can only be learned in situations that demand a lot of it. Getting everything I wanted quickly and consistently might teach me *something,* but it would not be patience.

And how about *faithfulness*? The very word contains the idea of something happening over an extended period of time. Like a couple still in love after 55 years of being married to each other - that long-term faithfulness is beautiful, Lord, and should be celebrated. A one-month relationship does not call for much celebration. It is kinship with You over the long, marvelous, difficult years that grows faithfulness.

Just interesting thoughts, Lord. Deep down, I know that You are running this show, and all is well. It is obvious that You could change anything, at any time. So I need to practice some patience with myself. One thing I realize from this train of thought - You delight in variety. We are taught in Your Word to live in unity, but that does not mean we are to be all alike. You made us to be different because You want us to be different. Your Holy Spirit, working through me precisely as You know I need, will produce exactly the final result that You want. How amazing is Your grace!

September 22
WALKING TOGETHER

Can two walk together, except they be agreed?
Amos 3:3

Walking with You, Lord, is no casual stroll down a country lane to view the beauties of nature. It is a purposeful *going* somewhere. You not only have a certain destination in mind, You also have a complete and detailed understanding of what is required to get there.

You choose the pace, and You choose the direction. You arrange the circumstances day-by-day to teach my heart the lessons that You have authored especially for me. You teach, and then You test to see if I've advanced in knowledge. Occasionally, I'm a bit over-confident about what I *think* I know. Then You might throw in a pop quiz to show me just how little I *do* know, get my attention and proceed with the next topic of study. My part is to be entirely dependent on You, thoroughly devoted to You and joyfully expectant about what comes next.

I remember the miles and miles my husband-to-be and I walked in our courting days, how much fun that was and what it took for us to walk together. Since we were still in college, most of our walking was done on campus. Sometimes we walked to a specific place at an appointed time, and sometimes we leisurely strolled with no other goal but to spend time together.

What did it take for us to walk together? It took agreeing on a destination and how long we had to get there. It took agreeing on a route - taking the long way, staying on sidewalks, or using shortcuts over wide expanses of campus lawn. It took holding hands (well, not necessary but more fun). Most importantly it took just loving to be together, enjoying each other's company.

Those things are true with us, too, Lord, except that You don't ask my opinion about where and how. I simply agree with You, not knowing where and how, but totally trusting that You have my best interests at heart, fully believing that You love me and knowing deep in my soul that You will not turn loose of my hand.

What an adventure it is walking with You! I don't know what is around the next bend in the road but I know it will be fine because You will be there. Looking back fills me with gratitude for Your faithfulness. Looking forward fills me with Your peace and joy. And that makes this present moment full of love for You!

September 23
MOTIVE FOR SURRENDER

And he answered and said, "You shall love the Lord your God with all your heart,
and with all your soul, and with all your strength, and with all your mind;
and your neighbor as yourself."
Luke 10: 27

What is my motive for loving You, Lord? What causes me to desire complete surrender to Your will? Am I loving and surrendering for what I will get in return? I must be honest. I *do* look at what I will get in return - being made holy, being filled with You, being used by You, having eternal life with You - all these and more are so valuable to me! But then I think about this verse: *"We love, because He first loved us." (1 John 4:19)* and I see that the reason I love You is that You loved me first. The wonderful things listed in this paragraph are the *result* of my surrender rather than the motive for it.

The only "right" motive is love for *You, Yourself.* I love You and prefer You over any other person or thing in my life. This is genuine surrender. So surrender is just another word for love, isn't it, Lord?

As I look deep within, I see that truly I do prefer You and love You more than any other person or thing. I know this because I own nothing that I cannot live without *if I have You.* And, as much as I love the people in my life, there is no person I cannot live without *if I have You.* But if I had material riches beyond measure, and many more people to love and didn't have You, I would not want to live. There would be no reason to live. You, Lord, *are* my reason for living. I don't even like to think about life without You! Desolation and darkness!

Your gift of salvation means that I'm being completely delivered from myself and placed into perfect union with You; You accomplish this in me through my loving surrender to You and Your loving surrender to me. My surrender to You I understand. Your surrender to me is a new thought. But You did give Yourself completely and wholly, totally, unconditionally, without reservation - *even unto death.* How can I do less? My heart says I cannot.

I see that to the degree that I allow myself to be consumed with You, I will become more perfectly one with You. I see that You have done (and are doing) Your part, and I must constantly *choose* to do mine. I see that, even in making those choices, You are within to encourage and strengthen and love.

It always comes back to choices, doesn't it? The awesome, terrifying power of choice! Thinking about it makes me exceedingly grateful for Your promise to never leave me. I am safe and secure in Your hands - absolutely nothing can reach me without Your permission. And Your grace is sufficient to see me through any choice You put before me. You, Lord, are my Beloved. Thank You for these truths.

September 24
THE BLESSING OF TRIAL

Behold, we count those blessed who endured.
You have heard of the endurance of Job
and have seen the outcome of the Lord's dealing,
that the Lord is full of compassion and is merciful.
James 5:11

You, Lord, have brought challenges into my life - difficult matters over which I had no control - to show me how loving and trustworthy You are.

I learned that my strength, my self-sufficiency, had to be set aside *because it was worthless*. You actually made it easy to look to You because, in reality, I had no choice. But wait, that's not entirely true, is it, Lord? I did have some choices. I could have chosen to run, to escape my problems that way. I could have chosen to end my life. I could have chosen drugs or alcohol as a way of coping with difficulty. And yet, those options never occurred to me.

And why didn't they? Because You had been at work in my heart, preparing me, teaching me, making me love You more and more. You *always* prepare us for every experience, don't You, Lord? That is only one of the many things I love about You.

But what I'm thinking about this morning is how You blessed me in the midst of those troubles. Even now, it seems odd to me that I learned to love You *so much more* through the rough patches. I would have thought that blessings would cause love. But in my life, the hard-to-bear struggles have *been* the blessings.

Perhaps it was my drawing near to You more often, or the more consistent looking to You for help, or just the sense of utter dependence upon You to get through the day. Whatever it was, as I look back now, Lord, I see those times as blessed times. And I see that You do not look at the minor distress of today - You look at the major result from the training of today. You *knew* that yesterday's burdens would become today's joys. You knew the blessings You would bring to me during and because of those trials, and You considered the suffering insignificant when compared to the end result.

When I look at today, Lord, I see that it also is blessed. I still have problems over which I have little or no control. I still have choices to make. I can try to out-maneuver circumstances, or I can simply give the whole situation to You - clicking an inward, invisible, attitude-changing switch. Switching *off* my attempt to control - switching *on* Your patience, gentleness and quietness within my spirit.

Putting it down in black and white makes it so clear. Thank You that this coming week will provide me ample opportunities to practice getting it right. Please help me to be both wise and faithful to what You have taught me. Thank You, Lord, for being compassionate and merciful to this needy child.

September 25
FRIENDSHIP WITH YOU

Greater love has no one than this, that one lay down his life for his friends.
You are My friends, if you do what I command you.
No longer do I call you slaves,
for the slave does not know what his master is doing;
but I have called you friends, for all things that I have heard from My Father
I have made known to you.
You did not choose Me, but I chose you, and appointed you,
that you should go and bear fruit, and that your fruit should remain,
that whatever you ask of the Father in My name, He may give to you.
John 15: 13-16

Those words from John create in me such gratitude and amazement. I have a few exceptionally close friends in my life, Lord, and with each one there is a sense of total, mutual acceptance. There is a commonality of likes and dislikes. There is a level of intimacy that isn't present with mere acquaintances. My close friends love me, and I love them. We take pleasure in spending time together. We enjoy going places and doing things together. We like talking to each other, sharing our thoughts and feelings.

All this and more is true of You and me. So I am bold and say, "You are my Friend." What an absolutely incredible thing it is that *You* are my Friend! The thought brings me to the subject uppermost in my mind this morning. A few days ago, I wrote in my journal about how, if I have given You control of my life, doubting myself was the same as doubting You. That thought is still circulating in my brain.

That particular truth gives me the freedom to move forward, confidently knowing that my decisions *are* Your decisions. I can feel the liberation, delight and assurance that come with knowing You will stop me if I'm headed the wrong way - I will feel Your hand tighten its grip on mine and slow me down; I will sense the restraint of Your Spirit, in which case I must obey immediately; I will discern that tug in my spirit that says, "Wait, let's talk about that."

I know the truth of those statements because I have experienced those very things, You have planted my feet in a spacious place - an expansive, beautiful, full-of-light place. I marvel at Your grace, my Lord. You love *first,* You love *best* and You love *always.* How can I not respond with all the love that is within me?

I wish that every person in the world could experience this joy of friendship with You!

September 26
CONFIDENCE IN INTERCESSION

And in the same way the Spirit also helps our weakness; for we do not know how to pray as we should, but the Spirit Himself intercedes for us with groanings too deep for words; and He who searches the hearts knows what the mind of the Spirit is, because He intercedes for the saints according to the will of God.
Romans 8: 26-27

The truth about Your work in me, Lord, is still in my mind this morning. I want to think with You about how this truth impacts intercessory prayer. Reviewing the concept: if I have given You total control of my life, inner and outer, and have not since then removed myself from Your control, then I am to consider that *You are at work.*

There are times of prayer when I am *aware* that Your mind is at work in mine - when it seems that You are doing it all, and I am simply cooperating. But the truth is that that is correct *even if I'm not* aware of it. This is simple faith in Your promise. Truly, I don't know how to pray as I should; so I trust Your unlimited ability, and Your complete knowledge about the situation. I am certain that Your faithfulness is forever. In other words, when I begin to pray for a person, I can *know* that You are there within me, praying through me.

Did You not instruct us to pray for one another? Did You, Yourself, not pray *for* us? Does Your Word not say that You are, even this moment, interceding for all the saints? So I know this is a subject dear to Your heart, too, Lord.

Your children's failure to believe these truths about prayer and failure to *live them out every day* grieves You. To understand Your work in our interceding is to be greatly encouraged! What bloody battles are fought in the spirit world over this subject of prayer! Prayer is the thing the enemy fears most because he *knows* it is powerful. Give me grace to live every moment of every day close to You and be faithful in this business of interceding. The rest of it is Your work.

September 27
THE DIFFERENCE YOU MAKE

Every good thing bestowed and every perfect gift is from above, coming down from the Father of lights, with whom there is no variation, or shifting shadow.
James 1: 17

As I read these words from James, I think about the many good and perfect gifts You have given me, Lord. And I am made to ask, "Do I understand what it means to have You in my life? Do I see the countless ways my life is different because of You?"

I need to spend some time thinking about this, Lord. I'm probably taking many of Your blessings for granted. They are all given through Your grace. I don't deserve *any* of them. Only because of Your mercy can I possess these shining and glorious gifts.

You Give	You Take Away
Right standing with You (forgiveness)	Condemnation and guilt
Acceptance, even love	Exclusion
Your sweet, blessed Presence	Emptiness! Despair!
Freedom from fear	Hopelessness and fear
Our talking to each other	Loneliness
The anticipation of all eternity with You	The dread of eternity in hell

These are only a few of the riches You give Your children. But what magnificent treasures they are! I need to ponder them, allow my heart to meditate and be fully immersed in them. Please Lord, may I never take even one of them for granted. *You mean more to me than anything or anyone else.* I know I've said this to You before, but reflection on the difference you make in my life makes me realize it even more. Thank You for Your grace!

September 28
TOTAL TRUST

Trust in the Lord with all your heart,
and do not lean on your own understanding.
Proverbs 3: 5

This little proverb says to trust in You with *all* my heart. This is a simple statement. Easy to say, easy to understand, but so profound in its application.

I see this total trust, Lord, as a childlike trust. When I was a little girl, I had total trust in my Daddy - that he loved me, that he would always be there, that he would always act in my best interest. My trust came from some deep level of knowing based upon how Daddy had lived all the days of my young life. He never varied in his actions toward me. He was consistently loving, kind and willing to listen to me. So I learned very early that he was trustworthy, even though as a child, I had no grasp of that concept.

This, to me, Lord, is a simple and beautiful picture of trusting You with my whole heart. You are unchanging; the same yesterday, today and tomorrow. You are a God who loves to bless. How many times You have shown me that! You possess all wisdom and so will always know what is in my best interest. How safe that makes me feel! I would be so foolish to lean upon my own understanding. It is partial and faulty and weak. My hand in Yours, Lord, is my security.

Just as I was unable as a 5-year-old to make big life decisions, so now I am just that helpless in seeing what is needed in my character/spiritual growth. Or in how my actions affect others. Or any other matter of eternal significance. The wisest thing I can do is look to You, trust You, walk close beside You, listen to You, every minute of every day for the rest of my days. So be it, Lord.

September 29
BLESSINGS FOLLOW OBEDIENCE

And Solomon did what was evil in the sight of the Lord,
and did not follow the Lord fully,
as David his father had done. Now the Lord was angry with Solomon
because his heart was turned away from the Lord, the God of Israel,
who had appeared to him twice, and had commanded him concerning this thing,
that he should not go after other gods;
but he did not observe what the Lord had commanded.
1 Kings 11: 6, 9-10

You had blessed Solomon abundantly up until this time. His reign over Israel was more splendid than even that of his father David. Solomon asked You for wisdom and You gave him not only wisdom but great wealth - incredible amounts of gold, silver, ivory and every other material that was considered precious.

You also gave him a few instructions to follow. And all was well for a while. But as his riches and power and prestige grew, he began to marry foreign wives - a thing You had forbidden all the men of Israel to do. And these foreign wives soon turned Solomon's heart away from You and toward their false gods. He made two bad choices - marrying foreign wives and then falling away from his faithfulness to You.

I can't help thinking "what if?" What if Solomon had married only suitable women of Israel and continued to faithfully serve You and his people? What if he had taught all his sons to be strong in faith? Is that not a beautiful picture? How much misery and heartache could the nation of Israel have avoided if only *this one man* had been obedient?

Well, that's all speculation because historically the generation immediately following Solomon's saw Israel divided into two warring factions. Consequently, Solomon's son, Rehoboam, ruled over a much smaller kingdom. Never has Israel regained the grandeur that was theirs under Solomon's reign.

Your best and perfect will for Your children is *always* to bless abundantly but when we make poor choices, You have to withhold blessings. That is what I learn from this story of Solomon's rise and fall. Another way to say "poor choices" is "disobey." So, if I were perfectly obedient, would I never have a problem? No, I'd surely still have some. But I believe I could avoid some, too, and in the bargain, receive more of Your intended blessings.

I believe our own country is suffering ills today from poor choices made in this generation. And I expect that suffering to become worse. Certainly the nations that make up the Middle East are living out their poor choices - so much hatred, violence and such seemingly unsolvable dilemmas. Our whole planet, Lord, is groaning for Your return. Only You have the answers for the problems caused by our disobedience. Come quickly, Lord Jesus!

September 30
TRUTHS CONCERNING FAITH

Thus says the Lord, "Let not a wise man boast of his wisdom,
and let not the mighty man boast of his might,
let not a rich man boast of his riches;
but let him who boasts boast of this, that he understands and knows Me,
that I am the Lord who exercises loving kindness, justice,
and righteousness on earth;
for I delight in these things," declares the Lord.
Jeremiah 9: 23-24

I cannot say that I am one who fully "understands and knows" You, Lord. You are far greater than my mind can grasp. But I *have* learned some life-changing truths about faith. Please help me think about these in Your presence.

Faith rests on Your Word alone. It does not need to be propped up by feelings or impressions or appearances. Faith, at its root, is believing a thing *because You said it.* So the way to peace is to simply believe what You have said. Internal conflict ends, double-mindedness flees and stability comes when my faith is lined up with Your Word.

You *will* exercise my faith. Like an unused arm muscle decreases in size and strength, so my faith, if unused, will decrease. Therefore, You bring me into situations that *require* my faith to work and through these challenges, my faith becomes stronger.

Trials are actually the food of faith. Food is for nourishment, strength, growth. Food is one of the blessings of life and only an unwell person does not desire food. Just so, *trials are a blessing* to my spiritual well-being. That is why James said "count it all joy…" He understood that working through trials produced spiritual maturity.

Faith is also increased by meditating upon Your Word. It is through Scripture, Lord, that You have revealed Yourself to me. Your Word, stored up in my mind and heart, teaches me about You, and helps me hear Your Spirit speak to my spirit. This learning never ends because there is always more to discover about You.

You are good, gentle, kind and You love to bless Your children. This has been the testimony of saints down through the ages. It is also my own testimony, Lord. I can relax in Your care because You are faithful. There may be numerous things I do not understand, plenty of questions I have on several subjects. But of this one thing I am certain - as long as You are in control of my life, all is well.

274

October 1
LESSONS FROM JOB

He who is at ease holds calamity in contempt,
as prepared for those whose feet slip.
Job 12: 5

I'm astounded by that moment in the far distant past, that moment that Satan appeared before Your throne in heaven and You asked this question of him, *"Have you considered My servant Job? For there is no one like him on the earth, a blameless and upright man, fearing God and turning away from evil." (Job 1: 8)* That question was the start of it all - manifold troubles in what had been a life of manifold blessings, the loss of every outward sign of Your favor upon Job. Poor Job! He had done nothing to anger You. You seemingly did not do this to teach him a lesson. So I am compelled to ask, "Why?" "Why did You do this?"

I know, Lord, that Your motive is always love. When You initiated this conversation with Satan, You *knew* that Job would ultimately lose his wealth, all his children and even his health. But through Your divine vision across the long span of time even until today, You understood that good *would* come forth after Job's tribulation; good that would more than compensate for the suffering, loss and grief that Job endured.

Who but You can measure the strength that is gained by one under trial as he reads Job's story? Only You know how many have found courage to continue trusting by hearing Job say, *"though He slay me, yet will I trust Him."* You, being the all-wise God, knew that Job's faith would not waver - that he would come through on the other side of this enormous trial, shining and much wiser.

Job's faith, like mine, was a gift from You, but he had to choose to exercise it. He could have chosen to turn his back on it (which Satan thought he would) and become bitter and resentful. He could have taken his wife's bad advice to "curse God and die." But without any understanding of why all this had happened, he chose instead to continue trusting in Your goodness and love.

Somewhere along the way, Job had learned a valuable truth: *For the child of God, all things are from You and therefore are for good.*

Naked I came from my mother's womb, and naked I shall return there.
The Lord gave and the Lord has taken away.
Blessed be the name of the Lord.
Job 1: 21
Shall we indeed accept good from God and not accept adversity?
Job 1: 10

So, from Job I gain courage, strong faith, and perseverance. I also learn that the reason for any event in my life may not be for *my* good, but it will be for *good* for someone. Or, in Job's case, millions of someones.

275

October 2
FREEDOM

It was for freedom that Christ set us free; therefore keep standing firm
and do not be subject again to a yoke of slavery.
Galatians 5:1

This verse reminds me that I am required to *do* something to continue walking in the sublime freedom that You have given me. Paul was teaching that right standing with You is obtained only through grace, not by futile attempts to keep the law. Not having been reared under Jewish law, I cannot completely appreciate the dilemma of Jewish believers, but I can identify with the bondage that modern legalism brings. It is a sneaky trap the devil uses to enslave people when Your desire is that we be free.

When I begin to think that I must do this or that in order to earn Your acceptance, I'm in serious trouble. The "this or that" may increase to a page full of things I must do, and then the questions start - is that enough? Do I need to do more? When do I know I've done enough? Let's face it, Lord. Legalism is a lose-lose deal, always going from bad to worse.

That is when grace appears to me the most beautiful, Lord - when I think about trying to *earn* my way into Your heart. *I'm there already.* I'm there because You chose for me to be there. If there is anything honorable in me, it is because You put it there. If I have ever done a worthwhile thing in my life, it was You doing it through me. Your beautiful, incredible, wonderful, freeing grace! How I love that word! And how I love You!

I see this freedom of Your grace as being like a well-cared-for child. Such a child doesn't worry about outcomes or how to get to those outcomes or tomorrow or yesterday. He lives in the moment and *enjoys* the moment, just doing "whatever his hand finds to do" knowing (if he even thinks about it) that what he needs will be provided when he needs it.

Is this too simple, Lord? Some, I'm sure, would say it is. But it seems that the more I know You and love You, the more Your wisdom becomes a basic principle of love and trust. I love You because You first loved me. I trust You because You have proven to me over and over that You are worthy of my trust. It *is* simple. I love You because You are good. I trust You because You are good.

You have spent the last two years of my life teaching me to relax and rejoice, to be less driven and results-oriented. I'm still learning, but I'm much better than I used to be. *That* is the freedom I'm thinking about here - to live every day of my life knowing that *You are in charge of everything*. All I need to do is relax, rejoice and do whatever You put before me to do, trusting You to supply all I need to do it.

What amazing freedom Your grace provides!

October 3
RELAX AND REJOICE

The steadfast of mind Thou wilt keep in perfect peace,
because he trusts in Thee.
Trust in the Lord forever,
for in God the Lord, we have an everlasting Rock.
Isaiah 26: 3-4

Thinking of those words above, Lord, brings more reflection upon truths You have been teaching me over the past two years. I finally see that to relax and rejoice is the very best thing I can do. It is not what I *ought* to do or would be a *good* thing to do; it is actually *the best thing to do.* Let me see if I can explain my thoughts…

When I am relaxed, You and I communicate more quickly and easily. There is no strain and effort on my part, only a clearness of mind and peace of heart that I have come to know as Your speaking within. When I'm not relaxed, it is impossible to hear You over the noisy tension of my mind and body.

When I am relaxed, I am able to see all of life from Your perspective. Consequently, I am more patient, kind, loving and well, Christ-like, all of which is Your answer to my fervent prayer for myself. And I've learned that when I'm not relaxed, it is *always* because I have decided to be in control. Bad decision.

When I am relaxed, I have this tranquil sense of well-being because You are in charge rather than me. This is just a blessed fact, Lord. There is no substitute for this peace - Your peace - filling me.

When I am relaxed, I am secure in Your strong arms and nothing can touch me without Your permission. This is the peace that I just talked about compounded with Your protection. There is no power greater than Your power.

I see, Lord, that You have plans and purposes in mind that have not even occurred to me. Things invisible to me are distinct and well-defined in Your mind. And experience teaches me that Your plans and purposes are always good. This knowledge helps me stay relaxed even in what could be difficult times.

Attitude is very important, isn't it? If I'm relaxed and ready to follow You, our journey together is so much more pleasant. If I balk, and stubbornly demand my own way, we pretty much camp there for a while until I grow sick of myself and repent.

Lord, I am so foolish to ever try to run my life myself! Thank You for allowing me to see these truths. Thank You for Your blessings to me when I follow Your loving guidance to simply relax. When I think of those blessings, rejoicing naturally ensues. Praise and gratitude mingle with that rejoicing to make my spirit sing. I love You, Lord!

October 4
YOUR GENTLE SPIRIT

But let it be the hidden person of the heart,
with the imperishable quality of a gentle and quiet spirit,
which is precious in the sight of God.
1 Peter 3: 4

We are making progress, Lord, You and I, at exhibiting Your patience instead of my impatience. I'm not perfect at it yet, but I do finally understand the concept of enjoying adversity; I see that it is the *only* way I will learn. It is only in times of testing that my fork-in-the-road decision is before me - will I allow *You* to control in this situation, exhibiting Your patience and gentleness, or will I jerk my hand out of Yours and show impatience and irritation? I'm improving at inwardly stopping, that very moment, and saying to You, "Please, Lord, remove the tension and anger from me and fill me with Your peace. I want only Your gentleness to come from me."

I also see that I am actually eager to allow You to evidence Your life in and through me. *Eager*, Lord. You have made me desire this strongly. It is so important to me that my outward behavior reflects *always* my inward peace, joy and love. These are the beautiful qualities You have placed in "the hidden person of the heart."

I have only recently seen this situation for the spiritual battle that it truly is. I now understand how it delights the enemy for me to fall back into my default behavior of impatience. I hate that, Lord! But more than I hate delighting him, I hate disappointing You. And I'm sure You are even more eager for me to learn this lesson than I am to learn it. How it must cause You to sigh when I am once again defeated! May this knowledge strengthen my resolve to respond to You, rather than react to the situation.

How good You are to continue Your work in me, transforming me from what I was to what You want me to be, teaching me to work out my salvation by submitting to Your plan, showing me how Your life is to be manifested through my body. Thank You for Your perseverance. Thank You for continuing to arrange circumstances which are exactly what I need for learning and testing.

You never take away our power to choose no matter how close we get to You. I must still choose, even after total surrender, to allow You to be my Lord. That is just part of walking by faith. I know that the day before us will present me with many more choices to make. You certainly have placed me in a situation to learn this lesson! May I consistently be Your obedient child all day. I love You, Lord.

October 5
PLEASING YOU

Therefore also we have as our ambition,
whether at home or absent, to be pleasing to Him.
2 Corinthians 5: 9

Some verses that I love from 2 Corinthians 4 (paraphrased)

I do not lose heart that my outer man is decaying
because my inner man is being renewed day by day.
The momentary light afflictions of today
are creating an eternal weight of glory far beyond all comparison!
So I look not at my present circumstances, things I can see,
but at the things that are not seen.
Because the things I can see are only temporary and will pass by quickly,
while the things I cannot see are eternal and I will enjoy them forever.

Those verses speak my heart for me, Lord. They are another way of saying that, as Your child, I walk by faith. This inner man renewal is what keeps me going! You renew my love for You. You renew my deep desire to be faithful. You renew my determination to allow You to control. You renew my strength, both physical and spiritual.

This living, ever-changing, growing relationship is simply amazing to me, Lord. Last night I had a very short, but vivid, dream. In it, both You and Bob were smiling at me and saying You were proud of me. This does not puff me up or make me smug. It makes me more determined than ever to keep my hand in Yours. It encourages me to just stay very close to You and keep walking in the right direction. It makes me love You even more.

I give You this day ahead and ask only that I might please You in every way.

October 6
THORN IN THE FLESH

And He has said to me,
"My grace is sufficient for you, for My power is perfected in weakness."
Most gladly, therefore, I will rather boast about my weaknesses,
that the power of Christ may dwell in me.
Therefore, I am well content with weaknesses, with insults, with distresses, with
persecutions, with difficulties, for Christ's sake;
for when I am weak then I am strong.
2 Corinthians 12: 9-10

A physically strong man is hard pressed to see that, in Your perspective, he is actually weak. This passage of Scripture teaches me, Lord, that it is also difficult for a *spiritually* strong man to see that he is weak. Even the great apostle Paul seemingly had to be afflicted with a thorn in the flesh to arrive at this great truth - that only when he acknowledged his innate weakness could You demonstrate the sufficiency of Your grace and allow him to appropriate Your strength.

We are not told what Paul's thorn in the flesh was, but it has been my experience that we all have one. I do not know anyone who does not have at least one challenging "something" in their life. This "something" is not here and gone in a couple of days. It is experienced in chronic proportions, day in and day out, and it carries with it the knowledge that it is here to stay, in one form or another, for as long as this body lives. For some it is living with a critical and over-bearing person; for many it is physical pain; for others it is a mental/emotional illness that causes them to be fearful and anxious; it may be a body which is handicapped in some way. *No matter the numerous ways in which we can experience a thorn in the flesh, Your grace is sufficient to enable us to bear it to the victorious conclusion of this earthly life.*

That truth, Lord, is vast in its power, in its ability to strengthen! Only when we understand its power can we say, as Paul did, "I am well content..." Only when I have been in this position of weakness and received Your grace can I say with confidence, "Your grace *is* sufficient!"

How wise we would be to relinquish what we *believe* to be our strength into Your hands simply because we see that, in truth, *the strongest among us is very weak.* That, indeed, would take great wisdom. In theory, it would allow us to step immediately from our weakness into Your strength without going through the trials and tribulations that sap our physical strength; without experiencing the problems for which we have no solutions. We would consider no other recourse *except* to look to You. I must confess, I've never known anyone wise enough to do this, Lord, so it is only a theory. It seems that most of us have to learn our lessons the hard way. How good that You are our patient Master Teacher!

October 7
PRAYING WITH POWER

"Not by might nor by power, but by My Spirit,"
says the Lord of hosts.
Zechariah 4: 6

Earlier this morning, Lord, I read a short essay about praying with power. It said that I am strong with You only to the degree that self is conquered. And that it is not by wrestling but by clinging that I can receive the blessing.

This resonates in my heart because I know that, only as I get myself out of the way, are You able to pray in me and through me. I do not mean to imply, Lord, that it is possible for me to wait until "prayer time" to get out of the way. No, I mean when my life, *in its entirety*, is surrendered to You, then can I come to You and allow You to pray through me with all effectiveness.

I know that it is only prayer which is in line with Your will that will be answered. And I know that all prayer that *is* in line with Your will *shall* be answered.

I see that "wrestling" denotes wanting my own way while "clinging" says, "I give You, Lord, freedom to do as *You* choose."

I know that "the blessing" - whatever it might be - is far more valuable than any personal sacrifice of time and energy to this work of prayer. What You desire to give me are things of eternal significance, things which I have not even dreamed of asking, wonderful blessings that can come from no one except You. *That* is what You want for all Your children.

How foolish I am to pass up any opportunity to spend time in this kind of prayer with You, Lord! It is like sitting in a dark and cold room, feeling hungry and chilled, when all I have to do is open the door into the next room where all is light and warmth, where there is a beautiful banquet table laden with food.

How I wish all Your children, this day, would see the light under the door, get up, walk over to it, turn the knob and enter into that full-of-wonder experience of allowing You complete control of their lives. There is no greater blessing than to be one with You, my Lord.

October 8
GRIEVING YOU

And do not grieve the Holy Spirit of God,
by whom you were sealed for the day of redemption.
Ephesians 4: 30

So, what have You taught me from the lesson just passed? I see that to do my will rather than Yours, even in a very small matter, is rebellion. Rebellion grieves You. I already was disturbed in spirit before I picked up my Bible this morning, so when I read these words in Ephesians, they were like a sharp stab to my heart. But You are ever faithful and merciful to teach me. Here is what I've learned.

I've learned that a poor choice will always result in negative consequences.

I've learned that disobedience is not fatal to our relationship. My confession and Your forgiveness restore the warm fellowship that means more to me than life itself.

I've learned that the hurt in my heart is a reminder that *my choices matter.* Though the disobedience was not sizeable, the spirit of rebellion present is what grieves me and humbles me.

On the other hand, this incident simply proves again that Your Word is true:

I am just an earthen vessel;
in me is no good thing;
left to myself I will always make wrong choices;
my free will is never taken away from me.

All those are true, Lord. I must focus on the truths of Your Word - all the things it teaches me about You and about me - and just keep my eyes upon You. You are my Master and Lord, even in the little details.

The fact that You and I are having this discussion is a good thing. Would I be concerned about it if my oneness with You were not the most important thing in my life? No, the entire incident would have slid by without notice. It is only a big deal to me because I love You so much that even a tiny issue between us looms large. I hope we never have to repeat this lesson, Lord.

October 9
A TIME OF REST

For thus the Lord God, the Holy One of Israel, has said,
"In repentance and rest you shall be saved,
In quietness and trust is your strength."
Isaiah 30: 15

My mind needs rest.
My spirit needs warmth.
My heart needs You, Lord.

So in the quietness of this morning
I come to You.
I shut the door against all that would distract us
and enter into the lovely, orderly place
You and I have created within me
so that we can simply be together.

How precious is this gift of Your Presence!

In Your warm and loving presence,
I realize anew that *You* are glad to spend time with *me.*
How amazing!

I feel the freedom to talk to You about the things on my mind,
no matter what they are.
In Your listening, You remove the anxious thoughts
and fill me with peace.

There is a power that flows from You to me, Lord.
It renews my commitment, my trust, my strength.
Everything needed for this walk of faith,
You provide and replenish.

Oh, that I could operate all my life from this blessed center!
Please give me the wisdom and clear thinking *this day*
to govern all of my actions from this
peaceful place where You and I dwell together.

Just for today.
Tomorrow, I'll ask again.

October 10
SUFFERING DEATH TO GAIN LIFE

That, in reference to your former manner of life, you lay aside the old self,
which is being corrupted in accordance with the lusts of deceit,
and that you be renewed in the spirit of your mind, and put on the new self,
which in the likeness of God has been created
in righteousness and holiness of the truth.
Ephesians 4: 22-24

I read an essay on "gentleness" this morning, Lord. The words touched me because You and I have been "renewing the spirit of my mind" concerning this quality in my life. And we have been working on gentleness because it is so *not* a part of my inherent nature. I thank You that I'm making progress; I confess that the work is not yet complete.

There are still times that the old temper takes over, and my words become harsh rather than gentle. I've learned that that contemptible behavior stems from both a control issue and a purity of heart issue, and that I have some important choices to make - conscious, deliberate choices to surrender all that I am to all that You are.

The point of the essay was that I can only arrive at gentleness by and through suffering death to self. That's true of every grace You give, Lord. It takes effort, pain and death to realize - to manifest - the wonderful gifts You bring with You when You move into a life. *None* of them are automatic or easily obtained. *All* of them come through dying to self and living to You, looking to You, focusing on You, loving You, wanting to please You in all I do, seeing all of my life through Your eyes - all this and more is what it takes for Your gifts to open and blossom.

What a patient and loving Teacher You are! I fail over and over, but You never give up on me. You may sigh a weary sigh sometimes, but You always let me have another chance. I wish I knew different words to say "I love You." My mother always taught me that "actions speak louder than words." Today I'll let my actions speak to You of my love by consistently reckoning the "old me" dead. So be it.

October 11
A GODLY HERITAGE

The Lord is the portion of my inheritance and my cup;
Thou dost support my lot.
The lines have fallen to me in pleasant places;
indeed, my heritage is beautiful to me.
Psalm 16: 5-6

The older I get, Lord, the more I appreciate the godly heritage and loving home in which I grew up. May my life prove to be worthy of such grace. Today I see so many families without the stability that was ours, and I know ours was secure *because* it was centered around You.

Without doubt, Lord, our culture propagates obstacles to having a stable, Christ-centered home. That may have always been true, but I'm thinking of the differences in the "outside" world today compared to how it was even when I was a child. The huge proliferation of drugs., the free access to pornography by even young children, the cultural emphasis upon wealth and beauty being worth whatever it takes to secure them, the mad rush for all things temporal rather than eternal. It makes me want to apologize for my generation, for allowing things to slide as far downhill as they have.

And then I contrast that with living for You, Lord. Living for You and with You is such an incredible privilege! Lost sheep don't know what they are missing. To be in Your fold and under Your care is worth far more than any so-called "freedom" could ever offer. To me, the comparison is like the difference between light and darkness - or life and death - or sweet and bitter.

My life with You, Lord, is light and life and sweetness. Without You, it would be darkness and death and bitterness. But, of course, the lost sheep don't know that. Part of what we are supposed to be doing is *telling them.*

How I wish every child today could be growing up in a Christ-centered home, a home where You are honored and loved, where Your grace is poured out upon parents and children alike. Lord, make us eager to tell the lost sheep about You at every opportunity. Arrange opportunities and send us out to act upon them. Prepare hearts to hear and then send us to speak. Allow us to tell them about the Good Shepherd and how much You love them.

October 12
ENCOURAGEMENT TO PRAY

Ask, and it shall be given to you;
seek, and you shall find;
knock, and it shall be opened to you.
For everyone who asks receives,
and he who seeks finds,
and to him who knocks it shall be opened
Matthew 7: 7-8

The significance of this statement is enormous, Lord!
You are saying,
"All I have is yours. Simply ask Me for it."
These words fill me with certainty
that You hear
and answer
requests made in Your name

In Your Word
I am given a wealth of petitions
from which to choose in praying for these I love.
Your Word, my Lord, is precious!
Its worth to me increases day by day.

Allow me to show my gratitude for Your great grace by
being faithful to pray as You have directed
claiming every good thing for every person according to Your will
asking wonderful and mighty things when such is Your will
asking for strength to simply stand firm when that is what is needed.
My prayer for me, Lord, is that You pray
in me and through me
for the glory of Your name.

Now to the King eternal, immortal, invisible, the only God,
be honor and glory forever and ever. Amen
1 Timothy 1: 17

October 13
MAKING ME HOLY

Blessed be the God and Father of our Lord Jesus Christ,
who has blessed us with every spiritual blessing in the heavenly places in Christ,
just as He chose us in Him before the foundation of the world,
that we should be holy and blameless before Him.
Ephesians 1: 3-4

I know, Lord, that Your goal is to make me pure and holy. You will be satisfied with nothing less. What an incredibly joyful thought! Because Your will *shall* be done. I am willing, as far as I know, for You to change me any way You choose in this business of making me innocent and spotless. And if we come to a place where I'm not willing, I'm willing to be made willing. The realization that this is true frees me to relax and rejoice in Your grace.

I think sometimes, Lord, about how it will be when this life is finished to look back and see clearly the truths You kept trying to tell me, and which I believed somewhat but maybe not "with a whole heart."

And when I think about that, it makes me determined to open up my entire being for Your work *now*...to change *today.* Change my relationships, change my motives, change my default attitudes, change me in areas I'm not even aware need to be changed. Let me believe *all* that Your Word says, taking it just as it says it, without watering it down, modifying it with man-made conditions or in any other way altering the simple meaning of Your truths.

I am willing
You are able
It shall be done.

287

October 14
FAITH FOR OBEDIENCE

Was not Abraham our father justified by works,
when he offered up Isaac his son on the altar?
You see that faith was working with his works,
and as a result of the works faith was perfected.
James 2: 21-22

My mind was caught and held by those words from James this morning, Lord. Abraham had faith at the time You spoke to him and told him to take Isaac and slay him. But through the difficult process of obedience, that faith was added to immeasurably.

He came down that mountain with a stronger, surer trust in You than when he went up. He came down with a heart overflowing with love for Your provision, for Your goodness, for Your faithfulness. This was a monumental test of faith You put before Abraham.

It profits me to put things in perspective by aligning them with Your Word. Being an all-wise God, You suit the test to the child. This means that, however difficult my present situation looks to me, by Your grace and Your provision, I *can* complete the task.

When Abraham went up the mountain, his mind must have been filled with questions, doubts and fears. His heart was heavy with what was before him. Mixed in with all that, however, was his solid faith that You *had been* his Provider and You *would be again.*

I am still on the climbing-up side of the mountain as it relates to this latest task You have given me. Like Abraham, I know from past experience that You are worthy of all my trust, that You are good and loving, and that Your grace is sufficient. May I be obedient as he was.

October 15
YOUR PURPOSE

Now to Him who is able to do exceeding abundantly beyond all that we ask or
think, according to the power that works within us,
to Him be the glory in the church
and in Christ Jesus to all generations forever and ever.
Amen.
Ephesians 3: 20-21

This morning my mind is full of thoughts about dear friends and their problems, about the changed dynamics of our own household with the addition of a new family member and about the personal challenge You have put before me. Three situations that *could* make me anxious. They won't, however, because You have taught me to be anxious for nothing, and I choose to follow that instruction.

What I long for, Lord, is just to sit awhile in Your presence and absorb into my very bones Your light, warmth and strength. I so need Your grace and all that it brings to me. You are the source of all that has value in my life. My need is great, but Your grace is abundantly greater. As the verses above say, You are able to do *so much more* than I can think or ask. As I ponder Your power and our needs, I am made to think about the reason behind these problems I bring to You today - what You are doing in these lives and how can I best fit my prayers and my actions to Your purpose.

I know that You do have a purpose for every child of Yours. And I'm seeing that it is *not* that we successfully complete each task You put before us. No, Your purpose is the change - the inner change - that comes to us *while* we complete that task. The finished task may be good, but it is not Your compelling purpose. I'm so prone, Lord, to emphasize "finishing the task" rather than paying close attention to the journey that gets me there.

I see that You are saying that the journey itself and its lessons are of primary importance. I need to pay attention to all the situations along the way, to learn from each of them the lesson You desire to teach me. I also need to carry this wisdom into the lives of others and encourage them to do the same.

So I give You the three challenges mentioned above that are now before me. I ask, Lord, that You work Your purpose in me as You see fit. I ask also that Your purpose be worked in the other people involved. May we all, moment by moment, walk in the circle of light that You give. Therein is forgiveness, safety and joy forevermore.

October 16
THOUGHTS ABOUT TRUTH

Sanctify them in the truth. Thy word is truth.
John 17: 17

You and I, Lord, have been thinking about the subject of truth. More specifically, about Your Word, which to me is absolute truth. Help me think through these concepts. *Truth is true whether I believe it or not.* Let's say there are six billion people on earth today. Of those, only one billion believe that You exist and that You supernaturally inspired the writing down of history, information, facts and promises. Overall then, a relatively small number of people see the Bible as Your truth. Does the refusal to believe of five billion people negate Your existence and Your power? Does it do away with the facts as they are? Of course not. Your truth is eternal - it has stood for billions of years and will stand forever and ever. My prideful mind may refuse to allow me to kneel in Your presence and acknowledge You as Holy God, but You are still God and You are still Holy.

I can believe a lie, really believe it, and it is still a lie. And how many of those five billion unbelievers are believing a lie? Five billion of them. Some of them have substituted some other god for You. Some think they are already 'sons of God.' Some simply want to believe *anything* other than Your truth and so are deceived. And who is telling all these lies? Ultimately, Satan. He is determined to thwart Your plan of redemption in as many lives as possible. He is full of hatred, evil and destruction and will stop at nothing to deceive. But, to me, Lord, the important fact is that sincerity will be worth nothing on that coming day of judgment when we each will stand before You and give an account of how we lived this earthly life. Here is what You have said about having no excuse on that day:

> *For the wrath of God is revealed from heaven against all ungodliness and*
> *unrighteousness of men, who suppress the truth in unrighteousness;*
> *because that which is known about God is evident within them*
> *for God made it evident to them. For since the creation of the world His invisible*
> *attributes, His eternal power and divine nature, have been clearly seen,*
> *being understood through what has been made, so that they are without excuse.*
> *Romans 1: 18-20*

You are the one who decides what is truth. This third fact, Lord, is awesome! Only *You* have the power to decide what is truth. How arrogant we creatures are to think we have that power. You are the Creator of all. We are only creatures whose genuine happiness lies in discovering and understanding as much of Your truth as possible. What we accept as truth will shape our lives, how we think and what we do. So there are life-long consequences to what we believe is true and, as the verses from Romans show, even eternal consequences. What a sobering thought.

October 17
TRUE REST

Come to Me, all who are weary and heavy-laden, and I will give you rest.
Matthew 11:28

We have come back around to this precious verse, Lord, and I can never pass it up without talking to You about it. Today I'm thinking about *how blessed* is one who is weary and heavy-laden - one who has decided that the battle is too fierce, the mountain is too high and all strength is gone. Because at that point we can *understand* that these beautiful words are being spoken to us.

Only You have the rest that I need. What I need is so much more than a good night's sleep. Rest for the body is beneficial but what I really need is rest for the soul. I need resolution of inner conflicts. I need to surrender to Your cleansing of my heart. I need to be filled with Your peace. That is the rest I need, and it begins by coming to You.

It is similar to the prodigal son returning home, finally willing to surrender to the father's authority. He has been out on his own and has discovered that "freedom" wasn't nearly as much fun as he thought it would be. It turned out to be bondage disguised as freedom. It was far more loss than gain. So now he is back, ready to do whatever is necessary to regain his father's acceptance. What a surprise when his father comes running down the road to meet him and does not even allow him to apologize for his stupidity in leaving! Talk about grace!

This, my Lord, is what it feels like to me when You say, "Come to Me." It is an invitation I cannot refuse. It is an invitation to have a heavy weight lifted, to be free of the constantly divided mind or the troubled heart with which I've been dealing. And then follows the joy. Now I am able to claim all the blessings - and *receive* them - that are conditioned upon surrender. To feel the light and warmth and peace of Your presence; Lord - *that* is rest.

It occurs to me that I *can* choose to continue to carry this heavy burden. But how foolish that is. You so desire to relieve me of it that it *will happen*. I can be wise and surrender early on in this life (and then often afterward) and so live in the blessedness of Your presence. Or I can struggle and fight and hold on until I die. And then I *will* turn loose of it. In the end, You will win. But how sad to have missed all the joy of walking with You - all the adventure of seeing You at work day after day.

Your way is life and light. Man's way is death and darkness. Please, God, open blind eyes to see this truth.

October 18
CONFESSION

For the sorrow that is according to the will of God
produces a repentance without regret, leading to salvation;
but the sorrow of the world produces death.
2 Corinthians 7: 10

The heartache I am feeling
is a consequence of my own harmful actions.
It is the law of sowing and reaping at work.
I'm so sorry, Lord.

Please change within me
the source of hasty, foolish words.

Remove this tendency to be critical
and judgmental.
I despise it in others
and I despise it even more in myself.

By Your grace, Lord, I *can* overcome this.
And by Your grace,
the damage I've caused can be healed.
Please give me wisdom and grace for apologizing.

I'm filled with sorrow at how much I love You
and the person I hurt,
and yet I *acted* so contrary to love.

Please forgive me, Lord.
My spirit bows at Your feet
admitting my failure to live out Your grace.

October 19
THINKING OF YOUR LOVE

And hope does not disappoint,
because the love of God has been poured out within our hearts
through the Holy Spirit who was given to us.
But God demonstrates His own love toward us,
in that while we were yet sinners,
Christ died for us.
Romans 5: 5, 8

You and I have spent a lot of time, Lord, thinking about this subject. As far as I can understand, Your love is the greatest subject which we could ever study. And perhaps it is the most talked about and written about subject among Your children. And, for all this, there are yet vast areas of unexplored knowledge.

That verse above says that Your love is lavishly poured out into my heart. This I know from personal experience. The words "the love of God" *can* mean, not only Your love for me, but also my love for You. So which is it? I think it is both. You poured into me Your love for me and because of that, there springs up within me the desire to return that love. It is not goodness on my part that causes me to love You. It is a heart-felt response to seeing the immensity of Your grace in loving me. So those who sense no springing up of return love have simply *not yet realized* how much You love them.

Thinking about love in relation to obedience, I see that my deep desire is to obey You in all things. I fail at times because I am weak and my life, like all Your children, is full of occasions that give me opportunity to fail. But my heartfelt goal is to always be obedient. What is the motive behind that desire? At one time in my life, it was to earn Your acceptance. I thought that was the way to go - do everything a "good Christian" does, and God will love You. So I tried. And failed. And tried again and failed again. After a while, I gave up. Only years later did I begin to understand grace. You had *already* accepted me and *were* loving me. When I began to understand this, Lord, it was an entirely new world for me! And the fountain of love opened up within that has never yet stopped flowing. *That* is the source of my desire to be obedient. You are worthy of my obedience and all else that I can give.

And here is an important thing about Your love - You are the only Person who wholly knows me. Even though You see all the bad stuff we have yet to conquer, You love me. That makes Your love of much more consequence than that of people because people only know what I have allowed them to know. You know me better, actually, than I know myself. And yet You love me enough to die for me! Hallelujah! You, Yourself, are amazing. An awesome and holy God are You! With all the praise and honor of my grateful heart, I bless You, my Lord.

October 20
FOUNDATIONAL TRUTH

Be anxious for nothing,
but in everything by prayer
and supplication with thanksgiving
let your requests be made known to God.
Philippians 4: 6

Once again I need to go back to basics..."be anxious for nothing." Your words, Lord, always have the power to reorder my thoughts, to bring peace to my mind and heart. My choice this morning is clear: to obey these words or go tromping off under my own steam and be miserable.

That's a no-brainer! Once more I place myself and my many needs into Your kind and capable hands to bless as You see fit. You know exactly what is needed. Allow me to be a vessel for Your use, Lord. I see that my part of this is to keep our connection, our relationship, strong and tight; to stay full of humble obedience, listening carefully to what You are saying. And then simply walk on, trusting You.

You are worthy of all my trust because You *are* Love. Your goodness is constantly at work - always *active*. Keep me fully in its flow. I'm so needy and weak without You, Lord. And those are not just words. They are truth.

See in my heart the gratitude for Your hand upon my life, the thankfulness for Your many blessings over years of walking with You. We have come such a long way, Lord! How could I walk away from You now? May it never be! Allow me to keep my hand in Yours all this day, and may the whole day glorify You. I love You so much!

And the peace of God,
which surpasses all comprehension,
shall guard your hearts and your minds in Christ Jesus.
Philippians 4: 7

October 21
RANDOM THOUGHTS

For I am convinced that neither death, nor life, nor angels, nor principalities,
nor things present, nor things to come, nor powers, nor height, nor depth,
nor any other created thing, shall be able to separate us from the love of God,
which is in Christ Jesus our Lord.
Romans 8: 38-39

Desire to be with You, need of You, thoughts about what must be done today, concerns about people I love - all this and more circles in my brain as I try to read Your Word, talk to You and listen to You this morning, Lord. I find it difficult to be focused enough to even read. At times like this, I'm so thankful that You know all about the human brain and its weaknesses. I'm also very glad for the verses above that say that nothing can separate me from Your love. Your love is a mighty river flowing through me. It will flow on in spite of obstacles for it is powerful! My body may be weak but you have made my spirit strong.

It is a mystery to me how the "brain" is an organ of the physical body and will die when the body dies, but the "mind" which is contained within it *will live forever*. Your creation is too full-of-wonder for my understanding! How You can divide mortal from immortal is probably a small thing in Your Eternal Mind. There *are* no mysteries to You. We humans may think we are quite smart sometimes but our knowledge is so partial, so pieced together on faulty theories. It impresses upon me again how much we, Your children, need to open up our minds and spirits to Your wisdom and knowledge.

How much I need to simplify! I seem to fall back into making things harder than they need to be. Teach me, Lord, to "will one thing." Give me insight into Your ways, Your will and Your wishes. May I align my ways, will and wishes with Yours because *that is all I'm seeing;* all else simply disappears from my radar because I recognize that all else is of no value.

This planet is covered over with war and famine and disease. It might seem that the enemy is winning. But I know better. I know that You have a bright and light-filled people - some in plain sight, some underground, some strong, some weak - a people preserving this earth from total destruction, because You have glorious plans for its future. When You come back to rule, there will be no more hatred, death nor disease. This new world is beyond my imagination and experience, Lord, but by faith I look forward to it. That will be a glorious day, indeed, when evil is expelled for eternity!

October 22
LIGHT

The people who were sitting in darkness saw a great light,
and to those who were sitting in the land and shadow of death,
upon them a light dawned.
Matthew 4: 16

Light and darkness - I've been thinking about this off and on all morning since reading this verse in Matthew. You *are* that light. When I allow You to, You fill me with Yourself, and so I am instructed to let my light shine. But it is not my light; it is Your light within me.

There is no need for light in an already light-filled space. That's why we will not need the sun in heaven. There, You will be our light. A flashlight turned on outside on a bright, sunny day would not even be noticed. But on a black, starless night, with no other light around, that same flashlight becomes an amazingly bright and helpful beacon. This is so obvious, but it leads me to the conclusion that You would never have told me to let my light shine if I were not in a dark place.

My logical list-making mind wants to make two lists of what is light and what is darkness, and that is easily done. All that You are, all the noble characteristics like love, mercy, goodness and faithfulness - those are light. All the characteristics of evil such as hatred, greed, fear and perversion - those are darkness. But I'm not sure the lists are necessary or even useful. I think the important point is that I really am living in a dark world, surrounded by evil, but *perhaps I do not perceive the evil as You do.*

I tolerate it, I ignore it, I purposely close my mind to it, I may even take part in it. I think, Lord, I don't *want* to see the evil and darkness for what it is. I don't want it to intrude upon my sheltered, happy existence.

But if I don't recognize how black the darkness is, how can I be the light I am put here to be? That verse above says the people "saw a *great* light." A tiny candle flicker would not have made the impact that was needed. Is Your light any less great today than it was when that verse was written? Is our darkness any less today than then? Of course, the answer to both is NO! Thinking about this makes me even more determined to open my mind to Your mind, to let Your Spirit fill my spirit, to be wholly and evermore transparent so that *Your light shines brightly.* Many people will remain in the land and shadow of death - eternal death - unless they see Your light. May *all* Your children shine! So be it, Lord.

October 23
PREPARING THE HEART'S SOIL

Read Matthew 13: 1-23

Yesterday I was thinking about Your parable of sowing seed into four different kinds of soil and the results of each. For the first time, Lord, I saw this parable as it relates to the critical responsibility that parents and grandparents have - to prepare the soil of our children's hearts to receive Your Word at Your time.

We don't have to teach them about the kingdom of the world. They begin to learn that every hour of every day from birth. But the seed of the Kingdom of God *must be intentionally planted.* Before that seed can be sown, however, there is work to be done preparing the soil. That is where my mind is this morning.

In gardening, it would be a waste of time (and seed) to sow on ground that has not been prepared. And it is physically demanding to break new ground. The soil is often packed and hard. It is not sufficient to simply scratch up the surface. The soil must be worked down deep so that the new roots will have freedom to grow. This is time consuming, back-breaking labor but absolutely critical to the success of producing anything worthwhile.

Then the soil must be cleaned up. It has already been growing things - things like grass, weeds, thorn bushes and scrub trees. All those have to go. It would be another waste of time to get rid of only what is visible of the undesirable growth. The *root* must be dug up and discarded. This calls for much hard work and perseverance, which in turn requires *keeping the worthy goal in mind.*

Then we must add whatever is necessary to make the soil fertile and rich so that all seed newly planted will sprout and enjoy sustained growth. Every soil is different. It takes great wisdom to know what is needed - Your wisdom, as revealed to us earthly gardeners.

The parallels are clear, Lord. How great it would be if every Christian parent and grandparent would make this project a matter of focused prayer! Help us to see the importance of this preparation of little hearts for Your truths to be planted in them. Because the day will come when Your Spirit will touch that child's heart, and You will give that most gracious of all invitations, "Come, be My child." Help us, Lord, so that Your invitational seed falls on good soil.

October 24
ENJOYING YOUR PRESENCE

How blessed is the one whom Thou dost choose,
and bring near to Thee,
to dwell in Thy courts.
We will be satisfied with the goodness of Thy house,
Thy holy temple.
Psalm 65: 4

At last - a quiet house and a quiet time to sit, to be with You, even though I know I'm *always* with You, to allow the pain to ebb away and to put out of conscious thought all that would distract me.

Now I can enter into that beautiful place within where You dwell. All is peaceful and orderly there. All is inviting and warm and accepting. Because *You* are all those things and so much more.

You are unfailingly better to me than I deserve. I deserve death and destruction but You give me abundant life - eternal life. I deserve punishment, but You give me love and healing. I deserve to be pushed away and ignored, but You draw me into Your strong arms and hold me close. How could I *not* love You, my Lord? Your grace never fails to amaze me.

I was thinking earlier about all I have learned through this latest adventure with You - this time of having to lean heavily upon You. I gained even more confidence in Your faithfulness. Having to depend on You always does that, doesn't it? Which I'm sure is one reason You orchestrated those circumstances.

I experienced the not-to-be-equaled fellowship of Your presence. You know, Lord, that I have many friends and family members that I enjoy being with and love dearly. But our fellowship - Yours and mine - is on an entirely different level altogether. There is no equal in human relationships.

I learned more of the pure joy of being a well-loved child. My heart aches for people who do not know what it is to be a well-loved child. Lord, may Your compassion flow through me and out of me, over and into the lives of those who do not know You. Use me any way You choose.

I keep thinking that I cannot possibly love You more than I do. But then I feel my love for You today surpass that of yesterday; and so it continues each day. What an astounding thing! This love which fills me up to running over, yet increases! May this whole day be lived out of that bountiful supply.

October 25
BEAUTIFUL THOUGHT

For by grace you have been saved through faith;
and that not of yourselves, it is the gift of God;
not as a result of works, that no one should boast.
Ephesians 2: 8-9

You dropped a beautiful thought into my head yesterday.

"I don't love you because you are good, My child.
I love you because *I* am good."

This is not a new thought, Lord.
I've known this for a long time.
But it was exactly the thought that I needed at the moment.

It liberated me immediately,
as grace always does,
from feeling like *I* was responsible for keeping the boat steady.
It put my entire situation in proper perspective.
It set me free from the bit of legalism that had crept into my thinking.
(I need to be reminded often that it is all about *You*.
It is all about *grace*.)

It released me from the burden of responsibility
for decisions and mistakes made by others.
I have no control over others.
Even *You* don't exercise total control over people.
You allow them to make choices and then to live with the consequences.
So why should I think I'm responsible?

Thank You, Lord, for clearing that up one more time.
I tend to slide easily into trying to be all things to all people.
Thank You for setting me free to relax and rejoice.
Thank You for teaching this slow-to-learn child.
Thank You for that beautiful thought.

October 26
A NEW CHALLENGE

But He knows the way I take;
when He has tried me,
I shall come forth as gold.
Job 23: 10

Sometimes, Lord, You give me a new song to practice before I'm through learning the old one, or at least it seems that way to me. Here I am, still working on control issues, and You have given me extra responsibilities which means less solitude (oh, woe), increased pain and the need for more strength. I'm not complaining, Lord. It's merely an observation.

Maybe it means I'm stronger than I think I am. Maybe this new situation will teach me faster about control issues. Maybe it means You think we've beaten this control thing to death, and *You* are ready to move on. What I know for sure is that You are good and wise and You love me, and that is all that matters. Come what may, I am safe in Your care.

I want to thank You for that word of encouragement last night. It does not puff me up. It makes me humble, joyful and eager to continue learning. You know, Lord, how often I feel such a failure, so weak and needy and worthless. And then I remember that it is exactly those conditions through which You can demonstrate Your strength. May it be so in my life!

From the beginning of our long walk together, You have reformed my personal goals and priorities; such things as integrity and transparency are now at the top of the list. I very much want everything in my life to be authentic, enduring and strong.

I finally understand that my physical weakness does not in any way affect achieving those goals, except perhaps in a positive way - to help me be more aware of my great and constant need of Your grace.

So I thank You for the fatigue and the pain for they remind me to lean hard upon You. I thank You for being my wonderful Teacher and Friend. I even thank You for this new and difficult song to learn.

October 27
THE TRANSFIGURATION

And He was transfigured before them;
and His face shone like the sun,
and His garments became as white as light.
Matthew 17: 2

I read Matthew 17 awhile ago, the first few verses of which are about Your transfiguration. What an awesome experience that was for Peter, James and John! What an astounding power was present that made Your face shine as the sun and even altered the molecules that made up the fabric of Your garments so that they became shining light!

But Lord, I can't help wishing that Peter had been silent for once and just listened to You, Moses and Elijah talking together. Then this trio of favored disciples could have come down the mountain and told us what was said. But, obviously, that was not Your intention or that is what would have occurred.

So I must use my sanctified imagination. I think this incredible visit was a wonderful gift from Your Father to You to help prepare You for what was ahead. Maybe the words of Moses and Elijah were to strengthen and give assurance. Maybe they were to give additional information. Certainly this was an extraordinary happening and had a divine and loving purpose.

My heart zeros in on Your Father's words, "This is My beloved Son, with whom I am well-pleased; listen to Him!" What more comforting, life-giving, energizing words could there be than "beloved" and "well-pleased"? And then those words, "listen to Him." They were spoken to Peter, James and John to focus their attention on what took precedence. Those words are for Your children today, too. So often I tend to get distracted and wander down a side path instead of concentrating upon what is important - *listening to You.*

There is no more blessed thing I can do than listen to You. You speak through Your Word. You speak in my mind. You speak in the happenings of my day, those circumstances designed by You. You speak through other people. In an unlimited number of ways available to You alone, You speak to me. May I listen - truly be awake and aware and *listen* - to all that You say to me.

That You even *want* to speak to me is amazing! I can never take that for granted. Your love never ceases to move me and astound me, Lord. I, too, like Peter, James and John, fall on my face before You, not in fear, but in worship and reverence and awe. You are my King, my Lord, my Everything.

October 28
HARD WORDS

It is the Lord of hosts whom you should regard as holy.
And He shall be your fear, and He shall be your dread.
Isaiah 8: 13

Sometimes, Lord, You speak hard words. Your responses as recorded in the New Testament are often unexpected and blunt. That's because You always spoke the truth - even if it offended the listeners. How many times in the Old Testament did You have to speak hard words to the nation Israel for their disobedience? But all those hard words came from Your magnificent heart of love. All of them were spoken to give the hearers every chance to understand truth and turn to You. Today, we call this "tough love."

Here is what I learn from that: Your primary desire is to bless Your children; however, if I wander away, become disobedient and insist on having my own way, the only loving thing You *can* do is speak hard words to me. Your love for me is too great to leave me in my disobedience. But here is the encouraging truth: *Your hard words are always followed by gracious words* - words of promise and blessings which You are storing up, waiting to pour out upon children of obedience. Perfect obedience would eliminate the need for You to speak hard words, wouldn't it, Lord? Perfect obedience would allow You to do every good thing for me that You wish.

The same concept applies to the trials You allow into our lives. You have led me down some paths I would never have chosen. But for this, too, You had a purpose. That purpose was to make me more like You, to change something within me that still wanted to demand my own rights, that was still bent on having my own way. Your purpose is always to lead me to a deeper surrender to Your love, to teach me to see all of life as You see it, to make me one with You. Thank You, Lord, for tough love that never gives up!

October 29
BURDEN OR PRIVILEGE?

With all prayer and petition pray at all time in the Spirit,
and with this in view, be on the alert
with all perseverance and petition for all the saints.
Ephesians 6:18

I'm thinking this morning about this work of intercessory prayer. At the moment it is like a heavy burden on me, Lord, and just stating that fact starts the red flags waving in my spirit. *Any time I feel burdened by a task You have given, it means I'm trying to do what only You can do.*

Please help me get to the bottom of this and resolve it. Praying is the most natural thing in the world to me. I write prayers in my personal journal as I am doing now. I write prayers for my church family in my Intercessory Prayer Journal. And when I'm not writing, I'm talking to You in my spirit - all day, every day, Lord, I'm talking to You! It is as natural as breathing. It is basic to my life. It is *vital* to my life. It is, without doubt, the most important work I could ever do.

Even as I write those words, I realize how absurd that seems to an unbeliever. To the natural man, such communication with an invisible God is the height of foolishness. But their opinion affects me not at all because Your Word tells me I am spiritual, not natural. I am indwelt by Your Spirit and, therefore, much of the praying that is taking place in me is actually *You* doing the praying. (Rom. 8: 26-27) So, I must ask myself, how can praying ever become a heavy burden?

Of course, the answer is, "It shouldn't." The sense of burden happens only because I have temporarily forgotten what is Your part of the work and what is my part. I have momentarily switched jobs with You - or tried to. That never works, does it, Lord?

Thank You for reminding me one more time. My part is to be faithful. It is Your part to work, change lives and bring about results. *This miracle we call redemption is Your work.* My part is to pray, listen to You and obey. My part is to live so close to You that hearing You is easy. I must admit, Lord, that sometimes this feels like doing nothing when the situation *seems* to call for action. And yet, I *cannot* do what only You can do. Therefore, I know You don't expect that of me.

Allow me to lay aside for all time and forever the idea that this blessed privilege of praying for others is a burden. May I simply be faithful to do it.

October 30
YOUR PERSPECTIVE

"For My thoughts are not your thoughts,
neither are your ways My ways," declares the Lord.
"For as the heavens are higher than the earth,
so are My ways higher than your ways,
and My thoughts than your thoughts."
Isaiah 55: 8-9

I need to talk to You, Lord, about what You have been showing me over the last 24-36 hours concerning the stepped-up-in-intensity attacks of the enemy that I am seeing. I know from experience that any time I desire to live closer to You, the enemy will do all in his power to thwart my efforts. So his attacks are in direct response to my prayers. But I have been praying only *what I believe to be Your will*:

for an increased hunger and thirst for You;
for Your total control in our lives;
to see work done which only You can do;
and that these things will be done at any cost.

This kind of praying is dangerous, isn't it, Lord? Because those are all things which the enemy will work vigorously to derail, hoping for crash and burn. Therefore, rather than be dismayed at the spiritual battles going on, I should be rejoicing at this evidence of heading in the right direction! The enemy does not fight those who pose no danger to him. I should be full of praise at Your work, full of faith and expectation as I look to You with full confidence in Your goodness. I should be full of anticipation as I expect You to work, bless, grow, teach and love. Much of what is going on right now *is* from the adversary, but all I need to know is that You are allowing it and that Your good purposes are being worked out.

I'm also seeing something that makes me a little sad. That is the fact that Your work is done according to Your timetable, and You do not measure time as I do. Abraham spent his entire life looking for "that city not made with hands" without seeing it. Just so, I may *never*, in this lifetime, see answers to many prayers. But here is the full-of-joy part - Your promise is to both hear and answer every prayer made in Your will, in Your name. When and how is Your business. Mine is to be faithful to pray. So be it.

October 31
A FRUIT TREE

For there is no good tree which produces bad fruit;
nor, on the other hand, a bad tree which produces good fruit.
Luke 6: 43

By paralleling nature's order to spiritual matters,
You taught Your disciples some Kingdom truths.

What a wondrous occurrence is a tree that bears fruit!
It is a thing that we can easily take for granted.
It reminds me that Your work is done
Your way
and at Your time.

Fruit bearing is a God-thing.
Who created the tree?
Who put within it the miraculous design to produce fruit?
Who provided everything needed for fruit-bearing:
the soil,
the nutrients in the soil,
the sunshine,
the rain,
the leaves performing their photosynthesis
to supply exactly what is needed?
Can man do any of this?
No.
All man can do is plant the seed
and wait for *You* to do the real work.

I, too, have everything I need to be fruit-bearing,
and I have it *only because You have provided it.*
This is a God-thing as well.
My prayers originate with You,
are renewed by You,
and the working out of them can only come from You
in due season.
Teach me, Lord, to trust with a simple faith
and to walk with a happy heart.

November 1
TAKING YOUR NAME IN VAIN

You shall not take the name of the Lord your God in vain,
for the Lord will not leave him unpunished who takes His name in vain.
Exodus 20: 7

In Luke 8 is the account of You casting out a legion of demons from a man who had been long possessed by them. Then You told him to go home and tell *everyone* what great things You had done for him. And the people were frightened! I find that very puzzling. I'd have thought they would be relieved to have the scary, demon-possessed man clothed and in his right mind. Aren't we strange creatures, Lord?

A few verses later, Jarius comes to get help for his little girl. You raise her from the dead and tell her parents to tell *no one* what happened - the opposite of what You told the demon-possessed man. Why the difference?

Maybe this was because casting out demons, while not an everyday occurrence, was still not unheard of - the priests, at least some of them, cast out demons. But raising someone from the dead *was* unheard of. And it was just too early in Your ministry for that kind of knowledge to be broadcast far and wide. That is only my interpretation, Lord, and subject to error. What is obvious to me is that *the words we speak about You are of great consequence.*

That brings up something I have been pondering for a few days concerning taking Your name in vain. I do not mean cursing. That is obviously wrong and unacceptable. But that is only one very specific way of taking Your name in vain. What I'm thinking is that we, Your children, can attach Your name to something that You not only had nothing to do with but that, in fact, You disagree with and refute. Again, I don't mean obvious things like the Ku Klux Klan. Rather, I'm concerned with the subtle way we can use Your name to lend strength to an idea or a statement that, in truth, came from our human thinking. This bothers me a great deal, Lord, and I do not want to do it. It shows a lack of respect for You. It shows a desire to exalt self. Both of those make my heart hurt. You are holy, and I want always to treat You as holy with an attitude of love and worship.

I can only ask You to please guard me from taking Your name in vain *in any way*. I know You are well able to both get my attention and make me understand. Thank You for being my Teacher.

November 2
BEING FOUND FAITHFUL

Be dressed in readiness, and keep your lamps alight.
Luke 12: 35

My mind is on the subject of faithfulness this morning, Lord, because I just read in the 12th chapter of Luke about the "faithful and sensible steward" who was assigned certain responsibilities and then his master left. The story's purpose was to teach faithfulness-to-the-master even if he is gone for a very long time. Just before this story, You gave instructions for us to be "be dressed in readiness and keep your lamps alight" in preparation for Your return.

At the time You spoke these words, the hearers of them may have thought the time would be short before You would be back. Now, here we are, many centuries later, still waiting. So, is it ever going to happen? Oh, yes. You *are* coming back for us. Either one at a time through the death of our body, or altogether in the rapture. In one of those two ways, this earthly assignment *will* come to an end.

Thinking about this brings a huge joy to my heart! And also the strong desire to be found faithful by You. My faithfulness, to my eyes, seems like a corporation's profit chart when it has been having some good months and some bad months - zigzags up and down, up and down. But Your Word tells me that You look not at the outside performance, but at the heart. In my heart, Lord, the love for You and desire to be faithful look like level ground reaching all the way to eternity - constant and steady.

Of course, I want my outward life to match my inward life. Yet I'm comforted by the fact that it is the heart that matters. Such an incredible gift is this grace in which I stand! When I think of what it cost You, the agony of the cross, and what it cost our Father to provide such grace, my only response is eternal gratitude, everlasting praise and all my love. This keeps my lamp lit and shining brightly. Come quickly, Lord Jesus!

November 3
REST AND STRENGTH

For thus the Lord God, the Holy One of Israel, has said,
"In returning and rest you shall be saved,
in quietness and trust is your strength."
Isaiah 30: 15

Isaiah wrote such beautiful words! Some very mysterious, some hard to understand, but all beautiful. I read these awhile ago and they so spoke to my heart, perhaps because they are both simple to understand and they are do-able, even by me. They tell me what *I* must do, and what *You* will do. I can return to You; I can rest; I can get quiet, and I can trust.

When I have been occupied for several hours with daily-living tasks and finally have a moment of quiet, I find that returning to the consciousness of Your presence is the most joyful thing in the world. It is only there that I find perfect rest. Only there can I truly get quiet. By Your grace I can do these things and by Your Word, You *will* do Your part - provide salvation and strength.

Sometimes, Lord, my rest is so total that I can't even speak. But You have taught me that wordless worship is both satisfying and *more restful* than searching for words to express the inexpressible. I can come to You feeling like a dried out sponge, hard and useless. And seemingly without effort on my part, I soak up contentment and joy and peace. All these and more gently wash through my spirit and bring quiet renewal. It is my desire never to leave this place of rest.

I know, my Lord, that this is a tiny glimpse of heaven - of being in Your visible Presence - of being held in Your feel-able embrace. See the deep longing within me for that time? In the present, even while enjoying the sweetness of shared time with You, there is the knowledge that I must "go back" to the physical world with its not-so-pleasant realities. But what a glorious future is mine! I am filled with quietness and confidence in You. You will do what is good because You *are* good. Thank You for Your wonderful grace. I love You very much, Lord.

November 4
ETERNAL FOOD

Do not work for the food which perishes,
but for the food which endures to eternal life,
which the Son of Man shall give to you,
for on Him the Father, even God, has set His seal.
John 6: 27

You, Lord, are the Blessed Controller of my life. You made me as I am. You have orchestrated the events and conditions of my life even to this present day. You have taken me under Your wing. You have taught, protected and loved me; not because I'm good and lovable, but because You are both good and loving.

You see potential when none is visible to the human eye. You see hurting hearts even when the exterior is hard and scornful. You see need - interior need - even when all physical needs are met. All that, Lord, is part of what You were teaching in Your words I just read from John 6 about the "food which endures to eternal life" being the primary need of our life rather than physical food.

We are so guilty, as parents, of seeing that all physical needs are met, sometimes to excess, and *failing to feed the spirit at all.* We, Your own people, are guilty of this. I, Lord, am guilty of this.

Allow me to repent and to give You my total self this day. The children are all home, all day. May I be aware of each teachable moment that occurs and use it to plant good seed. Grant me to see as You see - the potential, the hurting heart, the interior need - and then grant me wisdom to speak Your words of strength and healing. I can think of no greater honor than to be Your channel of love to a child.

November 5
FAILURE IS NOT FATAL

Remember my affliction and my wandering, the wormwood and bitterness.
Surely my soul remembers and is bowed down within me.
This I recall to my mind, therefore I have hope.
The Lord's loving kindnesses indeed never cease, for His compassions never fail.
They are new every morning; great is Thy faithfulness.
Lamentations 3: 19-23

Do I need to analyze and understand or just repent and learn a lesson?

I *do* repent, Lord, and I also learned. What I learned is that I allowed circumstances to dictate my behavior. Without even stopping to think, I acted. In an instant of time, my "surrender of control" was jerked out of Your hands. I took it back and let the anger flow unchecked. This is not only immature, it is alarming.

It is frightening to witness that kind of anger being expressed. Or that kind of anger even *being* there. I'm very aware that I used to have a bad temper, but for it to return with such a vengeance is a bit scary. So I also learned the *depth* of my need for Your control.

I do not like the spirit I exemplified yesterday. It was the opposite of the quiet and gentle spirit that is our goal. Please forgive me, Lord. Please give me grace and wisdom to more wisely handle my pain and frustrations. I do love You, even when I don't act like it.

Perhaps the most valuable lesson is revealed to me as I sit here and think about all this. And that is the *unending mercy and tenderness* which You show Your children. You allow me to fail and repent as many times as necessary. Without scolding or punishment of any kind, You pick me up from failure, turn me in the right direction again, take my hand and we move forward once more.

Such love is past understanding, Lord. It makes me determined to continue on with You, no matter what.

"The Lord is my portion," says my soul, "therefore I have hope in Him."
The Lord is good to those who wait for Him, to the person who seeks Him.
Lamentations 3: 24-25

310

November 6
DEATH

Precious in the sight of the Lord is the death of His godly ones.
Psalm 116: 15

This verse brings up a subject I've been thinking a lot about, Lord. It seems to me that, as Your children, we have a very warped view of physical death. The prevailing view seems to be that death of the body is an enemy to be avoided at all costs and for as long as possible.

We put people (including ourselves) through painful procedures. We pump in toxic chemicals that may be effective at fixing one thing but will do serious damage to another. We spend hundreds of thousands of dollars on medical care that so often simply prolongs the misery of the patient. We take so long to reach the point where we say "enough" and let nature take its course.

It *is* the natural thing for physical death to follow this life. Death for Your child is not some horrible monster waiting for us. It is simply a transition from living in this earthly, perhaps worn-out and painful, body to living in a glorious new existence that is beyond our comprehension to visualize. Our physical death is just a doorway through which we walk from this room to that room.

I see this transition as a *good* thing, Lord, not something to be dreaded. Because, in Your view, I have died already.

Truly, truly, I say to you, he who hears My word,
and believes Him who sent me,
has eternal life, and does not come into judgment,
but has passed out of death into life.
John 5: 24

So the grief we experience at the death of a fellow believer is not grief for them but for ourselves, for the empty spot their going leaves in our lives. My own experience, Lord, is that there is so much joy mixed in with that grief….joy in the fact that they have finished their race and have been promoted to glory! And this it true even when that life has been much shorter than normal.

I would never advocate that there be no medical intervention and treatment. And I certainly am not making the sudden death of a child or young person a thing of small consequence. I simply see, among my fellow believers, a dread of death that I find perplexing. Am I wrong to have these views? If so, I'm willing for You to change me.

November 7
INVESTING MY FAITH

Now faith is the assurance of things hoped for, the conviction of things not seen.
Hebrews 11: 1

Lord, please help me develop the thought You gave me earlier this morning - the concept that the gift of faith is a spiritual resource to be *used* or *wasted* just like financial resources. You give each of Your children a certain amount of faith and what we do with it has eternal consequences - just as what we do with our money today changes our tomorrows. What are some ways I can wisely invest my faith?

Your Word says I am to build myself up on my most holy faith. So it is *foundational.* My spiritual life is built upon it. A foundation must be *strong.* I would never build a house upon a foundation made of plywood because as soon as it got wet, the weight of the structure would cause the plywood to buckle and collapse. Concrete is required for a strong foundation. My spiritual life, if it is to be stable, must be built upon a strong faith - a firm belief that You are good, and Your Word, which tells me of Your love, is true.

I can use my faith to pray for myself and for others. In fact, if I am obedient to Your Word, I will *pray without ceasing.* This does not mean an endless repetition and litany of memorized words. It means real conversation, with a real Person about real situations. It means the blessed practice of being consciously in Your Presence at all times, sharing all of my life with You.

I can invest my faith by seeing Your desire for my ever-present surrender to You and willingly making that surrender. And when I have done that, perceive all that happens to me as coming from Your hand. This will take a constant exercise of faith because in some things it will be difficult to believe that the situation is Your work. Which brings me to the next use of my faith.

I *must* use my faith as my shield in spiritual battles. A shield left lying on the ground or leaning against the wall will do me no good. I must have it in my hand and in place for it to be effective. This means I must know Your Word and have it inscribed in my heart to extinguish the fiery darts of Satan.

Those are but a few ways to invest my faith. Now, how can I waste my faith? By not using it at all. By asking You for "things" which are not on Your list of priorities. By not taking time to understand Your will in a situation. By not *caring* what Your will is, just praying my own will. By making myself the center of my universe and believing You will bless that. By failing to see the enormous price You paid to redeem me. By ignoring the real blessings You desire to give, and craving only temporal ones. May it never be!

Please give me wisdom to use my faith wisely, Lord. It is far more precious than gold.

November 8
ONE DAY AT A TIME

Therefore do not be anxious for tomorrow;
for tomorrow will care for itself.
Each day has enough trouble of its own.
Matthew 6: 34

That verse holds so much wisdom. How good You are, Lord, to give us our lives one day at a time. I'm so thankful that You did not sit me down at age 18 when I got married and lay out my whole life before me saying, **"This is what you have before you if you take this step."** I would *never* have been brave enough to face the things that would come to us in our lives. I would have missed marrying the love of my life. I would have given up the desire to live at all because I would have considered the things ahead much too burdensome for me.

And I'm sure that, if we polled ten people past 40 years of age on the subject, we would get ten opinions that agree with mine. Obviously, knowing this, You arranged to veil the future from us. Then, You instructed us to not be anxious concerning things over which we have no control.

This is one of the main principles of the 12-Step programs for overcoming addictions - doing it one day at a time. We can get our mind around doing a difficult thing for one day. We cannot handle thinking, "I've got to do this every day for the rest of my life." You, Lord, made us with these limitations. When we work within Your design, good things happen.

Worrying about tomorrow, or anything else for that matter, will do nothing but harm. Anxiety creates physical stresses in the body which cause harmful chemical changes which, in turn, cause illness. People spend ten of thousands of dollars on counseling for various kinds of anxiety. How wise we would be to simply do what we are supposed to do - merely live today as well as we know how. Yesterday is past and cannot be changed. Tomorrow is unknown to us and being anxious about it will not change it one iota.

So, just for today, Lord, I ask You to fill me with Your love and joy. I invite You to flood my mind with Your peace and gentleness. Your grace will give me everything I need to accomplish what You have put before me today. Thank You for being my ever present help!

November 9
LIVING BY GRACE

Let us therefore draw near with confidence to the throne of grace,
that we may receive mercy
and may find grace to help in time of need.
Hebrews 4: 16

Lord, as I sit here in my quiet room on this beautiful morning, I'm aware of my need for You. I'm aware of my desire for Your touch or a word from You. I invite the fresh wind of Your Spirit to blow through the clutter of my life and leave me with only those things of eternal value. I give You permission to remove anything that You know is holding me back. I welcome Your correction, Your rebuke if necessary, because I know You discipline those You love. And I know that You love me.

How thankful I am to know that! I remember how long it took for You to convince me that You loved me. I had to learn a whole new way of seeing You and of seeing myself. I had to learn what grace is. You had to teach me, through several difficult, painful things, the truth that this life of faith is all about You and not at all about me. I had to accept the fact that I was not worthy of Your love, and will never be worthy of it, but that Your unconditional love is the foundation of Your grace. I even had to learn what unconditional love is!

You are an awesome and patient Teacher to bring me through such a long time of learning and into a place of yielding to You. And I'm *still* learning about this thing we call surrender. Surrender is an act which begins at a definite point in time but then becomes an ongoing process for as long as this life-in-the-body continues - a process of making right choices, or of making wrong choices, repenting, and beginning again.

I can draw near to You with confidence, my Lord, because You have invited me to do so. What a blessed way of life it is to belong to You. What a high and holy privilege it is to experience Your presence and to praise You. There is much gratitude mingled with my praise because You have blessed me in so many ways - blessings that are clear evidence of Your wonderful grace. I love You with all that is within me.

November 10
BACK TO BASICS

And without faith it is impossible to please Him,
for he who comes to God must believe that He is,
and that He is a rewarder of those who seek Him.
Hebrews 11: 6

We always come full circle back to the basics, don't we, Lord? In my strong tendency to make things difficult, I wander off down a side path and get lost in the woods. And time after time You remind me of the foundational facts, the eternal truths upon which my faith-life is built and You use them to bring me back. Like this one in Hebrews.

This verse speaks of pleasing You. I *do* want to please You, Lord. Sometimes I wish You would *force* me to stay within arm's length of You. But I know You don't operate that way. You give me abundant truth to follow and the promise that You are always with me. And then you allow me to choose.

This is everything needed to be successful at this business of pleasing You. This entire walk with You is to be by faith. You and I are on a journey that is brand new to me every day. I have no idea what the day will bring or what direction the path will take. I have only enough light to see the next couple of steps in front of me. The length of the journey is unknown to me. It may end today for all I know. Only You know what is ahead. And that is enough. Because I know, deep down *know*, that You are good, that You love me and that You have my hand in Yours. That is all I need to know.

Thank You, Lord, for keeping me safe even when I remove my hand from Yours. Thank You for bringing me back to Your side. It is the drawing power of Your love which does this bringing-back work in me. It somehow causes me to see that You want me close, but only if it is my choice. How awesome!

November 11
A SONG OF YOUR CARING

O Lord, how many are Thy works!
In wisdom Thou hast made them all;
the earth is full of Thy possessions.
Let the glory of the Lord endure forever;
let the Lord be glad in His works.
Psalm 104: 24, 31

I read this psalm earlier this morning, Lord. It is such a delightful song about You and Your loving care of all that You have created. What an amazing God You are!

Truly, You are very great!
You are clothed with splendor and majesty.
You are wrapped in light.
The clouds are Your chariot.
You walk upon the wings of the wind.
The angels minister to You
and they are also Your messengers.
All of creation tells of Your wisdom and power.

My response?
I will sing unto You as long as I live.
I will meditate on all Your full-of-wonder creation.
I will be *glad* in You.
All that is within me shall bless you, my Lord.

Singing and joy are so closely related. How kind of You to provide even the most poverty stricken their very own musical instrument with which to praise You. Not all of us have melodious voices, but we can still sing love songs to You. We can still sing songs of praise for Who You are. We can still rejoice in song because we belong to You. I'm thinking, Lord, that in heaven we will *all* have exquisite singing voices and that there will be abundant opportunity to use them. We will sing old favorites and learn new songs. We will sing alone and in huge groups. There will be music unlike any we have ever known. I can hardly wait! How great is our God!

November 12
JOYFUL TRUTHS

...I shall be glad in the Lord.
Psalm 104: 34

Truths that bring joy to my heart...

You, Lord, take my feeble expressions of love and praise
and return to me a enormous blessing;
sometimes an inner joy in Your nearness,
sometimes an encouraging word,
sometimes the assurance of strength to do what is before me.
always the certainty that You are at work in my life.
It doesn't get any better than that!

And another...
I can *never* have a need that You will not meet.
What an awesome thought!
And then...
because You are a good and merciful God,
I need not despair over past failures but rather,
learn from them the needed lesson and go on,
this time to victory.
Thank You, Lord!

Here is a great one...
though my ability to understand is limited,
Your ability to *make* me understand is unlimited;
thus, I can be sure that You will make clear to me anything I need to know.
By this I acknowledge that there are many things I might like to understand
but don't *need* to understand.
I therefore accept this with peace,
like that weaned child resting in its mother's lap.

You, my Lord, know me fully.
No one else knows me as You do,
no one else loves me as You do.
You truly bring heaven to my soul.

That is what this joy is.
Heaven in my soul!

317

November 13
A BURDENED HEART

Cast your burden upon the Lord, and He will sustain you;
He will never allow the righteous to be shaken
Psalm 55: 22

I have a burden that I must give to You this morning, Lord. Yesterday's incident of the so-called humor our entire family witnessed on television has left me with a hurting heart. I need Your perspective on the situation. My own thoughts tend to get extreme in one direction or the other - either ignore the situation and do nothing, or make a big deal out of it. And maybe one of those behaviors *is* Your will for how I should respond. Or perhaps Your way would be more middle-of-the-road. I don't know, but I *want* to know. I'm asking You for wisdom.

Here is what I do know: I worship You as holy and exalted; therefore, I cannot accept hearing You treated as *less* than holy. I know this dishonoring skit was created by unbelievers, and I realize it is unrealistic to expect unbelievers to honor You. But my concern is my family who saw and heard this. I love You, Lord and I so much want others, especially family, to love You also. Love does not belittle; respect does not ridicule; reverence does not treat as ordinary that which is holy.

Here is a wide-open door to speak truth, rebuke even, to these I love. Eli failed to do this with his sons, and dire consequences resulted. Love for You and love for these precious ones both seem to demand action. I know that You do not need my puny defense, Lord. You have all power and are well able to defend Yourself.

What comes immediately to mind is that the Father did not *need* You to chase out the money changers who were making a mockery of the temple, either. But You cracked the whip and spoke the truth to them anyway. I think, in all honesty, Lord, that a lot of my heart pain is that I didn't say something right then! But it's not too late. I give this burden to You knowing that You will, in return, give me the wisdom I need. You have promised.

But if any of you lacks wisdom, let him ask of God,
who gives to all men generously and without reproach,
and it will be given to him.
James 1: 5

I am willing.
You are able.
It shall be done.

November 14
OUR RELATIONSHIP

I am the Lord, I have called you in righteousness,
I will also hold you by the hand and watch over you.
Isaiah 42: 6

Maintaining the vital relationship that we have, Lord, means to me that on ordinary days - days without any big problem or crisis - my thoughts still are turned to You, still centered on You. Even on ordinary days, I'm aware of Your love, and my heart is thankful for it. What more, Lord? The gentle rebuke of Your Spirit tells me there is more.

"There is an ever-present temptation to look upon where you are spiritually as a destination - to stop and set up camp and rest. When this temptation is yielded to, there begins to grow a weed of spiritual laziness in your heart.

Yes, you are still loving Me, thinking of Me and thankful to Me. But you have stopped seeking Me. You have stopped expecting Me to teach you something new today. You have forgotten that we are on a journey, I am your Guide, and we have new ground to cover.

This weed is fast growing and invasive. It can soon have your senses dulled to My presence, your spirit growing cooler and dimmer. It will obscure from your view things I need you to see. You will begin to choose always to do the easy thing rather than the right thing. The easy thing pleases the flesh. The right thing glorifies Me.

Don't you see, My child? It is not your actions, your behavior, that I'm correcting; they are just the natural result of your choices. It is your heart that I want to fix. That is where that weed of spiritual laziness is rooted. Allow Me to pull it up by its roots so that it will disappear.

The light and warmth will return; the passion will burn again. My joy and your joy will combine to give you new strength for the journey. This is My will for you even on an ordinary day."

Oh! My Lord, I confess I allowed that weed to root and grow too long. Please pull it up. Please give me wisdom to resist the temptation to laziness. Please help me distinguish between physical and spiritual - to realize that my physical fatigue and need of much rest does not affect my spirit, because my spirit is strong, energetic and healthy. Thank You, Lord, for Your mercy and patience for this slow-to-learn child.

November 15
POOR IN SPIRIT

Blessed are the poor in spirit
for theirs is the kingdom of heaven.
Matthew 5: 3

Lord, I probably don't understand the full meaning of "poor in spirit."
But I'm thinking,
as I look at this latest assignment You have given me,
that is exactly what I am.
Poor in spirit.
May I talk to You about it?

I have no resources of my own from which to draw.
I am completely unable to do the task on my own.
I am certain that if You do not work in me
and through me,
it will not be accomplished.

Sometimes walking by faith is very difficult, Lord.
Not difficult to understand but difficult to do.
It requires wisdom I don't have.
It requires discernment that I do not possess.
It requires consistently putting Your wishes before my own.

"Have I not promised to supply all your needs?"
Yes, Lord, You have promised.

"Have I ever failed to keep My promises to you?"
No, Lord, You do not fail.

I am filled with confidence in You even while being totally without any in myself.
Truly, I know You are all-powerful.
You are able to complete that which You have begun.
I shall *look* to You,
listen to You,
trust You.
Even that will require Your help.
So be it.

November 16
LIVE THIS MOMENT

So teach us to number our days,
that we may present to Thee a heart of wisdom.
Psalm 90: 12

This morning, You are showing me yet again, Lord, the importance of fully *living* life today rather than postponing it for some future time or event. I confess that I'm guilty of doing exactly that. I know that, in You, I do have a wonderful future to which I can look forward. And this joyful future grows more important to me with every passing day. But I see that it is the "passing days" that You are concerned about.

"Yes, you tend to stoically plod through today knowing things will be better later on. In doing this you are missing the joys of today, of this moment. Every moment of life is precious and miraculous and to be treasured. Each small exchange of words with those you love or even with strangers is valuable.

You say you believe that I am in control of even the details of your life, but your heart does not yet fully understand that. Allow that knowledge to sink deep into you for it will change how you think, and thus how you react and respond to every moment of your day.

I have told you so often to relax and rejoice. You are learning, you are doing better, but you are not yet where I want you to be. It is a matter of what you perceive as truth. Accept into the deepest part of your inner being this foundational truth, and allow it to change the total structure of your outlook. It will bring the peace, gentleness and patience you want, because it will be My peace, My gentleness, My patience flowing through you. As you and I rebuild this way of looking at your life. you will see more and more of the power of My Spirit working in you and through you. Relax and rejoice. I am in control."

Gratitude fills me up and overflows! How blessed I am to belong to You! How good it is to be corrected by You. There is nothing I want more, Lord, than to allow You full control of my life. Make my heart wise and use all my moments to Your glory.

November 17
THE POWER OF GOD

Do you not know? Have you not heard?
The Everlasting God, the Lord,
the Creator of the ends of the earth
does not become weary or tired.
His understanding is inscrutable.
He gives strength to the weary,
and to him who lacks might He increases power.
Isaiah 40: 28-29

Nothing is more sure, more certain, than Your promises. Behind Your promises stands the all-powerful, all-knowing God of creation. You are without limits in Your ability to do what You have promised. There is no higher power that can thwart Your plan. There is no superior intelligence that can out-maneuver You.

You rule over all because You created all that exists and set all things in motion. You have a plan so large, so vast, so far-reaching that we creatures can only dimly perceive our tiny part in it.

But even in my poor perception, Lord, there is yet such a fear and trembling! For You are exceedingly high above all, so exalted and holy, existing from everlasting to everlasting outside of time and space. You are able to see and to know everything. How can a mere mortal stand before such as You are?

How amazing is the Love flowing out from You that provides a way for me to come to You and bow before You in all reverence. And then You lift me up to stand before You, and I see the joyful love in Your eyes! That never fails to astound me!

Thank You, Lord, for allowing me to be a part of Your kingdom. And thank You for all the riches of Your promises that are mine, a wealth so much more precious than gold or silver.

November 18
GIVING AND TAKING

"Bring the whole tithe into the storehouse,
so that there may be food in My house,
and test Me now in this," says the Lord of hosts,
"if I will not open for you the windows of heaven,
and pour out for you a blessing until it overflows."
Malachi 3: 10

This verse is about giving and taking. At first glance, Lord, it seems to be about Your people *giving* first and then *taking* the blessings You pour out upon us. And it is true that the pouring out of Your overflowing blessings does not happen until we are obedient to this instruction to tithe. But, in truth, *You* have given first because You have given us everything from which we are then able to give to You. All we do with our tithe is return a small portion of it to You.

I'm a firm believer in tithing money because I have seen first-hand, all my life, how You bless our faithfulness to tithe. Your creativity and Your ability to bless Your children in meeting material and financial needs is infinite. This promise, like all Your promises, is rock solid.

But I'm thinking this morning of the symbolic application of this concept - the idea of giving all You ask, no matter what it is You are asking. I read a statement recently that said, "Give all He asks; take all He promises." I like the sound of that!

So, what do I understand that You are asking? Well, everything. All of myself, all rights to myself, all that I am, all that I own, all my past, all my future, this present moment....*everything* is all You ask.

That sounds like a lot to give until I think about all You give in return. I don't even know where to start listing what You give in return! It is so much - so incredibly more precious than what You get from me - it is truly an overflow of blessings. Your promises to Your children from Genesis to Revelation are all mine when I am all Yours! It is not possible to put a value on this exchanged life that You give me.

You take my sinful nature and give me Your own. You take my sure and certain eternal damnation and give me heaven. You take my weakness and give me strength. You take my emptiness and fill it with Yourself. You take any good gift You have given me and teach me how to glorify You in the use of it. You take me and give me Yourself. That is the bottom line, Lord. You give me *Yourself.*

For as many as may be the promises of God,
in Him they are yes.
2 Corinthians 1: 20
Glory!

November 19
PRAISE

Through Him then, let us continually offer up a sacrifice of praise to God,
that is, the fruit of lips that give thanks to His name.
Hebrews 13: 15

A sacrifice of praise - I'm not sure what that means to You, Lord. To me it means praising You *for who You are* even when conditions of my life and/or the enemy of my soul try to make me think there is nothing praise-worthy at the moment. But I am not subject to conditions. I am not subject to the enemy. I am subject only to You. You are my King. You are my Sovereign God. You are always worthy of all the praise my heart can imagine!

All Your children have days and situations that contain more adversity than serenity. But we learn that You are just as worthy of praise in the bad times as You are in the good times.

All of us have an enemy who will take every opportunity to attempt to discourage and depress. He will do everything in his power to blind our eyes to Your goodness and to make us doubt Your love. But by Your grace, we have the power to resist his attempts.

That's why the verse above says, *"Through Him then...."* It is completely because of what You have done, are doing and shall do that we have any power at all. You truly are the Author and Finisher of our faith (Heb. 12:2). You are our changeless Christ...

Jesus Christ is the same yesterday and today, yes and forever.
Hebrews 13:8

You are eternal love, infinite wisdom, unlimited power. You are so much more than I can understand. If all that You are is likened to all the grains of sand in the world, I have in my possession only about a teaspoonful. But even that small grasp of Your reality is enough to make my spirit bow down in worship.

So from my spirit, through my mind comes worship; beautiful, reverent adoration for who You are and thanksgiving for letting me love You. Please, Lord, may it all please You and bring You joy.

November 20
NARROW WAY - WIDE WAY

Enter by the narrow gate; for the gate is wide,
and the way is broad that leads to destruction,
and many are those who enter by it.
For the gate is small,
and the way is narrow that leads to life,
and few are those who find it.
Matthew 7: 13-14

We are all on a journey, aren't we, Lord? Every person alive is traveling on either the broad way to destruction or the narrow way to Life. I wonder how many thought about that when they got up this morning and started their day. I wonder how many people on planet Earth today even *begin* to understand the spiritual significance of this life.

I'm thinking we, all of us, spend a lot of our days looking upon this life as a thing unto itself - a time of no real purpose other than staying comfortable, which means different things to different people. I wonder how many see that it is the prelude to eternity.

We are masters at deluding ourselves, aren't we, Lord? Especially when we are young, life seems to stretch out in front of us far into the distance. When the dark reality of death intrudes upon us, we somehow consign it only to others, never to ourselves. As we grow older, thoughts of our own death become harder to put aside. Many begin a spiritual search for answers, for some kind of peace to calm the troubling thoughts. And the answers are out there - scores of wrong ones and only one right one. I wonder how many are believing a lie, even at this moment.

The only right answer is what *You* have said about this life and the next. Your Word teaches that life is brief, and eternity follows. It teaches that *today* is the day of salvation for we do not know what tomorrow will bring. It tells us that *You* are that gate that opens onto the way to Life. It teaches that the narrow way demands repentance, denying self and walking by faith. It tells us that only in adversity (being uncomfortable!) do we learn the spiritual truths necessary for this walk. But this is only one side of the coin.

When we turn it over, we find that You walk every step of this narrow path with us. Your Word promises that You will never leave us. It teaches us to look forward to every new day of this adventure of walking with You, of being loved by You and learning to love You in return. We experience a deep joy that is *there* no matter the circumstances of life. Your Word tells us of a destination that is wonderful and beautiful, and we look forward to that. And, in Your grace, You give us a foretaste of it by allowing us to experience the blessedness of Your presence every day. I wonder how many hold this coin of the heavenly realm in their hand right now.

How I wish it were the "many" instead of the "few."

November 21
GREAT GRACE

For it is God who is at work in you,
both to will and to work for His good pleasure.
Philippians 2: 13

Thinking about the narrow gate and the narrow way takes my mind way back to the day of my salvation at age 12. My commitment to You that day was as complete as I knew how to make it. But, oh, how much I did not know! I knew I was lost and that the only way to be saved was through You. My concept of what took place in salvation and what happened after salvation was pretty vague, but I was clear on my part in being saved. And I knew that one basic of being a "good Christian" was reading my Bible every day. King James was all I owned so I started, that day, at Genesis, which seemed logical to me. I got through Genesis and Exodus pretty well. But then came Leviticus. There I got bogged down and quit reading. What 12-year-old has the discipline to plod through Leviticus in *any* version?!

After awhile I felt such guilt that I started again. With Genesis. I do not remember how many good intentioned starts and dismal failures I went through, Lord. But I distinctly remember getting to the place of saying to myself, "Well, obviously I can't live this Christian life. I can't even read my Bible!" My concept of being a Christian was *doing all the right things*. So, by age 15, I gave up trying. My thought was, "If I can't do it right, I won't do it at all."

How many times I've wished I'd been wise enough to talk to an adult about that. They could have told me to start with the New Testament rather than the Old. They could have encouraged me and helped me. They could have taught me how to love You and receive Your love. I think this is why I feel so strongly today about discipleship for new Christians, Lord. Because *so many will not ask.* They will just try and try and try, and then they will quit.

How many times I've wished I'd had more teaching of the role of Your Spirit in living this life. I had learned a lot about Your wrath against sinners, Your day of judgment to come and about the eternal fiery torture in hell awaiting anyone not fit for heaven. But nothing about Your blessed Holy Spirit who would come and live within me and be my Friend, Counselor and Teacher. I had heard about "grace" but had no understanding of it. However, the next 15 years - the ones I spent shutting You out of my life - were a demonstration of wonderful grace!

I saw the truth of that grace only later, after I came home to You. *All those years, You never abandoned me.* You were always there loving, protecting and guiding in spite of my dark confusion. How can I ever thank You enough for that?! How can I show my gratitude for Your faithfulness to me even when I was unfaithful to You? All I know to do is love You with all that I am for all the rest of my days on earth, and then for all of eternity. This is my desire, my Lord.

November 22
THE DISOBEDIENT PROPHET

Now behold, there came a man of God from Judah to Bethel
by the word of the Lord...
1 Kings 13: 1

There is a very interesting story leading up to this event, Lord, about the nation of Israel splitting, what caused the split and who was in charge. However, I want to zero in upon this prophet. I find this a most remarkable story, and the lesson it teaches worth some thought.

The man of God You sent, arrived at Bethel and delivered Your message to the king of Israel. The king invited the prophet to go home with him so the king could give him a reward.

But the man of God said to the king, "If you were to give me half your house I would not go with you, nor would I eat bread or drink water in this place. For so it was commanded me by the word of the Lord, saying, 'You shall eat no bread, nor drink water, nor return by the way which you came.'"
1 Kings 13: 8-9

So the man of God started back to Judah by another way.

During this time, there was an old prophet living in Bethel. When his sons came and told him all which the man of God had done that day in Bethel, he had them saddle his donkey and he rode out to find the man of God. When he found him, he ask him to come home with him and eat bread. But the man of God gave him exactly the same words he had spoken to the king.

Then the old prophet lied to him and said:

I also am a prophet like you, and an angel spoke to me by the word of the Lord, saying, 'Bring him back with you to your house, that he may eat bread and drink water.' "
I Kings 13: 18

So the man of God went with him and ate bread and drank water. But Your word came to the old prophet as they were sitting at the table, and he said to the man of God that, because he had been disobedient, his body would not come to the grave of his fathers. Sure enough, on the way home, the man of God was attacked by a lion and killed. The old prophet went out, recovered the body, and buried it in his own tomb.

The simplest understanding and clearest lesson I see from this strange story is this: *when You give me instructions, I am to follow them until or unless You directly give me different instructions. I am not to believe what someone else says You have told them about me. I must get my information first hand from You.*

This is actually a sensible rule to follow all the time, isn't it, Lord? If I know Your Word, I am able to measure everything anyone says by it, and thus verify the truth or prove the lie. Knowing what You have said is crucial. There is no substitute for first hand knowledge given to me by You.

November 23
FEELING YOUR LOVE

If you love Me, you will keep My commandments.
John 14: 15

At the beginning of our relationship, Lord, I remember the difficulty I had in believing You loved me. I believed it with my mind because I believed Your Word was true, and it plainly said that You love all who come to You. But I didn't believe it with my heart and, therefore, my emotions remained untouched. In other words, I did not "feel" love from You.

Some might say that since feelings are unimportant, mental assent should be enough. But my heart disagreed. I somehow knew that it was *important* for me to emotionally experience that love which You so freely pour into Your children. So I continued seeking and knocking. And being the faithful, awesome God You are, You gave me the answer in two ways. One, by showing me that my love for my son is a human example of Your divine love for me, and the second - totally unexpected - was this: You showed me that, just as my love for You is tied to obedience, as John says above, so is *experiencing* or *feeling* Your love for me.

"Your awareness of My love requires a couple of things, My child. First, that you live out all you know of My will. Second, it is necessary that every new revelation to you of My will be met with an attitude of eagerness to follow it. Obedience is important. Consistent obedience will involve your entire being in this life of faith, which is what I desire. It will provide the single-mindedness that is crucial to our relationship."

He who has My commandments and keeps them,
he it is who loves Me;
and he who loves Me shall be loved by My Father,
and I will love him, and will disclose Myself to him.
John 14: 21

"You see, the channels through which My love flow into you can be blocked by disobedience. Likewise, those channels can be made open and enlarged by obedience. Fulfill all joy for both of us by being My obedient child and all will be well."

November 24
MY SHEPHERD

The Lord is my shepherd,
I shall not want.
Psalm 23: 1

You *are* my shepherd.
Not 'were'
Not 'shall be'
But *are*, in this present moment.
I belong to You.

What a glorious freedom!
I don't have to be strong
or able
or sufficient.
Because You are all these and more.
I can simply rest in Your care.

You will find the green pastures and still water,
You know exactly how to restore my soul,
If I'm tempted to stray from the path, You will guide me back,
all for the sake of Your Holy Name.

Even death has no fear for me.
All this, Lord, makes my joy and praise overflow.
Your goodness and loving kindness fill me
and surround me.
How blest I am to belong to You forever!

November 25
AWESOME BLESSINGS

But by His doing you are in Christ Jesus,
who became to us wisdom from God,
and righteousness and sanctification,
and redemption, that just as it is written,
"Let him who boasts, boast in the Lord."
1 Corinthians 1: 30-31

This verse grabs my attention this morning, Lord, and I must talk to You about it. What a great collection of blessings Paul gathered up in such a few words! Because I am in You, I *have* all these wonderful things. It seems to me, though, that Paul's thought process worked in reverse as he wrote this list of blessings. I would put them in this order:

Redemption. Remember back in the 60's and 70's when merchants gave trading stamps when we bought their goods? Then we took the stamps home and glued them in special little books, collected enough books to take them to the Redemption Center and trade them for stuff. Free stuff, we thought. I'm sure we paid for those things but it *felt* free. The difference here is that when You redeem us, it truly is a *free gift.* By Your grace we are bought back from sin's bondage and set free to walk with You. We are redeemed from the dominion of Satan. We are now and forever a member of Your Kingdom!

Sanctification. Like redemption, this is one of those big church words. But it simply means that I am set apart for Your purposes and am made pure and holy in Your eyes. It is a thing *You* do in me - not something I do for myself. All I do is surrender and obey. How spectacular it is that, in Your sight, I am pure and holy! And You have promised to keep me that way until that day I stand before You when this life is over. Glory!

Righteousness. Another big church word. To me, Lord, this means that, because You have saved me and made me pure, *now* I have right standing with You. It means that I do not have to be timid or afraid to come into Your presence. It means I don't have to hang my head in shame for those things You have forgiven. They are all past and gone forever. I am a new creation, and I have right standing with You. I am accepted. I can come to You as often as I want and stay as long as I want. Righteousness is sublime!

Wisdom. Wisdom isn't just a one time gift, is it, Lord? We need Your wisdom every minute of every day. It is like a flowing fountain, there for us to drink from as often as needed. Through the manifestation of these divine blessings, You have entitled us to ask for Your wisdom. And Your promise is that You will give it when our single-minded intent is to be obedient. You are such an awesome God! It is all of You. *"But by His doing..."*

November 26
MY QUIET TIME

Thou hast dealt well with Thy servant, O Lord, according to Thy word.
Teach me good discernment and knowledge, for I believe in Thy commandments.
Psalm 119: 65-66

I've been thinking about something extraordinary. I have followed the same early morning process of Bible reading and prayer for years, Lord, and it has taken me through Your Word many times. The O.T. and N.T. readings are as long as I choose them to be - sometimes only one verse if my meditation gets deep, or sometimes two chapters if it's a book such as Numbers that doesn't lead to intense reflection. Now, one might think that this process is just a habit and a very old habit, at that. I choose to think of it as a divine appointment. But here is the extraordinary thing I've been thinking about.

So often I open my Bible to the end of yesterday's reading and amazingly discover today's reading concerns the exact subject about which You have been speaking to my heart. Or what I read today is the answer to a problem I've been trying to solve. Or through what I read, I hear Your quiet voice showing me something I've never seen before. This is, to me, a marvelous thing, Lord. It makes this an exciting part of my day. It confirms to me Your work in me, and proves again that Your Word is living and active.

I do not want this blessed time of my day to ever become routine. I want it always to be real communication with You - a time of speaking and responding to each other - a time of stillness in listening for Your voice - a defining element of our living, growing relationship.

You have been so faithful and good to me, Lord! Why would I not love You? Joy and thanksgiving overflow in my spirit, emerging as warm tears running down my face, as I praise You and try to find words to express my love. What a wonderful thing it is to be Your child!

Forever, O Lord, Thy word is settled in heaven.
Thy faithfulness continues throughout all generations.
Psalm 119: 89-90

November 27
YOUR PRAYER

John 17

For several days, Lord, I have been meditating on this prayer of Yours recorded by John. Your prayer time was usually private, and I do not know what You and the Father talked about. The fact that this one is set forth in detail makes it, to me, extremely significant and worthy of prayerful focus.

Unlike most of Your children, You did not fill this prayer with requests for Yourself. In fact, it was much like a summary of the task to which the Father had assigned You. You were nearing the end of the assignment and were reporting back some notable accomplishments. You still had the cross ahead of You and, since the time was very near, the one request You had for Yourself was *"Father, the hour has come; glorify Thy Son, that the Son may glorify Thee." (v.1)*

You were aware of the incredibly dreadful and daunting part of the Father's plan yet before You. In the second verse, You said that the reason You were asking to be glorified was so that You might *give eternal life*. Only because You finished the assignment by going through the crucifixion, burial and resurrection, do I have eternal life. If You had changed Your mind, the entire plan of redemption would have failed. No words are adequate for thanking You for seeing this task through to the end!

You did ask the Father for several things, however. You asked that I might have eternal life. You asked for me to be kept in the Father's name and to be full of Your joy. You requested that I be safe from the evil one. You asked that I be sanctified in the truth and thus to be made one with You and the Father. And then to be perfected in that unity. You asked for me to know that the Father loves me. You asked that I could be with You where You are and to behold Your glory. No, You did not pray for me by name. But You did pray for "those who would come to believe in You" and, by Your grace, I am one of those!

What an extraordinary list! Every one of these blessings is a God-thing! I, on my own, cannot do a single one of them. How can any child of Yours read these words and not fall down before You in adoration and gratitude?

One more truth occurs to me - if any prayer that has ever been prayed will assuredly be answered, it is this one! How that fills me with Your joy!

November 28
THE NEW COVENANT

And it will come about after this that I will pour out My Spirit on all mankind;
and your sons and daughters will prophesy,
your old men will dream dreams, your young men will see visions.
And even on the male and female servants I will pour out My Spirit in those days.
Joel 2: 28-29

The Bible tells me about several covenants You have made with mankind through the many years of recorded history. I like that word "covenant" because it is a strong word, a legal word. We speak of the Covenant of Marriage in which two people vow to love and honor one another until death parts them. We speak of the Last Will and Covenant through which earthly belongings are passed on to whomever the giver chooses. We even have neighborhood covenants which stipulate some things we can and cannot do in our subdivision.

I'm thinking this morning, however, about these verses from Joel. Your covenants, Lord, reveal much about You and Your feelings about us. They show me Your great, enduring love for a stiff-necked, rebellious people. They show me Your amazing grace in continuing to devise ways to reach out to us, to show us that You *want* to bless, You are *longing* to bless and not punish, if only we will realize that and cooperate with You.

This giving of Your Holy Spirit to dwell within every believer was a revolutionary concept to the first-time hearers of that good news. Peter used these very verses in his sermon in Acts 2 to explain what was happening on the Day of Pentecost. That day was a benchmark in the history of our faith. It is plain to see that this new wine could not be poured into the old wineskins. It demanded a mind open to new truths and a heart willing to be transformed by Your Spirit.

I'm afraid, Lord, that we don't fully appreciate the huge difference it makes to us that You, in the Person of the Holy Spirit, are with us 24/7. Like every other constant in our lives, we can begin to take Your presence for granted. Oh, God, may it never be! The holy fact of Your presence is the bedrock foundation of my life! Without Your presence, I would not want to live.

I *know* that You will continue to work in me, honoring Your covenant, until Your purposes are accomplished. So be it.

November 29
SELF SUFFICIENCY GONE

But we have this treasure in earthen vessels,
that the surpassing greatness of the power
may be of God and not from ourselves.
2 Corinthians 4: 7

What is "true repentance"?
Has my repentance been "true"?

Those words, Lord, attempt to push me back
into the life-long struggle I have had
with a sensitive conscience coupled
with an extremely high expectation of myself.

These two together
have, over the years
caused me lots of misery.

And You, too,
as You have had to listen to me
work through that misery
time and time again.

Good news!
This morning I have neither the strength
nor the inclination
to do this work.

I just want to tell You that
those two things,
be they liabilities or assets,
are *Yours*
along with the rest of me.
If You need me to understand something,
You are well able to make me do so.
My confidence level in You is of the highest order;
in myself, non-existent.

I rest completely in Your care.
Oh, Joy!

November 30
YOUR TEMPTATION
Part One

Matthew 4:1-11

In my time in the Word, Lord, I again come to Matthew 4 and the account of Your temptation. John the Baptist had come preaching repentance and preparing the way for You. You came to the river and were baptized by him. Immediately thereafter comes this event - all of this preparing You for the ministry ahead of You.

Verse 1. *Then Jesus was led up by the Spirit into the wilderness to be tempted by the devil.* It was obviously a good thing - this temptation by the devil - because God the Holy Spirit would not have led God the Son into it if it were not for good. So...

Was the purpose to strengthen You?

Was the purpose to strengthen us?

Was it to teach us truths about You?

Was it to teach us about the devil?

Perhaps, Lord, the answer to all those is "yes." We do not know if Satan had to appear before the Father and ask permission to do this as he did with Job. One thing that is certain: You are sovereign, so it was at least *permitted* by the Father if not *arranged.* Probably the devil was very excited at this chance to overcome the Son of God. This, however, proves that he is not all-knowing. If he were, he would never have started this confrontation.

Verse 2. *And after He had fasted forty days and forty nights, He then became hungry.* The words "after" and "then" stand out, Lord. It is as if You were not aware of being hungry *during* the 40 days. If so, that is by supernatural intervention. I know how weak I feel if I don't eat for 24 hours, so I cannot comprehend a 960-hour fast. I do understand that at the end of it, when the devil arrives on the scene, You were hungry. This clearly shows that he times his attacks for when we are weakest.

Verse 3. *And the tempter came and said to Him, "If You are the Son of God, command that these stones become bread."* I do not think for a minute, Lord, that the devil did not know that You were the Son of God. And I am certain that it was well within Your power to turn those stones into bread. I can only believe that he was trying to get You to go against the Father's plan, to take an easier way than the one You and the Father had already decided upon. The devil will always try to lead me into disobedience and away from the path of righteousness. You refused to fall for it!

December 1
YOUR TEMPTATION
Part Two

Matthew 4:1-11

Verse 4. *But He answered and said, "It is written, 'Man shall not live on bread alone, but on every word that proceeds out of the mouth of God.'"* This was absolutely not what the devil wanted to hear! He was appealing to Your physical needs, and You turned it into a lesson on what is truly important - meeting spiritual needs. I do need physical bread for my physical body, but You say here that the Living Word from the mouth of God is what gives life and nourishment to my eternal spirit. If I nourish only the body and allow the spirit to starve, I am dead already.

It is *You* speaking to *me* through Your Word, through Your Spirit, that kindles life within me and makes me strong; that enables me to do more than I could ever imagine. Your words are power, and they are life!

Verses 5 & 6. *Then the devil took Him into the holy city; and he had Him stand on the pinnacle of the temple, and said to Him, "If You are the Son of God throw Yourself down; for it is written, 'He will give His angels charge concerning You. On their hands they will bear You up, lest You strike Your foot against a stone."* Even the devil can quote Scripture. And correctly, at that.

Until this time, the two of you were in the wilderness, away from other people. But this scene takes place in the middle of a busy city filled with people. We do not know if it was day or night, if the two of you were visible or invisible to others. But what a strange place for the devil to take You - to the building erected for and dedicated to the One True God and the worship of God!

What if?...What if You had jumped, people saw You jump and then You stood up uninjured and whole? Would it have proven anything? You later performed feats equally miraculous. Did everyone who saw them believe? No. Did all proclaim You to be the Son of God? No, only a few.

But think what would have been lost if You had done as the tempter wanted. The devil would have won. That could have been the end of the plan of salvation right there. We would all be eternally lost. How thankful I am, Lord that You saw this for what it was. Even in Your weakened condition, You were strong!

Verse 7. *Jesus said to him, "On the other hand, it is written, 'You shall not put the Lord your God to the test.'"* This reminds me of the children of Israel testing You over and over again during the exodus. In spite of Your promise to go with them and provide for them, they doubted You at every turn. That is the same as calling You a liar. It is exactly that, also, when I doubt You - an insult of the highest order to my Holy God!

December 2
YOUR TEMPTATION
Part Three

Matthew 4:1-11

Verses 8 & 9. *Again, the devil took Him to a very high mountain, and showed Him all the kingdoms of the world, and their glory; and he said to Him, "All these things will I give You, if You fall down and worship me."* Since there is no mountain on Earth from which the whole planet can be seen, perhaps You went far out in space. Certainly You *could.* The important thing here, however, is that the devil has the power to give all the kingdoms and their glory into Your hands. If he didn't, these would be merely empty words. Elsewhere Your Word says that the whole world lies in the power of the evil one. (I John 5:19) And that it will continue to be this way until You return to set up Your righteous government.

For untold time, Satan has intensely desired to be worshipped as You are worshipped - in fact, to take Your place as Highest of All. How presumptuous, Lord, for this fallen angel to stand before You who created him, and say these words with any hope that You would actually do this! How could he not know that You would see right through this scheme to the result that would follow? Maybe he thought You would be truly tempted to take this path he offered in order to avoid the pain and suffering of death on the cross and hell. I'm so thankful You were both wise and strong!

Verse 10. *Then Jesus said to him, "Begone, Satan! For it is written, 'You shall worship the Lord your God, and serve Him only.'"* Satan had long before rebelled against worshiping and serving You from a willing heart. He still serves You, but only because his power is subservient to Your power. He does it because he has no choice. I believe, Lord, his time is short. The day is coming when You will rule totally, and all power will be taken from him. Certainly, we are closer to that day this moment than ever before in the history of man.

Verse 11. *Then the devil left Him; and behold, angels came and began to minister to Him.* What a great statement! What a glorious victory You won! I'm sure the angels were full of joy over how it all played out. I'm certain that they had watched the events unfold and held their breath a few times (if angels breathe). Those angels had been Your faithful servants for eons, and they *had* to realize that the outcome of these few days was pivotal to the Father's entire plan of redemption. All could have been lost right here.

I imagine they brought You all Your favorite foods to eat, Your favorite juices to drink, maybe a soft pillow for Your head and a blanket for the cool night. Maybe they sang beautiful, peaceful songs composed specifically for this blessed time of rest and restoration. Most of all, they rejoiced with You and for You, just as I do. Praise wells up within my spirit, my Lord, for Your wisdom, faithfulness, strength and perseverance in all You went through for us! Praise and everlasting thanksgiving!

December 3
THE DESIRES OF MY HEART

Delight yourself in the Lord; and He will give you the desires of your heart.
Commit your way to the Lord, trust also in Him, and He will do it.
And He will bring forth your righteousness as the light,
and your judgment as the noonday.
Rest in the Lord and wait patiently for Him.
Psalm 37: 4-7

This is one of my favorite Psalms, Lord, all 40 verses of it. But this morning I'm especially thankful for the promise that if I delight in You, You *will* give me the desires of my heart. I'm filled with praise for You this morning. I'm filled with expectation, thanksgiving and joy. Living for You and with You is not merely a *good* way to live; it is absolutely the best!

There is no doubt in me that I delight in You! My heart is filled up and running over with love and gratitude for You, for the awesome God You are! So I can, in all good faith, claim this promise as I pray for people I love. And I know that the desires of *my* heart concerning these are actually *Your* desires - for those who are Your children already and for those who are not yet Yours. The very drive and desire to pray for them is Yours. The words, emotions and thoughts are Yours.

So, what do I believe concerning those prayers?

I believe that everything I asked is Your will and, thus, You *will* answer. I do not know how or when or where - that is Your business - but You will answer. I believe that if You need me to do something other than pray, You will make it evident to me.

When I see Your work over the years, Lord, I feel sorrow for my small faith and for my erratic praying. Thank You for those who did pray consistently! Thank You for faithful-to-You brothers and sisters who do not give up in the face of daunting circumstances and spiritual opposition. Thank You for Your sovereign control of all that happens to Your children. Knowing You are in charge assures us that, even when things do not go the way we thought they would or hoped they would, still *all is well*! The Almighty God, Creator of all that exists, is good, and all that He does is good!

December 4
SELF SURRENDER

What then shall we say to these things?
If God is for us, who is against us?
He who did not spare His own Son,
but delivered Him up for us all,
how will He not also with Him freely give us all things?
Romans 8: 31-32

Two truths: (1) at the moment of salvation, I was filled with Your Spirit and all that You bring, and (2) I experience that fullness only to the extent that I am emptied of myself.

Surrender of self is like peeling the layers off an onion - layer after layer after layer until all that is left is - *nothing*. That is what I'm working toward, Lord, becoming *nothing*. And, like peeling an onion, there is almost always discomfort and tears involved in the process. You do not spare us any misery necessary to accomplish Your purpose. But the end result is so well worth any trial it takes to get there. My heart says, "Work faster!" I want to be 100% filled with You.

"He must increase but I must decrease." (John 3: 30) Those words of John the Baptist are also mine. He saw that his purpose was to prepare the way for You and then step aside. I see that my purpose, like that of every child of Yours, is to continue this process of self surrender for as long as it takes, because this *is* preparing the way for You.

Will finishing this process happen in this lifetime? Am I wanting something that is not possible in this dark world? Could I shorten my time here by peeling faster?

I'm seeing, Lord, that my surrender, step by step, is at *Your* instigation. I must cooperate, but *You* are the one who is driving this process. I need not be anxious about anything. No matter how much work You and I have yet to do, those verses above make me happy all the way down to my toes!

Relax and Rejoice!

December 5
PRAYING FOR OUR WORLD

And this is the confidence which we have before Him,
that, if we ask anything according to His will, He hears us.
And if we know that He hears us in whatever we ask,
we know that we have the requests which we have asked from Him.
1 John 5: 14-15

In my imagination, Lord, I look down upon planet Earth from the heavens You created. I see a big, round beautiful world, but it is covered over with problems - war, hatred, violence, poverty, illness, suffering and killing.

In my heart, I know that no human, or group of humans, has the wisdom or power to bring about earthly peace. The problems are too complex and the needs too great for a human "fix." So how should I pray? For what do I ask?

I know You have devoted children all around the globe that can make a difference where they are, and that is good. I pray we will listen to You.

I know that Your power to bless, to change lives, is not limited to working in any prescribed way, and that is better. Use that power, Lord, to do what only You can do.

I know that someday You *will* return, and then there will be peace and good will. That is the best. Oh, how I look forward to that!

In the meantime, please help me see this as You do. I ask that all Your children everywhere, even today, be filled with a burning passion to live their lives completely under Your Lordship. Touch those who have grown cool and distant toward You, Lord, and draw them back into Your nearness. Strengthen those who deeply desire to be used in Your work to do Your will even in adverse circumstances.

Joy reigns supreme in my spirit as I think of this verse - *"Greater is He who is in you than he who is in the world." (1 John 4:4)* Certainly, our problems are countless. But, Lord, I think again about Your devoted children scattered over the face of the earth; we are *each one* filled with Your much greater power! Combined, we are a force to be reckoned with - as long as we obedient to You.

This is my prayer today for all my brothers and sisters. Make us realize and *use* this incredible power You have placed within each of us to follow You more closely. Help us to love You with all that we are. Empower us to give ourselves totally to You, to be used up in Your service as You choose. You are Lord of all!

December 6
PRAYER FOR SURRENDER

For what will a man be profited, if he gains the whole world, and forfeits his soul?
Or what will a man give in exchange for his soul?
Matthew 16: 26

I am burdened this morning, Lord, about several people I love who are, by their own admission, struggling with their surrender to You. What a miserable place to be! To be under Your conviction, yet resisting, causes a pain deep in the spirit that is harder to bear than physical pain. Please allow me to pray for them.

Perhaps these who are living on the fringes of Your grace do not truly understand Your love - because to understand it is to be overwhelmed both by its magnitude and by Your grace in giving it. I ask You, Lord, to give them new insight into Your love for them - insight that will awaken their desire and determination to place You *first* in their lives.

Use that love to draw these precious ones into the center of Your will for them. Show them that they are in much greater danger from the enemy out there on the fringes. Help them understand that they are missing the incomparable joy of fellowship with You. May they see that they are wasting never-to-be-recovered days and God-given opportunities to be an agent of change in someone's life.

And then help them understand that they are missing the adventure of walking by Your side each day. Help them see that they are not experiencing the complete peace that follows complete surrender. Give them the knowledge, Lord, that there is an eternal significance in this present struggle.

Your will be done in every life, Lord. That is my prayer for these I love.

December 7
THE SECURITY OF YOUR PROTECTION

He who dwells in the shelter of the Most High
will abide in the shadow of the Almighty.
I will say to the Lord,
"My refuge and my fortress, my God, in whom I trust!"
Psalm 91: 1-2

Reading this beautiful psalm this morning, Lord, brings to mind the total security which is mine because I am Yours.

You know that one of my favorite "pictures" of You is as my Shepherd, maybe because I have so much in common with a sheep. As my Shepherd, You are constantly vigilant in looking out for my welfare; providing for my physical needs with plenty of green grass and water, a place to rest safely from predator enemies, my quick healing from injuries. Are these things that I, a sheep, can do for myself? No. I am quite helpless and totally dependent upon my Shepherd for everything.

Another beautiful-to-me picture of You is as my Father. You are always thinking about the future while closely supervising the present. Since You are wise, You are more concerned about my future character than my present happiness. You protect me in the present for the benefit of what You know is my future; yet there are times You purposely lead me into difficulties in order that I may grow into all godliness. You are not just a wise Father; You are a loving Father. I know I can always come and talk to You, and You will not be too busy to listen. I know that in Your presence I find courage, strength, wisdom and all else I need to continue this walk of faith.

One of the most effective safety measures You give us is light. You, Lord, are my Light. You illuminate any dark places within that, left dark, would breed deadly evil. How great that You can work in the deepest, darkest recesses of my heart and mind and reveal things I did not even realize were there. When Your light shines on them, I am appalled and sorrowful that such things were within me. And yet I am so grateful for your determination to complete what You have begun. Your goal is that I be holy and without spot or wrinkle. And the good news is You always reach Your goal.

Thank You, Lord, for being my Shepherd, my Father and my Light. Truly, You are all I need. I love You very much. I claim these paraphrased promises today.....

"Because she has loved Me therefore I will deliver her;
I will set her securely on high because she has known My name.
She will call upon Me, and I will answer her;
I will be with her in trouble; I will rescue her, and honor her.
With a long life I will satisfy her, and let her behold My salvation."
Psalm 91: 14-16

December 8
WITNESSING

But the goal of our instruction is love from a pure heart
and a good conscience and a sincere faith.
1 Timothy 1: 5

Sometimes, Lord, when witnessing to those who have never gone to church, I feel that I have to defend You because they have a warped view of You. They have seen only the world's view of You, and I feel I must have arguments prepared to overcome that view. Help me see truth here, Lord; You are able to do in their minds *exactly what You want done* in spite of their misinformation and ignorance about You.

Here is my part: I must be rooted and grounded in You. There must be no doubts in my mind concerning Your existence, the reliability of Your Word, Your presence with me, or any of the other truths You have taught me. My job is to tell them what I know and trust You to do the work of making them comprehend and accept.

All the wonderfully eloquent words in the world are fruitless without the work of Your Holy Spirit. It is *You* who makes understanding come about, who enlightens and convicts and works deep in the heart. My part is simply to speak the truth so they may hear - "faith comes by hearing." You have promised, Lord, that if You are lifted up, You *will* draw all men to you.

I am sure and certain of *You* - that is what matters. My confidence in You also assures me that You will provide words as necessary because this is Your work. I am the tool; You are the Master Craftsman creating new life where, at present, only death abides. Work within me as You will, Lord, to make this tool effective.

Now, the only thing left is results. Here, too, it is all of You. It is Your work to do in Your time and Your way. I relinquish all expectations to You, Lord - the beginning, the doing, the end result.

Now to the King eternal, immortal, invisible, the only God,
be honor and glory forever and ever. Amen.
1 Timothy 1: 17

December 9
OUR GREAT GOD

Remember the former things long past, for I am God, and there is no other;
I am God, and there is no one like Me, declaring the end from the beginning
and from ancient times things which have not been done, saying
'My purpose will be established, and I will accomplish all My good pleasure.'
Isaiah 46: 9-10

My mind is flooded with the needs around me this morning, Lord! So many people with so many needs! It would be overwhelming except for the sure knowledge that You are our mighty God, and Your purposes will be established. You are aware of every need. And You not only see the need, You see the causes and the solutions. How *good* to know that! How strong in faith that makes me!

That certainty allows me to ask in all confidence that *this* is Your will - may every person with any need turn to You first rather than last. May they each trust that You will hear their prayer and expect Your answer. May Your answer be understood and acted upon. May lives be strengthened and You be glorified by the results of this cycle of need-request-answer-change. You are such a great God!

This is a God-thing - this cycle of need-request-answer-change. Being the lacking-in-insight creatures that we are, we would rarely turn to You without a need. So possibly, for me to pray for You to remove the need would be like praying for that person to *not* come to know You better - the exact opposite of what You want! You want them all to *strongly desire* to surrender completely to You. So I pray that they will turn to You in their need.

I pray for them to exercise all the faith You have given them, to trust that You are gracious, will hear them and will supply their need. I pray that the answer to their need will meet with a surrendered heart, one totally yielded to Your will in their lives; that they will realize anew how much they are loved, how safe they are, how powerful is their Provider and Protector.

Please create in them the desire to draw near to You. You are the Alpha and the Omega. The beginning of our desire is You; the satisfaction of it is You. Our faith comes from You and is in You. Our love is a gift from You, both our love for You and Yours for us. Oh, how we need You to be in total control of our lives! We know nothing about our future except that You will be there. That is enough. Thank You, my Lord, for hearing my prayer for these I love.

December 10
THE POWER OF CONFESSION

I acknowledged my sin to Thee, and my iniquity I did not hide;
I said, "I will confess my transgressions to the Lord"
and Thou didst forgive the guilt of my sin.
Psalm 32: 5

The power of confession. My understanding, Lord, of the meaning of "confession" is to say what You say - to agree with Your viewpoint on any given subject.

As You know, my current definition of "sin" is simple. *Sin is anything in my life that separates me from You.* But when I was a new believer and had even more to learn than I do now, my concept of "sin" was of things far removed from me - like murder, robbery and adultery. You soon taught me that sin was, indeed, as close as my beating heart. And that we, You and I, had some sin issues with which we must deal. So, was I not forgiven my sin when I was saved? Yes, I was. But the working out of that salvation was just begun at that point. And here we are, many years on down the road, *still* working it out.

So I learned *the power of confession.* I learned that when I agreed with Your analysis of what was sin and agreed that it was present in me and repented of it, then I was cleansed and freed from it. That is powerful! That is a thing only *You* can do - that cleansing and freeing! That, my Lord, is a miracle of the first order - that interior work You do in changing me from what I was into what You want me to be. There is no other power in heaven or on earth that can do that incredible work!

What I began thinking about this morning, however, was the paradox of weakness becoming strength and how confession impacts that process. You dropped these thoughts into my mind - the stronger I grow spiritually, the more I see the desperation of my need for You. And that it is only the *admitted* weakness that is transformed into strength. Weakness that I try to hide creates more weakness. Only as I acknowledge and confess that weakness will I gain Your strength. These two facts, Lord, so obviously line up with the clear teaching in all the New Testament! Paul, especially, was quick to confess his weaknesses.

It would not be too strong a statement to say that acknowledged human weakness is the only soil in which spiritual power *can* grow - *that we have this treasure in earthen vessels, that the surpassing greatness of the power may be of God and not from ourselves. (2 Cor. 4:7)* Earthen vessels are fragile, easily cracked and broken, often worth little or nothing except for the useful purpose they serve. I am that earthen vessel. It is Your power within, Lord, for which I am so desperate. I ask You to take all my very real weaknesses and teach me to appropriate Your very real strength. All for Your glory.

345

December 11
LIGHT AND DARKNESS

Deliver those who are being taken away to death,
and those who are staggering to slaughter, O hold them back.
Proverbs 24: 11

We, Your people, are in Your light and it is in us.
We are surrounded by it and filled with it
but only to the extent that we are emptied of ourselves.

So, Lord, how brightly are we shining?

The darkness is full of people who are, themselves, full of darkness.
Do they see our light?
Have our man-made institutions we call church
put up walls that make them either
not see
or turn away if they do see?

To be in darkness and full of darkness is dreadful and fearful.
We, Your light-filled children, need to be reminded
of the desperate situation it is to be there,
how awful it is to live and how *really* awful to die in darkness!

We need to be aware and to *care*.
To care enough to take steps toward sharing with them
how they can find Light.

Oh, God, give us an unrelenting burden for doing just that.
A conviction and a strong burning desire
to be used in Your Kingdom's work of saving souls.

Today is the day of salvation.

But you are a chosen race, a royal priesthood, a holy nation,
a people for God's own possession,
that you may proclaim the excellencies
of Him who has called you out of darkness into His marvelous light.
1 Peter 2: 9

346

December 12
HONESTY

But He turned and said to Peter,
"Get behind Me, Satan! You are a stumbling block to Me;
for you are not setting your mind on God's interests, but man's."
Matthew 16: 23

As I think about this business of praying for others, I have to admit to some frustration, Lord. Week after week, the prayer requests we receive are almost entirely for health issues or job issues. I know You care about all the physical needs of our lives; however, I'm certain You are concerned equally, or more, with the far deeper reaches of our soul. *But very few prayer requests admit to the need for spiritual help.* There are some of us praying for those spiritual needs, not because we are asked, but simply because we know they are there. I wonder, Lord, does the fact that the persons involved *did not ask for the meeting of those needs* create a hindrance? Is this an instance where confession is needed for Your power to be at work? Is it enough to just hope *they* are speaking to You about their spiritual shortcomings?

Is our pride blocking us from asking You for what we so dearly need? Is illness or injury a "respectable" need but lack of love in our heart for You is not? Is pride preventing us from admitting a point of disobedience to You or a loss of fellowship with You? It's true that admitting we are faulty and broken is not easy to do. And yet *we all are faulty and broken.* If only we could see the truth of that! There is tremendous release of power in admitting truth. Oh, how we need to be honest!

What does honesty require? At least these two things:

Humility. My favorite definition of humility is *to see myself as You see me.* If I can do that, I will never be prideful, on the one hand, nor feel worthless on the other. Humility is also willingness to allow others to see me as I am. No façade, no pretending, just me. Humility requires me at times to be a "taker" (maybe even an "asker") of others. Pride always wants to be a "giver" but never a taker. Humility is not afraid to ask for what it needs. Humility is admitting my desperate need of You. Every day in every way, my Lord, I'm desperate for You.

The second thing that honesty requires is *knowing that I am loved.* I can be honest with You because I am certain that You love me just as I am. Maybe, if Your children were better at letting Your love flow through us to one another, we could have that same certainty of love from each other.

How sorely we need to be honest with ourselves, with each other and with You! You can manifest Your powerful work of transformation in us only to the degree that we are honest with You. This, complete honesty before You, is setting our minds on Your interests. In this direction lies true spiritual growth and maturity. So be it. Starting with me.

December 13
ENOCH

And Enoch walked with God; and he was not, for God took him.
Genesis 5: 24

Enoch is one of my heroes, Lord. I wish we were told more about his walk with You. What did he do differently than say, Moses, that made You decide to bypass physical death for him while Moses died like the rest of mankind? Enoch just disappeared. Here is the total of what we know about him:

And Enoch lived sixty-five years, and became the father of Methuselah. Then
Enoch walked with God three hundred years after he became the father of
Methuselah, and he had other sons and daughters. So all the days of Enoch were
three hundred and sixty-five years. And Enoch walked with God; and he was not,
for God took him.
Genesis 5: 21-24

By faith Enoch was taken up so that he should not see death; and he was not found
because God took him up; for he obtained the witness that
before his being taken up he was pleasing to God.
Hebrews 11: 5

And about these also (rebellious ones) *Enoch, in the seventh generation from*
Adam, prophesied, saying, "Behold, the Lord came with many thousands of His
holy ones, to execute judgment upon all and to convict all the ungodly of all their
ungodly deeds
which they have done in an ungodly way,
and of all the harsh things which ungodly sinners have spoken against Him."
Jude 14-15

So he was a prophet, he walked with You a very long time, and he was pleasing to You. That's pretty bare bones information. Guess I'll just have to wait until I meet him in heaven one day, and then he can answer my questions in person. I'll bet he has already done that about a million times for those who have gone before me!

Maybe this lack of information was designed for our benefit. We would have created an entire denomination called the "Enochists" by now!

348

December 14
TRUSTING YOU

And when Israel saw the great power which the Lord had used against the
Egyptians, the people feared the Lord, and they believed in the Lord
and in His servant Moses.
Exodus 14: 31

This verse follows upon the heels of Your deliverance at the parting of the Red Sea. And not only deliverance to the children of Israel, but destruction to the pursuing Egyptians. That is total deliverance! And that verse says "they believed."

What follows in chapter 15 is called in my Bible, "The Song of Moses and Israel." This song is *18 verses long*. And it says that, "Moses and the sons of Israel sang this song to the Lord." Being a former school teacher myself, Lord, I have a few questions. Like...

Were they much more intelligent than we are today? How long would it take to teach a very large group of adults 18 verses of words without any of the teaching aids we have now? They didn't have a word processor or copier or overhead projector. They didn't even have a wall on which to write the words! They had to learn by hearing and repeating and hearing and repeating. Maybe they *were* more intelligent. Or maybe they were just inspired.

Anyway, this song is, from beginning to end, words of praise and thanksgiving to You for all You had done in their deliverance from bondage. They exalted You for Your great power and salvation. They sang that there was, "none like You, majestic in holiness, awesome in praises, working wonders." The last verse says, *"The Lord shall reign forever and ever."*

And yet, before the next three days were over, they had forgotten their strong faith in You and all their words of praise and thanksgiving. They came to Marah and could not drink the water because it was bitter. *"So the people grumbled at Moses, saying, "What shall we drink?""*

Your Word, Lord, says You were testing them (vs.25). You were giving them a chance to exercise faith, to simply look to You trusting that You could and would do something to provide them water to drink. Obviously, they failed. But I cannot throw a stone. How many times have I been just that short-sighted? How many tests of faith have I failed, Lord? How long it takes for Your children to learn - *really learn* - that You are worthy of our total trust in every situation!

Deliverer, Savior, Provider. Your amazing grace at work!

December 15
THE BOOK OF LIFE

He who overcomes shall thus be clothed in white garments;
and I will not erase his name from the book of life,
and I will confess his name before My Father, and before His angels.
Revelation 3: 5

Some random thoughts about what is called the "book of life" in some places or the "book of remembrance" in others. First, Lord, I'm overjoyed to think that there are books in heaven! Hopefully, lots and lots of books. Maybe all the authors who have written through the ages, thereby blessing millions of Your children, continue writing and publishing there, too. I actually cannot imagine eternity without books.

Second, in Psalm 69:28 are these words: *"May they be blotted out of the book of life."* Now, this is only a speculation question, but since David was praying down manifold miseries upon his enemies in this psalm, not speaking of believers-in-God, does this mean that every baby born upon earth is entered into Your book of life? Then, further into the lifespan of each child comes a time of decision - to be Your child or not to be? And those who finally and forever choose not to be, are *erased* from the book (see Rev, 3:5)? This is one of those questions not essential to salvation, Lord. But we *do* believe that babies and young children who die go immediately to be with You, so it seems feasible to me.

In Exodus 32:32 we find, *"And the Lord said to Moses, 'Whoever has sinned against Me, I will blot him out of My book.'"* These words were spoken to Moses when he was interceding for the children of Israel. After receiving Your commandments and coming back down the mountain, he found them worshipping a golden calf. You are saying, to Moses and to us, that we will each pay for our own sin. But does the fact that those who sinned were to be blotted out necessitate that they first be written in Your book at birth?

Then in Daniel 12:1 are these words: *"...and at that time your people, everyone who is found written in the book, will be rescued."* These words are part of a lengthy prophecy concerning the end times. It is the promise to all of the children of God that they will be saved out of the coming time of distress *"such as never occurred since there was a nation until that time."* This is a wonderful promise! And, evidently, someone is going to check the book for whose names are there. All Your records must be on computers even faster and more powerful than we have! So in an instant of time, You have the complete list before You.

There are several other references to this book, Lord, but the truly important thing to know is that our names are written there. How they got there, how long they have been there - all that is unimportant. You said, *"...rejoice that your names are recorded in heaven." (Luke 10:20)*

And I do!

December 16
TEACHING ON THE BLOOD

Therefore even the first covenant was not inaugurated without blood.
And according to the Law, one may almost say, all things are cleansed with blood,
and without shedding of blood there is no forgiveness.
Hebrews 9: 18,22

From Genesis to Revelation, Your Word has much to say about blood. And the more I read and study Your Word and understand the plan of redemption, the more I see the perfection of that plan - a plan which only unlimited intelligence and wisdom could devise. Truly You are an Almighty God!

I was thinking early this morning, Lord, about a funny story that happened years ago when we owned the store. We had many salesmen who called on us regularly, and our favorites were ones who loved You as we loved You. It was a chance to talk about *important* things - the things of God - not just place our order for merchandise.

During an afternoon visit, this one favorite salesman told us of an article he recently read concerning medical researchers who had spent millions of dollars and years of work attempting to determine where, in the human body, was "life." They finally discovered that it was in the blood. He said, "Man, I could have saved them all that money and all that time. I could have read them one verse and they would have had their answer:

"For the life of the flesh is in the blood, and I have given it to you on the altar
to make atonement for your souls;
for it is the blood by reason of the life that makes atonement."
Leviticus 17: 11

You said those words to Moses instructing him how to, in turn, teach the children of Israel why Your several rules about blood were significant. Now, had those medical researchers known about this verse, they might have read it and still gone on to do their scientific proving.

But Your word on it is all I need, Lord, to know that Your very life drained out of You as Your blood dripped from Your awful wounds on Calvary. And the giving of Your life atoned, once and for all, for my sin in our Father's eyes. The life is in the blood. *My* life comes from Your shed blood. My heart is full of pain that You had to do it and, at the same time, full of thankfulness that You did.

Much more then, having now been justified by His blood,
we shall be saved from the wrath of God through Him.
Romans 5: 9

351

December 17
THE MYSTERY OF GOD

*To me, the very least of all saints, this grace was given, to preach to the Gentiles
the unfathomable riches of Christ, and to bring to light what is the administration
of the mystery which for ages has been hidden in God, who created all things;
in order that the manifold wisdom of God might now be made known through the
church to the rulers and the authorities in the heavenly places.*
Ephesians 3: 8-10

These words above, Lord, speak of "the mystery" as if there were only one. To me, still in this dark world, there are several mysteries, but the words in verse 10 always stop me in my tracks. Please allow me to talk to You about them this morning. Your wisdom, Lord, is not a mystery. From Genesis 1:1 to Revelation 22:21, Your unfathomable wisdom is shown to us. I know I don't understand all about it, but I know it *exists*. The two things that do surprise me in this verse are these phrases, *"through the church"* and *"rulers and authorities."*

The rulers and authorities, as explained in other portions of Your Word, are spiritual beings living in the spirit world. In our limited understanding, one might assume that, because they are spirit and You are Spirit, and they live in "heavenly places" and You live in "heavenly places," that they know all that is going on in "heavenly places." Obviously, this is not true because these words plainly state that You have been *making known to them* some truths about Your eternal wisdom.

And You are doing this through the church! That is, to me, the great mystery about which Paul is speaking. Up until this time in history, such a thing as the church was unknown. The very concept of the church is a New Testament one. Only as You called out these men, like Paul, to be Your apostles and teachers of the next step of Your vast unfolding plan, did the people who heard them *and the rulers and authorities in heavenly places* begin to understand what was signified by Your birth, life, death and resurrection - the forming of this new entity called "the church."

And, since I am a Gentile, here is the good news. Paul talks earlier in the chapter about his ministry to the Gentiles. He says, *"to be specific, that the Gentiles are fellow heirs and fellow members of the body,* (the church) *and fellow partakers of the promise in Christ Jesus through the gospels." (vs. 6)* In this new entity called the church, Gentiles are just as welcome as Jews. In fact, in 1 Corinthians 12:13-14 Paul says, *"For by one Spirit we were all baptized into one body,* (the church) *whether Jews or Greeks, whether slaves or free, and we were all made to drink of one Spirit."*

In the Old Testament, Your called-out-ones were the people of Israel. In the New Testament, Your called-out-ones are all who believe that Jesus Christ is the Son of God, sent to redeem them from the snare of Satan. These are called "the church." All dividing barriers are gone. We are made one *in* You and *with* You. What a great God You are!

December 18
A MIRACLE OF GOD

So the sun stood still, and the moon stopped,
until the nation avenged themselves of their enemies.
Joshua 10: 13

This astounding story in Joshua never fails to grab me every time I read it, Lord. I'm sure that many people don't believe that this actually happened - they choose to think of it as a parable rather than an event that historically occurred. I choose to think You truly *did* this marvelous thing.

Do I understand how You did it? No, I can't even begin to grasp what effect it would have on the earth to stop rotating for almost 24 hours. But for the sun and the moon to stand still, the earth *would* have to stop turning. In my limited knowledge, Lord, I know this would affect the ocean tides, the winds and all climate-related things. Surely, the law of gravity would be affected. And, without doubt, countless other geomagnetic properties as well.

Here is what I do know. You created our entire solar system containing our sun and moon. So it would not be a challenge at all for You to suspend, for what is a moment of time to You, the rotation of this big, round globe on which we live. You would know exactly down to the tiniest detail all that had to be done for the earth to come through this experience unharmed. Both Your wisdom to know and Your power to do are infinite. Why would I *not* believe You could do this?

And in verse 11 of this chapter are these words about You helping Joshua and his men defeat those coming against Gibeon, *"And it came about as they fled from before Israel, while they were at the descent of Beth-horon, that the Lord threw large stones from heaven on them as far as Azekan, and they died; there were more who died from the hailstones than those whom the sons of Israel killed with the sword."*

Again, there may be those who choose to believe that, since hailstones are a naturally-occurring phenomena, this was just a fortunate coincidence. This particular hailstorm came at exactly the right time to kill the enemy of Israel. But how would they account for the fact that they fell only on the enemy? Normal hailstorms are not respecters of persons. They fall where they fall. But this was no normal hailstorm - this was a God-thing, done for a God-purpose and achieving a miracle in the life of the young nation of Israel.

Just one day in the life of Your people. But what a day! You, my Lord, are so far above and beyond our understanding - so much greater than we can know!

And there was no day like that before it or after it,
when the Lord listened to the voice of a man;
for the Lord fought for Israel.
Joshua 10: 14

December 19
ONLY MOSES

So Moses, the servant of the Lord, died there in the land of Moab,
according to the word of the Lord.
Deuteronomy 34: 5

Even people who have never picked up a Bible to read it know some things about Moses. They know he was a larger-than-life figure in leading Your people out of bondage and toward the promised land. They know he was the one You called to the top of the mountain and gave the stone tablets upon which were written Your commandments. They might have heard that Moses is the man mostly likely to have written the first five books of the Old Testament.

But, Lord, there is so much more to know about Moses. Truly he was a giant of a man, spiritually speaking. No other man has endured what he did in leading the rebellious people of Israel for 40 years in the wilderness. No other man has been blessed with the closeness to You that he had and, at the same time, burdened with the load he had to bear. He was truly a one-of-a-kind servant of Yours, called to a ministry unlike any other.

My thoughts this morning, Lord, are on these verses which concern the very end of his remarkable life. You did not allow him to step over into the promised land because of an event which happened during the wilderness wanderings. (See Numbers 20:12) So he has come to the border - to the land of Moab. You took him up to the top of Mount Pisgah and showed him all that could be seen of the promised land from there. And You said to him, *"This is the land which I swore to Abraham, Isaac, and Jacob, saying, 'I will give it to your descendants.' I have let you see it with your eyes but you shall not go over there."*

Now comes something which many people do not know about Moses...something I find so amazing each time I think of it. *"So Moses the servant of the Lord died there in the land of Moab, according to the word of the Lord, and He buried him in the valley in the land of Moab, opposite Beth-peor; but no man knows his burial place to this day."* (vs.5-6)

Only Moses, of all the wonderful saints of the Bible, was buried by You! You, Yourself, buried him and in a place only You know. We only know it was in the valley. And yet, he died on the mountain! (See Deut. 32: 49-50) So this means, Lord, that You carried him down the mountain to his burial place. Just a few verses earlier than this story of his burial, Moses had prophesied, *"The eternal God is a dwelling place, and underneath are the everlasting arms."*

My Lord, the sweetness of those words breaks my heart. Your goodness, Your kindness, Your love for this man just flows out of these words. That You would hold him in Your arms and carry him down to the valley and gently place his body into the ground is so full-of-wonder! Only Moses...only our Great God! How I love You!

December 20
INTELLIGENT STONES

And He answered and said,
"I tell you, if these become silent, the stones will cry out!"
Luke 19: 40

These were words You spoke on that day we now call Palm Sunday. You were making a triumphal entry into the city of Jerusalem, and the streets were lined with people shouting praises to You. Some of the Pharisees in the multitude did not like that, of course, so they said to You, *"Teacher, rebuke Your disciples." (vs. 39).* The verse above was Your reply.

I find those words astonishing, Lord. I've heard them all my life and I still find them astonishing. Stones can speak?! I have never heard a stone speak. In fact, in our culture today we have a saying that when someone is mentally challenged, he is as "dumb as a box of rocks." In light of this verse, perhaps that is a poor choice of words. Maybe rocks are smarter than we know.

Because in Joshua 24:26-27, I find these awesome words about stones. Joshua has come to the time of his own death, and he is preparing the children of Israel to go on without his leadership. He has encouraged them to be obedient to all Your commandments, to love You and serve You faithfully. *"And Joshua wrote these words in the book of the law of God; and he took a large stone and set it up there under the oak that was by the sanctuary of the Lord. And Joshua said to all the people, "Behold, this stone shall be for a witness against us, for it has heard all the words of the Lord which He spoke to us; thus it shall be for a witness against you, lest you deny your God."* Stones can hear?! How amazing is that?

And implied in that verse is that the stone not only heard, but will witness against them if they deny their God. Likewise, in the verse from Luke, Your words implied that those rocks could not only speak, they could hear what was going on around them, and had a cognizant understanding of the events. This implies, therefore, intelligence of some level!

These wonderful thoughts affirm to me, Lord, that all of creation is Yours. You are Owner of all and thus can do as You please with any small portion of it. I like to think about this - if You can make a rock both hear and speak, think of what You can do with a surrendered heart that loves You above all else in this world. That heart is mine, Lord. Do with it as You please.

December 21
GOOD KING HEZEKIAH

And he did right in the sight of the Lord,
according to all that his father David had done.
2 Kings 18: 3

Hezekiah, king of Judah, was one of very few good kings. Verses 5 and 6 say, *"He trusted in the Lord, the God of Israel; so that after him there was none like him among all the kings of Judah, nor among those who were before him. For he clung to the Lord; he did not depart from following Him but kept His commandments, which the Lord had commanded Moses."* You prospered him and made Judah victorious in battles with the Philistines because of Hezekiah.

It might seem that Hezekiah could do no wrong. But the story of his life is not all sunshine and roses. He got crosswise with Sennacherib, the king of Assyria, who was a powerful king of a powerful nation. Sennacherib's power made him unwisely proud, and he made some threatening statements to Hezekiah and the people of Judah. Angered by Sennacherib's threats, You did some showing of *real power*. In one night, You killed 185,000 Assyrians! Then as soon as Sennacherib returned home, badly defeated, he was also killed. That was quite a boost in faith for Hezekiah and his people!

This all happened in the fourteenth year of Hezekiah's reign, which was supposed to have been his last year. He became "mortally ill" and Isaiah came and said to him, *"Thus says the Lord, 'Set your house in order, for you shall die and not live.'" (Isaiah 38:1)* Now Hezekiah was only 39 years old at that time and did not want to die. He prayed to You and wept bitterly; You sent Isaiah back to tell him You had heard his prayer and would add fifteen years to his life.

The king of Babylon heard of Hezekiah's illness and recovery and sent messengers with congratulations and a present. Hezekiah was pleased at this and showed the Babylonians all the treasures of Judah - everything. Then Isaiah said to him, *"Hear the word of the Lord. Behold, the days are coming when all that is in your house, and all that your fathers have laid up in store to this day shall be carried to Babylon; nothing shall be left,' says the Lord." (2 Kings 20:17)* But Hezekiah was not disturbed by this news because it was not going to happen in *his* days. So he lived his fifteen more years and died. And his son, Manasseh, became king.

Manasseh evidently had not learned from his father to follow You because he was one of the most evil kings ever to reign over Judah. And since he was only twelve when he became king, he obviously had been born during the additional years Hezekiah had lived. I can't help having some questions, Lord. How different would this period of Judah's history have been if Hezekiah had died at age 39? No Babylonian captivity? No evil Manasseh ruling Judah? Should we perhaps be more careful what we pray for?

December 22
JUDGMENT ON MY GENERATION

Woe to those who call evil good, and good evil.
Isaiah 5: 20

As I read these words this morning, Lord, my heart sinks because that is exactly what our culture is doing. We call it being "tolerant" or "politically correct," but that doesn't change the fact that it is evil in Your eyes. I tremble when I ponder what my generation will answer for because most of our slide down the slope of evil has occurred in my lifetime; I feel a burden of guilt for that slide even though I was never an active part of it.

I think about the world of entertainment as it was when I was a child and as it is now. How innocent it was then by today's standards! I think about abortion. It is incredible to me the millions of babies my generation has killed before they could be born. Lord, my heart tells me that the value You put upon life cannot be degraded as abortion has degraded it, and not cause serious ramifications. I think about the incessant push for the acceptance of homosexuality. This is not something the generation before mine would believe! There is no end to the means to which those pushing this "alternate lifestyle" will go to be accepted as normal and, yes, even *good.*

I know, Lord, we really cannot expect anything better from the world. They don't read Your Word and, therefore, they don't live by it. I believe they do have spiritual input but not from Your Spirit. I think Satan is working day and night to influence, advance and encourage evil in every way and every place possible. It is painful to see the results of his agenda, but it is to be expected.

No, the two things that really disturb me are the number of Your own people, at least Yours by their own confession, who totally disregard what You have said in Your Word. I'm appalled by the respected leaders of the organized church who stand before TV cameras (and in their pulpits) and speak the lies of Satan. They may be sincere, but they are also deceived. And the damage they do is enormous because they are supposed to be Your spokesmen and thus, many will believe them. Some of them, Lord, do not even believe in the virgin birth or in Your death and resurrection. I cannot fathom how they can think themselves to be Christian and deny the truth of these two enormous foundational stones of our faith!

And then there is the silence from the rest of us. *That* is what makes me tremble. God help us!

Woe to those who are wise in their own eyes, and clever in their own sight!
Isaiah 5: 21

December 23
OUR JOURNEY OF FAITH

And a highway will be there, a roadway,
and it will be called the Highway of Holiness.
Isaiah 35:8

A few days ago, Lord, we talked about the narrow way and the broad way, the road to Life and the road to destruction. Then today I come in Isaiah to these poetic words in the 35th chapter. They give us a beautiful description of the narrow way and some of the things we can expect along that way.

It says that the unclean will not travel on this road. It is only for the holy, the redeemed. And how am I made holy? How am I redeemed? Only by Your shed blood and Your amazing grace. You assure us that there will be no fools who wander onto this road by mistake. Nor will there will be any lions or other vicious beasts to do us harm.

On this road the eyes of the blind will be opened, the ears of the deaf unstopped, the lame healed and the tongue of the dumb made to shout for joy. I believe these miracles are physical healings for those who need them and spiritual healings for *every one of us.* We all need spiritual healing. Before we came to You, we were all spiritually blind, deaf, lame and dumb. The true miracle to me, Lord, is that You take us as we are at that point and change us so radically on the inside. What a great God You are!

Waters will spring forth where there was no water, and the dry land will become a pool. The streams and springs of water represent the constant rejuvenation of Your blessed Spirit as we make this journey of faith. How unable we would be to survive without Your Spirit! Physically, our bodies cannot go long without water. Spiritually, we are just as desperate for Your Spirit's constant flow and Life-giving refreshment.

The closer we get to the end of this highway, to Zion, the greater our rejoicing. What joy and gladness will be ours as we see the end of our long journey! May this encourage the exhausted and strengthen the feeble. May this give us peace, courage and strength to continue walking. Our God is with us!

And the ransomed of the Lord will return,
and come with joyful shouting to Zion,
with everlasting joy upon their heads.
They will find gladness and joy,
and sorrow and sighing will flee away.
Isaiah 35: 10

December 24
LOVING WORDS

Lord, I love this prophet Isaiah! I know You inspired him to write what he wrote, but he must have had a gift with words, too, to pen the beautiful prose he authored. My heart is full of worship and thanksgiving for the wonderful, sweet, encouraging promises for Your children, and this child in particular, that I have read this morning. Such as...

Like a shepherd He will tend His flock, in His arm He will gather the lambs,
and carry them in His bosom; He will gently lead the nursing ewes.
Isaiah 40: 11

These words so clearly describe Your gentleness and compassion. Oh, how needy I am of both. And then these words...

He gives strength to the weary, and to him who lacks might He increases power.
Isaiah 40: 29

As a younger person, Lord, I read those words without a second glance. I had not yet realized my need for your strength and power. How much I had to learn! Now I read them and rejoice that I am the weary who can claim Your strength, and I am the one lacking might; therefore, Your power will be increased in me. And then there are these...

A bruised reed He will not break,
and a dimly burning wick He will not extinguish;
He will faithfully bring forth justice.
Isaiah 42: 3

That, my Lord, is me so often - a bruised reed and a dimly burning wick. Nothing of any value to You whatsoever, and yet Your mercy endures, Your work continues, Your grace wraps me up and loves me back to wholeness. How much I love You! How blessed I am to be Your child! Then I come to these words...

When you pass through the waters, I will be with you;
and through the rivers, they will not overflow you.
When you walk through the fire, you will not be scorched,
nor will the flame burn you.
Isaiah 43: 2

Who of Your children can not identify with this? All of us have trials in this life that seem like deep waters and burning fire to us, and our natural instinct is to be full of fear and anxiety. Allow me to shout it from the housetops - as one who has been through some of these times, Lord - *I know Your faithfulness.* Here I am - neither drowned nor burned! Glory! Thank You for all these inspiring words this morning. Thank You for the joy in my soul!

December 25
HAPPY BIRTHDAY, JESUS

For today in the city of David there has been born for you
a Savior, who is Christ the Lord.
Luke 2:11

Christmas wears me out, Lord! Traditions of men have taken over. Why do I allow all this busy-ness to attack me, to overcome me, to sap my strength? Why do I spend time and energy on things that have nothing to do with celebrating Your birthday? I yearn to come away with You and have a *quiet* celebration. I long to simply think about that day You were born and what an astounding difference it has made in our world and in my life. How desolate I would be without You, Lord!

What can I give You for Your birthday? You already own everything, so material things mean nothing to You. Only "heart things" matter to You - such things as love, joy, honor and reverence. These I bring, my Lord.

I bring You love by giving all of myself to You - spirit, soul and body. I bring You love by putting You first in my thoughts. I bring You a love that is still growing, not yet perfect, often faulty, but so very deep. From somewhere beyond what my conscious mind knows, I draw from this reservoir of love.

I bring You joy by my obedience, my loyalty to You, my steadiness in all circumstances. When difficulties arise, my trusting Your motives for allowing the hard things bring You joy. My being certain that nothing is impossible with You brings You joy. I give You joy by sharing with You some of the incredible joy You give to me.

I bring You honor by exalting You always in my behavior - by acting as a daughter of the King should act. I bring honor to you with my language by speaking life-giving words when the enemy would have me speak words of death. I bring You honor with my heart by realizing that the praise bubbling up in me is completely for You and You alone.

I bring You reverence by bowing in Your presence to tell You that You are my Lord and my God. You are Almighty and lifted up, You are my Beloved Savior. You are such an awesome and holy Being, and I could never belong to You except that You drew me to Yourself. My worship is the only way I know, Lord, to give You the reverence You deserve.

These gifts I bring on this special day. As the three wise men of the East brought You gold, frankincense and myrrh on that long ago day, I bring my gifts to You today. They came to worship also, to witness this great thing that was told them by the heavens themselves. They were aware that something spectacular had happened. And indeed it had. A King had been born. Happy Birthday, Jesus!

December 26
YOUR GRACE TO THE GENTILES

Now there was a certain man at Caesarea named Cornelius...a devout man, and one who feared God with all his household, and gave many alms to the Jewish people
and prayed to God continually.
Acts 10: 1-2

Lord, I just finished reading the 10th chapter of Acts. It is a wonderfully informative 48 verses about the world of spiritual things and, in particular, about Your Spirit's work. Please help me as I think about it.

There probably were not many men like Cornelius - a Gentile who loved the God of the Jews and who had taught all his household to do likewise. I can see why he was the one You chose to receive Peter's visit. You sent to Cornelius an angel with clear instructions, and Cornelius obeyed the instructions. You prepared Peter with both a vision (repeated three times) and the spoken word, *"What God has cleansed, no longer consider unholy." (vs. 15)* You, Yourself, spoke to Peter, *"Behold, three men are looking for you. But arise, go downstairs and accompany them without misgivings; for I have sent them Myself." (vs. 19)* Only then did he understand the vision.

He went with the men and spoke to those gathered at the house of Cornelius.

"God has shown me that I should not call any man unholy or unclean." (vs. 28)
"I most certainly understand now that God is not one to show partiality,
but in every nation the man who fears Him
and does what is right, is welcome to Him."
(vs. 34-35)

Since, at that time in history, a huge barrier existed between the Jews and the Gentiles, especially concerning religion, I am impressed by the detailed arrangements You orchestrated for this series of events to take place. There are a couple of definitive characteristics about You that I need to learn and remember.

The first is that the inclusiveness of Your love and grace far surpasses what I think I know; there is *no one* outside Your mercy. And the second, You are exceedingly able, in ways of which I might never think, to make me understand Your will. When it is imperative for me to know something, I can depend upon You to make it clear to me. What an astoundingly wonderful, liberating thought that is!

December 27
OVERCOMING

You are from God, little children, and have overcome them;
because greater is He who is in you than he who is in the world.
1 John 4: 4

Lord, I need to talk to You this morning about this business of "overcoming." I see that overcoming can apply to situations as large as doubting You have forgiven me or as small as a bad-for-me-habit of eating too many sweets in my diet. The size of the problem is, in Your eyes, not at all important. The problem *itself* is not the problem, is it, Lord? The crux of the matter is how I respond to Your conviction concerning my need to overcome the problem.

Please help me think clearly about my choices. How many forks in the road are there at this intersection?

Fork #1: There is quenching Your Spirit. This is essentially ignoring You, tuning You out, intentionally switching my mind away from You when You are trying to speak to me.

Fork #2: There is listening to You but then going on with my plans, even though I feel guilty about it. I guess that is stubbornness - a harsh word, but what else can I call it?

Fork #3: There is outright rebellion - saying in my heart and by my actions that Your opinion does not matter to me. All that matters to me is what I want.

Putting it down on paper makes it clear to me, Lord, that *none* of those three forks in the road take me where I want to go! I can choose one of them, and You will not stop me, but each of those choices will create harmful consequences.

I will be turning my back on so much blessing. I will be putting distance between myself and You. I will be disappointing You. I will be forfeiting the joy of obedience. I will destroy the peace in my spirit that all is well between us. I will be pleasing the enemy of my soul. I will be a bad witness to those around me. I will go backwards in my spiritual maturity. I can probably fill several pages with the detrimental results of choosing any way except Your way.

Bottom line, the only life-affirming way is Your way. Why on earth would I give up all the divine blessings You have for me for *anything*?! There is nothing worth more than the fulfillment of being Your child and walking close beside You every minute of every day, Lord. Thank You for helping me see the truth about overcoming. Thank You for giving me Your power within to overcome. Thank You for caring about me enough to continue to teach me.

December 28
PERFECTION

Therefore you are to be perfect, as your heavenly Father is perfect.
Matthew 5:48

That radical statement, Lord, was the summation of a sermon overflowing with new, extremist teachings. I'm not sure how Your listeners felt about what You preached to them that day, but the next three chapters, in their entirety, are amazing to me. I find that if I measure the bulk of my behavior by Your teaching in those three chapters, I come up drastically short of my idea of perfection. But do I understand perfection?

An intelligent person once said that the best interpreter of the Bible is the Bible. Looking in Your Word for additional discussion of this concept of perfection, here is what I find...

Speak to all the congregation of the sons of Israel and say to them,
"You shall be holy, for I the Lord your God am holy."
Leviticus 19:2
You shall be blameless before the Lord your God.
Deuteronomy 18:13
Therefore, having these promises, beloved, let us cleanse ourselves from all
defilement of flesh and spirit, perfecting holiness in the fear of God.
2 Corinthians 7: 1

This all sounds unattainable and hopeless. Can any man make himself holy? Is it possible for any one of us to, on our own, become blameless before You, Lord? That kind of perfection *is* impossible and unachievable.

Here is the key - You never intended that we do it on our own. Even in the Old Testament, Your plan was that the people would love You and serve You; they would be Your people; You would be their God and provide everything they needed to live that life of faith successfully. It was grace then and it is grace now. And here is proof that it is You - not us - who does the work...

Not that I have already obtained it, or have already become perfect, but I press on
in order that I may lay hold of that for which also I was laid hold of by Christ
Jesus. Brethren, I do not regard myself as having laid hold of it yet; but one thing I
do; forgetting what lies behind and reaching forward to what lies ahead, I press on
toward the goal for the prize of the upward call of God in Christ Jesus.
Philippians 3: 12-14

If any man could have reached perfection in this life, it would have been the Apostle Paul. So the fact that he is pressing on means that it is something to which we look forward when this physical life is over. In the meantime, we are forgiven, cleansed, covered over and clothed with Your righteousness. We are growing more like You and maturing spiritually. *That* is our perfection for today - pressing on in obedience to Your Spirit.

363

December 29
YOUR HELP

And Jesus stopped and called them, and said,
"What do you want Me to do for you?"
Matthew 20: 32

The two men You said these words to were blind. They had heard of Your mighty miracles of healing, and now they heard that You were passing by. They realized this was their chance for their own miracle. I'm sure You didn't ask this question because You didn't know what they wanted. You asked this question *so that they would then ask You for help.*

This Scripture speaks to me this morning. You are saying to me, "What do you want Me to do for you today?" And the truth is, Lord, I *have* been carrying around some burdens I need to give to You. You *knew* that. I'm the one who needed to see that truth.

These burdens are probably no different from the baggage that all people carry day after day. No crisis situations, no huge heavy load. Just "small" things that accumulate one-by-one and which I put on a shelf in my mind. Occasionally, I go back, pick them up and carry them around for a time. I begin stacking more small things on these small things. Soon the stacks and piles begin to weigh down my mind and spirit. But, Lord, I've learned that small things can, in Your view, be quite large. And I've learned from Your Word that, as Your child, I am to bring them all to You, every one of them, and not carry them myself.

So what is necessary for Your child to come and ask for Your blessing of any kind? I must believe that You want me to ask, are *waiting* for me to ask. I must believe that when I give You a situation, You take control of it. I must believe that You *will* work all things out.

Then I can go back to doing whatever is before me to do, expectantly looking for Your solution.

Consistent, lived-out faith is what I desire, Lord. Faith for any and every situation that comes my way. Faith that is steady in every storm. And Your Word teaches that You want exactly that for me! So this is one of those times that I can say…

I am willing.
You are able.
It shall be done.

Thank You for asking me that question this morning. I very much needed to lay that bundle of burdens down. You are such a good and loving God!

December 30
PERSISTENCE IN PRAYER

I tell you, even though he will not get up and give him anything because he is his friend, yet because of his persistence he will get up and give him as much as he needs.
Luke 11: 8

You are teaching here that I should be persistent in my asking; don't give up. These verses bring up hard questions for which I have no answers, Lord; questions about accepting Your will and about taking "no" for an answer. I will leave those mind bogglers for smarter people to answer. Instead, I want to look at this whole concept of persistence as it relates to prayer and to our relationship. The margin reference in my Bible gives an alternate translation of the word "persistence" as *shamelessness*. I want to talk to You about this word.

Here is the situation - I have a need, for myself or for another, which can only be met by Your power. If I am shameless, I will repeatedly come to You, asking for what I need. And this implies, Lord, that I should begin to *look for the answer*. In this, I am shameless because I am, by my asking, simply being Your obedient child. The verses immediately following this passage instruct me to "ask, seek, knock" and to *continue* to do that, along with the promise that the answer *will* come. So I am brave and shameless in my asking, and also expectant because *this is what You want*.

The word "shamelessness" speaks volumes to my heart because it concerns itself with pride. Pride is so often the culprit that prevents honest prayer. Pride is such an invasive thing. It roots deep into the heart and shows its ugly self in a variety of disgusting ways. Pride can keep me from admitting my failures even to You, the One who knows all there is to know about me! When You look at my heart, You are able, in an instant, to see every flaw and fault; my feeble attempts to hide them are absolutely worthless. Shamelessness means that when I come to You, I come just as I am - warts and all - so pride is uprooted and cast upon the trash heap. It has no place in my heart.

Shamelessness means that, no matter how elementary a spiritual blessing might appear to others, if I need it, I will ask for it without shame. It means that the blessing I want from You is so esteemed by me that I will do whatever You require to obtain it. I am asking shamelessly because, more than anything else, I want the fullness of Your power at work in my life.

To me, Lord, it means seeing You as You are and seeing myself through Your eyes. When I see Your holiness and magnificence, I am awed and fearful. I could never even come into Your presence except that You have invited me, and You have taught me that Your presence is the safest place I can be. What an amazing thing it is to be loved by You! That knowledge, my Lord, gives me the boldness to be shameless and persistent.

December 31
THE LAST DAY

Therefore, let everyone who is godly pray to Thee
in a time when Thou mayest be found.
Psalm 32: 6

This is the last day of yet another year, Lord. Another year of living in my two worlds - the physical world which most think of as *reality* and the world of the spirit which is actually the more real one to me. You and I have been doing this year-end thing for a long time. I remember the old hymn that said, "Every day with Jesus is sweeter than the day before; every day with Jesus I love Him more and more." That is the absolute truth. I didn't grasp it when I learned those words as a child, but living all these years with You has taught me the truth of those simple words. I *do* love You more than I did at the close of last year. Or a month ago. Or even yesterday. Such an astounding truth!

This is a day for reflecting over the previous year and witnessing again Your faithfulness to me. As I flip back through the pages of my journal, Lord, I'm amazed at the number of struggles and difficulties I had, the number of times You had to correct me and, most of all, the immense grace with which You surrounded me. When I failed, You were faithful to forgive and get me back on track. When I was happy, You rejoiced with me. When I hurt Your feelings, You gently showed me what I should have done. When I brought You all my anxieties, You took them and gave me Your peace. In other words, my Lord, You were faithful to Your promises. In every instance, You were faithful. My heart overflows with love for You - with thanksgiving for all that You are and all that You do for this slow-to-learn child!

This is also a day for looking ahead to a new year. Endings can be sad until I think about the fact that, without endings, there could be no new beginnings. This year ahead of us and what it will bring are totally unknown to me. You and I will travel paths brand new and different. Any of the people and things in my life can be changed in an instant. My health could deteriorate in only a few moments of time. All this would probably make me anxious if I did not know who is in control. But because You see tomorrow, because You are all powerful and wise and full of love, I have no apprehension at all. You, my Lord, are my peace and my joy, today and forever.

And thinking about forever - someday will actually be my last day on this earth! I do not know when that will be, but I know it *will* happen. You will either return for all Your children, or You will call for just me. That last day will come. How thankful I am for Your promises to keep Your obedient children safe and ready for that day. How my spirit rejoices to think about that day - that last day - which is actually the beginning of a new and glorious day where there is no night! I have so much to which I can look forward, and I am filled with Your joy.

A FINAL WORD

How many of you remember the old days when our telephone service was set up on "party lines"? For those of you too young to have experienced this, it was simply four or five households all on the same phone line. So you might pick up the receiver to make a call and hear someone already using the line. Thankfully, phone service has improved since those days.

If you have read these pages daily for a year, you have actually listened in on conversations. Daily conversations between an ordinary person and an extraordinary, great and loving God - a God who is faithful to His promises, a powerful, all-wise, gentle Teacher of Truth.

As we finish this year together, dear reader, my prayer for each of you is that you are looking forward to a new year of walking closer to our Lord. He loves you so very much. If you have gleaned just one truth from these pages, I hope it is that His love for you is unconditional and eternal. He loved You before you were born, so since you did nothing to earn His love, neither can you do anything that will cause the loss of it. And included in that God-love is everything you need to live a life of joy, peace and daily fellowship with Him. He *longs* to spend time with You. I urge you, don't disappoint Him.

I want to express my heartfelt gratitude for the immense help of my former pastor and forever friend, Dr. Tim Deatrick, who read every word of every page, checked my theology, encouraged me, corrected me and in general kept me working toward the finish line. Only he and God know how he fit that into his full schedule as Senior Pastor of a busy church and husband and father to an active family. In my humble opinion, he should receive a sizable and sparkly jewel in his crown for all his help to me. Thank you, Tim.

And then I want to express my huge admiration and gratitude for Dawn Marsden, my second pair of eyes. She not only caught my many grammar and punctuation errors, but offered so many excellent suggestions which made the text flow more smoothly. And, being a child of God, she encouraged me by her sweet comments amidst all the red-lines. This book is infinitely better because of her work. Thank you, Dawn.

> *And now to the King eternal, immortal, invisible,*
> *the only God,*
> *be honor and glory forever and ever.*
> *Amen*
> *1 Timothy 1: 17*

Breinigsville, PA USA
29 September 2009

224967BV00002B/4/P

9 781432 734